THE ANATOMY OF SEX AND POWER

THE
ANATOMY
OF SEX
AND
POWER

An Investigation of Mind-Body Politics

MICHAEL
HUTCHISON

WILLIAM MORROW

AND COMPANY, INC.

NEW YORK

Grateful acknowledgment is made for excerpts from the following sources:

"The Delicate Sex" by Duncan Maxwell Anderson. *Science 86 Magazine*, April 1986. Copyright © 1986 by Duncan Maxwell Anderson. Reprinted by permission.

From *The Hare and the Tortoise: Culture, Biology and Human Nature* by David Barash. Copyright © 1986 by David Barash. Reprinted by permission of Viking Penguin, a division of Penguin Books USA Inc.

"Of Meese and Women: Porn Panic's New Face" by Lisa Duggan. *The Village Voice*, December 3, 1985. Copyright © 1985. Reprinted by permission of *The Village Voice*.

From *Sex and the Brain* by Jo Durden-Smith and Diane de Simone. Copyright © 1983 by the authors. Reprinted by permission of Arbor House (a division of William Morrow and Company).

Excerpts from "The Big T Personality" by Frank Farley. *Psychology Today* magazine, May 1986. Copyright © 1986 (PT Partners, L.P.). Reprinted with permission from *Psychology Today* magazine.

From *The Sex Contract* by Helen E. Fisher. Copyright © 1982 by Helen E. Fisher. Reprinted by permission of William Morrow and Company.

Excerpts from "Memetics and the Modular Mind" by H. Keith Henson, copyright © 1987 by Davis Publications, Inc. Reprinted from *ANALOG Science Fiction/Science Fact* by permission of the author.

"Interview" with Candace Pert, by Judith Hooper. *Omni*, February 1982. Copyright © 1982 by Judith Hooper and reprinted with permission of Omni Publications International, Ltd.

"Interview" with Helen Singer Kaplan, by Diane Klein. *Omni*, August 1981. Copyright © 1981 by Diane Klein and reprinted with permission of Omni Publications International, Ltd.

From *The Tangled Wing* by Melvin Konner. Copyright © 1982 by Melvin Konner. Reprinted by permission of Henry Holt and Company, Inc.

"When the Music's Over," written and composed by: Jim Morrison, John Densmore, Ray Manzarek, and Robby Krieger. Copyright © 1967 Doors Music Company (ASCAP). All rights reserved. Used by permission.

"On the Road Home" by Wallace Stevens. Copyright © 1942 by Wallace Stevens and renewed 1970 by Holly Stevens. Reprinted from *The Collected Poems of Wallace Stevens*, by permission of Alfred A. Knopf, Inc.

"The force that through the green fuse . . ." by Dylan Thomas: *Poems of Dylan Thomas*. Copyright © 1939 by New Directions Publishing Corporation. Reprinted by permission of New Directions Publishing Corporation; U.S. rights. For Canadian and British rights, refer to: David Higham Associates, Ltd., 5–8 Lower John Street, Golden Square, London W1R 4HA, England.

From "Interview" with Robert Bly, by Keith Thompson. *New Age Journal* 1982. Copyright © 1982. Reprinted by permission of the author. Keith Thompson lives and writes in Santa Cruz County, California.

"My Generation," words and music by Peter Townshend. Copyright © 1965 Fabulous Music Ltd., London, England. TRO–Devon Music, Inc., New York, controls all publication rights for the U.S.A. and Canada. Used by permission.

Prometheus Rising by Robert Anton Wilson. Copyright © 1983. The author thanks Falcon Press for permission.

Wilhelm Reich in Hell by Robert Anton Wilson. Copyright © 1987. The author thanks Falcon Press for permission.

Recognizing the importance of preserving what has been written, it is the policy of William Morrow and Company, Inc., and its imprints and affiliates to have the books it publishes printed on acid-free paper, and we exert our best efforts to that end.

Library of Congress Cataloging-in-Publication Data

Hutchison, Michael.
    The anatomy of sex and power : an investigation of mind-body
  politics / Michael Hutchison.
      p.   cm.
    ISBN 0-688-06588-0
    1. Sex customs—United States.   I. Title.
  HQ18.U5H88   1990
  306′.0973—dc20   89-14558
                                                            CIP

Printed in the United States of America

First Edition

1 2 3 4 5 6 7 8 9 10

BOOK DESIGN BY BARBARA MARKS GRAPHIC DESIGN

To Kelly

ACKNOWLEDGMENTS

Thanks to those friends and acquaintances whose conversations have contributed to my knowledge of and clarified my ideas about the nature of sex and power. Among this crowd, I offer special thanks to Alan Badiner, Courtney Hoblock, Catherine Houck, Ed Hershberger, Dr. Julian Isaacs, Tom Miller, Caroline Schneider, Maggie O'Bryan, Jill Niemark, Dr. Marcello Margini, Chris Michael, Cliff Cowles, and John Mage.

For friendship, encouragement, and support during the writing of this book, thanks to Rick and Lynn Henriksen, Rich Mitchell, Jerry Simon Chasen, John and Françoise Howell, Ann Walker, and my sisters, Cindy, Callie, and Suzanne. Thanks, mom and dad, for your lifelong demonstration to me that, in a world of sex and power, the greatest force is love.

My gratitude to my agent, Gail Hochman, who supported this project from the first, when it sounded like something even stranger than my last two books, and to my editor, Jim Landis (ditto). Editor Jeanne Bernkopf put her extraordinary energy and intelligence to work in shaping the manuscript into final form, and her suggestions and criticisms were invaluable.

Most of all, my love and thanks to my wife, Kelly Howell, who kept me going, made it all a voyage of discovery, and introduced me to some astonishing facts about the anatomy of sex and power; and, of course, to Galen, who, before I even knew I needed him, was there.

CONTENTS

Acknowledgments   7

Introduction   The Burning of the First Amendment Bookstore   11

PART I   THE BATTLE

1   *Schizosexuality in America*   23
2   *Revolutionary Sex*   29
3   *The Sexualization of the Masses*   40
4   *Strange Bedfellows and the Death of Sex*   51
5   *Halting the Decline of Western Civilization*   63
6   *The Rat Runners Meet the Freedom Fighters: The Conflict
    About Human Nature*   79

PART II   THE FACTS

7   *The Genesis of the Sex Contract*   89
8   *The Facts of Life*   111
9   *Different Strokes*   129
10 *The Brain-Mind Revolution*   149
11 *Sex in the Head*   166
12 *Who's on Top?: Biopolitics in the Sex-Power Nexus*   186
13 *Land of the Free and Home of the Thrill-Seekers*   206
14 *The Feminization of American Culture*   220

PART III   THE TRANSFORMATION

15 *Fear of Sex*   235
16 *Mind Wars: The Germ Theory of Ideas*   250
17 *Putting on the Armor: Sexual Imprints and the Emotional
       Plague*   271
18 *Meme Warfare in the Sex-Power Nexus*   287
19 *The Big Payoff*   299
20 *The Wild Man, the Sacred Prostitute, and the Quest for
       Power*   313
21 *Renegotiating the Sex Contract*   326

Bibliography   346
Index   365

INTRODUCTION

The Burning of the First

Amendment Bookstore

· ·

Long before dawn, within minutes of each other, two bookstores in the same town were set ablaze. When firemen arrived at one of the bookstores, they found a cheering, howling mob already on the scene, despite the early hour and the bitter cold. As the flames raged out of control, the mob celebrated the arson by singing songs and chanting slogans, linking arms as they danced around the burning building, attempting to keep the fire fighters from getting to the flames. With the help of their efforts, the bookstore was consumed totally, and two firemen injured.

I felt a sudden chill the morning I read about it in *The New York Times*. Grinning crowds in an act of communal book-burning. What a scene. Only a few days before, I'd watched a newsreel about the rise to power of Hitler and the Third Reich, and could still see the eerily vacant smiles on the faces of the German crowds as they piled "obscene, pornographic, and degenerate" books on the Nazi bonfires, books by Freud, Einstein, Hemingway, Dos Passos, Helen Keller, Jack London, Karl Marx, and Darwin.

But these bookstore burnings took place not in Hitler's Germany, but in Colorado Springs, Colorado, a skiing and university town. The cheering crowds were not Nazis but opponents of sexually explicit literature. Such literature has traditionally been protected in America by the First Amendment of the U.S. Constitution. So it seemed significant that the name of one of the shops destroyed in the Colorado Springs fires was the First Amendment Bookstore.

"Take a look at this." I handed the article to a friend of mine, and went back to my coffee as she read. I anticipated her outraged response. We'd known each other since the late sixties, had been to the same marches, chanting, "Make love, not war." She was a woman who had gone braless and had laughed at people who were too uptight to enjoy sex as recreational sport. She had spent years in a commune where sexual repression was considered a sign of mental weakness, where the degree of one's liberation was directly linked to the degree of one's sexual freedom. I remembered her describing the porn film *Deep Throat* to me with great bursts of laughter.

"Great!" my friend now sneered, looking up from the article. "It's about time they started burning out some of those terrorists. Vicious filth like that shouldn't be published."

At first I was too startled to say anything. Only a few minutes earlier, we had been talking about a book I had recently had published. It was a book about the brain, a discussion of new findings in neuroscience, and had been highly praised by neuroscientists, psychiatrists, and other authorities on the brain. It had nothing at all in it about sex. And yet I had just learned that it had been condemned by at least one group as a "work of the Devil." When I had told that to my friend, she had laughed at the absurdity of it. Now, I had a sudden mental image of someone in a jeering crowd running up to the burning First Amendment Bookstore to pitch a copy of my book onto the flames.

As my friend raged on about the evils of porn, I sat back and observed her with curiosity. She was still the same person, and yet something had happened. She spoke with an intensity and fervor that reminded me of people I had known who had suddenly undergone religious conversion or become members of cults.

A few days later I heard from Peter, a fellow writer, that he had made a big sale to *Playboy*. According to publishing-industry figures in 1985, *Playboy* has a readership of 11,839,000. That makes the magazine perhaps the most highly visible place to publish short fiction in America today. If, say, 10,000 people read your story in a literary journal, then having your story published in *Playboy* is like having it read by the combined readers of over one thousand different literary magazines. Peter and I had mutual friends who had published stories in *Playboy* that later led to National Book Awards, book contracts, movie deals, and more.

I was happy for Peter, and so was especially concerned when again I read a story in the *Times* over breakfast: The Southland Corporation, which operates the 7-Eleven chain of convenience stores, announced that all of its over seven thousand stores were ceasing to sell *Playboy* and *Penthouse* magazines.

The stores had been under fire from a variety of feminist and Christian fundamentalist groups, which had set up picket lines outside some of the 7-Eleven stores, heckling, and in some cases physically attacking, customers who had purchased the magazines. A group called Citizens for Decency, and their leader, a fire-and-brimstone southern Bible-pounder named Reverend Donald Wildmon, who had gained a bit of notoriety for his claims that CBS was run by the communists, had been attacking the 7-Eleven chain as apostles of the demon for selling the magazines. The president of the company that owned the stores had vowed to resist the coercion. So it was a shock to read about this sudden and total capitulation.

In effect, I thought, by banning the magazine, the 7-Eleven stores were denying their customers access to Peter's writing. In an odd but effective way, Peter was being censored.

I mentioned this to another young writer who knew Peter, a woman who was just finishing her first novel, struggling to get stories published while working at a boring, low-paying job. I assumed she would feel some identification with Peter. "I can't really get upset about the problems of hate publications like *Playboy*," she said. "Whoever writes for them deserves what he gets."

Shortly after that, I heard that Attorney General Meese was setting up a commission to find ways of combating pornography. A writer friend told me he was going to testify before the commission because one of his books—a children's book—had been banned in a midwestern state. The reason? In one scene the young heroine changes from street clothes into a costume: She is briefly naked.

Such events seemed threatening; but then, they weren't happening to me. I had other things to worry about. I was agonizing over my next book, which was to be an account of some years I had spent among revolutions and death squads in Central America. Now that was *real* censorship, the kind that came out of the barrel of a gun.

A holiday came along, and my family members had one of our infrequent gatherings. One evening after a long feast, we were sitting around the table, and the subject of handedness came up. As a left-hander, I've always been interested in the seeming brain differences between lefties and righties. I brought up a recent study that had suggested that more males than females were left-handed. Instantly a jolt went through several people at the table.

"Camilla Benbow!" cried one of my close relatives, a respected scientist and educator, identifying the author of the study. "Heresy! Bad science!" he joked, and some others around the table laughed with him.

"Burn it!" groaned one of my sisters—a highly educated businesswoman and human-rights organizer—a look of disgust on her face. I was a bit taken aback. The study—Benbow had compared the mathematical ability of certain male and female students—had seemed a paltry thing to arouse such responses. I began to explain Ms. Benbow's findings, but the scientist broke in. He was quite aware of the study, and explained that he had served on a committee appointed by an international scientific organization to award a prize for the best study in the field for that year. Camilla Benbow's study had been overwhelmingly selected by the panel, and then the group's selection was sent to a chairwoman to be approved. This approval, the scientist told me, was pure formality—never before had any chairperson refused to approve the selection of the committee. This time, however, the chairwoman refused the selection.

But why? I asked. "She said it was a bad study, and didn't deserve the award," said my scientist relative. "And she was right."

I was confused, and said so. "Look," the scientist said finally, with exasperation, "Benbow's study suggests that there are innate differences between males and females."

A hot argument ensued. "Hold on," I said. "I thought the program of science was to find out what's true, and then communicate the truth."

"There is no truth!" the scientist yelled at me. "Statistics can be twisted to say anything you want! And anyway, no one should be studying differences between the sexes—they should be studying *similarities!*"

"Wait," I said, "this is like the Catholic Church telling Galileo he shouldn't be studying astronomy. Science is supposed to be able to study anything with dispassion and objectivity."

"Such studies can only lead to harm" yelled the scientist. "Such studies should not be done!"

"Even if what they find is the truth?" I wondered.

"Even if what they find is the truth," my sister cried, "it should be ignored." The scientist agreed. I was stunned.

"But that's censorship."

"It's not censorship," said my sister, "it's fighting against evil."

I was almost in tears, bewildered. Here were were, scientists, intellects to some degree, lifelong readers and book lovers—around the table were half a dozen graduate degrees, several college professors, a Protestant minister, a former college president, people with expertise in areas including anthropology, theology, archeology, art, child development, educational statistics, philosophy, psychology, neuroscience, and ethics. It was a family that had taken some pride in being open-minded, fair, and honest, at times under difficult circumstances. And now, they, or at least some of them, were saying some truths should be covered up, some truths were too dangerous, freedom of speech did not include some speech.

I went up to bed but couldn't sleep, so offended was I by what had happened. As I replayed the argument in my head, I could see that my sister and the scientist were afraid of something. But what? As I analyzed it, it became clear that what they hated so much that they wanted it to be censored had something to do with the sexes.

As I tossed and turned, I suddenly remembered the old fifties science-fiction movie *The Invasion of the Body Snatchers*, in which aliens invade Earth by entering the bodies of Earth people. The human victims appeared to be unchanged, but were transformed, moved by alien, incomprehensible drives. I decided it was time to put away my Central America book for a while and investigate what was happening to transform people, to frighten them so much.

And so I began to gather information for a book on a subject I couldn't yet describe to myself. It had something to do with sex—that had to be the starting point. But it had to do also with what linked publications like *Playboy* to the publications of scientific articles exploring the differing qualities of maleness and femaleness. It had to do with censorship, fear, power, politics, and an eerie transformation that seemed to be overtaking a large segment of our culture today.

I mentioned my new project to a friend over lunch one day. A writer whose work was published mainly in women's magazines, she shared my fascination with the subject, and our discussion soon turned toward anthropology. Surely, we agreed, the powerful responses people had toward sexually charged matters had some basis in the evolution of our species. She told me she was a friend of an influential anthropologist I'll call "Robbie," and she offered to introduce me to him, to see if he could be of assistance. I thanked her, and later that day she called me to give me Robbie's number.

The very next day she phoned me and cried, "Don't call Robbie!" When I told her I hadn't, she ordered me, "Then throw away his number!"

She explained that she had just been talking with a friend of hers —a graduate student in anthropology. "I mentioned your book project, and that I'd offered to introduce you to Robbie," she said, "and my friend just blew up! I mean, she started shouting and screaming, and saying that Robbie's ideas are dangerous, and that I should stop you from talking to him at all! She said he represents a view of anthropology that has to be suppressed."

I felt that strange *Invasion of the Body Snatchers* chill creeping over me again. Robbie, I pointed out, was a respected member of one of the finest anthropology departments in the country, had done extensive field research, and published influential papers and books. Her friend was just a grad student.

And what could be so dangerous that it had to be suppressed? "Well, it's not just Robbie," she explained, "but the point of view he represents." That point of view, it finally came out, had to do with sex. Robbie, a physical anthropologist, was one of a large number of anthropologists who believed that through the forces of evolution, human males and females had developed some biological differences. "My friend says people like him believe that the only reason we exist is to reproduce, our only reason for living is sex! She says that their views are disastrous and can only lead to increased overpopulation and nuclear war. After all," pleaded my friend, who was not a mother, "ideas like that would mean there was no point for me to exist at all!"

It seemed clear that what had prompted her friend to blow up and attempt to suppress Robbie's ideas had to do with that same tangle involving sex that had caused my other friends to begin talking like censors. It had to do with fear. But what was it that frightened these people so much that they became irrational?

As I analyzed it, seeing how it manifested itself—with prestigious scientific prizes and publications at stake, with battles among academics over good and evil, with actual attempts to suppress perceived opponents—it became clear that it had to do not so much with sex as with power.

No, with sex and power.

It hit me in a flash. Sex and power were fused, and they were what life in this era is all about. The sexual revolution of the 1960's and the feminist movement had dismantled the old sexual and political structures, and they were now being reassembled in new ways. The question was, who would have the power to determine how the structure would be put together? An enormous amount of power was up for grabs, and everyone wanted a piece of it. It was happening on all levels of society, from the nation as a whole to the individual.

Immense groups, like the more than 40 million Christian fundamentalists in the nation, were engaged in full-scale battles to gain political power, to influence who would be president, legislators, Supreme Court justices. They were tapping the power of sexuality to do so, mobilizing their forces with sexual issues, such as sex education, abortion, and pornography.

On an individual level the culture seemed obsessed with the erotics of power. Masses of people were paying big money to learn how to walk on hot coals so that they could attain power over themselves; or they were going to seminars and workshops on "personal empowerment."

The boom on Wall Street seemed to symbolize a mania that had swept society. The naked lust for money, once considered as unseemly as public sex, was now being accepted as a virtue. And money, of course, was power. And from moguls like Ivan Boesky and Donald Trump down to yuppie stockbrokers two years out of business school and making more than a million a year, everyone spoke of the pure sexual pleasure of making The Deal.

Here, I thought, is a subject worth investigating.

For the next three years, in my investigation of the sex-power nexus, I read, spoke with, observed, and researched cultural anthropologists, cultural materialists, cultural feminists, postfeminists, radical feminists, feminist sado-masochists, Christian feminists, Christian sensualists, Christian fundamentalists, Neo-Freudians, Neo-Jungians, New Age Tantrics, Neo-Reichian quantum physicists, neuroscientific mystics, Republican pornographers, and more.

As I explored the terrain, I found that many of the people I encountered there are ideologues, true believers: They look out at the world through the lenses of their ideologies, and what they see is the world as it fits into their ideological structure. Their ideology, that is, is the Truth.

Because they know the Truth, ideologues are certain that those who don't share their ideology are Wrong. In fact, they are frequently so obviously wrong and dangerous that they are clearly mad, evil, "heretics," and must be silenced. Burn their books, at least.

As I interviewed and investigated, I began to feel like some curious, fairly innocent lad who has wandered onto a battlefield and taken a position seated in the crotch of a tree overlooking the grassy knoll where all the combatants are wailing away at each other. Amid the screams and curses, the flying sweat and blood, I can observe who's fighting whom, and I can look around at the surroundings and see just what this patch of ground is that these heroes are fighting for so desperately. And amid the din of battle, the whanging and clanging of swords, I can now and then call down to various combatants and ask what they think they're fighting about.

Perhaps from all their conflicting claims, I can arrive at some consensus. Ideologues may not see the actual "world that is," the absolute reality, but they do see *something* out there. Each ideology has *some* connection with reality. Most of us, when we look at a cloudless noon sky, would agree that what we are seeing is blue.

And so here I am, perched in my tree overlooking the battlefield, scribbling madly in my notebook, trying to understand if not the entire world that is, at least that part of it about which there is general agreement. No matter what their ideologies, the combatants tell me the sky looks blue, the blood looks red, they are standing on dirt, not water, they are humans, not giraffes. Thus, bit by bit, it should be possible to find out what's true. Not "The Truth," just some things that are pretty clearly true.

PART I

THE BATTLE

Life is, in fact, a battle. Evil is insolent and strong; beauty enchanting, but rare; goodness very apt to be weak; folly very apt to be defiant; wickedness to carry the day; imbeciles to be in great places, people of sense in small, and mankind generally unhappy. But the world as it stands is not illusion, no phantasm, no evil dream of a night; we wake up to it again for ever and ever; we can neither forget it nor deny it nor dispense with it.

—Henry James

SCHIZOSEXUALITY IN AMERICA

· ·

America is obsessed with sex. Americans' interest in and tolerance for overt sexuality has reached such a high pitch, some Rip Van Winkle wandering in after a twenty-year snooze would think he was still asleep but had merely got caught up in an adolescent wet dream or erotic filmmaker's X-rated satire on American culture.

The soap operas of twenty years back have now moved to prime time, where they explore the adulteries, orgasms, impotencies, and breast implants of wealthy families in Texas and other states. And on our talk shows the guests describe the joys of S&M, the heartbreak of genital herpes, the thrill of group sex, the pros and cons of incest, the esthetics of nipple-piercing.

Nearly half of all the films we watch, according to recent statistics, are hard-core pornographic movies. And while porn flicks used to be something only men watched, today figures show that over half the people renting porn movies are women.

Our ads look like stills from arty porn films, with piles of naked bodies advertising a cologne, bare-breasted young ladies becoming sexually aroused by their jeans while young ladies for another brand of jeans seem quite sultry and naughty by sharing some partly clad kisses with each other and then going off to the local truck stop to do a strip tease for the truckers and cowboys. In stylish women's magazines sleek ladies in black net stockings and garters and high heels but little else pose languidly with whips, chains, and sneering men in black leather accompanied by growling Dobermans, like a scene from some 1930's Continental sadomasochistic film.

Today, what the voters want to know about a candidate first is not where he stands on the issues but does he commit adultery? If he does, we get front-page pictures of him with one or two of his sex partners, and color spreads of the sex partner with her clothes off in the magazines. The sex partner then sells her story to national magazines, and Hollywood producers bid for the movie rights.

There's no doubt—American life is drenched in sexuality; our lives, our thoughts, are more intensely sexual than ever before. But that doesn't mean we like it. In fact, rather than enjoying the sexual profusion of our culture, we're oddly ambivalent about it. Actually, ambivalence is not a strong enough word to describe the excruciating feelings we have.

American culture is drenched in sex, yes, but we wear it like a hair shirt. It is itchy and irritating, a remorseless reminder that the flesh is weak and impure, that we should be directing our attention to "higher" matters; but at the same time the hair shirt rewards us for the misery it causes—we are constantly aware that we can stoically bear these physical itchings, that we are, in our self-denial, spiritually superior to others, so that self-abasement and self-torture become at the same time an act of spiritual pride. We are obsessed with sex, but insist it is something too low, too dirty, too shameful, for us to really be wasting our time on, at least in public. The result is our unique cultural schizophrenia that causes us to spend most of our time in a state of sexual arousal while pretending to disapprove of the very thing that's arousing us.

THE NAKED HART AND THE UNDERWEAR DOCUMENTS

It would be funny—and has been the subject of vast amounts of satire, particularly from Europeans, whose sexual foibles are somewhat different from ours—if it weren't so dangerous and destructive. One recent example is the case of politician Gary Hart. In mid-1987 he was the most widely recognized and most popular of a number of Democrats seeking the presidential nomination. Most political analysts considered him to be a shoo-in for the nomination.

At the time the story of Gary Hart and Donna Rice broke, the nation had been fascinated with the unfolding tale of how members of Ronald Reagan's administration had lied to Congress and the people, had broken dozens of laws, and had allowed a gang of thieves and murderers to operate a wildly dangerous secret government that was pursuing a foreign policy that was not only absurd but a threat to world peace. By any stretch of the imagination, it was a terrific story.

And yet the instant the Hart story became known, it pushed the Iran-Contra affair out of the top spot in the evening network newscasts, and took over the headlines. After all, the Iran-Contra affair was just the state of the world, but the Hart story was *sex*.

Meanwhile, as Hart was humiliated, Donna Rice was becoming America's darling. *Playboy* magazine offered her great wealth to pose for it. Barbara Walters welcomed Donna as her guest on a special that attracted scores of millions of viewers. Donna was such a hot ticket because she represented sex, but she was *safe*: the American hair-shirt mentality dictated that illicit sexual escapades had to be punished. Hart had fulfilled this stricture by sacrificing himself, his career hammered into rubble. As political analyst Hendrik Hertzberg wrote, "Gary Hart has now become the first American victim of Islamic justice. He has been politically stoned to death for adultery."

While this story was scorching the newspaper headlines, the Iran-Contra hearings were still going on—conceivably the biggest and ugliest story since World War II. But the public interest was low. Then, briefly, it appeared that one of the chief criminals, Oliver North, had a secretary, Fawn Hall, who was tall, attractive, with blond hair in the carefully windswept lion's-mane style of TV actresses. Fawn, we learned, had not only helped North shred thousands of pages of important incriminating documents, she had also smuggled many documents out of the White House. How did she smuggle them? From somewhere deep in the jungle the drums of voodoo Freudianism began to beat: She smuggled them in her underwear!

Instantly the Iran-Contra hearings were back at the top of the nightly newscasts; suddenly all eyes were on Washington as Fawn Hall came out and gave smiling press conferences, refused to talk about her underwear, hinted tearfully of her love affair with the son of the leader of the Contras, denied ever having sex with Oliver North. *Playboy* and *Penthouse* raised eyebrows with offers of vast sums of money for Fawn to pose naked in their pages. Heated speculation circulated as to whether Fawn and Ollie really got it on or not.

The sex follies of '87 rolled on at a breakneck pace as fundamentalist minister Jim Bakker, who with his wife, Tammy Faye, had turned their television PTL (Praise The Lord) ministry into a multimillion-dollar success story by preaching their gospel that God rewards born-again Christians with material success, was discovered to have had sex with a young church secretary who had been brought to his motel room in Florida.

As the story progressed, it appeared that the young girl, Jessica Hahn, had been paid some $250,000 hush money, but apparently she had taken the money and become unhushed. Jessica claimed Jim had had sex with her when she had come to him as a virgin, and as a member of his church (but the whole thing, America was fascinated to learn, had only taken twenty minutes!).

Jim claimed she performed like a professional. Soon it was learned that Jim was only one of several who had been in the sack with Jessica that night. Jessica claimed it was horrible. Jim claimed he only did it because his wife had been having an affair with the country musician known for those great American hits "Alley Oop" and "Monster Mash." His wife, recently out of treatment at the Betty Ford Clinic for addiction to alcohol and pills, tearfully denied that she'd had an affair. Jerry Falwell, head of the Moral Majority and a leading spokesman for the religious right, stepped in to take over the PTL ministry, claiming that he had information that Jim Bakker had not only been unchristian with Jessica, but with a number of young boys.

A variety of men and boys quickly made front-page headlines with their tales of sexual escapades with Jessica, all of them alleging that Jessica was sexually voracious. Jessica was not happy. "I am not a bimbo!" she proclaimed to the nation. To prove to America she was not a slut, she had her breasts enlarged and accepted a fortune to pose nude for *Playboy*. America was scandalized, and the magazine set a record for sales.

To all those conservative Americans who despised *Playboy* or any other magazine that published articles dealing with such perversions as group sex or homo-sex or what have you, here was something they could sink their teeth into. The result was an orgy of sex-talk among American fundamentalists the like of which has never been seen before—Christian talk shows, Christian call-in shows, newspapers, magazines, all were assiduously getting right down to the peskiest details, like did Tammy Faye have breast implants on PTL money? Just how many preachers were in bed with Jessica, and did she like it or not? They could wrestle around with the gritty stuff, you see, because this was about *religion*.

Then one of the most successful of all televangelists, Jimmy Swaggart—the man who had claimed that the sexual peccadilloes of Jim Bakker were "a cancer on the church"—was revealed to have been frequenting a prostitute. Swaggart made a public confession of his sins, and once again the fundamentalists could talk fervently and righteously about prurient matters. And once again it was quickly announced that the prostitute Swaggart had admitted to patronizing had signed a six-figure contract with *Penthouse* magazine to recreate the "precise poses and actions he paid for."

The point here is not so much that Americans are fascinated with sex. That would not make us different from anyone else. What is important is that Americans can only feel comfortable with sex when it's disguised as something else—like news, politics, or religion. Otherwise, it makes us nervous, it frightens us, it fills us with emotions and impulses we don't know what to do with. We still believe there is something dirty, naughty, or threatening about it, and so the only way we can allow ourselves to deal with it is by making certain that those who are dirty or naughty are punished, and then we watch what we take to be a morality play with consuming interest.

THE BEAST IN THE JUNGLE

What so fascinates us about these stories is not simply their sexual content, but their deep, almost mythic resonance. They reach into the depths of our unconscious, and threaten to reveal something about ourselves, about all humans, about the nature of human nature. They resonate with other stories we have grown up with, like the tales of Adam and Eve, Samson and Delilah, Salome, the Blue Angel.

They are all stories that carry a message: that sex cannot only undo power, it *is* power. Not the physical power of a Samson, or the political power of potentates and politicians, for those kinds of power are manifest and respected. But a power that is more subtle, secret, ungovernable, and therefore more to be feared. It is a power that, as Samson discovered, along with Gary Hart, Jim Bakker, and so many others, can undermine and destroy worldly power with insidious ease. If even the most powerful, respected, and disciplined among us are susceptible to this power, then who of us is safe from it?

We are like the inhabitants of some small village surrounded by jungle. As we go about our lives, now and then the wild beast emerges in the night and carries away one of the villagers. Some of the villagers, led by the priest, claim we should pray to the gods, make sacrifices, perform the correct rituals of worship, and we will be protected from the beast. The beast will only attack those who have angered the gods. Others angrily insist that we should arm ourselves and go out after the beast and hunt it down. Only when the beast is destroyed will the village be safe. Still others argue that the beast can be tamed. Rather than fearing and resisting it, we should welcome it, feed it, make friends with it, create a place for it within the village. Then, they argue, we will see that the beast is not so frightening, that it is at heart benevolent, playful, and will provide us with pleasure and teach us much about ourselves.

The argument escalates until it has become a fight about who has the power to force the rest of the villagers to follow their plan. Tempers flare. It has become a naked struggle for power, a battle for control of the village itself.

And so weapons are drawn, and the combatants confront each other. As the battle rages, now and then the beast emerges from the jungle to pounce upon one of the combatants and drag the body back into the thick brush. At this point, it's hard to tell who has the upper hand.

REVOLUTIONARY SEX

. . . .

*All bibles or sacred codes have been the causes of the following
errors:*

1. *That man has two real existing principles: viz: a body & a
   soul.*
2. *That energy, called evil, is alone from the body: & that
   reason, called good, is alone from the soul.*
3. *That God will torment man in eternity for following his
   energies.*

But the following contraries to these are true:

1. *Man has no body distinct from his soul; for that called body
   is a portion of soul discerned by the five senses, the chief
   inlets of soul in this age.*
2. *Energy is the only life, and is from the body; and reason is
   the bound or outward circumference of energy.*
3. *Energy is eternal delight.*

—William Blake, "The Marriage of Heaven and Hell," 1790

The struggle now taking place in the sex-power nexus has, as the
quote from Blake illustrates, been going on for centuries. But to a
large degree the present full-scale battle has emerged from and is a
response to an upheaval that occurred in the 1960's, what has come
to be called the sexual revolution.

That revolution was the result of a number of converging and
interlocking forces and events. One of these was the sudden availability to the mass public of a variety of erotic or even pornographic
materials that had long been suppressed. In 1957, in a case that came

to be known as the *Roth-Alberts* decision, the U.S. Supreme Court ruled that for something to be judged obscene, it must be "utterly without redeeming social importance." The decision went on to state, "The portrayal of sex, e.g., in art, literature and scientific works, is not itself sufficient reason to deny material the constitutional protection of freedom of speech and press. Sex, a great and mysterious motive force in human life, has indisputably been a subject of absorbing interest to mankind through the ages; it is one of the vital problems of human interest and public concern."

This case opened the floodgates for the publication not only of books that had clear literary value, such as *Lady Chatterley's Lover* and Henry Miller's *Tropic of Cancer*, but for other, more questionable works, since it is hard to say that any book is utterly without redeeming social importance. Within a few years after the Roth-Alberts case Charles Rembar, the lawyer who had defended *Lady Chatterley's Lover* and was involved in over sixty trials of *Tropic of Cancer*, stated, "So far as writing is concerned, there is no longer any law of obscenity."

These books, and others that followed, such as Terry Southern's *Candy*, and *The Story of O*, were avidly devoured, particularly by the millions of young people born in the postwar baby boom, who were then moving into their teenage years of sexual exploration. The books plunged them into a universe whose driving force was sex, and the sex they found there—raunchy, perverse, comic, transcendent, obsessive, shameless, intense, consuming, enraptured—was quite at odds with what their parents and the society had informed them was normal and acceptable.

Jack Kerouac's novel *On the Road* hit the best-seller lists (1957), the word "beatnik" entered the popular vocabulary, and for the next several years battered paperbacks of the book were passed from hand to hand among teenagers as a sort of bible of beatdom. In its ecstatic spontaneous prose, they found a joyous affirmation of the liberating powers of sex. The conformist world was deadly, said the book, and it would beat you down, but even though you were beat, there was salvation, and it came through experiential excess, through the Vision that could redeem all the suffering of living among the walking dead, a Vision found in plunging into experience with a kind of kamikaze energy. Kerouac's book sizzled, alerting millions of youths to the revolutionary news that sex was energy and vice versa, and that, as Blake explains it, energy is eternal delight.

And that spontaneous release of sexual energy had become safe. In 1960 had come the Pill. Almost overnight, like a science-fiction utopian novel come true, there it was, promising worry-free sex, allowing women to follow their sexual desires as freely as men— more freely, since men faced the difficulty (more difficult for some than for others) of finding a willing sexual partner, while women, freed by the Pill, were assured of as many sexual partners as they wished.

And then, as if to symbolize the new direction a whole generation was taking, the bald, grandfatherly golf-course duffer Ike was gone, and the vigorous young JFK had swept into the White House, with his long hair blowing in the wind, his glamorous wife, and a radiant aura of sex and sexual power. Even though the stories about Kennedy's affairs didn't become widely known until after his death, still his virility was magically transported through the TV screen. Golf, it was clear to everyone, was not this man's favorite game. If Kennedy's presidency represented to a young generation the powers of sexual energies, it also presented them with a clear lesson of how sex and power were inextricably intertwined.

His assassination taught them another lesson—that there were forces out there opposed to the youthful (and intrinsically sexual) energies Kennedy represented. This sudden understanding, this feeling of youthful energies threatened by powerful murky forces, blossomed among the suspicions and paranoia surrounding the Warren Commission investigation of the assassination. Among all the conspiracy theories, one thing became chillingly clear to the baby-boom generation: Whatever political machinations lay behind the assassination, *They* did it, and *They* had covered it up, and *They* had gotten away with it. And whoever They were, They were old, and They were powerful, and They had felt threatened by the freedoms being taken by the young, including sexual freedom.

THE ATTACK OF THE ROCK-AND-ROLL SEX VIRUS

The assassination served as a catalyst for fused energies, anxieties, tendencies that had already been there. Now, what had seemed to be unconnected individuals, random groups, became a phenomenon, a generation. And it was a generation that apparently had an enemy— the older generation. If They represented the dominant culture, then

We were the counterculture. And this, the youth movement came to realize, was not just another generation but something entirely new: a generation with a mission. The mission was no less than to bring about a great Awakening: the total transformation of society.

Not that this supreme mission came to all in a blinding vision. Rather, it was like a suspicion, a slow dawning of comprehension as individuals looked around to find themselves together with lots of other people who had an uncanny similarity to them, right down to the same (nonconformist) long hair, the same scuffed copies of *Coney Island of the Mind*, the same lust for vividness and intensity, the same fascination with drugs, and, perhaps most of all, the same knee-jerk and absolutely pure visceral response to rock music: *Hey, this is our language!*

The feeling was generational, not political; naive and spontaneous, not organized; not a movement but an eruption, or an infection, as if some mysterious virus had wafted across the nation, a virus to which only certain people were susceptible—those who had been exposed to quantities of rock and roll, pot, the Mickey Mouse Club, Little Richard, and grade-school H-Bomb drills ("duck and cover"). The goal was not reform. Everyone knew the grinding gray technocracy—which turned everyone into numbers, from the phalanxes of robot-fathers in their gray flannel suits to the students registered on each course computer card with their Social Security student ID number—was beyond reform. The idea was much more innocent, idealistic—to become human again, to be honest and "up front" with each other, to cut away bullshit, to be free, wild, pure.

The perfect mode for this radical openness was sex. As French phenomenologist Paul Ricoeur was pointing out at just that time (1964), "Eros . . . belongs to the pretechnical existence of man. . . . Sexuality remains basically foreign to the 'intention-tool-thing' relationship. It is a surviving example of noninstrumental immediacy. The body to body relationship—or better, person to flesh to flesh to person—remains basically nontechnical."

Though the counterculture was never a single movement, its components—the SDS Weathermen politicos, the macrobiotic vegetarians, the dopers and acidheads, the commune dwellers, the Zen meditators, the postbeatniks, the intellectuals, existentialists, and esthetes—however contemptuous of each other, were united in their total rejection of technological society and the sexual constraints that seemed an essential aspect of it, and in their acceptance of the absolute necessity of unrepressed sexuality as the key to human relationships. It was what separated Us from Them. As the Who sang in their 1965 hit "My Generation," a song that became a sort of counterculture anthem:

> *The things They do look awful cold:*
> *Hope I die before I get old.*
> *Talkin bout my ge-ge-ge-ge-ge-generation!*

It took some time for the growing counterculture to catch on to the fact that they represented a potential power—the power to explode in expressing their own identity. Lessons were learned from the civil-rights movement, as the young participants, blacks and whites, sleeping together in church basements and storefronts, engaged in sex made unforgettably intense and sweet, an affirmation of life, against the constant threat of death from firebombings, or murders by drunken rednecks and KKK death squads. Lessons were also learned from blacks in the inner cities, who in those "long, hot summers" erupted in wild uprisings, turning ghettos like Watts and Detroit into bombed-out battlefields—spontaneous expressions of rage and frustration in which violence became an act of celebration: "Burn baby, burn!" To a generation whose only real heroes were middle-class musicians like Bob Dylan, the Beatles, the Stones, and a murdered president from a wealthy and powerful family, these young black men, defying tear gas and shotguns right on the TV news, looting and burning against a soundtrack of Motown and soul records—these were bold heroes, urban guerrillas.

The idea that the students could themselves become urban guerrillas and bold heroes began to emerge in the mid-sixties, an emergence marked by the spontaneous eruptions of students and "nonstudents" at Berkeley. The uprising and the resulting Free Speech Movement, were, according to the press, sparked by frustrations caused by the faceless, impersonal university system. But in truth they were more of a spontaneous emission, a surprising wet dream in which the student is so full of energies and desires that he wakes up to find the sheets wet, or in this case, students awaken en masse to find themselves setting police cars on fire and rioting with joy and rage in the streets. And when the authorities struck back at the Free Speech Movement, they found themselves in a nasty no-win struggle with the Filthy Speech Movement. "Fuck Kerr!" chanted the demonstrators, using the name of the university chancellor. Quickly and instinctively they had seen the link between their energies and sex, between their human rights and their right to fuck, between free speech and filthy speech.

THE SECRET SEXUAL POWERS OF DRAFT DODGERS

Leftists, essentially powerless in America for decades, looked on this wild unselfconscious outburst as a resource to be directed, a historic opportunity to regain leadership and power, and began organizing furiously, trying to impart to the students that most un-American thing, rational ideology. It's unlikely the left would have made much headway with a movement whose participants were more interested in sex and music than in the dictatorship of the proletariat, if it had not been for the Vietnam War. But there it was, so totally wrong, such a blatant object lesson in the evils of capitalism and American imperialism, that even the most apolitical doper could see it clearly.

Even in its political actions, the counterculture had a clear, instinctive, if subconscious understanding that its opposition to the war was inextricably fused with its sexual energy. It had to do with the sexual jealousy of the old for the young: They were uptight and impotent old men, who got their own perverse kicks from using power, who struck out at the free sexuality of the young by sending the males off to war (or jail, or Canada).

Fuck the System! Fuck the War! These were incendiary slogans. Fuck the System was a weird idea, since of course the System was some grinding, monstrous contraption that did not operate in terms of being fucked: It only fucked you. But what you could do was fuck, make love, assert your freedom and energy, in the face of the System, and thereby show it by contrast for the antilife monstrosity it was.

As the counterculture organized, growing more sophisticated in its tactics, it found the opposition using more and more frightening and unbelievable tactics: Undercover agents took photos of demonstrators, infiltrated organizations, broke into offices to steal files, opened mail, and had agents provocateurs actually incite riots, teach people how to make bombs, encourage them to plant bombs, even plant bombs themselves. It became clear that They took this movement seriously. And it made sense that at the heart of their fears was sex: nightmarish images of braless promiscuous alluring young women locked in sexual embrace with long-haired communist draft-dodging young men or, the horror, arrogant young black men—Black Panthers—armed, filled with rage and secret sexual powers.

For the forces of reaction, sex was terrifying, for it unleashed terrors and drives they had spent their lives keeping hidden and controlled. Richard Nixon showed how clearly he understood this sex-power dynamic when, speaking out against "pornography" in 1970, at the peak of the countercultural upheavals, he warned the nation, "If an attitude of permissiveness were to be adopted regarding pornography, this would contribute to an atmosphere condoning anarchy in every other field—and would increase the threat to our social order as well as to our moral principles." Unsuppressed, unopposed, it was clear, sex bred chaos.

PARADISE NOW: THE DISCOVERY OF THE ORGASM

The core idea was simple enough: Sex can make you free. If you freed yourself sexually, cast off your clothes, became naked physically, openly and free of guilt, then you might become naked spiritually as well, casting off not just clothes but "roles," and "ego," and "hang-ups," and "mind games." The most effective way to become untangled, spiritually naked, free, according to the sexual revolutionaries, was through ecstasy (in the dictionary definition, getting out of your ordinary position, your *stasis*), induced by a direct experience of the pure mystical energy that is your true self and that also links you to the energy of the universe. That is, through orgasm: not only sexual orgasm, but also the orgasmic bliss of other experiences, such as, say, LSD, dance, rock music, and various mystical religious practices. To have such experiences, such wisdom, was a political as well as spiritual act: the politics of ecstasy (which was the title of LSD guru Timothy Leary's book published at that time).

That was the theory; the practice was, for many, sex, drugs, and rock music. And the euphoria, the almost inexpressible exploding release of energy and the sensation of freedom at large shout from the titles of the rock songs of the era: "If It Feels Good, Do It!" "Why Don't We Do It In the Road?" "Light My Fire." "Born to Be Wild." "All You Need Is Love." "Wild Thing!" "Celebrate! Celebrate!"

Couched in the language of the 1960's, it sounds quaint and a little mush-headed, but it is not a silly or faddish idea—it is an expression of one of the most ancient and persistent religions in human culture. Its history can be traced through the ancient mystery cults of Sumeria, Mesopotamia, Egypt, and Greece, in which wisdom was found in sexual experiences with temple prostitutes, and in ritualistic practices associated with sex goddesses, such as Ishtar, Astarte, and Aphrodite. It appears in ancient Chinese Taoism and in Tantric Buddhism, which taught techniques of "sexual alchemy" for reaching enlightenment through intensified and prolonged sexual experiences.

It blossomed in one of its most influential forms, known as Gnosticism (from the Greek word *gnosis*, or wisdom), several thousand years ago in the Middle East, during that period of upheaval and religious ferment that gave birth to Christianity. Springing from the same matrix, Gnosticism competed with and strongly influenced early Christianity. Many biblical scholars now believe that Jesus himself was an initiate of a gnostic sect, and that many early Christian sects were in fact based on this belief, until the new religion was taken over by the leaders of the new Roman church, who in their need to centralize authority and establish a single orthodoxy decreed that this early mystical form of Christianity was a heresy, and vigorously rooted it out.

The gnostics, too, believed the world had been created by a powerful god, but the gnostics believed that this god or demiurge was in fact evil or incompetent, and inferior to the supreme God. The physical world and life itself was evil, and the goal of the gnostic was to break away from, pierce through, the illusions of this impure world and experience fully the true God.

Behind the apparent, material reality, gnostics believed, lies the true reality. Behind the apparent self of every individual lies the true self, totally transcendent. This true self is like a spark of the divine, but each bearer of this spark remains isolated, alienated in this world, "asleep." Thus, gnostics sought to "awaken," to reunite this spark with the unknown true God, who is hidden behind the apparent (false) reality.

Gnostics went about the freeing of self from the bonds of this corrupt world and reuniting with the divine in several ways. One way chosen by many gnostic groups was ascetic withdrawal. Other groups, however, chose a more dramatic path—rather than withdrawing from the world, they intentionally violated its rules.

What this meant in practice for these gnostics was a rejection of the morality of sexual restraint, and a dedicated pursuit of sacred wisdom through plunging into ecstatic sexual experiences (the gnostic true God is, unlike the Judeo-Christian God, sexual in essence). This aspect of gnosticism posed a threat to both the Jewish and Christian religions, one they have combated and suppressed ruthlessly. Despite the suppressions, the heresy of sexual gnosticism has popped up in various forms throughout history, including the Jewish Cabalistic teachings, the arcane practices of the alchemists, and the secret societies such as the Knights Templar, all emerging out of the Middle Ages; such large-scale movements as the Albigensians of the thirteenth century (who were so feared by the Christian Church that they were burned at the stake by the thousands, their towns destroyed, and their writings wiped out completely), and the fourteenth-century Brethren of the Free Spirit; and the countless smaller apocalyptic cults and sects that have flourished in periods of social disorientation.

IN PURSUIT OF THE SEXUAL MILLENNIUM

In *The Pursuit of the Millennium: Revolutionary Millenarians and Mystical Anarchists of the Middle Ages*, historian Norman Cohn points out that the social situations in which these millennial gnostic cults flourished were "remarkably uniform." The outbreaks, he notes, took place in areas and at times when general social disorientation, anxiety, and inequality were catalyzed by a force or event that was both unprecedented and, apparently, uncontrollable. Such a catalyst triggers fear and revulsion, causing individuals to reject the institutions and dogmas of the day as inherently destructive, corrupt, and evil, and to replace them with a mystical, gnostic belief in a pure and divine reality that can be found only by "awakening," by piercing through the veil of the illusory reality. One such catalyzing force in the Middle Ages was the Black Plague.

The mass anxiety, discontent, and disorientation of the 1960's were largely a result of the rapid emergence of a world-transforming technology that was increasingly seen as mindless, out of control, rolling toward disaster. To the general cultural disorientation in the United States was added the catalytic event, the modern "plague" that confronted millions with the threat of their own death—the war in Vietnam, and its draft.

The result was the flowering of a true millennial cult, spontaneous, irrational, gnostic, whose goal was to "awaken" and transform society through "revolution," which was understood to mean not a seizing of the political apparatus or of the means of production, but a metamorphosis of the culture itself, a total altering of expectations.

Gnosticism offered its practitioners a system of wisdom that was concealed from all others, and throughout the sixties the counterculture's main form of communication, rock music, was treated as a secret code, carrying mystic wisdom for those who had ears to hear. Gnostics explored and pondered such mysteries as the real words of "Louie Louie," the secret meaning of "Sad Eyed Lady of the Lowland," the contents of Bob Dylan's garbage can, and the significance of Paul McCartney appearing barefoot on the cover of *Abbey Road*. The most mundane objects in the world were pregnant with meaning, appearances concealed mystic realities.

Drugs were endemic in the counterculture, used largely in a religious context, as "sacrament," with joints passed from hand to hand, and the religion was, of course, gnostic sexuality. Drugs were valued not only for their ability to remove inhibitions and produce a state of mind more open to transcendent experiences, but also for their power to increase the user's pleasure in sex. Timothy Leary must have caused more people to take LSD with the sexual promises made in an interview with *Playboy* magazine than through all of his other writings combined. LSD, he declared, was the most powerful aphrodisiac ever discovered. "Compared with sex under LSD," he claimed, "the way you've been making love—no matter how ecstatic the pleasure you think you get from it—is like making love to a department-store-window dummy." And making an explicit gnostic link between sex and the divine, Leary proclaimed, "The three inevitable goals of the LSD session are to discover and make love with God, to discover and make love with yourself, and to discover and make love with a woman."

One poll in 1968 by the McGlothlin polling group revealed that 85 percent of all people in this country who smoked pot claimed their main interest in the herb was for its power of enhancing sexual pleasure. Break on through to the other side! sang Jim Morrison, who then took out his penis and waved it to the audience. And was arrested.

Religious and civil authorities from Mayor Daley to Richard Nixon to J. Edgar Hoover to Cardinal Spellman saw foreshadowed in these long-haired freaks the loss of control, a world without structure, a crumbling of the hierarchies, chaos. And they worked zealously, and in general ruthlessly, to stamp out these flare-ups of the old gnostic heresy.

At its peak in the late 1960's, it's interesting how close that heresy came to actually posing a serious threat to the established state and churches. What was, and remains, a radical vision, became for a time the program not just of the cultural wildhairs and yo-yos, fringe groups, artists, visionaries, radicals, and youth, but also of the respected cultural leaders, the mainstream intelligentsia and literati, priests, professors, and preachers, who let their graying hair grow long and wholeheartedly took up the slogan "Make Love, Not War." It was the era of what writer Tom Wolfe labeled "radical chic," and for increasingly large numbers of people, sex was seen as a powerful tool not only for self-liberation but for political action and cultural transformation as well.

THE SEXUALIZATION OF THE MASSES

. . . .

Like an earthquake, the sexual revolution shook and altered the cultural landscape of America. Some structures collapsed, others began to show cracks, people's daily routines were disrupted, machines were temporarily thrown out of kilter, things were rearranged. As with all earthquakes, the power of this one was greatest at its epicenter. The epicenter of this earthquake was the youth culture, whose sexual gnosticism represented the purest and most explosive expression of the sexual revolution. And as the shock waves moved outward from the youth culture hot spots—New York City, San Francisco, Berkeley, Ann Arbor, Madison, Cambridge, Los Angeles—their disruptive force diminished, the "purity" of the energies at the core of the upheaval became progressively diluted and transformed.

WOMEN UNCHAINED: STALKING THE WILD ORGASM

As the upheavals moved outward, those who were most immediately and powerfully influenced were, naturally enough, those who were closest to the youth culture, who had in fact been a part of it: young radical females. These women, who had been freed by the Pill and who had eagerly plunged into the sexual revolution, were finding themselves frustrated by it. The Heresy taught that you had to free yourself from sexual constraints, the constraints placed on you by culture, by conditioning. But women, in freeing themselves, had to undergo a double revolution. For after the sexual revolution, the breaking free from repression, fear, anxiety, the exploring of full sexuality, they found themselves still locked into the same roles as women. What was needed was not just a sexual liberation, but women's liberation.

So radical women began to break free of what they believed to be a male-dominated counterculture, and met together to exchange ideas and feelings about sex with other women in "consciousness-raising groups." A basic text was Anne Koedt's essay "The Myth of the Vaginal Orgasm," from which they learned that vaginal sexuality was a myth created by men to keep women passive and dependent on men for sexual fulfillment. In truth, they learned, all orgasms came from clitoral stimulation, and women who were clitorally sensitive could attain sexual independence from males through masturbation. Masturbation, in fact, could increase the power of women, since if women could arouse and satisfy themselves, males would no longer be required, or, if allowed to participate, would no longer be in charge.

Soon feminist writers were turning out handbooks teaching women masturbation techniques. Women would bring mirrors to their consciousness-raising groups to observe and learn to appreciate the beauty of their own vaginas. Writer Alice Walker captures the gnostic spirit of the period in *The Temple of My Familiar*: "The women in her consciousness-raising group had taught her how to masturbate. Suddenly she'd found herself free. Sexually free, for the first time in her life. At the same time, she was learning to meditate, and was throwing off the last clinging vestiges of organized religion. She was soon meditating and masturbating and finding herself dissolved into the cosmic All. Delicious."

Feminists discovered the powers of sexual fantasy in promoting orgasms, and pornography for women (called "erotica") was seen as another tool of sexual liberation. After all, the Heresy attested that the true liberation of the self, the casting off of chains, the tearing down of the illusory structures of consensus reality, came in the ecstatic experience, the loss of self, and fusion with the All. Which meant, it seemed, the orgasm. Which did not necessarily require a man's presence.

And so, in discovering and exploring their sexual independence, women began to see that it could also be a key to increasing their power and self-determination in other areas—socially, politically, economically. The energies released by the sexual revolution, these feminists found, could be used to fuel a revolution in the relations between the sexes.

RADICAL CHIC AND HORSES' PENISES

As the waves of the sexual earthquake moved outward, the next group to be affected was the cultural intelligentsia. Leading figures in the arts, the media, fashion, and society quickly adopted the outward mannerisms of the sexual revolutionaries, letting their hair grow long, proclaiming their love for rock music, learning to smoke pot and experimenting with LSD, wearing beads and chains, dressing in the eclectic, flamboyant style of the youth culture, and discovering the virtues of spontaneous, uninhibited sexuality.

Liberated sexuality, they came to believe, would lead to new personal and cultural freedom. Indeed, it had been the repression of this sexuality that had created the angst, boredom, and loss of purpose that plagued modern American culture. Columbia literature professor Steven Marcus explained this process in his influential 1967 book *The Other Victorians: A Study of Sexuality and Pornography in Mid-Nineteenth-Century England.* In his discussion of the shift of sexual values that took place in Victorian England, Marcus emphasized that "a general restructuring of the personality occurred, and what emerged at the end was a character which was more armored and more rigidified, a character . . . less spontaneous, less openly sexual—and probably sexually thwarted. This is the character which the modern middle class has inherited and that everyone is miserable about; and it is not open to doubt that a loss of tragic magnitude was entailed in the change."

The cultural intelligentsia knew well the "armored," "rigidified," and "miserable" nature of contemporary middle-class sexual life, and enthusiastically set about to remedy their "loss of tragic magnitude."

One reason for this rapid and wholehearted acceptance by middle-aged liberals and intellectuals of radical and even heretical sexual beliefs was that they were already intellectually in a state of readiness: a watered-down, deenergized version of the sexual heresy had already been accepted by the intelligentsia in what had become for them a pallid secular religion—that is, Freud and psychoanalysis.

In his clearest and most mature explanation of his theory of the causation of neurosis, elucidated in his study of "the problem of anxiety," Freud had emphasized that anxiety is a product of perceived cultural constraints upon largely sexual instincts: Our instincts give rise to a desire that cannot be acted upon, or is viewed as dangerous or unacceptable by the conscious mind. Thus, the wish or desire must be repressed, and as a result we suffer anxiety.

As a guide for relieving this anxiety Freud provided his famous case study of young Hans, a five-year-old boy with a horse phobia. Freud's investigation revealed that Hans had an open interest in penises, loved his mother, wanted her to touch his penis, feared his father, and was jealous of his father's intimacy with his mother. Hans suffered increasing anxiety that led to a debilitating fear of horses mixed with an obsession with horses and their large penises, which he associated with his father. He spoke of many similarities between his father and horses, and obsessively described whippings of horses he had witnessed on the streets of Vienna. Clearly this whole complex of associations involved instincts leading to wishes that Hans knew were unacceptable or dangerous. Hans's deep fears of horrible dangers brought about by his powerful sexual desires were disguised and diverted into a much more acceptable fear of animals. Freud advised the father to guide conversations with Hans to these matters so that the boy could become consciously aware of the associations. Over a period of time the fears disappeared.

Freud's strategy, to remove at least some of the constraints on instincts, was a more socially acceptable and perhaps less effective version of the strategy advised by the sexual revolutionaries, which was, as succinctly expressed in the title of a song by the Beatles: "Why Don't We Do It In the Road?"

Against the image of a drunken, black-leather-clad Jim Morrison pulling out his penis in front of a screaming audience was posed the image of LBJ, at just about the same time, frustrated by the inability of U.S. forces to make any headway against the ghostlike Vietcong, unzipping his fly, pulling out his penis, and asking the reporters (according to one who was there), "Has Ho Chi Minh got anything to match that?"

Clearly it was time for penis-waving. The liberal intelligentsia had their own characteristic way of doing this. And so Alexander Portnoy reclined upon his psychoanalyst's couch and dutifully, with wit, irony, and erudition, pulled out his penis and, as he waved it around, began to talk about it.

PORN CHIC: NIXON CONFRONTS DEEP THROAT

In 1969 Phillip Roth's scabrous comedy of male masturbation and sexual confusion, *Portnoy's Complaint*, was immediately attacked by middlebrow critics as "pure pornography." But the book became an enormous best-seller and, more important, was highly acclaimed by the intellectual elite. For masturbation, in part as a result of its enshrinement by feminists as an almost sacred rite, was no longer taboo. And pornography, long-scorned by middle-class liberals as lower class, vulgar, tawdry, and tasteless, was now being seen as a positive good, a tool for sexual liberation, a means of repudiating sexual repression. Porn had become chic.

A key to the widespread acceptance of pornography as good clean fun was the antiestablishment zeitgeist. During the administration of LBJ, as it became clear to people in power that there was a link between the troublesome antiwar movement and sexual openness, a commission was established by the president to investigate the potential harmful effects of pornography. By the time the report was completed in 1970, the president was Richard Nixon. *The Report of the Commission on Obscenity and Pornography* found that there was no evidence linking sexual material to delinquency or criminal behavior. In fact, the commission found evidence that sexual criminals, such as rapists, actually had *less* use of sexual materials than did normal people, and also cited evidence that explicit sexual materials could have "social redeeming value." It concluded, "The Commission recommends that federal, state and local legislation prohibiting the sale, exhibition or distribution of sexual materials to consenting adults be repealed."

Nixon immediately repudiated the study, angrily asserting that the report was "morally bankrupt." But many people had doubts about Nixon's own moral solvency—this was, after all, the man who had just been found to be secretly carrying on an illegal bombing of Cambodia and Laos. His rejection of the report was, to the millions of people who despised him, a veritable imprimatur on pornography.

Plays featuring nudity and sex, such as *Oh, Calcutta!* and *Hair*, were immensely successful, and films followed. First came the imports, like the sexually explicit but critically praised *I Am Curious, Yellow*. Then came the hard-core porn movie *Deep Throat*, which showed the sexual adventures of a woman whose clitoris was in her throat, and who went to great lengths to stimulate it (striking another blow to the myth of the vaginal orgasm). The film was a sensation, becoming not only the most profitable porn film ever made, but the first hard-core porn film to attain respectability, attracting an audience of both men and women, and inspiring scholarly analyses in academic journals and coy acclaim in the popular press.

Riding on the coattails of *Deep Throat* came *Behind the Green Door*, starring an angelic-faced Marilyn Chambers engaging in acrobatic sex with enough men to make up a football team, and *The Devil in Miss Jones*. Both films were filmed with higher production values and with more wit and imagination than most previous porn flicks. It became an amusing diversion for open-minded couples or mixed groups to make the film a part of their evening's entertainment.

Porn became a subject of dinner-table or cocktail-party conversation, as women and men gaily conversed about deep-throat techniques and the size of porn actors' penises.

THE BODY POLITIC: HOT TUB TRANSCENDENCE

Having gained the cultural seal of approval from the famous and influential members of the intelligentsia, the sexual revolution swept quickly into the mainstream of American middle-class life.

Many psychologists had long emphasized the link between sex and the psyche. One of Freud's favorite disciples, Wilhelm Reich, had seen the orgasm as a key to releasing tensions and traumas that if held in the body would lead to physical illness and neurosis. A Marxist, Reich emphasized the political importance of sexuality, and in books like *The Mass Psychology of Fascism* analyzed the part repressed

sexuality played in the rise of fascism. The systematic suppression
and repression of sexuality, he emphasized, was a key to the maintenance of the established order in such irrational societies.

Other psychiatrists and psychologists continued to explore the relationship between the mind and body, and, as the sexual revolution
made such ideas acceptable and even fashionable, these teachers and
therapists gave birth to what has come to be known as the human-
potential movement.

These "humanistic psychology" teacher/therapists combined the
Freudo-Reichian stream of thought with ideas of personal liberation
through direct experience of higher states of consciousness, drawn
from various Eastern philosophies, such as Zen Buddhism. Having
found academia too rigid and repressive, and the psychology departments too wrapped up in their quantitative rat-running approach
to consciousness, the humanistic psychology movement found a more
congenial home in the dramatic natural beauty of Big Sur, and pursued
its explorations of the interaction between mind and body in the hot
springs of Esalen Institute.

To free people from their personal anxieties and cultural conditioning so that they could be capable of healthy sexuality, experiencing firsthand the vision expressed by Blake's words, "Energy is
eternal delight," the teachers of the human-potential movement
adopted a variety of methods: direct physical manipulation, ranging
from dances to deep massage, to help free the body from tensions
and anxieties; and group techniques—improvisational scenes, encounter groups, nude encounter groups, marathon encounter groups,
marathon nude encounter groups—in which participants were encouraged to "let it all hang out."

It was, beneath the surface jargon, an approach to the Heresy. "I
remember the first time I went to Esalen," a Los Angeles writer
recalled to me, "you would see people making love quite openly,
men and women, men and men, women and women. There were
no taboos! I was in the hot tub, and a couple got in next to me. In
a minute or so I heard the water thrashing and their breathing and
was amazed to see them fucking right beside me. The nudity was
one thing, not so extraordinary in itself, but the idea that you could
just fuck, anywhere and anytime, it made the place seem so free, so
revolutionary. I loved it!"

While not apparently radical itself, the human-potential movement provided intellectual support and numerous handy techniques for various other groups and individuals involved in the sexual revolution.

The antiwar movement's enormously successful "politics as theater" approach, for example—with demonstrators taking the roles of soldiers and of Vietnamese peasants being massacred, carrying dead pigs' heads impaled on stakes, placing flowers in the guns of National Guardsmen, performing a mass exorcism rite on the Pentagon, dancing naked, carrying coffins—was like a gigantic marathon encounter-group session. One lead player in the game was Abbie Hoffman, who had earned a graduate degree in psychology at Brandeis, where he had been strongly influenced by the ideas of humanistic psychology.

The feminist movement, too, made powerful use of the encounter-group concept, incorporating it into its consciousness-raising sessions.

In the arts, the ideas of humanistic psychology were widely influential. In the theater, performances frequently featured nudity, and nude performers mingled with the audience, encouraging them to take off their clothes, too, and join the cast onstage.

So what had been too radical, kinky, embarrassing, or threatening in the youth culture, radical feminism, and the antiwar movement, now, having been softened and made safe as "therapy," "self-help," "personal improvement," and "self-discovery," became chic, exciting, and fun to the mainstream. The transition was captured in the popular film *Bob & Carol & Ted & Alice* (1969), with its two couples tentatively going through an encounter session at an Esalenlike retreat, gingerly exploring the idea of mate-swapping (but, reassuringly to the mass audience, deciding not to), and coming out of the weekend a bit wiser and more sexually liberated.

Across the country, people found themselves in encounter groups in church basements and neighbors' living rooms. Husbands and wives were encouraged to vent their spleen in the name of honesty, and marriages crumbled in record numbers. Swingers' groups and parties multiplied and appeared in every community, even gained a sort of semirespectability as therapeutic opportunities, chances to cast off hang-ups, nasty possessive attitudes, and other excess cultural baggage, and do some valuable self-discovery.

Those who didn't have a sexual partner to swap could go to the local singles' bar, where potential sex partners put themselves on display, and where, according to a survey, published in *The Atlantic*

Monthly, the most popular opening lines for males were "You got a great pair of boobs," and "I'm a monkey tamer"; for females, "I like your ass," "I wanna play," and "My monkey's wild!," and for both sexes "Wanna fuck?"

Sex had, for millions of Americans, become a recreational sport: crotch aerobics, the horizontal bop. This, of course, was not the point of the Heresy, which saw sex as providing access to freedom and wisdom. This was not the point even of the early sexual revolutionaries, who had seen sex as a road to individual freedom and the liberating of the culture. It was not even the point of the human-potential movement. But real freedom, real change, real personal growth, came through breaking free of social conditioning, something that was not easy, something that took time. Americans are not big on things that take time and effort, and our attention span is short. We like things fast and we like them mass-produced: fast cars, fast food, and good sex right now. Tame my monkey, baby.

The misinterpretation of many of the ideas of the human-potential movement—and the absolutely correct interpretation of many others—seemed to justify as healthy the national wave of sexual hedonism and sexual self-expression: sex as fast food, sex as the Gong Show. Many of the ideas of the human-potential movement had been absorbed, synthesized, and reshaped by Hugh Hefner and his editors, and expressed as the *Playboy* Philosophy, which was validated by climbing sales of the magazine. By the early seventies *Playboy* was selling nearly 7 million copies of each issue, with an estimated readership of nearly 20 million. Other magazines arose to challenge it, particularly what now seemed to be its prudishness: Its models were bright young girls-next-door-who-just-happened-to-have-enormous-breasts, and the magazine's photos were rather modest. *Penthouse*, published in the United States beginning in 1969, had a more erotic style, with models with knowing, come-hither smiles and exposed labia, and by the early seventies its circulation was climbing by the millions.

Marketing surveys and a variety of approaches convinced publishers that women were also eager for sexually arousing materials, but not the same sort of visually erotic material that appealed to males (*Playgirl* magazine caused a brief flurry with its pinup nude shots of men, including Burt Reynolds, but it turned out that many of the magazine's buyers were gay males). A series of for-women-only sex books became best-sellers, including Nancy Friday's compendium of largely pornographic women's sex fantasies, *My Secret Garden* (1973), Betty Dodson's graphically explicit masturbation-instruction manual, *Liberating Masturbation* (1974), and Lonnie Barbach's primer on sexual pleasure, *For Yourself* (1975).

And publishers quickly locked onto the formula for sexually arousing materials for millions of women—the historical romance novel, or "bodice-rippers." Soon these erotic romances were not only outselling magazines like *Playboy* and *Penthouse* combined, but constituted some 40 percent of all paperback book sales. These pulp romances exasperated feminists, who called for a more liberated fictional heroine, one embodying independence, self-assertiveness, and open sexuality. Poet Erica Jong produced a novel called *Fear of Flying*, whose heroine expressed and acted out her sexual fantasy of the "zipless fuck." "For the true, ultimate Zipless A-1 fuck," wrote Jong, "it was necessary that you never got to know the man very well. I had noticed, for example, how all my infatuations dissolved as soon as I really became friends with a man. . . . I no longer dreamed about him. He had a face. So another condition for the zipless fuck was brevity. And anonymity made it even better."

Jong's zipless fuck, depersonalized, anonymous, fast, with no strings attached, sounded like the kind of sex for which women had been criticizing men for years, but in its apparent assertion that women were just as sexually charged, just as horny, as men, it was a message many mainstream women wanted to hear, and the book was a huge best-seller.

By those early 1970's, it seemed that the sexual revolutionaries, who had set out with a wild dream of transforming the American political and economic structure, were actually on their way to success. In only a decade or so a sexually reticent, repressed, still puritanical society had been transformed into a nation in which sex had become, like jogging, a recreational sport with well-known health benefits for both mind and body. Richard Nixon, the personification of strangled sexuality, had been trapped in lies and corruption and was on his way out. The long blunder in Vietnam seemed almost over. American feminists had established a new image of female strength and sexual openness, and were confident that Americans would support an Equal Rights Amendment to the Constitution. Homosexuals and lesbians were asserting themselves confidently. In its 1973 *Roe v. Wade* decision, the U.S. Supreme Court had established that a woman's right to obtain an abortion was guaranteed by the Constitution, and within a short time millions of women were receiving safe abortions in local hospitals and clinics. Americans could speak frankly about sex. It was a time of great expectations.

However, there were many Americans whose expectations were more uncertain. As Billy Graham told a White House prayer breakfast in December 1973, "Almost everyone I talk to seems to sense that a hurricane, of cataclysmic proportions, is about to break on the world."

4

STRANGE BEDFELLOWS AND THE DEATH OF SEX

. . . .

The fact is, that as Graham spoke, the sexual revolution was over, and a counterrevolution of unimaginable proportions was shaking its shaggy shanks, a rough beast slouching toward Bethlehem.

If the war and the draft had provided the catalyst for the counterculture's apocalyptic sexual politics in the 1960's, the end of the draft, by removing the immediate source of anxiety, fear, and rebellion, defused the movement. By 1971 the counterculture had disintegrated, or at least fragmented. For several years city-dwelling freaks had been declaring, "The city trip is dead, man," and leaving in successive waves seeking shelter and survival in more natural environments such as Vermont, New Mexico, Arizona, Colorado, and any place there were mountains, clear skies, green meadows. The city experience had turned progressively nastier and more depressing, with increasing crime and violence in the countercultural enclaves such as the Lower East Side and Haight-Ashbury, related to sharp increases in the numbers of junkies and speed freaks.

Then, too, the counterculture fell victim to its own success, as the mainstream culture embraced and appropriated its concerns. For as the folly of the war became apparent to more and more Americans, increasing numbers of people and groups joined in the opposition—labor unions, teachers' groups, politicians, celebrities—marching in huge, festive demonstration-parades whereas in earlier years the counterculture had been the targets of stones, clubs, and tear gas when its members demonstrated. So to many, the counterculture was now seen as simply another antiwar group. Or, in another way, all the antiwar protesters were members of a counterculture. Thus, as the mood of the country turned against the war, the counterculture found itself in the frustrating position of having won an extraordinary struggle only to lose its identity. For if everyone was in the counterculture, then no one was.

And as the "sexual revolution" spread to the masses, the 20 million *Playboy* readers, the millions of readers of Harlequin romances and bodice-rippers, it did so not as a form of cultural revolution, inspiring aggression and rebellion against an evil society, but as a way of making the unjust society bearable, a sort of bread and circuses.

Thus, sexual revolution became not a tool for fundamentally altering the social order, but a means for *supporting* the social order, by permitting citizens sufficient sexual freedom to keep them happy and by depriving them of the motivation and energy to criticize or overthrow it—a process Marxist philosopher Herbert Marcuse disgustedly called "repressive desublimation."

The youth culture's own look had been a spontaneous response to its hatred for "fashion" and conformist technological society. The young people's long hair and bizarre clothes made them objects of derision, and they were branded "freaks," a name they accepted gladly.

But then, as the society turned against the war, in essence joining the freaks, and became more sexually open, the look of the youth culture came to signify freedom, sexuality, youthfulness. And so, a look that had been despised by mainstream America was absorbed and co-opted by Madison Avenue. Middle-class men were told the long-haired look was in, and put on bell-bottom pants, took off their ties, opened their shirts, and hung chains and beads from their wattled necks. Women went to the hairstylist to have their hair fashioned into the long, straight "natural" look, and wore their nail polish, lipstick, and assorted makeup in "natural earth tones." And the "hippie look" became simply another style, which if "in" at the present was, by the very nature of the endless flow of fashion styles, very soon to be "out."

And so, fatefully, the youth culture looked into the mirror of the media and found that they were young and beautiful, envied in their freedoms. The media had seized on their story and inevitably misread it, but the youth culture had seen what was apparently itself on TV, and enshsrined on the cover of *Time* magazine as "The Person of the Year." And with that vision of themselves came self-consciousness, an awareness of themselves as playing a role, a narcissism that began to undermine the spontaneous innocence that had made them seem such an attractive story for the media.

The Beatles, whose presence and music had for seven years provided the musical nexus that linked all the different musics that were essential components of counterculture experience—rock, the blues, heavy metal, pop, folk, African, and Middle Eastern exotica—announced in 1970 that they had irrevocably split up. And in 1970 Jim Morrison, Jimi Hendrix, and Janis Joplin died. Each, through his or her visionary ecstatic music and reputation for extreme appetites for mind-shattering sexual and drug experiences, had come to embody and express the wild energy and desperate drive of the counterculture's sexual gnosticism.

Also in 1970 came the arrest of Charlie Manson and the revelation of the murders committed by his followers. Despite his clear derangement, Manson was an embodiment of the sexual gnosticism of the counterculture, envisioning a coming worldwide upheaval, ordering his followers to open themselves to a variety of "forbidden practices," seeking self-transcendence not only through sexual activity (all the members of the Manson "family" had freely delivered themselves to Manson and willingly acted out his bizarre sexual fantasies with each other and anyone else Manson ordered them to), but even through murder.

The deaths of Joplin, Morrison, and Hendrix, along with the appearance of the Manson cult, made members of the counterculture examine their own lives, become aware of the darker aspects of the sexual revolution they had been pursuing. These deaths mirrored similar confrontations with darkness, confusion, and despair faced by many on an individual basis. One cause was the increasing paranoia and distrust in the community caused by the intensified campaign of surveillance, harassment, and infiltration by the FBI and other government agencies. The Lower East Side community was shocked in 1970, for example, when Prince Crazy, one of the most colorful of the Yippies, turned out to have been a longtime FBI informant, who caused the arrest of several who had looked on him as a friend.

So the growing paranoia, loss of trust, violence, and the effects of the increasingly available hard drugs undermined whatever sense of community existed among the counterculture. Discouraged and confused, seeking security, fellowship, and moral certainty, former sexual communards found these comforts by committing themselves to authority, particularly the authority represented by cults such as the Hare Krishna movement, Scientology, Guru Mahara Ji, the Unification Church of Reverend Sun Myung Moon, and the comforts of ecstatic Jesus-freak, born-again Christianity.

ABANDON SHIP: WOMEN AND CHILDREN FIRST

The most devastating blow to the counterculture had come when, from all appearances, the movement was at its height of popularity: Suddenly it was abandoned by many of the women who had played such an important part in it from the beginning. As they had explored their uniquely female vision of transformation through consciousness-raising sessions, sexual experimentation, and demonstrations with their sisters from the counterculture, they had developed a vision of their feminist gnosticism as linking them through historical gnosticism (such as witches and ancient mystery cults) to mythic goddesses and a prehistoric past when human culture was, they believed, organized around matriarchy, and when uniquely female values were dominant. The evils of technocratic America, they concluded, were a result of the systematic suppression and oppression of this feminist gnosticism and of the ancient matriarchy by a patriarchical society expressing the uniquely male values of "phallic power." All women were victims of oppression, they decided, and the oppressors were not simply those in power but all men: Women were victims of an ancient and continuing conspiracy to oppress them, and the conspirators were all men. And since the male members of the youth culture were, despite their opposition to the patriarchal regime, indisputably male, then they too were oppressors, as much the enemy as the corporate and political representatives of phallic power.

The effect of the split between radical feminists and the counterculture was disastrous. It was as if a ragtag guerrilla band had won a string of brilliant upsets over a well-armed, well-trained army, when suddenly nearly half of its forces deserted—not only deserted but turned around and began sniping at them, claiming they were as corrupt as the evil army they had been fighting.

So, embattled by hard drugs and police-state paranoia, co-opted by Madison Avenue and the media, simplistically mimicked by a mass culture seeking to be hip, defused by the end of the draft and the inevitable end of the war, divided by sexual warfare, the counterculture slipped away and disappeared into the rest of the nation.

BABY'S COME A LONG WAY

Feminists, too, found themselves in danger of being co-opted and splintered at the moment of their greatest success. Radical feminism had started as part of the cultural upheaval of the early 1960's, and shared the counterculture's commitment to a free-spirited sexual gnosticism. But now the transcendent experiences were sought through systematic cultivation of the orgasm—or multiple orgasms —through extended masturbation sessions, and through experimentation with lesbian and group sex.

Like the counterculture, the radical feminists had a powerful appeal to the middle class. Mainstream women were attracted not only by the persuasiveness of the message, but by its "glamour"—the movement had an edge of the forbidden, the dangerous, the exotic, and the appeal of the underdog. But while the middle class welcomed part of the radical feminists' message—the need for an end to the oppression of women, the assertion that women could be just as aggressive and independent as men—they were not so open to the sexual gnosticism at its heart. The core message, that sex and power were one, that by altering one, you inescapably altered the other, was simply too threatening for middle-class women, who wanted changes, not total transformation.

So, as the movement grew, the sexual message became subordinated to the political program. As it spread into the middle class, the movement began to focus almost completely on traditional politics, seeking to effect changes in the social order by working through the existing political apparatus, in electoral politics, in efforts at welfare reform, legalization of abortion, and so on. In this way sex and power could be seen as simple political allies, attending each other's fund-raising cocktail parties so to speak, rather than as the nexus, the single unified energy dynamic that could be the source of a total revisioning of life.

The glamour of feminism was not overlooked by the elves of Madison Avenue, and they lost no time in changing ideas into commodities. Feminism became a "style," a means of selling everything from cars to cigarettes (You've come a long way, baby).

A classic example of the Madison Avenue process at work was a Ma Griffe perfume ad that presented a stirring drama of feminism in action:

> *You're liberated.*
> *You don't believe in marriage.*
> *You tell him so.*
> *You wear Ma Griffe.*
> *He slips on the ring.*
> *(It's five carats.)*

So feminism, too, like the counterculture, found itself co-opted, transformed because of its energy and attractiveness into something quite different. Many radical feminists resisted, arguing for a continued emphasis on revolutionary sexuality, and extending their explorations into such areas as feminist S&M, and feminist group sex. But the middle-class women who now made up the majority of the women's liberation movement were in general horrified by the suggestion by the radicals that such practices were the heart of true feminism.

So, while the Reverend Billy Graham was prophesying cataclysm, while the feminist movement seemed poised on the edge of achieving real power, while the sexual revolution seemed to have been won, the real revolution was over, a failure. Many Americans, however, the Americans to whom Graham was speaking, were not aware of that failure. They were convinced that it was growing stronger than ever, and forces were combining to make them believe it was essential for them to do something to stop that revolution before it was too late.

THE RISE OF THE RIGHT

These Americans had been of this opinion for a long time. Good, law-abiding, sexually repressed citizens, they had been appalled by the flagrant sexuality of the counterculture, had feared and made fun of radical feminists as hairy-legged dykes and bra-burners. The Vietnam War was not hard for them to understand—it was a battle against godless communism, and even if some of it didn't make sense, it was the duty of patriotic Americans to support their nation, right or wrong. They were the embattled defenders of goodness, America, and the moral certainties of idealized family life: monogamy, sexual restraint, law and order, respect for authority.

They were, after all, God's people, and America was God's country. So the sexual rebels, threatening to undermine America and the moral certainties, were not just people holding views that one could disagree with; they were bad, immoral, un-American, ungodly—evil. It therefore followed that it was acceptable—no, necessary—to use extreme methods to eradicate them. Thus, for these Americans, the struggle against open sexuality became a holy crusade against anarchy and chaos, communism, and the forces of Satan.

Mainstream Americans, confronted by the same rapid social and economic change that had triggered the counterculture's rebellion (the inexorable advance of seemingly uncontrollable technology, its destruction of tradition, devaluation of the past, and homogenization of culture), blamed much of their disorientation and anxiety not on these causes, but on the nation's "moral decay." The country was in a state of decline, like the Roman Empire, which fell, so the popular assumption went, because of its sexual immorality.

And just as many members of the counterculture relieved their anxieties and disillusionment by delivering themselves into the firm embrace of authoritarian cults that promised freedom from doubt, so these mainstream Americans escaped a future that promised disaster by being "born again," to be held securely in the powerful arms and on the loving bosom of the Christian fundamentalist churches. Against the minority of sexual perverts and subversives, they proclaimed themselves the Moral Majority.

In the 1970's membership in the Pentecostal and fundamentalist churches climbed sharply. This growth was spurred by blow after blow to the nation and the nation's pride, especially the loss in Vietnam. No matter how it was disguised, the fact remained that America, which had never lost a war, had been humiliated by a bunch of skinny little Orientals in black pajamas. Then, too, the president the Moral Majority had elected by such a wide margin over that commie creep McGovern had been sabotaged by the left, raked over the coals, and forced to resign for a minor mistake, a second-rate burglary—the whole thing was nothing but a black eye for America.

Then had come the attack on the CIA, the Senate hearings that revealed the bungled assassination attempts on Castro and the clumsy covert-operation fiascos all over the world. The OPEC oil cartel jacked up oil prices, causing skyrocketing costs, gasoline shortages, and the frustration of having to wait in long lines to fill up the tank, and only on alternate days. America was supposed to be self-sufficient, and now it turned out we were so dependent on foreign oil that a bunch of raghead camel jockeys could bring us to our knees! Then a howling mob of Iranians seized the American embassy in Teheran, holding hundreds of decent Americans hostage and humiliating us by burning Uncle Sam and calling America the Great Satan, and there was nothing America seemed to be able to do.

The only thing a good Christian and a patriotic American (for these two had now become conflated) could do was what Jimmy Cagney or John Wayne would have done, come out punching, battling against the forces of evil. The clearest target was sexual immorality: the source of the antiwar movement that caused America to lose the war; the source of the feminists, who had caused all the increased divorce and the breakup of the family, and who had entered the workplace and taken jobs away from family breadwinners; the source of the increase in venereal disease; the source of the increasing sexual activity of teenagers; the source of the nation's moral decline, which had perhaps caused God to become displeased with His favorite nation, the way He became angry at the Israelites for their licentiousness and golden calves.

So to return America to her position of power and authority, the most important first step was to eradicate sexual immorality. The fundamentalist churches committed themselves and their vast wealth to a number of battles: against sex education, which was only an excuse for indoctrinating children with immoral ideas; legal abortion, which simply encouraged promiscuity, premarital sex, and allowed sinful fornicators to escape the penalty for their sins; "secular humanists," who were a conspiracy of leftists dedicated to spreading anti-Christian, un-American, and immoral propaganda through the schools, colleges, and leftist-controlled media; and pornography, which caused immoral behavior.

The battles included attempts to censor school texts, to remove "immoral" books from school libraries, to force the media to end its bias against Christian values, and to defeat the feminists in their attempts to undermine the family.

With the support of the right-wing fundamentalists, who provided the campaign with millions of dollars, and who urged their congregations to turn out en masse on election day and to vote for the candidate who had vowed to restore morality to America, the Moral Majority elected Ronald Reagan president by the largest landslide in American history. The sexual revolution had had its day. The counterrevolution was now under way.

As their battles against immorality began in earnest, the Moral Majority was joined by allies from an unexpected source—the camps of the feminists.

THE TAMING OF THE MALE ID: FROM CHAIN SAWS TO LIMP PENISES

As we have just seen, when women's liberation became chic, the influx of middle-class, liberal women altered the direction and energy of the movement. Mainstream feminists saw the movement as a way of speeding the advancement of working women in the business world, but the radical feminists, finding American corporate capitalism pure evil—the embodiment of the corrupting, destructive force of the male-created technocracy—rejected the idea that feminism should be used to assist women in becoming dehumanized cogs in the patriarchal machine.

Bitter struggles ensued, threatening to splinter the movement irrevocably. Clearly some rallying point, some cause that would unite all women and give direction to the movement, was needed.

In 1975 Susan Brownmiller's book *Against Our Will: Men, Women and Rape* argued that rape was not aberrant behavior, but a strategy devised by men to maintain their control over women; that, in essence, all men were guilty of rape, all women victims of rape. Every rape, Brownmiller argued, was an act not of sexual desire but of violent aggression against women; and conversely, every act of violence against women by men was rape. All acts of violence/rape, that is, were political acts encouraged by the male (or patriarchal) system as a means of oppressing women. The oppression of women, then, is an act of continuing rape, an ongoing crime of violence against women.

The needed feminist rallying point had been found: not simply rape, but violence against women. The feminists pulled together, and within a short time had achieved impressive results, with rape crisis centers, retreats for battered women, and associated programs, funded by both the federal and state governments.

As the struggle progressed, women became more sensitized to the violence against them that seemed endemic to the culture. In movies and on TV, women were slashed, shot, raped, chased by zombies, chopped with chain saws, and in general accorded fairly shoddy treatment. Campaigns were waged against violence in the media. Television executives responded with a well-publicized but minimal effort to purge some of the violence from their shows.

Violence in the media (including violence against women) was highly popular with huge numbers of Americans—among them the young and working women who were the natural constituency of the feminist movement—and therefore immensely profitable. Vast sums of money were being made by the television networks from advertisers who supported popular violent shows, by Hollywood movie studios and their investors, by makers of children's toys related to television or film violence, by publishers of women's bodice-ripper romances and male-oriented adventure fiction. To take on violence against women in the media, feminists discovered, was to take on not only all the media, but corporate and mainstream America.

So the feminists retreated a bit and aimed their wrath at a more vulnerable target: violence against women specifically in male-oriented graphic sexual materials. This type of pornography, depicting males acting violently or aggressively toward females, was, they insisted, a direct cause of violent acts against women. Social scientists persisted in pointing out that there was simply no credible evidence that pornography was linked to actual violence or aggressive behavior (Dr. Martha Kirkpatrick, for example, feminist and associate clinical professor in the Department of Psychiatry at UCLA, after an exhaustive study of pornography and its effects, concluded that "the evidence from all sources is dramatically clear: Pornography does not, per se, encourage sexual violence"). But when confronted with such objections, Susan Brownmiller asserted, "We supply the ideology; it's for others to come up with the statistics."

When it was pointed out that pornography that depicted violence or aggression constituted only a tiny fraction of all the erotic materials being sold, the feminists insisted that all pornography, even sexual imagery with no hint of sexual aggression, led to violence against women. Susan Brownmiller explained that a simple photo of a naked woman, with no males depicted, is capable of leading to violent acts by men, since the viewer provides his own violence by creating a fantasy of rape. Feminist lawyer Catherine MacKinnon, urging passage of an antipornography law, was asked by a feminist artist if such a law would lead to the suppression of her paintings of female nudes. MacKinnon declared that such paintings should be banned, since they might reinforce "male supremacist sexuality." Feminist organizer Robin Morgan made the pronouncement that was to become the motto of this group: "Pornography is the theory, rape is the practice."

Marcia Womongold agreed, asserting that pornography is "the ideological basis for the systematic persecution of females by males." Susan Brownmiller claimed, "Pornography is the undiluted essence of anti-female propaganda." Writer Andrea Dworkin, whose book *Woman Hating* (1974) made her a key figure in this campaign, went even farther, by asserting that "the eroticization of murder is the essence of pornography."

Ultimately, however, it was not enough to oppose pornography, since the sexual oppression of women could evidently exist without it (after all, male domination of women had apparently persisted for thousands of years, while pornography had only been widely available for a few decades). The target had to be male sexuality itself. Robin Morgan expressed it succinctly: "I claim that rape exists any time sexual intercourse occurs when it has not been initiated by the woman out of her own genuine affection and desire."

The goal was stated by feminist Alice Echols, in her influential essay "The Taming of the Id": "To curb the promiscuity and rapacity spawned by the sexual revolution, cultural feminists propose that we impose upon the culture a female sexual standard."

And just what that female standard might be was summed up by lesbian Andrea Dworkin: "Sexual relations between a man and a woman are politically acceptable only when the man has a limp penis," and "Coitus is punishment!"

* * *

In the progressive narrowing of their field of interest, from battling the oppression of women to battling violence against women, to battling violence against women in the media, to battling violence against women in pornography, to battling all sexual imagery no matter how nonviolent, to battling male sexuality itself, these feminists lost the support of many of their sisters—who felt that there were more pressing needs, like passing the Equal Rights Amendment and dealing with the economic woes of women; who did not agree that the *Sports Illustrated* swimsuit issue represented the eroticization of murder, and who, in the midst of a struggle to free their own sexuality from ideas of "politically acceptable" sex, were wary of a movement limiting sexual liberties and dictating "politically acceptable" sex.

So throughout the late 1970's the movement against pornography remained a noisy but small minority within the feminist movement. Their tactics—such as heckling customers at erotic bookstores and cinemas, pouring ink onto the pages of men's magazines in local newsstands, or shooting out the windows of stores that sell such magazines (as one group did in Harvard Square)—made them seem to many just another single-issue crank group. They had little money, and no real access to mainstream media attention. The election of Ronald Reagan, however, changed all that.

5

Halting the Decline of Western Civilization

· ·

During the ascendancy of the counterculture, the fundamentalist churches were largely viewed by the moderate-liberal mainstream as illiterate rednecks and tobacco-chewing bigots. Jimmy Carter had restored some respectability to born-again Christians, and heightened their sense of self-respect, but he had resolutely opposed their efforts to halt the moral decay of God's country by suppressing constitutional rights. This was a president, after all, who readily admitted that when he looked upon lovely women he did indeed feel lust in his heart—an admission he made to *Playboy* magazine.

Still, during Carter's presidency, the religious right capitalized on its growing respectability to develop its churches into television ministries. The ministers, men like Jerry Falwell, Pat Robertson, and

Jimmy Swaggart, were able to raise millions of dollars for "Christian" causes, which were actually sophisticated political organizations devoted to electing officials on the local, state, and federal level who would advance the far right's campaign against sexual permissiveness. With the election of Ronald Reagan, these political groups not only received a go-ahead, but were actively encouraged and assisted by the Justice Department and other arms of the administration. The Justice Department began to offer legal assistance to these groups in drafting new and more severe local and state antipornography statutes, and in devising ways to limit the freedom of women to obtain abortions.

Throughout the 1970's the religious right had preached that one of the greatest dangers to America was feminism, and the feminists had asserted that the religious right represented one of the most patriarchal, repressive, antifemale forces in the country. But as the effort to place greater restrictions on sexual activities gained momentum in the early 1980's, both the right-wing Christians and the antipornography feminists found that it was to their advantage to coordinate their efforts toward a common goal.

Radical lesbian Andrea Dworkin, for example, began couching her attacks on pornography as a danger to Christian womanhood. As a result, she found increasing favor among women of the far right, and even began speaking in positive terms about individuals like Jerry Falwell. She quickly wrote a new book that presented a highly sympathetic portrait of reactionary women, *Right-Wing Women*. As their part of the bargain, the preachers of the far right also changed their tone, and began to speak of how pornography was harmful to women.

Each group brought to the antiporn struggle something that the other lacked. The religious right had used the power of its numbers and money to bring great pressures to bear on communities to clean up erotic filth, but used a language of zealotry (pornography was "the work of Satan" and furthered by evil "secular humanists") that made them unacceptable to the moderates and liberals of the mainstream.

The antiporn feminists spoke like secular humanists, using the language of sociology and psychology, and thus could command the attention of the mainstream, which had considerable goodwill toward feminism in general; but they lacked funds and access to the media and to political power. The combination of the immense wealth, great numbers of devout followers, political clout, vast computerized mailing lists, and media access of the far right with the credibility (among liberals) and the skills in confrontational tactics gained from the counterculture experience of the antiporn feminists, created a juggernaut.

ATTACKS UPON THE DEVIL: ROMEO, JULIET, AND HOLDEN CAULFIELD

The combined antisex forces pushed forward, from grass-roots organizing in local communities and churches to nationwide boycotts and demonstrations to political lobbying for more stringent obscenity laws, to violent attacks on outlets of sexual evil, to a well-organized media campaign, to the creation of a U.S. Attorney General's Commission on Pornography.

The confrontations and demonstrations against pornography continued, but with a changed emphasis. Now, the targets became not only the producers of the sexual materials, but also the corporations that offered the erotica outlet, such as the television networks, advertisers, and the convenience stores. Unlike the makers of erotica, who seemed largely impervious to pressure groups, these corporations were sensitive to public opinion. With write-in campaigns and petitions calling for grand-jury indictments, the forces were successful in forcing many cable-television networks to drop shows like the Playboy Channel. Similar pressures were brought to bear on network television for what were called "pornographic" shows dealing with AIDS, abortion, adultery, and adolescent sex, and were combined with boycotts against sponsors of such shows, such as Pepsi, Procter & Gamble, Lever Brothers, McDonald's, Colgate Palmolive. Similar boycotts were undertaken against "subsidizers of porn"—advertisers in magazines like *Playboy*. Also targeted were the corporations owning the chains of convenience stores and drugstores where such magazines were sold.

These campaigns became most visible in the battle against the Southland Corporation, parent company of the 7-Eleven chain of stores, called by the Fundamentalist Christian National Federation for Decency "the nation's largest retailer of pornographic magazines." The combined antipornography feminists and religious-right groups carried out a nationwide boycott against the stores, with groups heckling and at times physically attacking customers of these stores who bought the targeted magazines.

Southland resisted the campaign for some three years. Then Alan E. Sears, who had been appointed executive director of Attorney General Edwin Meese's Commission on Pornography, sent a letter on official Justice Department letterhead to retail outlets and bookstores (including 7-Eleven), claiming that *Playboy* and *Penthouse* had been linked to "violence, crime and child abuse," and suggesting that they might be prosecuted as accessories to such crimes and listed in the report of the Meese Commission as "identified distributors" of pornography. Shortly thereafter, Southland gave in and ordered that the magazines be banned from the chain's more than forty-five hundred stores.

Jerry Falwell claimed this victory would "cause a domino effect among many retail outlets and grocery chains across the country." In short order other convenience stores (which had also received letters on the attorney general's commission stationery) succumbed to the pressures and banned sales of the magazines in their stores, including Revco Drugs, (2,010 stores), People's Drug (more than 800 stores), Rite Aid Drug Stores, the Dart Drug Corporation, and Gray Drug, Inc. In a period of less than three years, over twenty thousand convenience stores, supermarkets, and drugstores that had once carried the hated magazines cleared them off their shelves.

It was later revealed that the letter sent by Sears and purporting to be an official letter from the attorney general's commission was in fact *not* official. *Playboy*, the Magazine Publishers Association, and other groups brought suit, claiming that the letter threatened a "blacklist." A federal district judge ordered the letter to be retracted, claiming that it appeared "to contain an implied threat to the addressees" and "the only purpose served by that letter was to discourage distributors from selling the publications, a form of pressure amounting to an administrative restraint of the plaintiffs' First Amendment rights." By the time of the ruling, of course, most of the addressees had already ceased carrying the magazines.

The strategy of write-in campaigns combined with direct community pressure was carried over to attacks on schools and libraries for carrying "pornography" and other "objectionable" material. Cultural vigilantes in virtually every state made full-scale efforts to delete "pornographic" material from school texts and to remove "dangerous" and "pornographic" books not only from required reading lists, but even from the shelves of school libraries. The groups, such as Phyllis Schlafly's Eagle Forum, objected to biology texts that mention the theory of evolution, such novels as *The Catcher in the Rye* (labeled "the dirtiest book ever written" and removed from some high school English classes), "obscene" dictionaries (which include some four-letter words), and classic literature such as Shakespeare's *Romeo and Juliet* (publishers of high school literature anthologies were forced to remove over four hundred "pornographic" lines from the play). The groups went far beyond this, determined to censor any written material, courses, and activities that showed signs of "secular humanism"; i.e., that were "human-centered" rather than "God-centered."

UNSPEAKABLE ACTS, UN-AMERICAN PRACTICES, LEONARDO DA VINCI

Among the material and activities these censors actively struggled to eliminate from schools were: discussions of values or morals, politics, religion, or Eastern religious practices; curricula pertaining to alcohol and drugs, nuclear war, human sexuality in any form, feminism, population, or population control; guided fantasy or imagery techniques; evolution; the writing of autobiographies, diaries, or log books for assignments; role-playing games; and anything that smacked of a psychological approach to life. For many, the campaigns against sexual decay were seen as battles against communism, to restore America to its former greatness. Thus, book-banning and porn-busting were seen as patriotic acts. The objectionable materials and practices were described as "un-American activities." So when parents' groups and other groups that opposed such censorship spoke out, they were quickly labeled "un-American," became the recipients of floods of hate mail, and found their children ostracized in schools.

One example of the struggle to keep public schools from being taken over by secular humanists and purveyors of pornography and filth was the fierce battle in Tennessee. There, a group of families brought suit against a local school system for exposing their children to offensive and anti-Christian ideas. Mrs. Vicki Frost, a leader of the group, described some of the books and ideas she opposed:

—any discussion of Leonardo da Vinci, since his paintings glorify man instead of God;

—discussion of the spirit of the Renaissance as exemplified in paintings in the National Gallery of Art, because "a central idea of the Renaissance was a belief in the dignity and worth of human beings. The painters of this time glorified or elevated the human form in paintings," which is objectionable, since only God should be glorified, not man;

—the book *Anne Frank: The Diary of a Young Girl*, because it implies that all religions are equal, and the plaintiffs state, "We cannot be tolerant of religious views on the basis of accepting other religions as equal to our own";

—any texts that attempt to stimulate the imagination of the young readers, for "our children's imaginations have to be bounded";

—*The Wizard of Oz*, which concludes that people have a power within themselves to change the way they are;

—the fairy tale "Cinderella," which mentions magic;

—all references to feminism, to males acting like females and females acting like males, and to pacifism.

This fundamentalist group was provided financial support and lawyers from the staff of Concerned Women of America, the Washington-based organization led by Beverly LeHaye, and by a conservative lawyers' group founded by television evangelist Pat Robertson.

Federal Judge Thomas Hull ruled in favor of the plaintiffs, noting that they were acting on "sincerely held religious convictions," and were afraid that their children "might adopt the views of a feminist, a humanist, a pacifist, an anti-Christian, a vegetarian or an advocate of 'one-world government.' "

According to the American Library Association, library censorship increased 300 percent in the years between 1980 and 1985. Among the books "challenged, burned, or banned" in the United States from 1980 to 1986 with some descriptions given by their censors, were: *Brave New World* by Aldous Huxley, *The Catcher in the Rye* by J. D. Salinger, *Catch-22* by Joseph Heller ("dangerous"), *Charlotte's Web* by E. B. White ("blasphemous"), *The Color Purple* by Alice Walker, *The Crucible* by Arthur Miller ("sick words from the mouths of demon-possessed people"), *The Diary of a Young Girl* by Anne Frank ("sexually offensive passages"), *East of Eden* by John Steinbeck ("ungodly and obscene"), *A Farewell to Arms* by Ernest Hemingway ("a sex novel"), *The Grapes of Wrath* by John Steinbeck ("dangerous"), *Huckleberry Finn* by Mark Twain ("dangerous"), *Lord of the Flies,* by William Golding ("demoralizing"), *1984* by George Orwell ("pro-

Communist . . . explicit sexual matter"), *Of Mice and Men*, by John Steinbeck ("dangerous"), *Ordinary People* by Judith Guest ("obscene"), *The Red Pony* by John Steinbeck ("filthy, trashy sex novel"), *Slaughterhouse Five* by Kurt Vonnegut ("dangerous"), *Superfudge* by Judy Blume ("profane, immoral and offensive"), *To Kill a Mockingbird* by Harper Lee ("dangerous"), *The Valley of the Horses* and *The Clan of the Cave Bear* by Jean Auel ("obscenity and pornography").

ON THE SECRET MEANING OF ROCK AND ROLL

In addition to books and magazines, the censors also targeted "porn rock," claiming that the lyrics of rock songs were "obscene" and promoted Satanism. Columnist George Will angrily complained, "Rock music has become a plague of messages about sexual promiscuity, bisexuality, incest, sado-masochism, Satanism, drug use, alcohol abuse, and, constantly, misogyny."

In Washington, a group called the Parents Music Resource Center initiated a campaign against explicit lyrics. The organization included the wives of ten U.S. senators, six representatives, and a Cabinet secretary. In response, the president of the Recording Industry Association of America quickly announced that many American record companies would include warnings—"Explicit Lyrics—Parental Advisory"—on albums containing potentially offensive lyrics, or print the records' lyrics on the back of the jackets.

Televangelist Jimmy Swaggart led a campaign against the pornography of rock that included not just the albums, but rock magazines as well. In a nationally broadcast condemnation, Swaggart mentioned the Wal-Mart chain, and promptly the 890 Wal-Mart stores announced the removal of thirty-two rock and teen-oriented publications, including such titles as *Rolling Stone, Creem, Circus, Song Hits, Teen Beat, Tiger Beat,* and *Teen Machine*.

For many, such activities were far too mild. Across the country, clinics specializing in abortion, women's health, and birth control were the targets of hundreds of bomb threats. Over one hundred actual bombings took place between 1982 and 1985, causing several injuries and at least one death.

The feminist forces reserved such tactics for sources of sexual materials: bookstores, theaters, convenience stores and newsstands in many cities and towns had their windows smashed or shot out, received bomb threats, were bombarded with paint, and were fire-bombed.

Up Against the Law

The feminist-church coalition worked diligently to enact sweeping and stringent local and state antipornography laws, and to elect officials pledged to enforce existing laws in novel ways. District attorneys and mayors across the country, in response to urgings from the Justice Department, pledged to crack down on smut, and created well-organized antisex squads. Among the results:

In Decatur, Georgia, a man was sentenced to five years in prison for having oral sex with his wife in the privacy of his home.

In Los Angeles, a producer of erotic films was arrested for "pandering" when he hired several women to act in a film, despite the testimony of the women that they were professional actresses. He was convicted and sentenced to a mandatory three years on each of five counts. The case drew great attention from the media, and had the effect of driving other film producers and performers out of Los Angeles.

In Prince George's County, Maryland, police padlocked six erotic entertainment businesses because, according to the county, "There exists an emergency situation constituting an immediate threat to individual life, property or the public safety."

In Kansas, the state legislature prohibited vibrators and any other devices used primarily for "stimulation of human genital organs."

A Georgia florist was busted for selling "obscene" greeting cards, such as the back view of a naked man emerging from a birthday cake.

The U.S. Supreme Court in its 1986 ruling on *Bowers v. Hardwick* upheld the right of states to ban oral and anal sex even when these acts take place between consenting adults in the privacy of their own bedroom. By doing so, they upheld the criminal status of sodomy in twenty-five states. In Georgia, such acts can bring sentences of twenty years in prison. In its ruling the Court rejected as "facetious" the argument that such a law invades privacy and endangers deeply personal, basic liberties.

North Carolina, which once had an anti-obscenity law so vague it was difficult to enforce, passed a law in 1985 that seemed extraordinary even by the standards of the Reagan era. Written with the assistance of the U.S. Justice Department as a test effort to create more severe state obscenity laws, it made the dissemination of porn a felony punishable by up to three years in prison. Under the law it is a crime to show anyone under eighteen a bare buttock or a bare or lightly clad female breast; nudity and simulated sex acts in words, recordings, or photos are also prohibited. Many magazine and book-shop owners were forced to take virtually anything with sexual con-notations off their shelves. In some areas of the state even PG-rated videotapes were threatened, and a Superior Court judge ruled that films such as *Splash* and *Summer of '42* were obscene. The new law banned the use of sexually explicit material even when used for ed-ucational purposes, thus threatening sex education in public schools. University of North Carolina law professor Thomas Tedford, a re-spected First Amendment scholar, changed his graduate course on the First Amendment for fear the illustrations he used in a lecture would lead to his arrest.

Setting a significant precedent, the new law also made it a felony for adults to view what the state considers obscene material even when alone in their own home, making it a crime for a husband and wife to watch a sexually explicit videotape on their own television.

The North Carolina law was pushed through the state legislature by a sophisticated, well-funded Christian-right lobby in cooperation with antiporn feminists and the U.S. Justice Department, and a key to its passage was the fact that it was disguised as a child-pornography bill.

OUTLAWING THE *ILIAD*

Perhaps the most ingenious attack on erotic material was that pi-oneered by lawyer Catherine MacKinnon and writer Andrea Dwor-kin. Discouraged by the difficulty of proving it legally "obscene," they devised the strategy of claiming that pornography is harmful to women as a class—that is, it violates women's civil rights. They drafted a model law for local governments to follow that would outlaw pornography and allow women to bring a civil suit against any individual or company they feel has harmed their civil rights through pornography. Among the law's many sections, the broadest would allow any woman to bring a suit against anyone who produces, sells, exhibits, or distributes pornography.

What the law attempted to do was what philosophers, judges, lawyers, artists, and writers had been unable to do—to define pornography. Currently the only sexually explicit speech and expression that can be censored without violating the Constitution is that which is "obscene," which has been legally defined as something that when viewed by an "average person," applying community standards, appeals to prurient interests, or that offensively depicts specifically defined sexual conduct, and, that when taken as a whole, lacks serious literary, artistic, political, or scientific value.

The MacKinnon-Dworkin formulation ignores the whole concept of obscenity and defines "pornography" as: "the graphic sexually explicit subordination of women whether in pictures or in words," including when "women are presented as sexual objects for domination, conquest, violation, exploitation, possession or use, or through postures or positions of servility or submission or display," or are "penetrated by objects." The breadth of the law is increased by the fact that it stipulates that the use of men "in the place of women" in the subordinate situations mentioned, "shall also constitute pornography under this section."

Columbia anthropologist and epidemiologist Carole Vance pointed out that the assertion that pornography is a kind of discrimination against women is "actually a very old approach because it reasserts that women are sexually different from men and in need of special protection. Yet special protection inadvertently reinforces the ways in which women are legally and socially said to be different from men."

Despite such objections, the feminist group Women Against Pornography, working with the support of the Moral Majority and other groups of the far right, quickly proposed versions of the MacKinnon-Dworkin Act in a number of cities, and organized sophisticated, well-financed campaigns to bring pressure on legislators to pass the law. It was introduced in Cambridge, Massachusetts, as the Human Rights Ordinance. Emily Culpepper of Women's Alliance Against Pornography, sponsor of the measure, said, "Using the victim's rights" would get "justice for women without censorship because it puts power to decide what is pornographic in the hands of the victim rather than the police." It failed in Cambridge, as it did in Madison, Wisconsin, in part because of organized opposition from anticensorship feminists. Twice it was passed as a city ordinance in Minneapolis, but each time was vetoed by the mayor. It failed by only one vote in Suffolk County, New York.

The ordinance was passed in Indianapolis, with the strong support of the mayor. However, it was unanimously declared unconstitutional in 1985 by a U.S. Court of Appeals in a case brought on behalf of a variety of organizations including the American Booksellers Association, the Association for American Publishers, the Freedom to Read Foundation, and the National Association of College Stores. The judges concluded that the ordinance could outlaw writings from the *Iliad* to Joyce's *Ulysses*, since they "depict women as submissive objects for conquest and domination." Under the ordinance, wrote one judge, speech that was "disapproved" would be unlawful no matter how significant its artistic or political value, while "speech treating women in the approved way is lawful no matter how sexually explicit. The state may not ordain preferred viewpoints in this way. The Constitution forbids the state to declare one perspective right and silence opposition." Another judge characterized the law as "thought control."

OF MEESE AND WOMEN

In 1985 Attorney General Edwin Meese appointed an eleven-member panel, composed entirely of individuals known for their opposition to pornography, to the newly established National Commission on Pornography. The commission's charter stated that its goal was "to make specific recommendations to the Attorney General concerning more effective ways in which the spread of pornography could be contained." Thus, as legal scholar Alan Dershowitz pointed out, the attorney general "imposed an Alice in Wonderland style of justice in which the sentence precedes the trial."

After hearing from an array of politicians and government officials, a wide range of antiporn activists, and a few token representatives of anticensorship organizations, the committee issued its report in July 1986. It concluded, "Substantial exposure to sexually violent materials bears causal relationship to antisocial acts of sexual violence and possibly to unlawful acts of sexual violence."

The commission reached this conclusion despite the fact that none of the scientists who had testified before it could find any direct link between pornography and violent behavior. The commission impatiently rejected the cautions of experts such as psychologists Edward Donnerstein and Neil Malamuth, who had been carefully investigating the effects of pornography for many years, and who painstakingly explained that their studies showed that pornography by itself does not influence the attitudes of viewers, and that increases in aggression are related to violence, rather than pornography.

The social scientist the commission hired to summarize existing studies, sociologist Edna F. Einseidel, reported, "No evidence currently exists that actually links fantasies with specific sexual offenses," and went on to suggest that explicit sexual materials could have positive effects, noting that therapists have used such materials "to help patients with sexual dysfunctions overcome their fears and inhibitions."

In addition to calling for mandatory twenty-year sentences for twice-convicted sellers of erotica, the report recommended forming a vast computer system, combining state and federal resources, to prosecute porn merchants more effectively, and the surveillance of virtually every form of communication, from modems to satellites, to insure freedom from taint. Despite its repudiation by virtually all experts in the field of sexual behavior, Attorney General Meese praised the report and echoed its call to concerned citizens to form "watch groups" to combat pornography. Meese also called for a "prioritization" of pornography, elevating it to the same level as that of drug trafficking and organized crime: a national emergency.

Shortly thereafter, the Defense Department introduced sweeping new regulations on sexual activities that affected nearly 3 million military and civilian employees and defense contractors. The new regulations ruled that individuals had to inform the department if they had engaged in a number of sexual practices, including sodomy, spouse swapping, adultery, and "group sex orgies." In addition to divulging information about their own practices, individuals also were required to provide information about the sexual activities of their co-workers.

THE END OF SEX (AS WE KNOW IT)

The growing wave of victories engineered by the feminist-fundamentalist coalition was facilitated by the growing disillusionment of many people with the sexual revolution. In September 1980 (just two months before the election of Ronald Reagan), a *Cosmopolitan* magazine survey of over 106,000 women indicated that "the emotional fruit the sex revolution has borne" was not so sweet for many women. Said the report, "So many readers wrote negatively about the sexual revolution, expressing longings for vanished intimacy, and the now elusive joys of romance and commitment, that we began to sense that there might be a sexual counterrevolution underway in America."

Other polls, from rigorously conducted random surveys to an informal poll by the "Dear Abby" newspaper column, showed the same turn from impersonal sex to intimacy. Abby asked women whether they would rather be "cuddled" or have sex, and received an unprecedented response, with over 80 percent of the women claiming they would rather be cuddled. A growing number of books and articles indicated that women who in the previous decade had been asserting their independence of men were now seeking "commitment" from men, blaming males for what they saw as a "fear of intimacy," "flight from commitment" or the "Peter Pan Syndrome."

Along with the disillusionment came fear. Increasing numbers of sexually active people found themselves infected with herpes, a disease they were horrified to learn had no cure. This was, after all, the antibiotic generation, the first generation to grow up with the assumption that if you got sick, you could have a shot or some pills and get well. Now, they were told they were stuck with a highly communicable venereal disease for the rest of their lives.

The disease skyrocketed during the seventies, reaching epidemic proportions. Popular magazines began running cover stories with huge headlines like: FEAR OF SEX! Herpes victims created herpes hotlines, herpes support groups, Herpes Anonymous groups. The question became "When do I tell him (her) that I have herpes? On the first date? Before we go to bed? After we've come to know each other? Never?" The fear of herpes among those who did not have it was so high that in many cases to admit that one had the disease meant the immediate end of a relationship, or, if one was meeting someone new, it meant the relationship never began. Many herpes sufferers became totally celibate.

But herpes paled to insignificance compared to the next disease down the pike. AIDS first became widely discussed in 1981, as increasing numbers of homosexual men began dying from a breakdown of their immune systems. It soon became clear that the disease was growing rapidly, and that everyone who got it died. Initially the disease seemed limited, almost always striking homosexuals and intravenous drug users. But as increasing numbers of heterosexuals were struck, the realization began to hit home: AIDS could be transmitted through heterosexual sex. Scientists were quoted in the press as saying AIDS was "the greatest disease threat to the human race since the Black Plague."

Some heterosexuals who were certain they'd never had sex with a drug addict or homosexual felt safe. Then evidence indicated that someone could be infected with the AIDS virus and show no signs of infection for as much as eight years, yet be a carrier of the virus during the entire period. Heterosexuals realized they not only had to worry about who their prospective sex partner had engaged in sex with for the last eight years or more, but who his or her sex partners' sex partners had engaged in sex with for the preceding eight years, and so on. Sexually active people realized they could be exposing themselves to thousands of potential AIDS carriers in a single individual. Fear of AIDS quickly became one of the most powerful forces for sexual restraint in human history, as people began to ask themselves, "Is it worth dying to have sex with this person?"

The epidemic was seen by the religious right as retribution for years of immorality, the "wrath of God" striking down sexual sinners—and all the more reason to pursue relentlessly their antisex agenda. If people had sex only when married, and remained monogamous, then AIDS was no threat. The supporters of decency, seeing AIDS as clearing away the immoral deadwood from society, were not eager to support efforts to curb the spread of the disease. Antisex forces consistently tried to stop the funding or public use of educational videotapes or pamphlets that warned of the disease and advised safe-sex techniques, claiming that these methods served to approve promiscuity. In Los Angeles, for example, one county supervisor voted to withhold funding from one such safe-sex pamphlet, calling it nothing but "hard-core pornographic trash," and insisting that he was sure taxpayers wanted AIDS to be combated with "decency and good taste."

And as if AIDS weren't enough, newspaper headlines and magazine features spread more bad news: SEX CAUSES CANCER. A disease caused by an obscure virus called papilloma became the most rapidly spreading sexually transmitted disease in America by 1985, with millions of new cases each year. And research indicated that the virus was "strongly implicated in cervical cancer," which kills some seven thousand women a year in the United States. Investigators had already known that women who had multiple sexual partners, or who began to have intercourse at an early age, were at the greatest risk for cervical cancer. Now, it appeared that the papilloma virus was a cause. Carried by both men and women, the virus is frequently undetectable, and the incidence of infections by the virus had increased tenfold since the late 1960's. One study of sexually active girls, fourteen to eighteen years old, found that nearly one in five was infected with the papilloma virus. The clear conclusion of the scientists: Women increase their risk of infection, and potential cervical cancer, with each new partner.

The response to all this bad news was, for many, sexual shutdown. Popular magazines carried features on "The New Celibacy." Prominent figures such as Erica Jong discussed the richness of their celibate lives.

And so, as the antisex forces of the eighties moved onward toward their goal of restricting the sexual activities of the American people, they encountered less resistance than they might have had the American people been in a more sexual mood.

In Pursuit of the Red Herring

But just as the forces for sexual restriction seemed to be gaining the high ground, they began to encounter increasing opposition. Among the most angry opponents were feminists, who found the alliance between antiporn feminists and the forces of the far right a most threatening and ominous development. "Get off the pornography kick," Betty Friedan advised her antiporn sisters. "No matter how repulsive we may find pornography, laws banning books or movies for sexually explicit content could be far more dangerous to women. The pornography issue is dividing the women's movement and giving the impression on college campuses that to be a feminist is to be against sex. More important, it is diverting energies that need to be spent saving the basic rights now being destroyed."

The danger to the women's movement, Friedan warned, "is an enormous diversion of energy that could end the women's movement. I call to mind the historical analogy, at the early part of this century, when women had been fighting a century for women's rights, and they won the vote. And then they got diverted on some idea of sexual purity, and outlawing drinking, temperance, prohibition, and the whole century-long struggle came to an end."

Pornography, wrote feminist Marcia Pally, "illuminates our discomfort with the nakedness of sex, our panic at our arousal and loss of control, and men's lust for and anger at the female figure. But pornography didn't start any of this. And getting rid of porn won't end it. . . . I'm afraid the antiporn brouhaha of the past few years is a red herring, luring us away from the sources of sexism and its solutions."

The fear that many feminists began to voice was that the forces of the far right, determined to divide and destroy the feminist movement by stopping it from effecting meaningful political and cultural change, had intentionally nurtured the growth of the antiporn feminist movement.

Feminists saw the Dworkin–MacKinnon law as a dangerous tool that would be used against feminists, and began to organize against it, forming groups like Feminist Anti–Censorship Taskforce (FACT). Said FACT leader Carole Vance, "The push to restrict material is very mistaken in this political climate: any ordinance is going to be used primarily by right-wing groups against women. A great deal of writing and art and films produced by women will be prosecutable under these laws."

Betty Friedan warned, "In a period of growing right-wing power, feminists should be wary of lying down with the lion on this issue. If obscenity is in the eye of the beholder, many of those who would actually be the censors will see feminism itself as obscene."

6

THE RAT RUNNERS MEET THE FREEDOM FIGHTERS: THE CONFLICT ABOUT HUMAN NATURE

. . . .

The more one observes the battle on the sex-power nexus, the clearer it becomes that beneath all the statistics and counter-statistics, the calls to action, the warnings of danger, are two radically different views of the nature of human beings.

From one point of view, humans are born "empty," their minds a *tabula rasa*, a blank slate, upon which virtually anything may be written. Humans assume their "human nature," or personality, in response to the stimuli they encounter in their environment. Some stimuli make people feel good, and these "rewards" cause them to "learn" to behave in ways that will bring more rewards. Some stimuli make people feel bad, and these "punishments" cause humans to learn to behave in ways that will avoid further punishments. From birth on, humans are bombarded by stimuli: that is, humans are learning at all times. And as they learn, they become what they are, their personalities. What they are is, essentially, what they do.

This is, for many people, a very comforting point of view, because it means that people can be shaped or molded in desired ways: With the correct punishments and rewards, people can learn the right behaviors and become happy, peaceful, productive human beings. It also means that people who do not behave in desired ways do so because they received rewards and punishments for the wrong things when they were growing, which caused them to "learn" the wrong behaviors; but with the right training, the right program of punishments and rewards, they can "unlearn" the wrong things; their behavior can be modified. Humans, in this point of view, are wonderfully malleable.

Countering that is another point of view that contends that humans are indeed malleable, but not *absolutely* malleable. They are born open but not empty, with a slate that is not totally blank. In this view humans, by virtue of the structure of their genetic material, the architecture of their brain, the unique balance of chemicals within their nervous system, are innately predisposed, or "hard-wired," to behave in certain ways. These predispositions can be modified in many ways, and in many cases can be ignored or resisted. But they can never be totally eradicated. The slate cannot be wiped clean.

This hard-wiring view means that no matter how perfectly people are taught, no matter how precise and beneficial the rewards and punishments, not all people will act in the desired ways. Still, for people holding this second point of view, there are other comforts: the knowledge that there is something that can be called "human nature," and that each individual possesses a nature or self that is uniquely his or hers; the knowledge that through the personal self each individual is linked to all other humans, so that no matter how each human is modified by rewards and punishments, there will always remain this storehouse of shared secrets; the knowledge that through this personal self humans are fused with all the human and protohuman creatures of evolution, so that each human can confront feelings and desires and abilities that are ancient, mysterious, and seem to offer access to an awesome wisdom.

BEYOND FREEDOM AND DIGNITY: THE RAT RUNNERS AND THE BENEFITS OF TINKERING AROUND

Both these points of view have unique attractions for Americans. The first, with its belief that life offers the possibility of constant improvement—this is the dream that brought so many immigrants to America, the dream of beginning anew, with a clean slate and infinite possibilities. This is the basis for our program of mandatory education for children: Provide them with the right rewards and punishments, and they will grow into law-abiding citizens.

If you are not happy, then alter your stimuli by building a newer house, purchasing a new car, a dress. If you are a ninety-seven-pound weakling, then don't let those bullies kick sand in your face—only a few months of altering your stimuli by pumping iron will turn you into a he-man all the girls will be proud to be with. It is this viewpoint that has led to the peculiarly American belief in the essential benefits of tinkering around—whether it is tinkering with your car, to adjust the carburetor and get a few more miles per gallon, or tinkering with the brain, zapping it with a bit of electricity or some interesting molecules just to see what effect it might have on depression: The secret meaning of the American tinkering impulse is the unspoken belief that if you adjust the stimuli in the right way, giving the right rewards and punishments, then things will get better and better.

In psychology, this point of view, developed and systematized by John B. Watson, B. F. Skinner, and Clark Hull and their students and colleagues, came to be known as "learning theory," or, more popularly, behaviorism.

These practical, anti-introspective Americans had little patience with ideas of what had been called "the mind." These mental ghosts we call thinking have, they said, no more reality than the spirits of the dead, and to believe in them is pure superstition.

The behaviorists did extensive work with laboratory rats—observing how rats could learn (or become "conditioned") to do very specific things (such as press bars) in response to very specific stimuli (such as flashing lights) by providing them with rewards (such as food pellets) or punishments (such as electric shocks). These scientists, who came to be known as "rat runners," believed it would be possible to discover the laws not only of rat behavior but of all organisms. Including humans. B. F. Skinner even went so far as to place his

infant daughter in what he considered an ideal environment for learning, or conditioning—an environment, called a "Skinner Box," that
provided suitable rewarding stimuli for desired behaviors. "Give me
the baby and my world to bring it up in," declared John B. Watson,
"and I'll make it a thief, a gunman, or a dope fiend. The possibility
of shaping in any direction is almost endless."

The behaviorists' views leave no room for concepts such as individual "freedom." Freedom and free will, the behaviorists argue, are
obsolete concepts, superstitions. Once humans learn how their behaviors and beliefs are a product of conditioning, of rewards and
punishments, then they can move beyond such dangerous superstitions, or, as Skinner phrased it in the title of his popular book, they
can move "beyond freedom and dignity."

THE WIZARD OF OZ AND THE HUCK FINN TRANSCENDENTALISTS

The second point of view is also one that has been powerfully appeal-
ing to Americans from the time of our pioneers. Its acceptance that
humans, like the forces of nature, are unpredictable, driven at times
by impulses and energies that cannot be easily understood or altered,
made sense to people struggling to secure a safe home for their family
in the boundless and dangerous lands beyond the edge of civilization.
And its assertion that the mysterious forces at work within humans
can fill them with feelings of indescribable wisdom, with experiences
that are transcendental, was a plain fact of life to people who were
pushing into the uncharted and unknown of a wild country, immense,
seemingly infinite, beyond the dreams of Europeans.

The second point of view is best expressed not systematically,
statistically, in scientific journals, but in the American works of astonishment: the Deerslayer novels of James Fenimore Cooper, with
Natty Bumppo and his Indian companions confronting the deep forests; the New England transcendentalists, with their vision of individuals linked to the cosmos; Melville's *Moby Dick*; Mark Twain's
Huckleberry Finn, voyaging down the great river; and on and on
through its Wild West novels that created a myth out of the West
even as it was still being settled; its Wild West movies, and its Hollywood movies that embodied the bizarre, often violent, often warm
vision Americans had of themselves—a vision of people stumbling

onto treasures by accident, blundering through gunfights and romances.

If this view has a counterpart in psychology, it would be in the psychology of Freud, with its model of obscure instincts and drives; or, even more, in the work of Carl Jung, with its assertion that we all contain not just ourselves, but our *other*, our "shadow self"; and that we are all linked, through our unconscious minds, to a deeper level of awareness, our "collective unconscious," from which mysterious drives and forces emerge in the shape of gods and goddesses, wise old men and women, demons and angels.

SEIZING CONTROL: SEXUAL TINKERING AND THE COMING OF HUMAN PERFECTION

In the struggles within the sex-power nexus, we can see these two views of human nature pitted against each other. On one side are the antisex forces, who have put their faith in behaviorism.

As feminist writer Deirdre English explains it, "The ideological affinity of feminism and behaviorism arises from the fact that this particular bent in psychological thought helps to eliminate such knotty problems as whether or not there are any built-in differences between the sexes. This greatly simplifies (in theory) the project of equality. . . . Everything that was once considered part of a male or female sexual nature—from the maternal instinct to the tendency to become aggressive—is reinterpreted as a behavior that has been taught. . . . The hope of those who uncritically borrow this thinking is that to make men and women equal, all we need to do is seize control of the programming mechanisms of society and substitute a nonsexist input."

As an example, she quotes the attitude of Women Against Pornography activist Dolores Alexander: "[She] told me that she believes there is no essential difference between men's and women's sexual nature. It is just that men have been exposed to material that has corrupted them—'They took the wrong turn,' she said—with tragic consequences."

Though they do not speak in terms of seizing the programming mechanism, altering stimuli, or reinforcing desired behaviors, the Christian fundamentalists share the antisex feminists' belief in behaviorist learning theory. In the largest view, life itself, they believe, is a vast Skinner Box, with God playing the role of the white-smocked lab psychologist, meting out punishments and rewards to the sinners and the saved. Sinners receive punishments from the Great Teacher in the form of suffering in this life or by being denied access to heaven and eternal life, while those whose behavior is correct are rewarded or reinforced with "blessings"—wealth, success, or happiness in this life and eternal life hereafter. In the upbeat gospel preached by evangelicals such as Jim Bakker and Jimmy Swaggart—the "Be-Happy Attitudes"—worldly wealth and success are seen not as things to be scorned or denigrated, but as signs of God's pleasure, a reward to those who act in accordance with His will.

The ideal Christian fundamentalist Skinner Box will surely "lead us not into temptation, but deliver us from evil." And so its agenda includes the suppression or elimination of evil stimuli. The public schools, as these Christian behaviorists are keenly aware, are an extremely powerful conditioning system, offering those who control what stimuli children receive there an opportunity to shape the children's behaviors and attitudes for the rest of their lives. Thus, the fundamentalists see it as a most urgent duty to seize control of the school curriculum, to insure that the students receive good stimuli (the teaching of Creationism, and daily prayers), and to eliminate bad stimuli (the teaching of evolution, sex education, any mention of feminism, pacifism, communism, and any texts or library books that might expose the young to evil stimuli).

DEFENDING THE FREEDOM TO GET LOST

Confronting the antisex juggernaut is a diverse and motley assortment of groups, including defenders of civil liberties, feminists, publishers, academics, artists, church organizations, gay and lesbian groups, and individuals who simply don't like the idea of other people dictating to them what they should read or view, or what sexual activities they may engage in.

It is a heterogeneous and pluralistic band asserting that heterogeneity and pluralism are absolutely essential to a democratic society. Some of them make it clear that they have no fondness for some of the viewpoints they are defending, but that they are doing so for reasons of supreme importance. Lawyer Harriet F. Pilpel, a general counsel to the National American Civil Liberties Union, points out that freedom of expression "means freedom of expression for the ideas we hate. The ideas that are acceptable to a majority do not ordinarily need constitutional protection. . . . Freedom of expression has been called our 'first freedom' not only because it is guaranteed by the First Amendment to the Constitution but because without it all other freedoms falter. . . . The dictators of this world have always known that: their first official act has almost invariably been the suppression of speech and the press."

These groups are united in a belief in the overriding importance of freedom. Personal freedom is not, to them, a superstition or voodoo concept, it is not outmoded, and it is not something we must move "beyond." There is, they believe, a greater good than social order through conformity, and that is the freedom of each individual to move along an unpredictable path toward personal fulfillment or knowledge.

The behaviorist-fundamentalist social engineers insist that there is a single path toward that goal, and that everyone should walk it; after all, we're all born the same, with the same blank slates, the same capacities, the same desires—clearly we all must have the same goal. And so they would like to bring in the bulldozers and widen the path, pave it, and turn it into a freeway, and, by using the necessary rewards and punishments, insure that everyone moves in orderly fashion along the cultural freeway, with no unauthorized side trips into the wilderness. If all the traffic moves along smoothly, they argue, what is the point of concepts like freedom?

But to their opponents, the path to the goal is different for each person, and must be discovered through an exploratory process called living. Essential to this exploratory process is freedom: the freedom to discover the path even if it means taking a roundabout route. Even if it means blundering off in the wrong direction and getting lost. No higher authority can dictate what path a person must take, since each person's path depends on that person's unique capacities and characteristics.

All individuals are unique not because they have been conditioned to be that way, but because they are born with unique capacities and characteristics. In this core assumption, it becomes clear that these foes of the antisex forces represent the second view of human nature, the view that humans are not the pure product of environmental influences, but are born carrying with them drives and instincts, information and influences from preceding generations carried on by genes.

Only if individuals have the freedom to explore and act upon and come to understand their biological roots, they argue, can they find their own path toward fulfillment, and succeed in becoming fully human. And so they have come out upon the sex-power nexus to do battle with the antisex forces not out of a desire to silence them or change their beliefs, since those forces are clearly following their own path, but to keep them from restricting the freedom of others to find their personal paths, and to assert their own freedom to act as human beings and not as laboratory rats.

IN SEARCH OF THE FACTS

The question arises: Who's right? Everyone has a right to an opinion, but in this case the opinions claim to be based on facts, and the facts asserted by different groups are contradictory. For example, the anti-porn feminists, members of the Meese commission, the Christian right, all claim that pornography is a direct cause of violence, aggression, and acts of criminal violence. Their opponents, including psychologists who have studied the effects of pornography, insist that there is absolutely no evidence that this is so.

Some insist that the experience of unimpeded sexuality is the key to transcendent wisdom, and offers access to healing powers. Others seem to see the sexual experience as a potential source of evil, unleashing powers that are frightening and harmful.

The antiporn-feminist cultural determinists believe that the only difference between men and women is that men have been "conditioned" differently, that men simply "took the wrong turn" as they were growing up. Others believe there are significant differences between men and women that have their roots in biology. What is the scientific evidence?

Let's talk with the people in the white lab coats, the anthropologists with their skull fragments and their studies of the evolution of human sexuality, the neuroscientists and neuroendocrinologists with their careful analyses of the structure of the brain and the effects of brain chemicals and hormones on human sexual behavior, the social scientists with their tests and surveys and personality profiles and their sophisticated statistical analyses of human behavior.

PART II

THE

FACTS

· ·

The force that through the green fuse
Drives the flower
Drives my green age
That blasts the roots of trees
Is my destroyer
And I am dumb to tell
The crooked rose
My youth is bent
By the same wintry fever.

—Dylan Thomas, "The Force That
    Through the Green Fuse Drives the
    Flower"

It is dangerous to show man too clearly how
much he resembles the beast without at the
same time showing him his greatness. It is
also dangerous to allow him too clear a vision
of his greatness without his baseness. It is
even more dangerous to leave him in
ignorance of both. But it is very profitable to
show him both.

—Pascal, Pensées

7

THE GENESIS
OF THE SEX CONTRACT
· ·

"Mommy, where do we come from?"

The answer to that question is something that many adults do not like to be reminded of. In immediate terms, we "come from" sex, from the lustful, sweaty coupling of our own parents (a disquieting thought to many). In terms of eternity, we "come from" God, from some incomprehensible Ultimate Cause that created the universe for reasons we do not understand (another disquieting thought). And if we come from both sex and God, then somehow, in some mysterious way, sex and God must be linked (something many people find even more disquieting).

Between the immediacy of sex and the mystery of the Ultimate Cause lies the material universe, which scientists have now concluded is some 18 billion years old. Within that framework there is another answer to the child's question: We humans have "evolved"—we have developed or grown, gradually and over a long period of time, from other, simpler, more "primitive" forms of life. We have "come from" the beasts, we are descended from apes, we are brothers and sisters of gorillas and chimpanzees.

"Well, darling," says the parent to the child, "the stork brought you."

THE BISHOP'S WIFE AND THE DANCING BIRDS

In the years following the publication of Charles Darwin's *On the Origin of Species* in 1859, most of the mainstream society of the time rejected as absurd the idea that humans were descended from apes. As the wife of the bishop of Worcester exclaimed: "Descended from monkeys? My dear, let us hope that it isn't true! But if it is, let us hope that it doesn't become widely known."

In time, the evidence of the link between man and apes became indisputable. By the mid-1970's molecular biologists had developed techniques to analyze human genes, and discovered that they are more than 99 percent identical to African apes (chimpanzees and gorillas). In other words, if the information carried by the genes is compared to a thick book, then a change of less than one percent of the book's words would change a human into a gorilla. A change of a different fraction of a percent of the words would turn a human into a chimp. Furthermore, a chimp, or a gorilla, is just as closely related to a human as either is to the other. And humans are genetically more closely related to chimpanzees and gorillas than those apes are to other apes (such as orangutans and gibbons). As zoologist Richard Dawkins observes, "We are not, then, merely *like* apes or descended from apes; we *are* apes."

Scientists have also discovered that the average IQ of a chimp is 80, which is not that much lower than the human average IQ of 100. What makes humans humans, then, is a very slight genetic difference.

As a result of such advances in genetics, and vast amounts of fossilized evidence uncovered and analyzed by geologists, biologists, and anthropologists, the fact of evolution can no longer be questioned. And yet, a 1982 Gallup poll revealed that 44 percent of the American population preferred the statement, "God created man pretty much in his present form at one time within the last ten thousand years," over statements that included the idea of evolution, with or without the help of God. Millions of Americans are joined together today in a crusade to erase from school textbooks the "theory of evolution," even though evolution is no more of a theory than that the earth revolves around the sun. Evolution is a fact.

The idea of evolution did not originate with Charles Darwin. It had been widely accepted by many scientists, including Darwin's grandfather, long before the publication of *Origin of Species*. What had not been clearly understood was the mechanism by which evolution actually worked—exactly how new species emerged from older ones. What Darwin "discovered," and explained in his seminal work, was this mechanism. He called it "natural selection."

All creatures reproduce in one way or another. Those creatures who reproduce sexually (through the interaction of a male and a female) need to produce only two surviving offspring through their entire lives to replace themselves and to maintain a constant population. If they do not reproduce enough surviving offspring to replace themselves, the species will diminish in numbers and eventually become extinct. But if the creatures produce too many surviving offspring, the species faces another danger: The population of the species will become too large for the environment to support it, and it will be reduced by mechanisms such as disease, starvation, or mass suicide, like the Scandinavian lemmings.

All creatures have the capability of producing far more offspring than is necessary to replace themselves. Some fish, for example, produce a million eggs each time they spawn. If all these eggs survived and each went on to produce a million eggs, in a very short time the oceans would be a solid mass of fish. If the reproduction of the common housefly went unchecked, it would quickly produce a mass of flies bigger than the earth. But of course reproduction does not go unchecked, not all offspring survive, and most individual creatures rarely fulfill their reproductive potential.

But why do some offspring survive and not others? And why do some individuals fulfill their reproductive potential, producing many offspring, while others leave no offspring? Because some individuals are better *adapted*, more capable of meeting the challenges of the environment. An individual with dense fur and a thick layer of sub-cutaneous fat will survive an icy arctic environment better than an individual with no fur and no layer of fat. And such a better-adapted individual will also be more likely to fulfill its reproductive potential than will the poorly adapted individual: It will reproduce and pass along its genes to the next generation. That is, the individuals better adapted to survive are *selected by nature* to be the reproductive winners, to pass on their genes to the next generation. If an animal has a trait that enhances its reproductive success, it will pass its genes on to the next generation; it will pass a disproportionate amount of genes on compared to other members of its species less well adapted.

This process is what has been called "differential reproductive success," or more popularly, "survival of the fittest." But that phrase —and the process—have been widely misunderstood as having something to do with violence, aggression, and battles to the death, what Tennyson described as "Nature red in tooth and claw." This misunderstanding seemed to sanction the concept of "Social Darwinism," under which the wealthy and powerful capitalists of the late nineteenth century could justify enormous greed and inhuman treatment of the weak as a natural law: survival of the fittest—the big tough guys beat up on the little weaklings.

But natural selection is not a process of rewarding aggression. In fact, too much aggression is clearly nonadaptive—individuals who are driven to violent confrontations and fights will in many cases be too busy fighting to pass on their genes, or will not survive long enough to fulfill their reproductive potential. Survival of the fittest, students of evolution pointed out, did not mean survival of the most physically aggressive or powerful, but rather that those who have characteristics that increase their chances of producing more offspring are more likely to produce offspring, which will in turn carry on that genetic legacy.

Those "adaptive" characteristics may be the ability to emerge victorious from conflicts, but they also may be the ability to communicate well, to avoid conflicts, to withstand stress, to throw accurately, to find food, to attract members of the opposite sex, and to interact well socially. It's easy to see that an individual who cannot or will not communicate with other members of the species, who cannot find food, who cannot attract sex partners, would be less likely to leave offspring to carry on those maladaptive genes, while those who do possess those characteristics would produce more descendants, who would also possess those adaptive genes and would in turn be more successful at passing those adaptive genes along, until over scores and hundreds of generations, those behaviors would become more widespread through the entire population.

In evolution, then, the "winners" are those who reproduce, who pass along their own unique genes. "Are you the richest man in America," asks anthropologist Helen E. Fisher, "the most powerful woman in business, the smartest kid in the class? Nature doesn't care. When Darwin used the term 'survival of the fittest' he wasn't referring to your achievements or your endowments. He was counting your children. You may have flat feet, rotten teeth, and terrible eyesight, but if you have living children you are what nature calls 'fit.' You have passed your genes to the next generation and in terms of survival you have won."

The way humans pass their genes on to the next generation is through sex. That is, to become winners, humans must not only survive as individuals—avoiding death via childbirth, disease, famine, wild animals, accidents, and other kinds of violence—but must also pass another test of "fitness" by being able to attract and sexually reproduce with a human of the opposite sex.

This mechanism of evolution, complementary to natural selection, was also discussed by Darwin, who called it sexual selection. The concept is explained by evolutionary biologist Ernst Mayr of Harvard: "Natural selection normally concerns such things as better adaptation to climate, a greater ability to find or utilize food, a greater ability to escape enemies or to resist sickness. If one individual acquires any one of these traits and leaves it to his or her descendants, it benefits the whole species. There is another category of traits that merely add to the reproductive success of an individual and do not benefit the species. For example, male birds of paradise have gorgeous plumes. If one has plumes more gorgeous than his brother's, he may attract more females and leave more offspring. The gorgeous plumes, however, don't do anything for his species. That's what Darwin saw more clearly than the geneticists between 1900 and 1970, and what he called sexual selection."

These genetic traits or behaviors favored by sexual selection are also hard-wired: They cannot be intentionally altered. The birds of paradise mentioned by Mayr cannot "choose" not to have flamboyant plumes. Other birds, when approaching a sexually receptive female, go into elaborate mating dances, bouncing, turning, and strutting. These mating dances have been favored by sexual selection: that is, at some point in the evolutionary past, a bird must have been in competition with another bird for the sexual favors of a female, must have delivered some early primitive version of a mating dance, and been rewarded when the dance increased its opportunity for repro- duction. Through succeeding generations, the genes that favored that behavior would have been passed along, while the genes of those birds who did not dance would have been eliminated. So after hundreds of thousands of years of reproduction, the genes for the mating dance have become hard-wired into the brains of these birds—the dance is a matter of instinct, not choice.

Humans, of course, are a product of evolution just as much as birds of paradise. Our genes are the product of thousands of generations of winners in the genetic competition, and our bodies, ingenious protective devices for carrying around the genes and reproducing them, are those that have proven to be adaptive.

How Flat Feet Led to Big Brains

To a large degree what has proven genetically successful has been the same for all humans. When we emerged from the trees—whether forced out by some other primate competitor or by an increasingly dry climate, or attracted by the better hunting on the ground—we found that it made sense to stand upright. The upright posture, what anthropologists call "bipedalism," opened up extraordinary possi- bilities. It was an efficient way to walk or jog long distances, which made it possible to roam further afield in search of food. Hands that had evolved for gripping tree branches now could be used for gripping tools, weapons, and, perhaps most important, for carrying. When primate ancestors went on all fours, or swung through the trees, freshly killed game, or abundant patches of berries, fruits, or tubers, had to be consumed on the spot—only small quantities could be carried away held in the mouth. Now, upright, on flattened feet, humans were able to gather food and carry it back to a place where it could be consumed more safely, more leisurely; and where it could be shared. Mouths that had been used to carry food were now freed to enunciate sounds, to discuss plans.

Bipedalism offered tremendous evolutionary advantages. So those whose genes favored strong legs, strong ankles, flatter feet, knees rotated inward, pelvises realigned and strengthened to bear the weight of the upper body, survived to pass along those genes, while those who could not make the transition from jungle treetops to savanna were not favored by natural selection. Anthropologists have found the fossilized remains of a number of apelike species who apparently could not make that transition and as a result died out.

The upright posture then produced a constellation of interwoven behaviors and traits: Tools could not only be carried, tools could be made—thus the evolutionary leap from the use of a simple stone or bone or branch to chipping a stone into a sharper edge, shaping a branch to a point. With the creation of better tools came the possibility of more effective hunting of larger, more dangerous animals, spurring the development of better communication. And with the possibility of carrying food came the need for more efficient communication, to describe where the food spots were. With the increased toolmaking skills came the possibility of weaving carrying bags, so that larger amounts of foodstuffs could be gathered. And intermingled with these developments came the increasing use of another tool: the word. Those areas of the brain that controlled fine-motor movements, and expanded rapidly as a result of toolmaking, were the same areas involved in speech. So humans learned to use the intricate tool of language, enabling them to discuss the past and the future, philosophize and moralize, tell jokes and lies, describe where the best hunting or water hole was found, organize a hunting or nut-gathering expedition, or devise a plan to defend the group against intruders.

This complex of new invention triggered an enormous surge in the size of the human brain. Anthropologists have determined that the brain size of our quadripedal primate ancestors did not change much in size for nearly 12 million years—about one-third the size of the brains of modern humans. Then our ancestors became bipedal runners of the savanna, and suddenly (in evolutionary time) their brains expanded at a fantastic rate, ballooning from a chimp-sized 21.3 cubic inches to a modern-sized 86 cubic inches in less than 2 million years. Toolmaking and language-using had great adaptive advantages, but they required brainpower. Those whose brains made them clever or skillful in this area were favored by evolution. As University of Washington zoologist and psychologist David Barash points out, "Tool use, communication, and brain evolution thus interacted to produce a positive feedback ('vicious circle') loop. The ability to utilize tools and to coordinate our activities exerted initial selective pressures for increased brain capacity. This in turn made increased tool use and interpersonal collaboration possible, while the availability of increasingly sophisticated devices and opportunities further enhanced the desirability of a large brain."

But while the forces of evolution were molding all humans, male and female, in similar ways for millions of years—selecting for survival those who walked upright, manipulated a variety of tools, communicated by means of a subtle language, and developed large brains—there were also evolutionary forces at work that required males and females to adapt to them in different ways.

O Hunter! O Gatherer!

For well over 99 percent of our history, human beings lived lives that were, in their essentials, changeless. Anthropologist Helen E. Fisher sums up what we know "for certain," which is that "they were nomads who moved from place to place, hunting when the time was right, gathering when it wasn't." Over several million years the small (just over four feet tall when adults) hominid hunter-gatherers known as *Australopithecus afarensis* evolved into the larger-brained, toolmaking *Homo habilis*. Then, about 1.7 million years ago, came *Homo erectus*, as tall as modern humans, and heavier, with a dramatically increased brain size (twelve hundred cubic centimeters in volume), well within the normal range for modern human beings, who probably looked very much like us, and who thrived for well over a million years. Then, at least four hundred thousand years ago, emerged the almost modern *Homo sapiens*, and, at last, over ninety thousand years ago, the anatomically modern human—*Homo sapiens sapiens*—the direct ancestors of every human living today.

That long period of time saw extraordinary changes in humans and the way they lived, including the expansion and reorganization of the brain, the development of tools, weapons, language, the migrations out of Africa into the rest of the world, the control of fire, the construction of shelters and houses, the development of religious ceremonies, the fashioning of clothes, the creation of art. Yet during that immensely long period when humans were evolving with great speed, one thing was changeless: They remained hunters and gatherers.

During those millions of years, then, when our ancestors were changing dramatically in physical size, brain size, and behavior patterns, the traits and behavior patterns that became hard-wired into the expanding human brain were those associated with hunting and gathering.

It is a fact that males and females played different roles and performed different tasks in hunting and gathering societies. Clearly, then, some of the traits and behavior patterns that had survival value in hunting and gathering, and thus became hard-wired into the human brain, were different for males and females. Male and female contributions were complementary, and both were essential to the survival of the species. Speaking generally, males were in charge of hunting, and joining with other males in the defense of the group; while females were responsible for reproducing and caring for the young, and gathering roots, berries, fruits, and other foods. Males roamed far afield, alone or with bands of other males, in search of game. Females, burdened with infants, remained closer to the camp. Males exerted certain powers, but females also exerted power, particularly over such essential matters as healing, sex, and social life.

Many anthropologists see this sexual division of labor as a key factor in the adoption by our early ancestors of the upright posture, and thus in the extraordinary evolutionary leaps forward produced by bipedalism. As anthropologist, anatomist, and orthopedic surgeon Owen Lovejoy of Kent State University points out, our early quadripedal primate relatives were very much like us, but what they did *not* do was forage for food together. Therefore, a female, forced to fend for herself, could only manage one infant at a time. This meant that these primates had a very low birthrate, and were barely able to maintain their population. "Early man, you see, faced the same problem," says Lovejoy. "And evolutionarily speaking, there's only one way round it. Put up the calorie intake of the female and allow her to spend more time parenting, preferably in a protected spot, so that she can take care of more than one infant at a time. The male, in other words, has got to start providing food. How can he do this? He can't carry it in his mouth, as foxes and birds do. He has to walk upright and use his hands. And why should he do this? What does he get in return? Reliable sex and reliable care for his genetic investment."

This sexual division of labor, a key to human evolution, was complementary and interdependent—the labor of each sex was different but necessary, neither more important nor prestigious than the other. As anthropologist Colin Turnbull has written, "Sexual differentiation is indeed a major principle of social organization, being used—together with age—as a structural means of dividing the labor and authority—but without any sense of superordination or subordination."

Many people today, influenced by a culture in which "men's work" has, however erroneously, been more highly valued than "women's work," find it hard to accept the reality that for millions of years men's work and women's work were different but equally valued. But the evidence continues to accumulate that throughout our hunter-gatherer phase, the division of labor worked, with each sex satisfied and fulfilled within its own domain, balancing and cooperating with the other to create a uniquely flexible and interdependent social organization.

PELVIC MATTERS: THE OBSTETRICAL DILEMMA

While the sexual division of labor, with females caring for the young and males providing food and protection for their "genetic investment," contributed to the adoption of the upright posture, the adoption of the upright posture in turn seems to have increased and magnified the differences between the sexes. Our quadripedal female primate ancestors had been able to give birth and then return to their ordinary activities relatively quickly: Even though they had a baby clinging to them, they could still hunt and keep up with the males in the band. But as humans became two-footed runners, natural selection favored those with powerful legs and stronger, narrower pelvises. And this reshaping of the pelvis also reshaped the roles of the sexes. As anthropologist Sherwood Washburn explains:

> The emergence of man's large brain occasioned a profound change in the plan of human reproduction. The human mother-child relationship is as unique among the primates as is the use of tools. In all the apes and monkeys the baby clings to the mother; to be able to do so, the baby must be born with its central nervous system in an advanced state of development. But the brain of the fetus must be small enough so that birth may take place. In man adaptation to bipedal locomotion decreased the size of the bony birth-canal at the same time that the exigencies of tool use selected for larger brains. This obstetrical dilemma was solved by delivery

of the fetus at a much earlier state of development. But this was possible only because the mother, already bipedal and with hands free of locomotor necessities, could hold the helpless, immature infant. . . . Bipedalism, tool use, and selection for large brains thus slowed human development and invoked far greater maternal responsibility.

In this case, natural selection favored that minority of females who gave birth somewhat prematurely. "These mothers delivered infants with smaller heads—heads that easily navigated the shrinking birth canal," according to anthropologist Helen E. Fisher. "For these mothers birth was easier. They lived. Their infants lived. And gradually the descendants of these females proliferated."

So natural selection had solved one problem, but in doing so it had created a new one; "now females were left with a new burden —premature infants," says Fisher, "who would require many extra months or even years of care. In former days, when protohominids had traveled through the woodlands on all fours, each female had easily delivered her infant in the presence and security of the group. . . . But now their infants were premature and more vulnerable. They had to be fed and protected much longer. Moreover, because the protohominids walked upright, females had to carry their infants or strap them to their backs. It was harder for them to catch their own meat." This was a crucial difficulty, because the limitation of brain size at birth necessitates a very long period of brain development after birth, and this means large amounts of protein are needed by the infant for several years: Protein deficiencies during this time restrict the brain's growth and result in permanent retardation.

In fact, anthropologist Robert Martin of University College, London, looking at the problems surrounding human births, found that when a human child passes through the female's pelvis, it then has to *quadruple* in size. This growth requires a reliable high-protein food supply, which meant our ancestors had to hunt for meat. Since, Martin thinks, human females are not well adapted for hunting—the wide pelvis makes them unsuitable for cross-country hunting, their arms are not as highly geared as the male arm for throwing—it meant males had to become hunters, the providers of protein for their partners and offspring.

In addition, the slow period of brain development required a long time during which the infant was totally dependent on adults for

protection, training, and guidance. Giving birth, then, for these bipedal females, meant a prolonged period during which much of their
time had to be invested in caring for the young. Because of this
burden, the females were, in Fisher's words, "forced to make a deal
with males. With this bargain the sex contract would begin."

THE SEX CONTRACT: THE ADVANTAGES OF AMOROUS FEMALES

As many anthropologists and evolutionary biologists now agree, the
sex contract hinges on an interesting phenomenon called "loss of
estrus." Our early human female ancestors, like the other female apes,
and like females of most species, were sexually receptive to males
only during a brief period of fertility known as estrus. For the rest
of the time they would have no interest in sex and would react very
aggressively to any attempt by males to engage in sexual intercourse.
Males of most species are very aware when females are in "heat,"
usually through their sensitivity to chemical signals produced by the
females during that time. Thus, since sexual activity is limited to
these brief periods, sexual intercourse is a relatively rare occurrence
for most animals.

Observers have noticed an interesting characteristic of apes that
they believe was also true of our early ancestors: When a male ape is
successful in hunting, he determines how he shares his catch. In his
sharing, he pays attention to who is in estrus. Helen E. Fisher describes
this: "If a subordinate male made the catch, a senior male was forced
to beg like all the rest. Furthermore . . . some female chimps got
more meat than others did: *The females who were in heat received much
more meat than did those who were not in heat.*"

Now this makes evolutionary sense: A female in estrus is fertile,
and therefore offers the male a reproductive opportunity. It is to the
male's advantage to see that the female in estrus is fed, and to impress
upon her his own prowess and status by sharing his catch with her.
Fisher emphasizes the significance of this for early humans: "If a
female protohominid advertised sex when a kill was made, she also
received more meat." Millions of years ago, Fisher notes, during
periods when meat was hard to find, "this single ability to provide
sex at the right moment could have meant life or death to a hungry
female protohominid."

Most primate females are in heat only about ten days each month. Once the female becomes pregnant, her sexual receptivity stops and stays stopped for at least two years after giving birth while she nurses the infant. Only after the child is weaned will her monthly cycle return, and along with it her ten-day period of sexual readiness. However, variations in behavior always exist—some females will have a longer period of estrus, or longer periods of sexual receptivity. "And so it was among the female protohominids," says Fisher, "some were sexier than others."

Before humans walked upright, these females would have no particular advantage. But with the development of the upright posture, Fisher points out, "the more amorous females acquired enormous benefits—particularly as new mothers." Since natural selection favored mothers who gave birth too soon, "all the females had to carry, protect, and feed their young for longer and longer periods of time. But those females who came back into heat soon after delivering their young received the attentions of an entourage of suitors. . . . This had tremendous gains. . . . If a male carried an eland back to camp in the evening, everyone begged. But she received extra meat. . . . Thus, the new mother who came into heat soon after parturition received extra meat and protection for the part of every month she provided sex. These profits she shared with her infant. And because of these special benefits, her baby had a better chance to live to adulthood than did the infants of nonestrus mothers. More of the infants of sexier mothers did live, grow up, and breed—passing this genetic anomaly to a greater percentage of the next generation. Selection had begun to favor those unusual females who resumed sexual activity soon after delivering their young. . . . those who offered sex during pregnancy received the benefits of male attention too. When meat was hauled back to a central spot, these females got more meat than did pregnant females who couldn't offer sex. . . . As generations passed, selection gradually produced more and more female protohominids who copulated for a longer period of their monthly cycle; who made love during pregnancy; who had sex sooner after parturition. Protohominid females were beginning to lose their period of heat."

Here was the origin of loss of estrus, a key to what Fisher has called the sex contract. "With the stimulus of constantly available sex," she writes, "protohominids had begun the most fundamental exchange the human race would ever make. Males and females were learning to divide their labors, to exchange meat and vegetables, to share their daily catch."

Both males and females sought the same goal, which is the instinctive goal of all living things: to produce as many offspring as possible. Life forms have been evolving through reproduction for over a billion years. No matter what else life forms must do, they must reproduce. The sex contract made it clear that human males and females would have to pursue this goal in very different ways, to develop quite different "reproductive strategies." And so, beginning millions of years ago, males and females began to follow different evolutionary paths.

Since males were expected to hunt, and to provide protection from predators and attackers, natural selection favored those males who had strong legs and a powerful cardiovascular system, to make them better at ranging great distances and running down game; powerful arms and torsos to increase the male's ability to throw weapons, to fashion tools, and to carry meat home from the hunt; and a higher capacity to shift emotional gears and quickly enter an aggressive state for those times when the long hunt suddenly turned into a fight to the death with a wild animal, or when predators or attackers appeared unexpectedly. For all of these reasons—hunting, defense, conflict— a capacity for violence and aggression would be strongly selected for.

Since the female part of the contract did not involve hunting, there was no need for great size or a strong torso. However, it was essential that the female care for and nurture her young, so evolution would have favored females who felt a powerful bond with their children. Since the females would spend their time of gathering food, caring for the young, and training the young in the company of other females, natural selection would favor females who had good communication skills, who could interact effectively and cooperate with others, whose violent impulses did not erupt so rapidly as males, and who could restrain and channel their aggression in ways that could serve their ends most effectively.

Today, survival of the fittest no longer requires hunting or gathering traits: Natural selection no longer needs to favor men who are physically large, or who have strong upper bodies, or who are quick to act with violence. Violence, at least, seems to be distinctly unadaptive behavior today. And similarly, female survival no longer depends on a powerful mother-child bond, or strong nurturing behavior. However, our culture has only been moving away from the hunter-gatherer phase for some ten thousand years, and, as anthropologists agree, physical evolution is extremely slow, and there is no evidence or reason to believe that contemporary human bodies or brains differ from those of ten thousand years ago. In fact, recent evidence indicates that humans anatomically identical to modern humans were hunting the fields of the Middle East over ninety thousand years ago.

So despite the fact that we live in a culture with little resemblance to the hunter-gatherer culture we evolved in, there's no doubt that we are creatures genetically adapted to that vanished environment. The evidence is clear. Today, human males are 20 to 30 percent larger than females, consistently, in every culture; males are capable of much higher oxygen consumption than females—their hearts and lungs are 10 percent larger; males consistently possess far greater muscle strength, particularly in the upper body, than females; males are more aggressive and violent than females; and females are more nurturant than males.

WHAT'S THE DIFFERENCE?

Yes, yes, these are clichés, stereotypes. They are also true. There is simply no other way to interpret the evidence. Some who have not studied the literature reject the findings as sexist stereotypes. But many of the leading scientists who have made contributions in this area are females and feminists, including Margaret Mead, Anke Ehrhardt, Helen Fisher, Sarah Blaffer Hrdy, Corinne Hutt, Julianne Imperato-McGinley, Carol Nagy Jacklin, Annelise Korner, Jerre Levy, Eleanor Maccoby, Alice Rossi, Dominique Toran-Allerand, Beatrice Blyth Whiting, Doreen Kimura, Jeanette McGlone, Diane McGuinness, Sandra Witelson. All of these women are tough-minded scientists who have spent considerable time and effort determining whether differences between males and females are in part the product of biological, evolutionary causes; and all of them have concluded that they are.

Consider the evidence about some of the characteristics we have mentioned so far. In her studies of remote societies, for example, Margaret Mead demonstrated that there was a wide variation in sex roles; but in all the societies she described there was homicidal violence, and in all it was men who committed the violence.

Eleanor Maccoby and Carol Jacklin have made a systematic review of hundreds of studies of sex differences in their book *The Psychology of Sex Differences*, and found that out of scores of dimensions studied (vision, self-esteem, crying, conformity, and many more) the most overwhelming evidence for sex differences is in aggressive behavior, with males far more aggressive than females in virtually every study that compares such behavior.

From all indications, humans have evolved out of a violent past. Some feminist anthropologists in the 1970's wanted to believe that our primate progenitors were peaceful, nonviolent vegetarians, and that our ancient ancestors were naturally selected because of their peaceful and cooperative traits. Recent research has exploded this as myth. We now know that the primates and our early ancestors were much more aggressive and violent than we had imagined. Anthropologists such as Jane Goodall have described male chimpanzees patrolling the boundaries of their territory killing strangers and eating infants, bands of female baboons murdering the infants of mid- and low-ranking females; human bones from a half-million years ago reveal that two groups of humans had a bloody conflict, in which more than sixteen of one group were killed, roasted, and eaten.

In the last decade and a half, in fact, field researchers have found that despite all our wars and murders, modern humans kill a smaller proportion of their own kind than do other primates and vertabrate species, smaller than the hunter-gatherers from whom we have evolved. Apparently humans have grown not more violent, but less. But in all cultures studied, males are more violent than females.

As for nurturance, biological anthropologist and medical doctor Melvin Konner points out that "there is no society in the ethnographic or historical record in which men do nearly as much baby and child care as women. This is not to say anything, yet, about capacity; it is merely a statement of plain, observable fact: men are more violent than women and women are more nurturant, at least toward infants and children, than men." Maccoby has summarized fifty-two studies in "nurturance and affiliation"; in forty-five of these studies females showed more of it than males; five studies showed no differences; in only two did males show more. And in their classic six-culture study, Beatrice and John Whiting used uniform methods to make extensive direct observations of children's behavior in cultures around the world, and submitted their findings to statistical analysis. The data showed that the children varied widely on dimensions called "egoism versus altruism" and "aggressiveness versus nurturance." In all cultures, the boys showed greater egoism or greater aggressiveness—usually both—while girls showed greater nurturance.

It might be argued that these universal differences are the result of some sort of universal sex-role training (the cause of which, if it exists so universally, could itself be an evolutionarily determined behavior pattern). But in fact, many of the studies involved children who were very young, or in cultures with widely differing sex roles. Annelise Korner has made many studies of newborn infants, and she, as well as other scientists, has found that even *at birth* boys have more muscle strength than girls. On the other hand, Korner has found that girls show greater skin sensitivity at birth. This greater sensitivity extends into adulthood. In fact, research shows that female skin sensitivity is so extraordinarily greater than that of males that in many tests there is no overlap between the skin sensitivity scores of the two sexes—the *most* sensitive male is less sensitive than the *least* sensitive female. This too is significant, because lack of skin sensitivity is linked to aggressive behavior: There is evidence that those born with *less* skin sensitivity were more likely to behave aggressively by attacking and climbing a barrier at the age of five.

And Harvard psychologist David C. McClelland voices the objections of many scientists to the idea that differences in aggression are the result of some universal sex-role training. He points out that "practically all cultures train their boys in one direction—for assertiveness—and their girls for another—interdependence. If there were no biological basis in these directions, would it not be more likely that the differences in training would be randomly distributed between the two sexes?" Anthropologist John Tooby and psychologist Leda Cosmides argue, "The assertion that 'culture' explains human variation will be taken seriously when there are reports of women war parties raiding villages to capture men as husbands."

THE TORTOISE AND THE HARE: AN ASIDE ON CULTURAL VERSUS BIOLOGICAL EVOLUTION

I cannot emphasize too strongly that in discussing sex differences and differential reproductive strategies I am not discussing what is right or wrong, what should be or should not be, but what scientific evidence indicates was the case during the immensely long hunter-gatherer phase of our evolutionary history. Nor am I in any way favoring determinism over free will: Reproductive success is a key to evolution, but there's no doubt that at any time individuals could have chosen to act in ways that did not favor their reproductive success. We know, for example, that millions of people throughout history have chosen not to reproduce.

When I talk about reproductive strategies, then, I am not talking about what males or females "choose" to do, but rather of impulses, drives, and behavior patterns that have evolved by natural selection because they are the types of impulses, drives, and behavior patterns whose possessors' genes tend to get multiplied most. The human brain, evolved by natural selection, is built to promote the survival of the genes that created it, not to understand itself or be conscious of its own motives.

And, finally, when I talk about reproductive strategies favored by evolution, I am not talking about reproductive strategies favored today. Today, many reproductive strategies that have served to propagate genes for millions of years are outmoded, undesirable, socially unacceptable. We are no longer hunter-gatherers. But we have only stopped being hunter-gatherers for a few thousand years, and the reproductive strategies we may now disapprove of have been hard-wired into us over hundreds of thousands or millions of years. We can and do override these closed-programming circuits; it is good and desirable that we override many of them. And yet—they are still there, as much a part of us as our tendency to smile, to speak, to create. The more aware we are of these ancient evolutionary tendencies or potentials, the more we can learn to override them or use them wisely. Zoologist-psychologist David Barash emphasizes that a general truth of animal behavior is that "among progressively smarter animals, the role of genetically influenced and hormonally activated behavior declines as the cerebral component increases."

Again, I am most definitely *not* implying that the purpose of life is to reproduce one's genes. The reproductive strategies are products of *biological evolution*: alterations in the information encoded in our genes, changes that are the result of natural selection operating over thousands of generations. There is another type of evolution known as *cultural evolution*, whose laws and tendencies are quite different.

Cultural evolution involves alterations not in the information encoded in genes, but in information stored in minds, changes in the habits, attitudes, and capabilities humans have *acquired* (not been born with) in society. While biological evolution created us with sexual tendencies formed over millions of years—and as a result of which we may feel many of the same things humans felt one hundred thousand years ago—cultural evolution may change our sexual attitudes and capabilities virtually overnight. Between 1963 and 1973, for example, a sexual revolution took place.

David Barash has compared the two types of evolution to the tortoise and the hare, with biological evolution moving along at its painfully slow pace, while cultural evolution can race so rapidly it is difficult for humans even to keep track of it.

Today, cultural evolution has overtaken biological evolution as the most influential and important evolution in our lives. All scientists who are involved in the fields relating to evolutionary biology are quite clear about this. The hare is now outrunning the tortoise.

Thus, while our genetic reproductive strategies may be concerned with finding ways to successfully propagate our own genes, cultural evolution is selecting strategies that include somehow countermanding our own hard-wired self-propagation drives and ending the catastrophic growth of world population.

The only hope for humankind is through learning, education, increased wisdom, and heightened awareness of what we are up against. Part of this essential wisdom must be a clear awareness of our own natures, our own sexual drives—however outmoded they may be— clinging to us from the days we were chasing the woolly mammoth across the savanna.

INVESTMENT STRATEGIES: THE LAW OF SUPPLY AND DEMAND IN THE EGG AND SPERM MARKET

In evolutionary terms, both males and females have the same goal— to reproduce and multiply their own personal pattern of genes. However, since the process of reproduction is so different for each sex, so are the strategies they evolved for attaining that goal.

Females invest far more of their time, energy, and reproductive potential in each birth process—and risk more in terms of personal danger—than do men. A female can release only about four hundred eggs in her lifetime, and she must carry her offspring and feed it in her womb for nine months, reducing her own mobility and capabilities for defending herself from predators or attackers; she must undergo some risk to her life in giving birth; if she feeds the child at her breast, it is at some cost to her own nutrition and physical strength; she must carry it with her for several years, again reducing her mobility and capabilities for defending herself.

For males, the personal investment in reproduction—until the baby is born—is minimal. In a single ejaculation a male can release 300 million sperm, enough to fertilize every woman in the world who is fertile at that time. Theoretically, a male could invest only the few minutes necessary to fertilize a female, and then be on his way, never to be seen again, and yet still come out of the encounter with the same genetic payoff as the woman: reproductive success.

In actuality, if a male wants to insure the survival of his offspring, he must provide food for both the mother and the child, protect them, and teach the child what he has learned about how to survive. Also, the male is faced with an uncertainty that the female can never share: She is always absolutely certain that the offspring is hers, knows that it carries her genes; the male, however, can never be sure that the child he is feeding and protecting is his.

No matter how carefully he watches the female he has mated with, there will be many times when he is otherwise engaged that his mate may be having sex with another male. If this was the case, and he expended his effort in feeding and protecting another male's offspring, he will have reduced his own reproductive success. Thus, for males, it would seem to make sense, in cold genetic terms, to fertilize as many females as possible.

The Double-Standard Stuff and Reproductive Oblivion

A male can theoretically fertilize thousands of females and produce thousands of offspring in his life. But there are factors that make this difficult. First, there are other males also eager to reproduce themselves, so the competition for fertile females can be difficult and dangerous. Also, since the female reproductive strategy involves mating with a male who will help insure the survival of the offspring, females are less apt to have sex with a male who is not likely to stay around.

For males, then, the sensible course—the course dictated by evolutionary pressures—is to mate with a fertile female, to keep a close watch on her, and to use force or threats to discourage any potential rivals, to support her and the offspring that he is confident are his, and also to have sex with other fertile females, whether by making them additional mates, or by mating with unattached females or, when he can safely get away with it, with the mates of other males.

For females, of course, there are severe evolutionary pressures against indiscriminate copulation. While it's to the male's advantage to *maximize* the dissemination of his sperm, it's to the female's advantage to *optimize* in her matings, to entrust her genes only to male partners carefully selected for their abilities to provide and protect the offspring.

THE SOURCE OF FEMALE POWER

The kind of male who will insure reproductive success for the female is one who is capable of providing and insuring food, shelter, and safety for both the female and her offspring, and one who is likely to remain alive and capable of providing support for many years to come. That means the male must in some way be powerful, strong, reliable, and have a high status within the band. But such males are in a minority; and the more powerful, strong, reliable, and high status they are, the rarer they are likely to be, and the more fertile women there are likely to be competing for them.

Thus, the female is under evolutionary pressure not only to attract a desirable mate but to make sure that mate remains sufficiently attracted to her to remain with her, and support and protect her and, later, her offspring. One way she could increase the likelihood of his remaining with her was with the loss of estrus.

By concealing estrus and appearing to be sexually receptive at all times, females gained power. The sexually receptive female could choose the most desirable mate from among the males who were competing for her, and allow him to mate with her. Since it was difficult for males to know when the female was truly fertile, they were attracted to her at all times, not just during the ten days of estrus. And for the same reason, it was to his reproductive advantage to have sex with her frequently and regularly. In other words, it meant he had to invest much of his time and energy in her. It was the beginning of pair-bonding, out of which would evolve such institutions and behaviors as the nuclear family, sexual love, and, perhaps, the female orgasm.

Anthropologist Sarah Blaffer Hrdy, of UC at Davis, author of *The*

Woman That Never Evolved, observes, "When the possibility of males providing food and protection exists, a whole new range of possibilities for female reproductive strategies is opened up. And this is what I think primate female sexuality is all about: devising ways to manipulate males to get at their services and resources to provide for their children." In response to feminist critics who are appalled by Hrdy's enthusiastic exploration of female "cunning, duplicity, and manipulation," she points out, "Cunning and duplicity—these are the strategies of a creature that can't win a fight that depends on muscle mass."

Loss of estrus, an act then of "cunning and duplicity," transformed human physiology. It transformed human behavior. It transformed human culture and the human race. Most of all, it transformed sex.

For humans, sex became not only the key to the reproductive game, but the central organizing force of the entire culture. For both males and females, sexual drives tended to shape their bodies, their brains, and the way they lived. Over thousands of generations each sex evolved its own sexual agenda. As a result, there developed deep differences between the sexes, an effect known as "sexual dimorphism." "Only by regarding males and females as if they were two different species," says Tim Clutton-Brock, a Cambridge University ecologist, "are we likely to understand why it is that the sexes differ so widely in anatomy, physiology and behavior."

8

THE FACTS OF LIFE

. . . .

If any human society . . . is to survive, it must have a pattern of social life that comes to terms with the differences between the sexes.

—*Margaret Mead,* Male and Female

There are a number of sexual differences between men and women that seem to have existed persistently throughout human history. These differences, according to many anthropologists and biologists, are probably universal—the result of biological tendencies.

But before we get into these, it's important that we clear up how genes directly influence our behavior.

How Genes Shape Personality

As we noted earlier, the behaviorist school of thought claimed that under ideal circumstances scientists could take any baby born and by using the proper type of conditioning of a number of basic reflexes, turn out a lawyer, criminal, artist, priest, madman.

During the 1930's behaviorism spread out to join with the broader beliefs in environmental or cultural influence on behavior that then formed the mainstream of American cultural anthropology. In this view the only reason people grew up to be greedy, aggressive, brutal, was because the pressures of the environment or social training made them so. All human behavior was determined by the culture or environment: a point of view called *cultural determinism*.

Much has happened since the 1930's, including revolutions in the fields of genetics and anthropology. The unraveling of the mystery of the double helix, our breaking of the genetic code, has showed us how it is possible to store a vast library of information in our genetic material and pass it down from generation to generation. We now know beyond doubt that humans are not born as *tabulae rasae*, that we are born with a wealth of information within us. Cultural determinism, the belief that we are *exclusively* determined by the environment, or "nurture," is no more defensible than the idea of Creationism, the so-called "science" put together by people who believe we were created by God as fully evolved humans at some point in the last ten thousand years. It just is not so.

There is no doubt that a genetic program controls and gives shape to our biological life cycle. We are not programmed to wither away and die as soon as our reproductive years are over. We are not programmed to hibernate during the winters. We are not programmed to be born, grow old, and only in our old age become fertile and reproduce. The fundamental definition of our lives is laid out by our genes.

Our genes have also defined other aspects of our life, such as our basic needs for food, water, sleep, sex, reproduction, warmth, physical movement, and so on.

Perhaps the time we become most aware of how our lives are shaped by genetic influences is when the genetic programs (often in combination with environmental influences) cause us trouble; we now know genetic factors are implicated to some degree in such problems as schizophrenia, manic depression, some other types of depression, alcoholism, autism, hyperactivity, reading disabilities, speech disorders, some obesity problems, phobias, color blindness, and diseases such as hemophilia, Huntington's chorea, Tay-Sachs disease, Parkinson's disease, Down's syndrome, sickle-cell anemia, albinism, phenylketonuria, arthritis, diabetes, epilepsy, and some allergies.

In 1987 the Minnesota Center for Twin and Adoption Research dropped a bombshell with its eight-year study of 348 sets of twins raised separately. The conclusions attracted a lot of attention, including cover stories in national news magazines that trumpeted headlines like HOW GENES SHAPE PERSONALITY. The institute's researchers concluded that "how people think and act—their very personality—is determined more by the DNA in their cells than by society's influences." Said psychologist David Lykken of the Minnesota project, "The evidence is so compelling that it is hard to understand how people could *not* believe in the strong influence of genetics on behavior."

In another study psychologist Sarnoff Mednick at the University of Southern California traced the lives of fourteen thousand adopted children and found to a remarkable degree that those whose biological parents were criminals were much more likely to become criminals themselves. When some colleagues heard of his findings, they told Mednick to burn them. Said Mednick, "Some people had built their careers on the assumption that heredity was not a key player in human behavior. They just could not separate scientific fact from political dogma."

As examples of how personality traits are determined by heredity more than or as much as by culture, the Minnesota Center, using sophisticated computer analysis of lengthy tests taken by all the hundreds of twins, found that qualities like extroversion and conformity are very much influenced by genes (61 percent and 60 percent respectively), as are the tendency to worry (55 percent determined by heredity), creativity (55 percent), paranoia (55 percent genetically determined), optimism (54 percent), cautiousness (51 percent), aggressiveness (48 percent), ambitiousness (46 percent), orderliness (43 percent) and intimacy (33 percent). Other traits, according to the researchers, who are still analyzing the figures, may show even more genetic influence—as much as 85 percent.

In groupings of traits, the Minnesota psychologists found these things "mostly genetic": *social potency* (forcefulness, leadership qualities), *traditionalism* (respects authority, principles); *positive emotionality* (optimistic), and *negative emotionality* (ready to feel anxiety, anger).

Those found to be "mostly environmental" were: *social closeness* (sociable, affectionate) and *control* (cautious, plodding).

The researchers doing the study found themselves being changed. Psychologist Auke Tellegen said, "When I was developing the traditionalism test, I thought, that's a wonderful scale because it, at least, will show a strong environmental influence. At first when we started getting a strong heritability, I thought it was a fluke. How could respect for church, traditional values, a certain amount of prudishness—how could this strange conglomeration of traits be inherited?" It quickly became clear that this complex of traits was strongly genetic. "Now it's changing my ideas about liberalism and conservatism," Tellegen has said. "I'm now more of a believer that there is a genetic, knee-jerk quality to being liberal or conservative."

As all scientists studying the influence of genes agree, genes *do not* "determine" behavior, but only produce a tendency that can be ignored or controlled. Says Harvard biologist Edwin O. Wilson, "Admitting that we are all influenced in different ways by our genetic code doesn't reduce our freedom to do what we want to do." Twins researcher and psychologist Gerald McClearn of Pennsylvania State University points out, "A gene can produce a nudge in one direction or another, but it does not directly control behavior. It doesn't take away a person's free will." And Harvard evolutionary theorist Ernst Mayr says emphatically, "It's only the 'nurture' people who say behavior is determined by nurture to the exclusion of nature. The 'nature' people have always said it's both. They realize that believing in a genetic component of behavior does not mean believing in genetic determination."

LIES, DAMNED LIES, ET CETERA

Before we begin looking at "gender-linked sex differences," it's important to note that we will be talking about statistically significant *average* differences between males and females. Such a generalization requires qualifications. First, we should keep in mind Mark Twain's observation that "there are three kinds of lies: lies, damned lies, and statistics."

So, though these statistics if intelligently used can be very valuable, we must remember that they do not refer to *individuals*. For example, statistics say that the fastest male marathon runners average around two hours and nine minutes while the fastest female marathon runners average around two hours and twenty-four minutes. Statistically, elite male marathon runners are about fifteen minutes faster than elite female runners—or about thirty seconds per mile faster. Nevertheless, many female marathon runners can leave many male runners in the dust.

Furthermore, the average differences between groups are generally far less than the differences among individuals within the groups. That is, if overall the average difference between male and female marathon runners is about fifteen minutes, that is much smaller than the difference between elite female runners and slower female runners, and elite male runners and slower male runners—in each case, the slower runners will finish three, four, or more hours behind the leaders.

Speaking in social terms, the differences that are most important or relevant for each individual will be the differences among *individuals*. Thus, if we conclude that statistically males tend to have a greater variety of sex partners (and this is statistically true), that has nothing to do with the fact that many females will have a far greater variety of sex partners than most males.

And finally, we must remember when we talk about genetically or biologically based sex differences that each of these sex differences has also been subject to environmental or culturally based influences. Thus, while it is statistically true that males have on average a greater variety of sex partners, and that this behavior has a genetic basis, it is also true that throughout history it has been socially more acceptable for males to seek a greater variety of sex partners than females. But right now, let us analyze gender-based sex differences.

THE GATEKEEPERS OF SEX

Everywhere and at all times, sex has been seen as a service or a favor that women choose to provide or offer to men. There are no cultures in which the opposite is the cultural norm. It is males who hire prostitutes, and engage them purely for the purposes of having sex, while the use of male prostitutes is extremely rare, and usually involves a woman purchasing not simply sex but also companionship and perhaps a stable relationship. It is men who court women, give them gifts, take them to dinner (just as protohominid hunters millions of years ago shared their meat with the female in estrus), woo them, and ask indirectly or directly for sex. It is women who resist, are coy, reserved, cautious, "modest," calculating (to ascertain the man's potential value as a loyal and protective mate), and who choose indirectly or directly to have sex.

This is true throughout the world. Margaret Mead has described this sex difference in Polynesia: "It is the girl who decides whether she will or will not meet her lover under the palm trees, or receive him . . . in her bed in the young people's house. He may woo and plead . . . [but] if she does not choose, she does not lift the corner of her mat, she does not wait under the palm trees."

As Donald Symons, professor of anthropology at UC Santa Barbara, asserts, "Women control what males have always needed—the ability to carry and reproduce their genes for them. And so a man tends to pursue sex aggressively—it's a trivial expenditure of energy with a potentially big payoff. For a woman, though, sex is something else. Women, after all, have always had one of their few, expensive eggs and their bodies on the line. And so sex for a woman remains a valuable *service*, a service that has to be carefully traded."

In the early years of modern feminism many women assumed that female sexual reserve was a lack of assertiveness caused by sexist, male-oriented prescriptions for sex-role behavior, and therefore set out to alter the behavior through consciousness-raising and assertiveness training. But by 1980 women were demanding a return to "intimacy" and claiming that the sexual revolution was largely a men's event—in the words of feminist writers Barbara Ehrenreich, Elizabeth Hess, and Gloria Jacobs, "a victory for men and a joke on women."

Seen as a highly successful evolutionary reproductive strategy, the female reluctance to engage in quick promiscuous sex emerges not as a lack of assertiveness, but springs from an authentic, biologically based female assertiveness, and so any true assertiveness training would have the effect of enabling women to say "no" more decisively.

The biological difference between men and women is stated in its most exaggerated form by feminists such as Robin Morgan, who asserts that "rape exists at any time sexual intercourse occurs when it has not been initiated by the woman out of her own genuine affection and desire."

Despite its ignorance of the affection or love between mates that causes them to engage in and enjoy sex that they have not initiated out of their own genuine desire. Morgan's motto, in its assertion that acceptable sex can only be initiated by a woman, not a man, does, at least, demonstrate her understanding that the differences in sexual strategies between males and females spring not from sex-role training but from hard-wired, ancient, naturally selected-for behavior patterns.

HIGAMOUS HOGAMOUS

Males tend to seek more than one mate. "Monogamy is rare in mammals, almost unheard of in primates," according to zoologist David Barash, "and it appears to be a relatively recent invention of certain human cultures. . . . Prior to Western colonialism and Judeo-Christian social imperialism, the vast majority of human societies were in fact polygynous."

George Peter Murdock's *Ethnographic Atlas* lists 849 human societies, of which fully 83 percent (708) are based on the marriage form polygyny (one man married to two or more women). Less than half of one percent (four) of the societies are characterized by polyandry (one woman married to two or more men), and it is practiced only under adverse conditions—when women are extremely scarce or when the environmental resources are so limited that it takes more than one man to support a woman. All the other societies (137, or 16 percent) are characterized by monogamy; but as Melvin Konner points out, "in most of these a single individual may have more than one mate in succession, and because of the starkly different reproductive life spans in men and women, men . . . are much more likely than their female counterparts to have more than one family." And in virtually all monogamous societies there is female prostitution, while male prostitution is virtually nonexistent.

Of 116 societies in a cross-cultural study, 65 percent were more tolerant of adultery by men than by women; none was more tolerant of adultery by women.

Even without ethnographic evidence, man's polygamous tendency would be clear simply from the size differential between human males and females. Scientists have discovered that species in which monogamy or the pair-bond is the reproductive norm usually have little or no size differential between the sexes (or are "monomorphic"). Sarah Blaffer Hrdy explains this: "Since males [of monogamous species] are not competing among themselves for harems, and since both sexes must compete for territories and resources, there is little selection pressure for a larger male sex endowed with unique male weaponry."

At the other end of the scale are what are called "tournament species," in which competition for females is fierce, and the males are much larger than the females. Male elephant seals for example, which are up to four times larger than the females, fight for control of harems of up to fifty females, and in one breeding season ecologists found that only 4 percent of the males accounted for over 85 percent of the copulations, while the other 96 percent of the males had to fight for the attention of the few remaining females. As Konner remarks, "This is sexual selection with a vengeance."

Human males are 20–30 percent bigger than the females, which means that while they have polygamous tendencies, they also have mild pair-bonding tendencies, and they are certainly not a tournament species.

As David Barash explains the human preference for polygyny, "it is possible for such arrangements to enhance the evolutionary fitness of all—except for the excluded bachelors." Polyandry, on the other hand, "would likely reduce the fitness of the participating males, since it would lower the probability of any single one of them being a father; at the same time, it would do little for the fitness of the woman, since her maximum reproductive success is unlikely to be greatly enhanced. She can only have one child at a time, no matter how many husbands."

While many women seem to think that polygyny works to the advantage of males, in truth it works to the advantage of women in many ways. For it is the woman who is the possessor of the evolutionary treasure—potential reproduction—and she is the one who parcels out that treasure, and only to those who she finds satisfactory. As Harvard anthropologist Irven DeVore insists, "Males are a vast breeding experiment run by females."

As possessor of the treasure, the female can require males to do whatever she wants. Among the things she requires is that the males compete with each other. Evolutionarily speaking, she is separating the strong genes from the weak. And so, when she has found the male she feels is an acceptable father for her offspring, she will join with him. That the male may have other wives does not diminish his genetic fitness. And once she is pregnant, it does not matter how he expends his sperm. Sperm is cheap, but her egg is dear.

Which may explain a mysterious occurrence in the life of great American psychologist and philosopher William James. He is said to have awakened one night to scribble down something that came to him in a dream and that he was convinced contained the key to understanding the meaning of life. After writing, he fell back asleep and awakened in the morning with great excitement, eager to see this wisdom he had captured. He looked at the notebook by his bed and read:

> *Hogamous higamous*
> *men are polygamous*
> *Higamous hogamous*
> *women monogamous.*

COMPETITION

Students of preliterate cultures consistently report that competition for females is a central theme of life—great hunters, warriors, leaders, are rewarded with sexual access to females, and their females are a sign of high status. Violence between individual males and warfare among groups of males takes place to acquire mates. Competition between two males for Helen was said to have been the cause of the Trojan War.

Even if there were one female for every male, there would still be competition among males, since the reproductive strategy that they have inherited is to fertilize many females. In addition, males are not competing for all females, but only for those who are the right age to be fertile—a much smaller number. Thus, the male's physical size has evolved not just to make him a more effective hunter, but to help him win out over other human males in the competition for females.

As the only source by which men may participate in reproduction, females are, for men, an essential resource. They are always—in the minds of men—in short supply. And when there is a scarcity of any essential resource, like water or food, or females, men will compete for it, and groups of men will be willing to compete for it in organized fighting or killing—warfare—with other groups.

FEMININE WILES

It was long thought that female primates were not highly competitive, but recent, more sophisticated methods of field research have overturned that assumption. It is now known that primate females are quite competitive, but their competition is with other females, and is directed toward protecting their offspring at the expense of those of other women.

A wealth of recent field research has revealed that primate females have a wide array of competitive strategies, most of them directed toward sabotaging each other's reproductive output—strategies that include intentional aborting, abusing, starving, and even arranging the murder of other females' offspring. Many primate females harass a low-ranking female, either attacking her in early pregnancy, causing her to abort, or putting her under such stress that her reproductive system shuts down.

Other primate females (such as langur monkeys) have more subtle strategies that include luring bachelor bands of males to attack the dominant, or "alpha" male—if a new alpha male takes over, he quickly kills all the suckling infants in the troop, since he is not their father, and females are infertile while nursing. According to anthropologist Jim Moore, who has observed such behavior, "a female *with* an infant sure doesn't want it to happen—but one with no infant at risk might. That would eliminate the infants that would compete for food with *her* future infants." Also, Moore points out, it is a good way to test the prowess of the troop's alpha male: "Say a female is between kids—she's about to get pregnant. She'll be pregnant for six months, and then need another eight to nurse the kid. For the next 14 months, she needs peace and quiet—but will the current male hold on? If he's dumped in that time, her kid could get killed by the new guy. So for her . . . maybe it's best to provoke a takeover fight *now*—either you find out your male is still tough, or you get a new male at the beginning of his reign." Or, as anthropologist Sarah Hrdy concluded from her study of langur monkeys, "Essentially, what allowed infanticide to persist was competition among females for breeding success."

It has been learned that just as female primates can have their fertility suppressed by stress and competition from other females, so can human females suffer. According to Sam Wasser of the University of Washington's School of Family Medicine, who studied the problem, "Stress is a very important contributor to reproductive failure in women . . . including everything from ovulatory failure, delay of sexual maturation, spontaneous abortion, low-birth-weight kids, prematurity, insufficient breast milk, infant mortality, child abuse—you name it."

The primate females most susceptible to this kind of reproductive suppression, scientists have found, are low-ranking females, who are picked on by most of the other females and have few allies: Among human females, according to studies by Wasser, those with a strong support network or social support have fewer reproductive problems than the others.

Primate females attack the reproductive output of others by damaging their support network and inflicting stress, and human females follow a similar strategy using gossip and insult. For example, anthropologist Richard Lee has noted that women of the Kalahari Bushmen at times of extreme anger attack other women by sexual insult, using expressions like *Du a!gum* (Death on your vagina!), to which the response is usually suicide, violence, or a division in the tribe.

Irven DeVore, professor of anthropology at Harvard and a student of how evolutionary forces are manifested in human societies, observes that television soap operas are clear expressions of female competition: "The female-female competition is blatant. The women on these shows use every single feminine wile." He points to a segment of *Dynasty* when a divorcee sees her ex-husband's new wife (who is pregnant) riding a horse and shoots off a gun, causing the horse to throw its rider, who miscarries, thus protecting her own children from rival heirs. In the popular TV sitcom *Murphy Brown*, written, directed, and produced by women and widely hailed for its keen insights into women's lives, a younger female competitor of reporter Murphy Brown watches her fail in her attempt to serve as a stand-in mother and sympathizes venomously: "This must be particularly hard for you, knowing there's no one special in your life and you're probably not ovulating anymore."

"Whole industries turning out everything from lipstick and perfume to designer jeans are based on the existence of female competition," DeVore points out. "The business of courting and mating is after all a negotiation process, in which each member of the pair is negotiating with those of the opposite sex to get the best deal possible, and to beat out the competition from one's own sex. . . . I get women in my classes saying I'm stereotyping women . . . And I say sure—

I'm stereotyping the ones who make lipstick a multibillion-dollar industry. It's quite a few women."

Many women who in the past were claiming that female-female competition did not exist or was only a product of sex-role training are now admitting the importance of female competition. Susan Brownmiller, a decade after her book *Against Our Will*, writes, "As unprecedented numbers of men abandon their sexual interest in women . . . female competition for two scarce resources—men and jobs—is especially fierce."

Knowing what we do about how female competition sabotages the reproductive capabilities of other females, or sabotages their bond with potential mates, we would assume that our society would show a decline in female fertility or birthrate, and a decrease in the stability of pair-bonds. And there is evidence that females are experiencing the highest rate of infertility ever known; the divorce rate in the United States is now almost one in two; there are about 1.5 million abortions performed each year; and the birthrate (about 1.8 births per woman in her lifetime) is also the lowest in history. Apparently, female competition is having its effects.

SKIN DEEP

Susan Brownmiller was one of many feminists who in the 1960's and 1970's vehemently attacked the use of cosmetics by women. But more recently, in her book *Femininity*, she writes, "My congratulations to the cosmetics industry—they have weathered the storm. . . . It was probably inevitable that the anti-makeup forces should lose. We were bucking too much of history."

The reason women support the makeup industry is that cosmetics serve an important role in their reproductive strategy. It is one more of those apparently universal, biological sex differences. Males, in general, are attracted by physical qualities, particularly youth and physical beauty, while survey after survey continues to show that females are attracted by qualities such as status, power, skills. University of Michigan psychologist David Buss, for example, spent several years investigating human mating preferences. He administered a questionnaire to thirty-seven groups of men and women in thirty-three different societies, the largest such sample ever amassed. He found that despite their geographic and cultural diversity, the subjects had the same pattern of preference. Again and again males were attracted by signs of youth and fertility, while females valued wealth and ambition. In all thirty-seven groups "good looks" were more important to males than to females, while in thirty-six out of thirty-seven groups, a mate who is a "good financial prospect" is more important to females than males. And in every group males preferred younger mates, and females preferred older ones.

As Donald Symons points out, "Men in all cultures prize health and cleanliness—good skin, good teeth. They set store on physical attractiveness. And this attractiveness is always associated with *youth*. Why? Because youth is when a woman is most valuable, reproductively speaking. . . . Detecting and being attracted by signs of female youth are part of the male's genetic program."

Males seek females who are fertile, sexually receptive, and healthy. The signs of fertility are many, and include tight, smooth, youthful skin.

Other signs of youth and health include ruddy cheeks, big, bright eyes, and rosy lips. Females who are moving inexorably away from the smooth skin and ruddy cheeks of youth (and the fertility they denote) can fool males into thinking they have more years of potential childbearing than they really do by skillfully applying cosmetics, which is why all the antimakeup forces couldn't make a dent in this ancient industry.

While standards of female beauty vary widely from culture to culture, a youthful complexion seems to be a universal standard of female beauty. "That's why women wear makeup and try to look young," says Dr. Helen Singer Kaplan, physician, psychoanalyst, teacher of human sexuality at Cornell Medical Center, and director of New York Hospital's human-sexuality program. "And it's foolish not to recognize the universal appeal of the younger woman. I think it's ludicrous to say this is due to advertising or social conditioning."

Many feminists of the 1960's and 1970's perceived this "universal appeal of the younger woman" to be a simple matter of male sexual oppression of women—males seeking not equals but youthful "sex objects"—and they disdained the use of makeup. Today, feminists not only have returned to the use of makeup, but also endorse the use of cosmetic surgery to attain the universally desired tight skin. In 1986 over half a million American women submitted to such procedures as breast augmentation, liposuction to remove fat, and face-lifts to remove wrinkles, and the numbers of women having such surgery is increasing enormously every year. To show its approval of such strategies, *Ms.* magazine put the entertainer Cher, who had been newly sculpted by the surgeon's blade, on its cover, and proclaimed her a feminist "role model" and a "real" woman. Plastic surgery, announced the editors of *Ms.*, is a way of "reinventing" yourself, and is "for women who dare take control of their lives." And feminist novelist Fay Weldon proclaims that plastic surgery is a tool for self-transformation, and issues a call to arms: "Sisters, to the clinics!"

RELEASERS: THE INEFFABLE ATTRACTION OF BREASTS

The popularity of breast-augmentation surgery no doubt has some connection to the fact that, along with a tight skin, a clear sign of female fertility is swollen, firm breasts. And in the course of evolution humans have developed breasts that are, compared to those of other primates, extraordinary, true wonders of evolutionary biology. Helen E. Fisher points out, "These have no physiological use whatsoever and biologists agree that their original function was sexual invitation. These sensitive, fleshy, delicate areas expand by one third during intercourse. The nipples harden at the slightest touch, and for most women fondling of their breasts stimulates their desire for intercourse. Perhaps the breasts mimic the fleshy, rounded buttocks that attracted males during rear-entry intercourse. Whatever the case, protohominid males liked them in yesteryear. Those with breasts had more young than those without. And gradually breasts became the norm."

It is noteworthy that breast size among human females has no correlation with milk production, and David Barash observes that "Large, fatty breasts may therefore be biologically deceitful, giving the illusion of mammalian plenty, but when push comes to shove, not necessarily any more substance."

Ethologists have observed that many species are hard-wired to respond to certain stimuli, which are often presented by another member of the species. Once the correct signal appears, the animal responds with a behavior pattern that is automatic and instinctual. These signals or stimuli are called "releasers."

As Barash describes it, "Male European robins will attack a tuft of red feathers mounted on a stick and placed inside their territory, while ignoring a much more realistic stuffed robin that lacks the color red, which apparently releases robin aggressiveness. . . . These reactions are automatic, not rational. . . . if the appropriate characteristics that make up a releaser are artificially exaggerated by an experimenter, animals will often prefer them to the naturally occurring signal, or will perform their particular behavior more intensely or for a longer time. These exceptionally successful manmade signals are called 'supernormal' releasers."

Scientists speculate that female breasts may act on males as releasers. Just what is released is not clear, but it is something males find pleasurable. Charles Darwin is among the many who have noted the ineffable attraction of breasts: "In our maturer years, when an object of vision is presented to us which bears any similitude to the form of the female bosom . . . we feel a general glow of delight which seems to influence all our senses."

Barash suggests that the exaggeration of breasts, "as for instance the 40-inch chest of the topless dancer or Playboy bunny" could represent a sort of "supernormal releaser." It is also possible that other sexual stimuli act on males as releasers. For example, it has been suggested that full red lips exaggerated by lipstick mimic the swollen lips of sexual arousal, or the labia, and trigger unconscious male responses.

Another set of releasers men are susceptible to are those associated with children: an unusually large head and eyes, no protruding ears, a high voice, and an uncertain, stumbling gait. We view those who possess these releasers as being "adorable," "cuddly," and "cute." Again, women have traditionally tried to elicit these responses from men with such stimuli as styled hair (making the head appear unusually large and covering the ears), mascara (making the eyes appear large), a high voice (the baby-doll tones of Marilyn Monroe, Cyndi Lauper, Bernadette Peters, Madonna), and high-heeled shoes, which make them walk like toddlers.

Females, too, respond automatically to certain stimuli, but their stimuli are quite different from those that trigger responses in males. One well-known releaser for females is a sound: The crying of their baby acts as a releaser of milk, causing their breasts to lactate and eliciting instinctive nurturing responses. Scientists now believe this response is the result of the release of a neurochemical called oxytocin. All women have far higher levels of oxytocin than males, release more oxytocin during sex, and the amounts of the hormone released when a woman gives birth increase enormously. It's believed that these high levels of oxytocin can produce powerful nurturant responses in women, and scientists suspect it is the cause for the cases in which women whose own babies have died or been separated from them have felt driven to go out and steal other women's babies.

HERE'S LOOKING AT YOU, KID

Another legacy of evolution is that men are much more likely to be sexually aroused by visual stimuli than are women. Scientists have many explanations of why this might be so, among them the speculation that males, as hunters, developed a keener sensitivity to certain visual stimuli that were essential for survival (such as the ability to pick out the shapes of potential prey from the surrounding jungle or bush, or to distinguish a small animal from a shrub at a great distance), or developed a highly sophisticated visual-spatial awareness as an essential hunting skill (being able to see a running animal and mentally plot its speed and course to determine the right trajectory to throw a spear, rock, stick).

Another possible explanation is that the heightened responsiveness to visual stimuli is a result of the female loss of estrus. Other primates advertise their fertility with chemical signals, which makes the sense of smell of great importance to males. But human females, in concealing ovulation, reduced the importance of smell in sexual attractiveness, and, at the same time, began developing other signals of fertility, including breasts, buttocks, and so on. So the primary mode of arousal for the human male shifted from smell to sight.

Regardless of the explanations, the fact that males are more likely to respond strongly to visual stimuli of a sexual sort has been demonstrated in a variety of psychological experiments. Research shows that even men who claim that they have no interest in sexual images, and who make conscious efforts to ignore them, still show powerful arousal responses when exposed to such images. Men's brains are so responsive to visual sexual stimuli that even when they are presented with a vast array of neutral images, their eyes zero in on barely noticeable erotic photos or images with uncanny speed and accuracy, almost as if guided by some sixth sense.

This strong visual response in males is a result of natural selection.

Stated bluntly, evolution favored men with powerful and immediate sexual responses to healthy (potentially fertile) young women, and those males who were able at a glance to evaluate the visual sexual signals and characteristics were better able to decide whether that female was worth competing with other males for, or worth investing courtship time in. Those males with highly developed responses to visual signals were more likely to be successful in reproducing; and their offspring would receive those same "response to visual sexual stimuli" genes.

As long as thirty-five thousand years ago, when the first fully modern humans, *Homo sapiens sapiens*, were fashioning their tools and weapons, they also began creating works of art. Among the most numerous of these works were skillfully carved figures of females with exaggerated sexual characteristics—breasts like bowling balls, huge buttocks. These ancient "Venuses" are evidence of a powerful, almost mystical response to the visual stimuli of female sexual characteristics. John Noble Wilford, a science writer for *The New York Times*, observes, "The ice age artists seemed to have an eye for the female form. From stone, ivory and antlers they sculptured figurines of voluptuous women whose torsos leave little to the imagination. . . . Perhaps they were simply prehistoric pornography."

Wilford believes these works "represent a revolutionary shift in the pace and direction of human culture. Indeed, it could be said that this was when culture as we know it began." If this is the case, it would suggest that there is a close link between the arousal of males in response to visual stimuli and the origins of modern human culture.

While there is evidence that females become sexually aroused by some visual stimuli, it is clear that their response is far less powerful and less automatic than that of males. The lack of female counterpart to the extraordinary amount of visual sexual material produced by males throughout history—sculptures, nude paintings, drawings, photographs, films, and so on—is striking. And recent experimental evidence indicates that females do not respond with high sexual arousal to images of male genitalia, and are not as aroused as males by graphic erotic photos or films that simply involve anonymous people copulating.

Some have attributed these differences between males and females to sex-role training, but the differences seem too universal and stable to be produced by social learning, while the evolutionary explanation is far more convincing. Natural selection would have favored males who could become aroused by all the youthful, healthy, fertile women they saw. In females this response would be counterproductive to their reproductive strategy of being highly selective and requiring proof of fitness (intelligence, skills, power, evidence of long-term interest) from potential mates.

9

DIFFERENT STROKES

. . . .

THE COOLIDGE EFFECT

Calvin Coolidge is not one of our nation's most celebrated presidents, but Silent Cal secured himself an assured place in the indices of evolutionary biologists and students of sexual behavior when he and his wife were being conducted on separate tours of a model government farm. Mrs. Coolidge stopped to observe the chicken pens and asked her guide how often the rooster there would perform his sexual duties every day. "Oh, dozens of times," said her guide. Mrs. Coolidge raised her eyebrows, clearly impressed. "Please tell that to the president," she requested.

When the president later came to the pens and observed the rooster's performance, he was informed of his wife's request.

"Same hen every time?" asked the taciturn president.

"Oh, no, sir," said the guide, "a different one each time."

The president nodded, and said, "Please tell that to Mrs. Coolidge."

It is another of our apparently universal facts that men are far more
likely than women to desire a variety of sex partners. When a male
mammal is first introduced into a cage with a sexually receptive
female, he will copulate with verve. After a period of time, however,
he will begin to lose interest, even though the female is as sexually
receptive as ever. Finally he will reach a point where he has no in-
clination to copulate at all. However, if the female is then removed
and replaced by a new female, the male will immediately begin copulating with renewed enthusiasm: a phenomenon now dubbed the
Coolidge Effect.

Rams, for example, will lose interest in ewes after four or five
copulations. But when a new ewe is introduced, the ram will be
restored to his former vigor. This will happen every time another
ewe is substituted, and the ram's rate of ejaculation will be the same
with the *twelfth* ewe as it was with the first. A similar sexual dynamic
exists between bulls and cows. Researchers have tried to fool the rams
and bulls by disguising females they have already mated with, covering their heads and bodies with canvas sacks or masking their vaginal odors with other smells and reintroducing them, but the males
are not fooled. As psychologist Glenn Wilson has observed, "These
male animals know where they have been and do not like going over
the same ground again."

The increased intelligence of human beings has made it more likely
that mates can find more to arouse and maintain their interest in each
other than can other mammals. And of course the female evolutionary
strategy of loss of estrus, and the resulting dramatic increase in sex-
iness, have been designed for the purpose of keeping males bonded
to their mates. There's no doubt that an intelligent, imaginative,
sexually creative woman can keep a man's attention, devotion, and
love for a lifetime. Nevertheless, to a lesser degree the Coolidge Effect
obtains among humans.

The classic "seven-year itch" is one that many males can become
afflicted with after a single night, while some happily married males

are simply not susceptible. Many a male who has been involved in a long-term relationship with a woman recalls that in the early days of the relationship he was intensely aroused and would initiate sex frequently, but that as time passed the sexual episodes would decrease in frequency and in intensity. Males may reach a point where they appear to have no interest in sex, and yet if they encounter an attractive new sex partner they will initiate sex with renewed enthusiasm, as frequently and vigorously as they had years before. Anthropologist Donald Symons wryly observes that it's inaccurate and unfair to describe male sexual desires as "indiscriminate," since males are sufficiently discriminating to reject females they've already had enough sex with.

Evidence that the desire for variety is more characteristic of human males than of females came from research into the sexual attitudes of homosexuals, who are free to act on their gender-specific sexual drives without having to modify those drives to fulfill the expectations of members of the opposite sex. That is, scientists believe that male homosexuals behave in many ways like heterosexual men, only more so, and lesbians in many ways like heterosexual women, only more so. Before the threat of AIDS caused great changes in sexual behavior, male homosexuals showed a high degree of desire for variety, with from ten to one hundred times the number of sex partners as heterosexual men. And the sexual encounters were very likely to be impersonal, even anonymous, with knowledge of or intimacy with a partner tending to *diminish* the male's sexual interest. Lesbians, on the other hand, have been found more likely than homosexual men to form stable, intimate, paired relationships; and their sexual interest is more likely to be based on a prior knowledge of the partner.

While a woman's involvement in an extramarital relationship usually signals that the marriage has gone awry, research has revealed that there is no such association for men. In fact, as researchers S. P. Glass and T. L. Wright discovered in their study of "The Relationship of Extramarital Sex, Length of Marriage and Sex Differences on Marital Satisfaction and Romanticism," there is strong evidence that for men who have been married for a long time, extramarital sexual experience actually has a positive effect on marital happiness.

Surveys show that far more males commit adultery than females. In recent years this gap is closing, but there is evidence that increasing female infidelities are the result of a general loosening of sexual standards, rather than a change in female attitudes. When surveys look at beliefs rather than behavior, the sex differences remain wide: Surveys that ask whether people would *like* to engage in extramarital sex indicate that the difference between males and females is far greater than in actual extramarital sex. Psychologist Glenn Wilson found, "A very high proportion of men, but very few women, are attracted to the idea as a theoretical proposition. It appears that men are prevented from having extramarital sex mainly by lack of opportunity, whereas women are more often inhibited by their own attitudes, morals and preferences."

JEALOUSY

The Coolidge Effect leads us to another difference between males and females that is so universal that scientists believe it is a genetic legacy of naturally selected mating strategies: Males are more sexually jealous than women, and more likely to respond to the infidelity of their mates with violence. Cross-cultural studies have also revealed that by far the most frequent cause of violence among spouses is sexual infidelity and jealousy, in the majority of cases female sexual infidelity and male sexual jealousy. Researchers have found that in all cultures male jealousy constitutes the leading cause of spousal homicide, and is also the cause of most wife-beating as well.

Also, more than half of all divorced men report that sexual infidelity by their wives was the major cause of the divorce, while only about a quarter of women cite their husbands' infidelity as a major cause.

Clearly there are cultural traditions at work here, but the cultural patterns seem to emerge from powerful biological patterns: It is women who get pregnant, not men. If a male accepts parental responsibility for a child that does not carry his genes, while remaining sexually faithful to his mate, he is sacrificing several years of reproductive possibilities, while the woman's reproductive capabilities are fully invested in the child no matter who the father is. Sexual infidelities by women, then, are far more likely to damage the "fitness" of their husbands than vice versa.

The roots of this behavior are evident among primates, where males who assume leadership of a pack often proceed to kill all existing infants, since they bear other males' genes. There is also overwhelming evidence among humans that stepparents feel less responsibility for their stepchildren than for their biological children. This is an example of the well-established evolutionary biology principle of "kin selection," which dictates that any creature will tend to favor genetic relatives over nonrelatives, since the survival of one's genetic relatives will ensure the survival of some of one's genes.

Martin Daly and Margo Wilson of Ontario's McMaster University analyzed a huge amount of cross-cultural data dating from the Middle Ages to the mid-1980's, and discovered powerful evidence of kin selection: "Blood kin may be relatively immune from lethal violence," they found. However, stepchildren are not blood relatives, and Daly and Wilson found that they are far more likely than natural children to die of abuse: An American child, they note, "living with one or more substitute parents in 1976 was approximately 100 times more likely to be fatally abused than a same-age child living with genetic parents." Statistics show too that much father-daughter incest is not incest at all, but sexual relationships between a stepfather and his stepdaughter.

Also, sociologists have recently found that 17 percent of remarriages that involve stepchildren on both sides end up in divorce within three years, compared with only 10 percent of remarriages without stepchildren. Researchers Lynn White and Alan Booth of the University of Nebraska claim, "Our evidence indicates that if these couples divorced, it was because they wanted to get rid of the stepchildren, not the spouse." Evidence also indicates that the stepchildren tend to leave the combined household earlier than do other children—in many cases apparently pushed out (such as sent away to school, encouraged to set up their own apartments, or asked to live with their other parent). Studies such as this demonstrate clearly that the ancient evolutionary forces—in this case the desire not to invest in offspring that do not carry one's own genes—are still at work.

One would think that with recent advances in the technology of birth control and the increased access to abortion, the biological consequences of adultery—a male being cuckolded and having to raise a child that is not his—would have decreased substantially, which would mean males should have less reason to feel greater jealousy than females. Quite the contrary, there is strong evidence that the greater fear by males of female infidelity has real causes: Recent developments in tissue-typing have made it possible to state with complete accuracy whether a man is the biological father of a particular child; and in one recent survey in suburban London, as many as one third of all children born were sired by someone other than the man who assumed he was the father.

While females are less biologically inclined to experience sexual jealousy, they have a corresponding trait: fear of desertion. Anthropologist Helen E. Fisher points out, "A female knows her young belong to her, so the desire to kill her young would not occur. But if her mate deserted her, she might not survive and her children might not either. Thus evolved within females a heightened fear of desertion. If her mate wandered off to have sex with others, this was of small concern—as long as he returned with meat and continued to protect his family."

Female jealousy, then, is more likely to be driven by a fear that another female will steal the male's economic resources and time from her and her offspring than from an instinctive aversion to the idea of his copulating with another female.

THE NEW WOMAN MEETS THE DOUBLE STANDARD

Again I emphasize that the fact that something is natural, that some trait has a genetic basis, has nothing to do with whether it is "right" or not. As many have argued, the innate difference between the sexes constitutes a "double standard." There's no doubt that many of our biologically influenced emotional responses are inappropriate or intolerable, and that they can be significantly altered. Certainly Western society has moved in recent years toward providing equal opportunities for women to seek out variety and novelty in sex partners, and to seek satisfying employment and intellectual challenge in all areas of life.

And yet it's simply a fact that surveys like *The Hite Report*, the *Cosmopolitan* poll, various Gallup polls, and the writings of feminists from Betty Friedan to Germaine Greer indicate that few women seem to have been satisfied with casual, impersonal, spontaneous sex (though many are puzzled or guilty that they don't). Overwhelmingly, women are interested in sex with feeling, intimacy, while there's much evidence that males feel differently.

In a survey released in late 1987, Shere Hite asked women from her sampling group (largely readers of women's magazines and members of women's groups) what their greatest dissatisfaction was in their sexual relationships. She found that virtually all women listed the number-one problem as lack of *verbal* communication with their partners. Almost none of these women felt they weren't getting enough sex, and those few who did gave it far lower priority on their list of problems than those having to do with communication and intimacy.

On the other hand, virtually every poll conducted of males has found that their number-one problem with their sexual relationships is that they are not having sex as frequently as they would like.

Certainly women's roles have been changing at a breathtaking and accelerating rate in the last few centuries. The advent of reliable birth-control methods has made it possible for women to break free of many sexual restrictions: No longer must sexual activity be more "expensive" for women; no longer must they select sex partners with an eye toward reproduction and with attention to their suitability as mates. Today, men and women can agree to ignore genital differences and compete for the same goods, services, and jobs. Statistics reveal, for example, that in 1986 over 50 percent of all those holding jobs classified as "professionals," such as doctors, lawyers, educators, and so on, were female.

And just as women can now pursue new, independent sexual strategies, so they can pursue new reproductive strategies. Now, women need not select a male partner at all, but only a sperm donor. And today many women have decided there is no need for them to invest themselves in the future, no need to project copies of their genes into the next generation.

But because the biological forces may not seem fair, or relevant, or convenient does not mean they have disappeared. Evolution is not fueled by fairness but by what has worked for millions of years. Evolutionary biologists assert that well over 99 percent of our genetic makeup was complete over 12 million years ago, and that of the tiny part of our genetic heritage that is the result of the last few million years, virtually all of it is a product of our hunter-gatherer phase. These forces may be denied or ignored, but they continue to operate below the level of consciousness. Reason is directed toward modern life, but emotional responses can lag behind, still stuck in the Pleistocene epoch. The mind may say that anything is possible, but some inchoate urge or slow, powerful current within insists that some things are necessary.

And so women find themselves caught in a double bind—torn by two powerful but conflicting needs: the possibilities of new wisdom, independence, new things, versus the longings to create life, to participate in the ancient mysteries of reproduction and motherhood.

The continuing power of the drives imbedded in the genes can be seen in some of the confusions women are experiencing today. For example, in 1985 a French study was released showing a direct link between the age of a female and a decline in her fertility. The study found that 26 percent of the women under thirty were infertile, while 39 percent of those thirty-one to thirty-five were infertile.

Then, in 1986, a study by Yale sociologists Patricia Craig, Neil Bennett, and Harvard economist David Bloom was released indicating that women who had passed the age of thirty without marrying faced increasingly diminishing chances of ever marrying. Said Bennett, "As they defer marriage it becomes less and less likely, whether by choice or involuntarily, that they will ever marry. The marriage market may, unfortunately, be falling out from under them."

According to the study, which analyzed census data from seventy thousand households, white, college-educated women who hadn't married by age twenty-five, had a 50 percent chance of marrying; women who reached thirty without marrying had only a 20 percent chance of ever doing so; and of those women who reach age thirty-five without marrying, only 5 percent will marry. Whereas only 9 percent of college-educated women born in the mid-1930's never got married, according to Bennett, "it appears that 22 percent of college-educated women born in the mid-1950's can be expected to never marry." Yet, Bennett pointed out, in other subgroups of the population, fully 90 percent of the women married.

"I think people up until this point have suspected that well-educated women were deferring marriages," said Bennett. "However, it appears from this analysis that much of this marriage deferral is translating into marriage forgone." Economist David Bloom pointed to the huge increase in the participation of women in the labor market, concluding, "The fundamental point is both marriage and work are very time-intensive. Essentially, it's hard to do both. It turns out that a lot of those women who thought they were delaying marriage subsequently find out that their marriageability declines."

This study made it clear that while many women may have been altering their reproductive strategies, men were not: As always, men were selecting females on the basis of their fertility. And after women passed thirty, their fertility and their years of potential childbearing steadily decreased.

When this study was made public, it immediately became front-page news, and caused howls of rage, particularly from women who were past thirty and unmarried. Some of the objections were to the way the study had ordered its statistics: They pointed out that women over thirty who had a strong desire to marry had a much higher chance of marrying than the figures seemed to indicate. But the real rage came from a whole generation of liberated female baby-boom high achievers who for their entire lives had been told that they could have it all, who had worked their way into high-powered and demanding careers, who had put off the whole thing about family and baby until later, and who were now rudely awakened to the fact that later was now. That harmless pipe-smoking hubby and the baby they had been assuming would come along might never happen.

Suddenly a major topic of concerned conversation among women was "the male shortage." As Letty Cottin Pogrebin, a founding editor of *Ms.* magazine, explained it, "There has been a lot of superficial change: we can wear sneakers with our suits and we have a sense of entitlement about the professions we did not have 10 years ago. But women still value themselves positively if they have been claimed by a man. That hasn't changed at all."

Statistical studies of the generation of women born between 1945 and 1960 revealed that unprecedented numbers of women were passing through their prime childbearing years without having children. The birthrate for those women was so low that for the first time since such statistics were kept, a whole generation was not even replacing itself.

In 1986 the fertility rate of American women fell to a record low of 64.9 births per 1,000 women in the childbearing years of fifteen to forty-four. In 1957, by comparison, the fertility rate was 122.7, nearly twice the 1986 mark. The meaning of those figures was clear enough. Here were the highest-educated women, the highest paid, most liberated and independent, most successful and powerful in terms of careers, the most extraordinary generation of young women in history, and instead of reproducing and multiplying their excellent and assertive genes, they had taken a ticket on the evolutionary express to extinction. What a bitter irony, what a sad epitaph that might be—here lies a generation so successful they disappeared.

At the same time the popular magazines were full of cover stories and features on the problems of infertile women and couples. Experts claimed the United States was in the midst of "an epidemic of infertility." About one in every six married couples in their childbearing years in 1985 had fertility problems, and the proportion was on the rise. In part, it was men's fault: The sperm count of American men had fallen more than 30 percent in the last fifty years, with environmental pollution a prime suspect. Nearly 25 percent of all American males had sperm counts so low as to be considered functionally sterile.

Using new, highly sensitive measurement equipment and techniques, researchers at the National Institute of Environmental Health Sciences found in 1988 that 31 percent of all pregnancies end in miscarriage. Other studies revealed that of some 1.5 million women in the country suffering from involuntary sterility, some 40 percent were found to be sterile because of diseased fallopian tubes, which are easily scarred by disease or infection. Scarring results from pelvic inflammatory diseases, other gynecological infections, or IUDs. The researchers concluded, "Contemporary social patterns, including increased sexual contact of young people with a variety of partners, appear to be linked with increased infertility in women." The rise of infertility was also linked by researchers with "increased activity, both athletically and in the business world. Women who exercise strenuously have frequently experienced irregular or cessation of menstruation (amenorrhea), as have female executives under a great deal of stress." Here was more irony: The sexual revolution, which was to have liberated women, had made many of them infertile.

Ever since the flowering of the woman's movement in the 1960's, an article of faith had been that the goals were equality of opportunity between men and women, and the need for women to assert their independence, free of the domination of males. This included freedom from economic domination: Feminists asserted that they must pay for their own meals, contribute in proportion to their income to the household expenses, and so on. In one way this could be seen as an assertion that women now wanted to make it clear that sex was something they could give or share at will, free of economic influence. Women's freedom, they insisted, required an end to the ancient sex contract, whose terms were now obsolete.

But as the "male shortage" became apparent, the feminists' goal of economic independence was modified. Where once the statement by a male that there might be such a thing as a natural mother-child bond was enough to inspire a reputation as a sexist oppressor, now those same feminists began actively attempting to change laws so that in child-custody cases courts would be forced to give preferential treatment to mothers because of those very mother-child bonds. Pop radical feminist writer Phyllis Chesler, for example, produced a 1986 book, *Mothers on Trial*, contending that in divorces mothers as a class should be granted custody of children *automatically by virtue of their sex.*

Those same groups were pushing for laws that would actually increase the amount of child support males were forced to pay for babies over whose conception and birth they had had no say (since the feminist groups insisted males had no right to determine what happened to the baby). Many feminists also began struggling to pass quota laws forcing employers to hire a certain percentage of women, even though their qualifications for the job might be less than those of men applying for the jobs.

According to feminist writer Janet Richards, in *The Skeptical Feminist*, "What we want to achieve is not compensation but an improvement of the position of women . . . and, as a matter of fact, probably the best way to achieve this is to appoint to positions of importance women who are rather less good at the work than the men who are in competition with them."

In other words, the feminist movement in the 1980's went through an extraordinary about-face. An example of the change in orientation came with the 1985 prosecution by the government of Sears Roebuck & Company for discrimination against women in commissioned sales jobs. At the trial a feminist historian, Professor Rosalind Rosenberg of Barnard College, testified for Sears, demonstrating that women had never sought the jobs in question.

As a result of her testimony, Dr. Rosenberg was subjected to vituperative attacks from feminists at scholarly conventions, in historical and feminist journals, and in the feminist movement, where her testimony was called "an immoral act." At the Organization of American Historians, a committee of female historians passed a resolution saying that "as feminist scholars we have a responsibility not to allow our scholarship to be used against the interest of women struggling for equity in our society."

The evolutionary gender-based behavior differences between males and females, long denied by feminists, could no longer be ignored. The original feminist impulse of attacking all sexual bias was abandoned. The struggle openly became one of obtaining for females as many economic benefits as possible, even if it meant giving females preferential treatment (what earlier feminists would have called "sexism").

And so, by 1985, Erica Jong, who once celebrated "zipless sex," was proclaiming that women should "live by the motto, 'I'm not going to give sex away until I'm taken care of.' It's really not incumbent on men to be good providers in an age of 'free' sex."

PETER PAN AND RAMBO MOVING WEST

At the same time millions of dissatisfied women made huge best-sellers out of a series of pop-psychology books pointing out that the whole complex of economic and romantic problems women faced was the fault of men, who were "afraid of intimacy," would "flee from commitment," and were "fly-away lovers." Women were smart, intelligent, sophisticated, but made silly choices when it came to romance, argued *Smart Women/Foolish Choices*, which spent months at the top of the best-seller lists. Women are full of love, in fact they love too much, since many males are uncaring or inappropriate or unable to return the women's love, said *Women Who Love Too Much*, which inspired the spontaneous flowering of Women Who Love Too Much groups all over the country. Women were full of love for men, but men hated women, claimed another best-seller, *Men Who Hate Women and the Women Who Love Them*.

Not only was a good man hard to find, but there were, in fact, according to the title of another best-seller, *No Good Men*. Instead of growing up, men suffered from the "Peter Pan Syndrome." They were cut off from their true feelings, unable to express emotions. Men suffered from arrested development, emotional immaturity, and if they would give up their childish ways, settle down, act responsibly, and learn to express their emotions, then this whole problem in which women weren't happy and didn't have babies and loyal husbands would be over. Once men threw off this absurd macho cultural conditioning and learned how to cry, to get in touch, they would discover that they could be mature, loving, intimate, committed, emotional, and healthy. They could, in other words, be like women.

While superficially these books paid lip service to the fashionable dogma of cultural determinism—men could be trained to become healthier—their core message was the continuing, inescapable influence of the ancient drives that evolution had hard-wired into males:

that no matter how modern or enlightened they may seem, they are still back on the African savannas chasing down woolly mammoths with their buddies.

The readers of these books would probably not have understood if there had been a flood of best-selling books by males with titles like *Women's Flight from Adventure*, or *No Good Women*, dealing with questions like, "Why are women afraid of quick, impersonal sex?," "why do women cling?," "why are women so concerned with security?," and "why don't they have enough courage to take risks and stand alone?"

These male emotions were expressed in a flood of Hollywood movies featuring bare-chested, hard muscled, hard-boiled tough guys carrying machine guns, hand grenades, and sleek, murderous blades. With no women. These new All-American heroes were a direct response to the demands from women for intimacy and commitment. Played by actors like Sylvester Stallone (*First Blood, Rambo: First Blood Part II, Cobra, Rocky*, parts one through infinity), Arnold Schwarzenegger (*Raw Deal, The Terminator, Predator, Commando, The Running Man*), and Chuck Norris (*The Delta Force, Invasion U.S.A., Any Eye for an Eye, Lone Wolf McQuade*), these heroes simply don't have time to pay attention to women or their distracting demands for intimacy and commitment. They have a mission far more important, which is to save the world (or some important part of it); they are too committed to their self-sacrificing mission to give in to the desires of the heart.

Later, perhaps, they seem to hint, once the quest is completed, then these heroes will be able to find time for love, but the man's first duty is to fight for his convictions with his entire being. A man's gotta do what a man's gotta do.

A cultural touchstone of the post-Vietnam era was the Oscar-winning film *Coming Home*, in which the warrior, played by Bruce Dern, could only drown himself, while the sensitive male, wheelchair-bound Jon Voight, won the exemplary feminist woman, Jane Fonda, because he did not "flee from commitment," or "fear intimacy." But the cultural tides have shifted. As film critic Lawrence Christon writes, "The kind of character that Dern exemplified has been hauled out of the surf and sent back into the jungle to fight on, even if the jungle is the city. It's the Voight character who has been washed away now."

Says Christon, "I suspect the women's movement intimidated and

confused a lot of men through its own size and complexity, its mounting suddenness and through the pettiness and spiteful tone of some
of its own elements. And it didn't help a lot of the men who took a
chance on 'sharing their feelings' and 'getting in touch with their
feminine side,' to see themselves by the late '70s and early '80s dismissed as wimps—by women."

But of course there's a stronger myth at work here, one that is so
deeply rooted in the American male psyche that it has been the core
of classic American literary works, both highbrow and lowbrow,
since at least the eighteenth century: the conflict between women and
adventure, between civilization and real life. The true story of America, according to these works, is that of the idealistic and individu-
alistic male, the hunter, the warrior, the frontiersman, the pathfinder,
the explorer of the unknown, the voyager down the river on the raft.
We've grown up with these men—from Fenimore Cooper's Natty
Bumppo-Leatherstocking-Hawkeye-Deerslayer, treading into the
woods away from the fair-skinned Christian maidens of the city; and
Huck Finn, who has to "light out for the territory" because the
Widow Douglas wants to "sivilize" him; to Puzo's Michael Corleone,
who becomes a man only when he declares his independence from
his genteel WASP wife and becomes a wholehearted killer; and Kesey's noble McMurphy, who, with his Indian buddy Chief Broom,
tries to break through to the new horizon only to be lobotomized by
the big-breasted Big Nurse.

In this mythic tradition the only time males are safe is when they're
out in the unknown, the pure and mystical wilderness, on their idealistic and perhaps deadly quest, sitting around the campfire eating bear
meat or cruising the highway in their car or on the raft with their
male buddy, the noble savage, Chingachgook, Queequeg, Big Chief
Broom, Nigger Jim. Out there, cruising, exploring, they are on their
mission, free of the corrupting influences of civilization and its dis-
contents, unfettered by the demands of wife and family and culture,
free of the threats of the blond-haired bankers' daughters of Chris-
tendom who want to marry them and make them settle down.
(Though they are, of course, quite open to a bit of purely sexual
ecstasy with one or another of the dusky-skinned maidens they meet
out there on the quest, a maiden who understands that sex is something fine to do around the campfire at night before you have to get
up the next day and go wipe out that encampment of commies).

As film critic Christon says, " 'Rambo II's' final image—shirtless and weaponless and unavenged Rambo standing at the edge of a treeline, ready for re-entry into the hunt—is classic Americana. It's a jungle out there, full of all the evils of an anti-American world. But many men will choose that fight over the complications of self-surrender that come of loving a woman. . . . Or maybe women are the jungle too, and we let off psychic steam by seeing it all blow up in our heads. The simplifications of these films are a measure of the complexity of our state."

In this telling, the myth has a uniquely American flavor, but its driving force is ancient, biological, linking males to the thousands upon thousands of generations of hunters and explorers who secured their survival, and what must have seemed like the survival of their civilization, only by continuously venturing out into the unknown, leaving behind the women and the children, and focusing their attention, skills, and wisdom on the quest.

TAMING RAMBO WITH LOVE

Females, too, have their myths embodying truths of evolutionary biology. By the mid-eighties, as Rambo was flexing his muscles, the female counterpart of the male adventure fantasies—the romance novel—was more popular than ever before. Adult romance books were by then, according to *New York Times* reporter Edwin Mc-Dowell, the "fastest-growing category of paperback publishing, accounting for annual sales nearing $300 million—almost 40 percent of total paperback sales."

In 1985 Harlequin and Silhouette were turning out fifty-four titles per month, tales of women who are far smarter than the dolts they find around them, women who encounter jaded, wealthy, noble men who are also tough as any Rambo, with notches on their swords and a history of female conquests. Their hero is a man who saves the heroine from a rape worse than death, or takes her in when all her family dies in the crash of a Zeppelin; and who has never found what real love is, but now, under the guidance of the smart, sexy heroine, learns how to love, and loves her not only for her body but also for her mind. And so at last the fighting beastly primitive male in him has been tamed by the feeling, sensitive, loving female: Now, he is hers, tamed, submissive, caring, unafraid of intimacy, eager for commitment.

IN SEARCH OF THE WILD ORGASM

Human males, like most other male mammals, have an orgasm whenever they are engaged in sex. Human females do not. As evolutionary biologists all agree, male orgasm is a highly adaptive, naturally selected capacity. Zoologist David Barash explains, "Vaginal fluid is acidic, potentially lethal to sperm; male ejaculate therefore compensates by being appropriately alkaline. Discharge of the necessary fluid requires vigorous muscular contractions by the tubes that carry it, and the pleasurable sensation accompanying its release is closely connected with the release of tension as the tubes are physically emptied. It is thus interesting that the physiology of male orgasms does not differ significantly from humans to most lower mammals."

Most students of evolution agree that female orgasm is not an essential part of reproduction. In fact, there is no evidence that orgasmic women have any breeding advantage over nonorgasmic women.

According to Barash, "There is no compelling evidence for a female orgasm in any animal other than Homo sapiens." Dr. Helen Singer Kaplan observes, "The female orgasm probably doesn't occur in a natural state among most mammals, because the clitoris doesn't receive sufficient stimulation in the usual intercourse and love play of most mammals, including humans. The clitoris receives little stimulation since mounting is usually from the rear."

There are many human societies in which female orgasm plays little role. Margaret Mead has observed, "That whole societies can ignore climax as an aspect of female sexuality must be related to a very much lesser need for such climax."

Even in those rare cultures where female orgasms occur in virtually every sexual coupling, such as the island of Mangaia (one of the Cook Islands in the Pacific) and other Polynesian islands, this is a result of a systematic training process: Young boys are taught sexual techniques, including cunnilingus and the delay of their own ejaculation, then take actual hands-on learning experiences in intercourse with experienced women; while girls are given detailed instructions by older women. In other words, in these places there is no assumption that female orgasms will occur spontaneously.

According to psychologist Glenn Wilson, "It appears that a certain amount of caution and control is natural to the females of most primate species, and perhaps especially the human female. In order to become orgasmic and fully enjoy sex, some women may need to learn to override this control, but the inhibition is mainly of biological origin, not the result of political or social expediency."

Part of the biologically rooted inhibitions may have to do with fear. As Melvin Konner points out, "It has been said that a basic response of women to sex is fear. This should not be surprising, since one basic response of any creature to the approach of any other is fear; especially if (as may be the case with sex) the other is not yet the object of intimate trust." This hard-wiring of the brain to link fear with sex makes sense in evolutionary terms, says Konner, since "natural selection can be expected to have favored a system that could detect conditions jeopardizing either survival during copulation or survival of the resulting young, and to terminate sexual activity in the face of such conditions."

In addition, Konner suggests that "women have special reason" to respond to sex with fear. "In our species, as in most mammals and birds, males are better equipped to inflict damage than females." He points out that in many bird and mammal species, the male gestures of courtship are the same as those of dominance or threat.

Laboratory studies have revealed that some of the same conditions that trigger fighting behavior in males can also trigger sexual behavior—painfully shocking a male rat will cause him to fight if he is in the presence of a male, but will stimulate his sexual activity if he is in the presence of a female. As Konner remarks, "Considering the many situations in nature in which males have to fight for the sex they want, this association is not surprising." If, then, females engaging in sex find the experience tinged with an edge of fear, it would explain why orgasm might be more difficult to attain.

Some social scientists believe the female orgasm is a development to assist in pair-bonding. According to Barash, orgasm "gives women a direct stake in copulation, making regular sexual activity more likely and with it, the increased coordination of male-female behavior that is the evolutionary payoff. . . . natural selection, working through the advantage gained by a strong bond between parents, evolved mechanisms to achieve and maintain that bond, most notably the liberation of sex from its purely reproductive function. This may well have been achieved in part by endowing women with the capacity for orgasm." By encouraging the female to participate in sex with her partner, orgasm could induce the couple to fall in love, stay together, and help raise the offspring.

Another important fact is that the length of time it takes women to reach orgasm might lead to bonding with more dominant (and therefore more evolutionarily desirable) males. Barash explains that among many mammals, dominant males take longer to ejaculate than do lower-status, subordinate males, who, "obviously hurried because they are harried, spend most of their mating time looking over their shoulder, alert for the possible appearance of the dominants. Not surprisingly, they ejaculate very quickly."

Assume, as do Barash, Helen Fisher, and others, that sex among humans is not just for procreation but also for recreation, serving purposes of increasing human bonding. "Then," says Barash, "it is not surprising that female orgasm, which may well be related to bonding, is more likely when the sex act itself is prolonged, and hence, when the male partner is more likely to be successful, effective, and desirable, the human equivalent of social dominance among animals."

However, there is no evidence to support this pair-bonding theory of orgasm. It is, claims Donald Symons, a supposition supported by people who want to claim monogamy as the natural human condition. "They want to root monogamy in evolution," Symons notes. "The argument is that year-round sex enhanced the pair bond and made family life more rewarding. Somehow proponents of this view think it dignifies woman to claim that female orgasm is an adaptation; it makes it her birthright. I think this is a misguided effort to create an evolutionary parable in order to moralize about human beings."

Another possibility is what psychologist Glenn Wilson calls the "jackpot theory." As he describes it, "there are two main functions of orgasm: (1) to reward people for engaging in sex, and (2) to terminate intercourse at a suitable juncture, rather than have the couple pump on forever." The first function would increase a woman's evolutionary fitness by encouraging her to have sex; but the second function would decrease her fitness if it terminated sex before the male ejaculated. Therefore, evolutionary forces have selected for women who have the capability of being rewarded with an orgasm, but who don't have their orgasm more quickly than the male.

Another view is that the female orgasm serves no evolutionary purpose but is an "artifact," arising out of the fact that in evolution males and females will maintain physiological similarities unless there is an important reason for them to develop differences. This reduces the genetic-coding difficulties that would arise if males and females developed as two totally different creatures. Thus, males have nipples, though they serve no evolutionary purpose: They are artifacts. There is no real reason for males to derive sexual pleasure from their nipples, though for many males their nipples are a source of great erotic pleasure. In the same way, say some anthropologists, the clitoris is an artifact, the female counterpart to the penis. To derive sufficient erotic pleasure from the clitoris to lead to orgasm is a capacity that some women develop more than others.

This is a view supported by Dr. Helen Singer Kaplan: "Female orgasm is an artifact from the viewpoint of evolution. In other words, we could have survived successfully as a species without female orgasm, but we could not have survived without male orgasm. . . . From an evolutionary standpoint, the female orgasm is a luxury."

Donald Symons compares female orgasm with learning to play the piano. Our hands evolved for grasping, moving through trees, not for playing Beethoven piano sonatas. However, our hands have the *capacity* to learn to play the piano—with practice and skill. Most women can learn to play the piano. Playing the piano can give one great pleasure. It can be pursued alone and provide pleasure. One can play the piano for others, in doing so give them pleasure, and still receive pleasure oneself not only from the playing but from the pleasures others experience in the hearing. To say that piano playing is an artifact, while hanging from a tree limb is an evolutionary adaptation, does not mean that hanging from a tree limb is somehow more valuable or "dignified" or human than playing piano.

HOW MUCH IS ENOUGH?

Which brings us to our next universal and biologically influenced difference between the sexes; perhaps it is the basis of all the other differences mentioned above. Dr. Helen Singer Kaplan, speaking from a lifetime of research and clinical experience in human sexuality, asserts, "I think all the differences between male and female sexuality are due to the strength of the male sex drive, which seems much higher than the female's. All other differences follow from that.

"The male sex drive is so compelling that it's less subject to inhibition by learning than the female's, which is more variable, flexible, and influenced by experience. A woman can be aroused and have more orgasms than a man, but she isn't driven to sexuality the way a man is. The male sex drive is much more difficult to suppress. For example, if you tell a little girl not to masturbate, she's likely to listen to you, but a boy will continue to masturbate, in part because his urge is much stronger. I'm not saying there aren't crucial cultural factors present in sexuality, of course, but I believe the biological factors in our sexual behavior have been neglected."

But how do we measure the intensity of something called a sex drive? Scientists have tried everything from penis meters that gauge the intensity of erections to tiny transmitters placed in the vagina to send messages about the quantity of secretions, to sampling the amount of adrenaline in the bloodstream while watching pornography. But who's to say that x amount of vaginal secretions indicate a higher sex drive than y degree of penile erection?

Certainly it has been males who have throughout history been the overwhelming consumers of pornography. It is mostly males who use prostitutes, give gifts in exchange for sex, and commit rape. There's overwhelming evidence in the form of surveys and psychological studies that a greater percentage of males than females masturbate, and do so earlier, and far more frequently, than females. As we have seen, males are more likely to desire more than one mate and to seek variety and novelty in sex partners. Surveys of the frequency with which males and females engage in sex indicate that males *at all ages* have sex more frequently than females (though males reach their peak at the ages of thirty–thirty-five, with an average of three times per week, and females reach their peak somewhat later, with an average of two times per week). And everywhere, sex is something that males urgently seek, and that females withhold, sell, barter, or use as a tool.

But such facts and behaviors are imprecise and inconclusive. That is why more and more scientists are seeking to understand human nature not by reference to behavior but in the actual structure and electrochemistry of the brain.

10

THE BRAIN-MIND REVOLUTION

· ·

It's hard to imagine that many people are unaware of the fact that a "brain revolution" has been taking place in the last decade or so. What has been happening is so extraordinary that scientists, who normally try to be understated and careful in their statements, have been talking as if the world is being totally transformed.

"It's difficult to try to responsibly convey some sense of excitement about what's going on," says UCLA neurophysiologist John Liebeskind. "You find yourself sounding like people you don't respect. You try to be more conservative and not say such wild and intriguing things, but damn! The field is wild and intriguing. It's hard to avoid talking that way. . . . We are at a frontier, and it's a terribly exciting time to be in this line of work."

"There's a revolution going on," says neurochemist Candace Pert of the National Institute of Mental Health. "There used to be two systems of knowledge: hard science—chemistry, physics, biophysics—on the one hand, and, on the other, a system of knowledge that included ethology, psychology, and psychiatry. And now it's as if a lightning bolt had connected the two. It's all one system—neuroscience. . . . The present era in neuroscience is comparable to the time when Louis Pasteur first found out that germs cause disease."

THE LIGHTNING-BOLT PARADIGM SHIFT, OR, THE FALL OF THE MASTER BUILDERS

Since at least the 1920's America had been guided and ruled by the belief that human behavior is always the result of environmental factors. All wisdom, all crime, all aggression, all mental illness, all genius, all psychological disorders, are culturally determined, the result of "nurture" and totally free of "nature."

The ascendance of cultural determinism (rooted in the behaviorist psychology of J. B. Watson and B. F. Skinner, the cultural anthropology of Bronislaw Malinowski, the sociology of Emile Durkheim, the psychiatry of Karen Horney, and the historicism of Max Weber) was mirrored in the nearly total acceptance of the idea that nature could be shaped, controlled, and ordered by humans, made healthier, safer, more "civilized." And thus during this period humans made great efforts to alter their environment, and succeeded in changing the face of the planet more than any other civilization in history. Without any attention to the effects on the ecology of the planet, humans constructed vast interstate-highway systems that encouraged hundreds of millions of Americans to travel by automobile; erected towering skyscrapers, created huge dams, and altered the course of rivers to provide water to the growing cities and to turn vast dry areas of the nation into irrigated fertile land.

The concept that one should accommodate the human in the totality of the biosphere, including all other fauna and flora, was scoffed at. Theoretically, the biosphere could be continuously "improved." "Master builders" like Robert Moses, who changed the face of New York with his immense public works, and Arthur Levitt, who created the new controlled and civilized environment in his Levittown housing development, were the architectural-engineering counterparts of social engineers like Skinner.

America, at its apogee as a world power, came to believe that by exercising its vast military and economic strength, it could "clean up" and improve the entire world, like some huge Tennessee Valley Authority. Other cultures and peoples were backward, or poor, or communist, or violent, or irrational, only because they had not been properly educated, because they had grown up in the wrong environments. If we could only educate them in the truths of the Judeo-Christian capitalist system of American democracy, so the cultural determinists believed, then they would grow up to be happy, red-blooded, freedom-loving, capitalist consumers.

And so, during the 1960's, America's "best and brightest" undertook what must at first have seemed to be a simple environmental mop-up action—something on the order of building a new superhighway, or cleaning up a spill of chemical waste—in Vietnam. When it was discovered that the Vietcong were hard to find in the jungle that covered much of the country, the answer was simple: Get rid of the jungle. And so the largest "defoliation" project in human history was undertaken, with vast quantities of the poisonous Agent Orange poured over the land. When they wiped out the town of Ben Suc because of suspected Vietcong sympathies, the American military claimed they had to destroy the town to "save" it.

Through the fifties and sixties and seventies this orthodoxy ruled the American social sciences. Increasingly its principles became dominant in such liberal-arts disciplines as history and literary scholarship. Among the tenets that came to rule in academia were a denial of any transcendence of cultural conditions, and an insistence that intellectual life is determined and limited by the forces at work in any historical culture.

The rigid cultural determinism, and the determination to deny or ignore aspects of human nature and human experience that did not fit into this ideology, dominated American academe, even as evidence accumulated that the forces of biology and evolution had substantial influence over the way humans behaved. Dissenters who voiced such views were cut off from research funds, denied tenure, found their doctoral dissertations rejected, or were cast out of the academic community as heretics.

But during the 1970's and 1980's an astonishing and ironic thing happened: What at first seemed to be a brilliant victory for cultural determinists turned into the beginnings of collapse.

The collapse was caused, in part, by the clear and humiliating defeat of the American geopolitical engineers in Vietnam; in part by the emergence of ecological awareness, the understanding that the civilization's immense achievements in altering the environment were actually poisoning the planet. But just as clearly, and even more astonishingly and undeniably, it was shattered by the work of the brain scientists. Beginning around the mid-1970's, it was as if, in Candace Pert's words, a lightning bolt had struck, and everything became one: neuroscience. Or, as she said in 1982, "There's a revolution going on. We have grossly misunderstood how hard-wired we are."

What happened was a combination of events. Brain scientists had some inspired insights about how the brain worked, they developed new tools for pursuing those insights, the new tools revealed more information that led to other inspired insights . . . and in an accelerating feedback loop our knowledge of how the brain worked increased more in ten years than it had throughout all of human history before.

Due to advances in microchip technology and other technological tools, brain scientists were at last able to see what was going on in those billions of tiny brain cells that linked together in a network of unsurpassed and almost infinite complexity. Neuroanatomist Floyd Bloom of Scripps Clinic in La Jolla, California, described the new capabilities: "A neuroscientist used to be like a man in a Goodyear blimp floating over a bowl game: he could hear the crowd roar, and that was about it. But now we're down in the stands. It's not too long before we'll be able to tell why one man gets a hot dog and one man gets a beer."

Let's start with the key discoveries.

Brain Drugs: The Molecules of Mind

The billions of brain cells communicate with each other and with other parts of the body by means of a variety of specific molecules or brain juices that the brain cells secrete in response to changes in their electrical activity. As late as the early 1970's scientists had identified only about twenty different brain chemicals. Then, in 1975, researchers found that the brain created its own opiates, pain-killing counterparts to morphine, which they dubbed *endorphins*. That led to the discovery of scores of other brain juices, including natural neurochemicals that acted as an appetite suppressant in the brain, brain drugs that acted like Valium, and brain juices that increased memory. Within a decade hundreds of brain drugs had been identified, with new ones being discovered with increasing frequency.

These brain chemicals, the scientists found, are not only transmitted between adjacent brain cells, but also to cells in different parts of the brain, and often to distant parts of the body, turning on, turning off, or modifying certain types of activity in those other cells. Depending on their structure and the way they operate, the brain chemicals are known as neurotransmitters, neuropeptides, or hormones.

Each of these brain drugs seems to have a different effect depending on where in the brain it is released. Some of them seem to have very general effects, such as increasing or decreasing arousal (the general excitation level of the body). Others, composed of long chains of amino acids, apparently can carry quite complex messages, and have very specific effects on behavior and attitudes. Some of them are fast-acting and have relatively brief effects, but others can have extremely long lasting effects over such slow processes as growth, aging, and reproduction.

It is now known that these brain chemicals, in various mixtures and locations, determine our emotions, attitudes, and behaviors. Scientists assert that every imaginable mental state is the result of a specific pattern of chemical activity in the brain. Depending on what chemicals are circulating in various areas of the brain, you will feel euphoria, fear, reverie, sexual excitement, deep concentration, creativity, alertness, boredom, recall of childhood experiences, thirst, grief, depression, and so on. Certain neurochemicals will influence the strength of our immune system, help our bodies repair themselves, determine whether or not we fall in love with someone, and increase dramatically our ability to learn.

That these brain drugs can have such profound influences over what we feel and how we behave was a revelation, and cast new light on questions such as how it might be possible for behavior patterns, such as extroversion or introversion, to be genetically influenced. Recently, for example, neuroscientists found that males who are intensely shy have abnormally low levels of one specific brain drug called dopamine.

THE NEUROPSYCHOLOGY OF LUST

Numerous exciting discoveries have been made in the influence of these brain drugs on sexual behaviors. It has been found that people in the first flush of "falling in love" generate large quantities of arousing brain drugs such as phenylethylamine, dopamine, and norepinephrine. In the proper combination, these brain drugs have an effect like cocaine—in fact, cocaine produces its effects by exciting these neurotransmitters, while at the same time inhibiting a brain drug that normally calms things down, serotonin. So it makes sense that many people can become "addicted" to falling in love in the same way they can become addicted to cocaine: They spend their lives moving from one romantic fling after another, quickly tiring of one lover when he or she fails to stimulate the pleasurable neurochemicals, and seeking after new lovers to provide another high. And scientists have discovered that when these "love addicts" are given drugs that control or normalize their production of norepinephrine and dopamine, they soon end their compulsive falling in love.

Part of the euphoria of mad, head-over-heels romance, of course, is sexual attraction and sexual desire. The essential link between sexual desire and neurochemicals such as dopamine and norepinephrine, as well as neurohormones such as testosterone, has been well established. Specific molecules released in the brain fit directly into receptor sites on certain brain cells—like keys into locks—turning on specific moods, emotions, sensations, or activities, including sexual attraction and lust.

People who for some reason are unable to secrete the right brain molecules in the right area of the brain are unable to experience sexual desire or love. For example, certain people who have had surgery for a pituitary tumor, or have a malfunction of the pituitary, lack the ability to feel powerful sexual desire or to fall in love, since the pituitary secretes or causes to be secreted a number of powerful mind chemicals.

There is now evidence that abnormal levels of certain brain drugs are also linked to hypersexuality and nymphomania, jealousy, obsessive infatuations, and separation anxiety. One hypothalamic chemical, LHRH, has been called "the ultimate aphrodisiac," since it directly stimulates not only the sex glands but also the brain. Extraordinarily tiny amounts used in rat studies can make an animal engage in sexual behavior for eight hours at a stretch, and in human studies tiny amounts have had dramatic effects on impotent men, in many cases producing erections and sexual arousal immediately.

Another neurochemical, phenylethylamine, or PEA, seems to be the brain's equivalent of amphetamine, and accompanies sexual attraction and arousal. Imbalances of this chemical can produce obsessive sexual arousal and the "Don Juan Syndrome." One scientist leading the research into this chemical has called it "the base of what Freud called the libido."

What this means is that processes we used to call "mind"—our thoughts, dreams, visions, emotions, insights—are products of the electrochemical activity of the brain. It also means that some of the mysteries of human sexuality are becoming more comprehensible; that what were once loosely described as drives, impulses, desires, can now be seen as linked to certain genetic influences, and to other influences that alter the chemistry of the brain, ranging from diet to exercise to air pollution to mental imagery.

THE NEUROCHEMISTRY OF POWER

Neuroscientists have recently begun investigating the mysteries of power and the way it flows through and alters societies, and are discovering that power, and the social manipulations that are used to secure and maintain power—that is, *politics*—are a function of biochemistry.

In fact there is such a flood of new evidence into this fusion of neurochemistry and power that an entire new field of research has begun to take shape, a field the scientists call *biopolitics*. Among the extraordinary findings in this field are those demonstrating that male power and dominance is linked to high levels of the neurochemical serotonin. In studies of primates ranging from monkeys to baboons to chimps to humans, a variety of researchers have consistently found that dominant males have high levels of serotonin; that when a dominant male is removed from his position of dominance, his levels of serotonin plummet, and his former unshakable confidence and self-assurance turns into insecurity and anxiety; that when nondominant males are given chemicals to boost their serotonin levels, they begin to behave like dominant males, confident, self-assured, assertive, even aggressive.

This connection between brain chemistry and power seems inseparable from sexual chemistry: Scientists have discovered that there is a direct link between social dominance and sexual potency, between power and sex. Interestingly this link works in both directions, in what is known as a "bidirectional feedback loop" between sex and power. Sexual access to females, research is revealing, is in many ways dependent on a certain amount of dominance (and its associated qualities of confidence and assertiveness), which means high levels of serotonin (among other things). But it has also been found that sexual activity and potency itself will raise the level of serotonin in formerly submissive or passive males, and when dominant males are removed from access to sexual activity, or denied sexual activity, their levels of serotonin (and their dominance) decline sharply. Thus, in ways that are still to be fully understood, sex and power are interdependent.

INTO THE HEMISPHERES

A second area in which the brain scientists made astonishing discoveries has to do with the way the convoluted gray matter of the brain's "thinking cap" or cerebral cortex is organized into two hemispheres, each of which thinks or operates in fundamentally different modes.

While much is still not understood, it seems that for most people the left hemisphere processes information analytically, sequentially, logically, dealing with details, and is oriented in time. The right hemisphere (for most people) tends to process information in a non-linear, synthetic, large-scale, global, free-of-time-orientation manner that makes much use of visual-spatial modes of thought.

Also, intriguingly, it seems that for most people, the left hemisphere is optimistic, innocent, involved in expressing positive emotions, while the right hemisphere is involved in expressing negative emotions, viewing the world as hostile.

There is also fascinating evidence that sexual satisfaction depends on the ability to shift brain dominance from the left to the right hemisphere—one recent study, for example, revealed that those subjects who did not show such increase in right-hemisphere activity during sex were impotent or did not reach orgasm.

There is now evidence that humans can learn to shift their dominant brain activity back and forth between the hemispheres at will, making it possible to select desired states of consciousness or modes of information-processing.

BRAIN AND BODY

But if the new discoveries have revealed that our brains are more divided than had been imagined, they have also revealed that our brains and bodies are far more closely connected. In fact, one of the most exciting revelations has been that far from being two separate entities—a brain in which thoughts, emotions, nonmaterial mental activities, and "mind stuff" take place; and a body, the material, mechanical structure that houses the brain—the brain and body are truly one. Scientists discovered to their surprise that anything that influences the body causes an accompanying change in the brain (and in the mental or emotional state of that aspect of the brain called mind), and that anything that influences the brain (and its mental or emotional states) causes an accompanying change in the body.

Using a variety of approaches and tools, ranging from electrical stimulation of the brain to the use of biofeedback devices, scientists have found that simply by using their brain/mind in a certain way, humans can control parts of the body that had always been thought to be beyond conscious control—the autonomic system. People can alter the electrical activity of their brains, raise or lower their heart rate and blood pressure, increase or decrease their galvanic skin resistance (or skin conductivity), control their blood flow so well that they can cause one hand to grow hot while the other hand grows cold. The mind is operating the body.

Scientists have found that hay-fever sufferers who look at a picture of ragweed begin to sneeze. Many cancer patients who are taught to perform certain mental activities—visualizing their white blood cells eating the cancerous cells—discover that those mind activities alter their bodies, as their white blood cells actually begin to work more effectively against the cancer. This new knowledge that our mental states can alter our physical states, including our immune systems, resulted among other things in an entirely new field of medical research called *psychoneuroimmunology*.

And just as the brain/mind can alter the body, so physical events can alter the brain/mind. Running and some other exercises cause the release of endorphins, producing a mental state of euphoria, the "runner's high." Looking at certain colors, lights, hearing sounds, actually alters the brain's chemistry and produces dramatic changes in mental state. Looking at a member of the opposite sex can cause the release of a neurochemical cocktail in the brain that, depending on the chemicals involved, can be called lust, arousal, affection, or love. The new discoveries about the interplay between brain and body have created thriving scientific disciplines such as psychobiology, biopsychology, and psychophysiology that only a few decades ago would have been inconceivable.

The link between brain and body is now so widely accepted that it is accepted, at least in theory, by virtually everyone. But now some neuroscientists are insisting that to say the brain and body are one does not go far enough. Recent studies have revealed the astonishing fact that our very skin tissue can respond to certain stimuli, such as touch, by releasing a variety of hormones and other neurochemicals, such as interferons, interleukens, and peptides, some of which can cause alterations in consciousness or mental states, some of which can actually have powerful effects on the body's immune system and its ability to heal and regenerate itself.

And so it can be said that certain types of "thinking" take place as far away from our brain as the epidermis (and not incidentally, it shows how the physical touch of body to body that takes place in the act of sex can have powerful effects on the chemistry of the brain and even on the body's immune system). Candace Pert, for example, points out that recent studies have shown that "the lining of the digestive tract, from the esophagus through the large intestine, is lined with cells that contain neuropeptides and their receptors. It seems entirely possible to me that this is why a lot of people feel their emotions in their gut—why they have a 'gut feeling.' "

Another recent study observed babies who received light massages —that is, had the surface of their skin touched and rubbed—and a second group of babies who received exactly the same treatment in every way except that they were not massaged. Eight months later, the babies whose skin had been stimulated showed dramatically higher levels of mental and motor ability. In another study, psychologist Theodore Wacks of Purdue found that infants who had more skin-to-skin contact showed greater mental development in the first six months of their lives. Other studies have shown that touching of

infant rats by mother rats causes dramatic alterations in their production of beta-endorphin, and studies of rats and monkeys have
revealed that physical contact with the mother appears essential to
reducing the harmful levels of neurochemicals that are released by an
infant when subjected to stress: Physical touch has been shown to
reduce stress and its effects.

Neuroanatomist Marian Diamond of Berkeley recently discovered
that rats that received more tactile stimulation developed larger and
more densely interconnected neurons in that area of the brain that
processes the sensations of touch. Stated simply, the studies of Diamond, Wacks, and others have clearly demonstrated that certain types
of stimulation of the body produce brains that are larger, more densely
interconnected, and *more intelligent* than the brains of those who do
not receive such stimulation.

Studies of this sort are now leading scientists like Candace Pert
and others to believe we should look on the body itself not just as
linked with, or "connected with" the brain, but as an actual part of
the brain. According to Pert, "The more we know about neuropeptides, the harder it is to think in more traditional terms of a mind
and a body. It makes more sense to speak of a single, integrated
entity—a bodymind." That is, our entire physical being is one large,
ambulatory brain.

MAN AND WOMAN

The neuroscientists have kept pulling out nuggets of new information
about the brain with all the excitement of gold-rush prospectors who
have stumbled on a gold vein of unimaginable richness—fantastic
finds just keep popping up. Of all the new findings of the late 1970's
and 1980's, one thing could not escape the neuroscientists' attention:
the noticeable differences between the brains of men and women.

Neurochemical Differences
What goes on in the brain and in the mind depends on the levels of
neurotransmitters, neuropeptides, and hormones. And the brains of
men and women differ in the quantities of certain neurochemicals
they secrete, as well as in the way they respond to doses of these
neurochemicals. A neurochemical such as dopamine has a sexually
stimulating effect on men but not on women, while serotonin seems

to be sexually exciting for women but not for men. Yet, as we have seen, men classified as "dominant" show high levels of serotonin, while males who are not dominant have low levels of that brain drug; as soon as a dominant male is removed from his position of dominance, there is a pronounced drop in his level of serotonin. Females, on the other hand, show no such connection between dominance and serotonin.

Hemispheric Differences

Males and females, it is now becoming clear, differ not only in the way the hemispheres are organized, but also in their very structure and physiology—the right hemisphere of one sex, for example, is noticeably larger and heavier than the right hemisphere of the other sex. The verbal capacity of one sex is largely confined to one hemisphere, while that of the other sex appears to be spread more diffusely across both hemispheres. And scientists have been finding a variety of other anatomical differences in the brains of the sexes as well.

Body-Brain Differences

The brain and body are one, true, but the systems seem to function somewhat differently in women than in men. The brain influences the immune system, for example, but women's immune systems seem much stronger than men's in many ways.

Of course, these sexual differences in the brain make sense in the light of evolutionary biology. After all, males and females developed different physical shapes and tendencies and reproductive strategies under the pressures of natural selection. Since these different physical systems are operated by mechanisms in the brain, you would assume the brains of males and females had developed some anatomical differences. Unless, that is, you had a powerful reason for not making that assumption.

NEUROSCIENCE MEETS CULTURAL DETERMINISM

And there are many people who have such powerful reasons. The behaviorist and cultural-determinist establishment had no doubts that human mental states, ideas, thoughts, goals, strategies, are wholly a product of culture; that the noblest products of the mind are responses to healthy social influences; that when the mind goes wrong, it is a result of unhealthy environments (frequently unhealthy family influences in the early years of life). But now the neuroscientists were looking at their CAT scans and Nuclear Magnetic Resonance scans of brains in action, analyzing brain chemicals in their gas chromatographic–mass spectrometers, and providing proof that mental activities are the product of the movement of molecules, of hundreds of different chemical juices; that the mind is fused with the brain, and both are inseparable from the body; that much mental illness, rather than being caused by childhood traumas, or poor social influences, is a product of genetic influences that can be traced back through many generations.

The orthodox shouted out that any differences between the sexes are not inborn but the product of environment; that humans are products of culture, which means that biology and any biological sex differences are irrelevant; that men and women are not only born equal but the same, so that any differences between them are the result of cultural restraints, psychological damage, differential training, unequal upbringing, and biased education.

And now here were all these brain scientists, many of them liberated females, producing study after study, brain scan after brain scan, proving that certain differences between the sexes are innate, the result of genetic influences, and can be seen throughout the brain, from the relative size of the hemispheres to a sexual dimorphic nucleus in the preoptic area of the hypothalamus twice as large in males as in females, to differing levels of a variety of neurochemicals, to differing organization of the verbal and visual-spatial areas of the brain.

EVOLUTIONARY LEAP

The new understanding of how individual neurochemical molecules operate like keys, fitting exactly into the chemical "keyholes" called receptors on the brain cells, makes it possible to design synthetic neurochemicals that can unlock or turn on certain brain cells as if they were natural brain juices, and to do so safely, without affecting other areas of the brain or body. This makes it possible for neuroscientists to talk seriously about the possibility of wiping out types of mental illness, creating substances that will increase intelligence, alertness, creativity; synthesizing juices that will carry within them information, like a library in chemical form; producing chemicals that will slow down or stop the aging process.

Millions of people died over the centuries as a result of infectious diseases we now have virtually eliminated with antibiotics like penicillin and tetracycline. Neuroscientists now believe that it is possible to design penicillins and tetracyclines for the mind—drugs that will wipe out certain types of mental illness: schizophrenias, depressions, anxieties, psychoses, aggressions. Brain scientists are even now designing special neurochemicals to help outwit the AIDS virus. Others focus on eliminating Alzheimer's disease. The revolution that has taken place in brain science may make possible a new age for us all.

If biological tendencies, the result of outmoded evolutionary strategies, have got us into our present suicidal jam, contributed to our folly of daily making scores of species extinct, poisoning our environment, and threatening to blow up the whole planet out of stubbornness and hatred, then we need to investigate biological solutions to our problems. The biologists insist that the more intelligent the creature becomes, the less it is ruled by its hard-wiring; with greater wisdom comes greater freedom from biological constraints. And the recent discoveries give us reason to believe that by using neuroscientific techniques—chemicals to increase memory, and intelligence, electrical stimulation directed to parts of the brain, grafting of brain tissue from one brain to another, implantation of microscopic "biochips" that will live like tissue in the brain while interfacing directly with vast computer networks and data banks—it is possible to make ourselves much, much smarter, far wiser, and free from those outmoded behavior patterns hard-wired into our brains. What we are seeing is the possibility of a new type of evolution.

In the past, evolution has been a process of genetic accident—random mutations occur, of which certain prove to be successful, enhancing the creature's ability to survive, and thus increasing its reproductive potential, its "fitness."

Today, for the first time, humans have the opportunity to take control of their own evolution. If evolution involves the development of new mental powers, boosting the brain to new levels of achievement, then the work of the neuroscientists can be seen as evolutionary developments: revolutionizing evolution. The fact that humans may be able to control and alter their brains in ways they have determined themselves presents us with an unprecedented situation: Now, humans can consciously direct their own development.

Seen in this way, the process of evolution can become goal-oriented, teleological: Now, the process involves not only surviving and reproducing, but developing toward desired goals. Once we accept the idea that we now (or will soon) have the capability of choosing and directing our own mental evolution, questions arise: What should be the goal of human evolution? What kind of mental development should we pursue? What kind of creature should we desire to become? What sort of life is worth living? Human survival may well depend on our ability to increase our mental powers and develop new strategies for overcoming our present crises.

But the cultural orthodoxy feels its hegemony threatened by such discoveries, since each new development emphasizes again that much of its ideology is based not in science but in wishful thinking, like the belief that the universe revolved around the earth. And so it continues to insist that this work, the exploration of the biological differences between the sexes, should not be done.

WHY DO IT?

Biopsychologist Jerre Levy of the University of Chicago, one of the leading researchers into the differing functions of the brain's hemispheres, asserts, "What we ultimately want to know, of course, is everything we can about the connection between genes, brain development, chemistry, hormones, the environment and behavior. Well, that's a pretty tall order, given that we have a brain of a hundred billion nerve cells, hundreds of thousands of genes, a varying environment and all kinds of behavior and all kinds of psychology to cope with. So we need a way of focusing. One important way of focusing is to compare and contrast different classes of individuals— left-handers and right-handers, for example. Schizophrenics and non-schizophrenics. . . . But the most important of these classes of individuals are males and females. They're important because sex is a *major* dimension of human difference, just as it's a *major* dimension of difference all the way across the animal kingdom. And we know that both genes and the sex hormones are involved in this difference, this basic difference in sexual functioning. If we find *other* differences between males and females, then—differences in behavior—we have a working hypothesis that we can test in both humans and animals, that these differences are an expression of genes and hormones in the development and function of the brain."

As Levy points out, scientists know much about how the genes influence the growth of the male and female body and brain; about how the sex hormones work in the body and brain; and about the sex differences in behaviors and skills shown by humans and animals. And they are learning much about how these behaviors and skills are altered by certain imbalances or abnormalities. "We have information on several levels, in other words," says Levy. "And what we're now trying to do is to argue *between* the levels, to find as many connections as possible between them. This isn't easy. It's like trying to do a three-dimensional jigsaw puzzle of an unknown size, when all you've got to go on are different bits and pieces of the puzzle—from different levels and from different parts of the picture—arriving almost daily. It's going to take a long time to complete the whole puzzle, decades perhaps. . . . But already parts of it are beginning to come together. They're actually beginning to make some sense."

In talking about sex differences in the brain, Levy is speaking as a biopsychologist. She is talking about differences that exist now, in humans like you and me. Differences that might make you, if you're female, see a painting, hear a piece of music, exercise political power, differently from me. The differences in our brains are in all likelihood remnants of those Pleistocene ancestors and the behaviors they found most effective for survival and reproduction. But those evolutionary strategies are, in many ways, outmoded now, while their remnants, the physiological distinctions between the brains of males and females, are still locked in place, churning out their neurochemicals, altering our perceptions, influencing our behaviors, right now.

And it's important for us to know this information. If our future depends on learning how to improve our brains, on learning to overcome the outmoded biologically based behaviors we have inherited, then this work is essential. Jon Franklin writes in his study of the new wisdom gained through the recent discoveries of how neurochemical molecules influence behavior: "As we extend that wisdom into the new science of molecular psychology, we begin to see that the key to freedom is the ability to override commands from below. And the way to override commands is to anticipate them, and arm ourselves against their seductive ways—to understand, in short, what they are and whence they come."

To claim, like the behaviorist-environmentalists, that this research should not be done, and if done should be suppressed, or ignored, or twisted to fit their ideology, is the attitude of intellectual Luddites. This reactionary attitude toward science simply doesn't work: The way out is the way forward.

SEX IN THE HEAD

· ·

The idea that men and women "think differently" has been around a long time. Many women, for example, have received the dubious compliment, from bosses or work partners, that they "think like a man." Nevertheless, it seems undeniable that there are certain styles, behaviors, and modes of thinking that most people would characterize as masculine, and others most people would characterize as feminine.

Cultural determinists have always insisted that these perceived sex differences are the result of environmental influences, that every baby is born with the capacity to develop an entire spectrum of styles, behaviors, and modes of thinking, and only develops masculine or feminine patterns in response to cultural expectations and role-training. Many feminists in the 1960's and 1970's adhered to this cultural-determinist view with extraordinary tenacity, and vehemently condemned any scientists who dared suggest that there were any innate differences between the sexes.

Academic communities, sympathetic to sexual equality, decried and at times cast out or excommunicated members performing studies that hinted at biological sex differences, and denied grants to scientists who wished to explore this area. The Sociobiology Study Group of Science for the People, comprising nearly forty eminent scientists, many from Harvard, called scientists investigating the biological basis of human behavior "sexist," "elitist," and "chauvinist pigs." Colleagues of Harvard biologist Edward O. Wilson, who contended that certain sex differences had a biological basis, accused him in print of reviving the ideas that "led to the establishment of gas chambers in Nazi Germany." At the annual convention of anthropologists in 1976, one opponent called such research "a political plot, a vicious, pernicious disease." A feminist took the floor to shout her demand that all books that incorporated such research be banned from the curricula of universities.

But no matter how fiercely the cultural determinists defended their ideology, an overwhelming flood of new, astonishing, and absolutely convincing evidence pouring out of the laboratories was proving them wrong.

WHAT'S THE DIFFERENCE?

Research into the differences between right-brain and left-brain hemispheres led to evidence that the brains of men and women not only are actually organized differently, but even have discernible anatomical differences.

Studies by researchers like Doreen Kimura of the University of Western Ontario showed that males tended to rely almost exclusively on a single hemisphere for verbal tasks, while females apparently spread verbal tasks throughout both hemispheres. Psychologist Jeanette McGlone discovered that damage to the left hemisphere (the one usually dominant for language) caused less language disorder in women than men.

Other researchers, such as Sandra Witelson at McMaster University in Canada and Jerre Levy of the University of Chicago, reached similar conclusions. Witelson's research, for example, revealed that men seem to be able to do visual-spatial tasks simultaneously with verbal tasks better than women can, because their left and right hemispheres operate more independently than women's. According to Levy, "What evidence there is, from different approaches and different laboratories all over the world, indicates that the female brain may be *less* lateralized and less tightly *organized* than the male brain."

Research psychologist Diane McGuinness, who holds positions at UC Santa Cruz and Stanford University, has devoted much of her professional career to studying the differences in male-female behavior. Along with Eleanor Maccoby and Carol Nagy Jacklin, also of Stanford, she has done research involving thousands of boys and girls, from early infancy to young adulthood, and has succeeded in putting together a clear statistical analysis of the brain differences: "The fascinating thing is that they seem to be independent of culture—as true in Ghana, Scotland and New Zealand as they are in America. First, women are more sensitive to touch. And they have better fine-motor coordination and finger dexterity—there may be cerebellar differences. Second, there are differences in the way information is gathered and problems are solved."

McGuinness has summarized these differences in general terms as: "Women are communicators and men are takers of action. . . . Males are good at tasks that require visual-spatial skills, and females are good at tasks that require language ability. Males are better at maps, mazes and math; at rotating objects in their minds and locating three-dimensional objects in two-dimensional representations. They're better at perceiving and manipulating objects in space. And they're better at orienting themselves in space. . . . Females, on the other hand, excel in areas that males are weak in, especially in areas where language is involved. They're not as good, in general, at anything that requires object manipulation and visual sharpness—they're less sensitive to light, for one thing. But they're much better at almost all the skills that involve words. . . . Their verbal memory is also better. And they can sing in tune, six times more often than males can."

Jerre Levy notes, "Human beings use language in two different ways: as tools for communication and as pure organs of thought. Although each sex has both these capacities, males seem to be superior in using language as a tool for thinking (typified by mathematics), and females excel in using language as an agent of social communication."

Denver neurophysiologist David Shucard, who used an EEG to

study how infants processed speech and music heard through ear-phones, discovered that almost without exception "girl babies process both speech and music with the left hemisphere and boys with the right."

Male babies, McGuinness and her colleagues have found, direct their attention toward lights, patterns, three-dimensional objects: visual things. They are more curious about their environment, explore it more, and play with objects in their environment as often as with toys. Female infants respond to people in the environment: They pay attention not to objects but to faces. They are far more sensitive to sound, and respond more to sounds in their environment. McGuinness points out that throughout their lives women are more sensitive to sound.

Like Levy, McGlone, and others, McGuinness became convinced these differences were inborn. "Just as the *capacity* for language is prewired into our brains before birth—as Noam Chomsky, among others, has shown—so, in females, is a special skill in it. So is the male's special visual and spatial skill. And so, perhaps, are all the other abilities and behaviors I've talked about. What comes easy to either sex is likely to be biologically programmed . . . stamped, primed, waiting to be developed."

SEXUAL MATHEMATICS

The researchers who have faced the greatest storm of condemnation from the cultural-determinist establishment are Camilla Benbow and Julian Stanley of Johns Hopkins University. These two psychologists began testing mathematical ability in youngsters in 1971. Over an eight-year period they studied thousands of youngsters, mostly seventh- and eighth-graders, who made unusually high mathematics scores on the College Board Scholastic Aptitude Test—a test designed for seventeen- and eighteen-year-olds. In other words, these were students who had not been taught higher mathematics and yet seemed to have a natural aptitude for mathematical reasoning. In 1980 they reported that they had found ten thousand such youngsters, and that there were far more boys than girls among this number. Furthermore, the boys' average score was far higher, and no girl ever scored highest on the test.

When they published this report in 1980, it set off a firestorm of controversy, with the authors being accused of sexism and even immorality in scientific journals, conferences, and the halls of academe. By 1983 Benbow and Stanley had accumulated data covering about sixty-five thousand youngsters, by 1985 over one hundred thousand. The figures continued to confirm the results of their earlier study: Of those who scored 600 or more in math, there were four boys for every girl, and of those who scored 700 or above (about one out of ten thousand seventh-graders), there were thirteen boys for every girl.

In further research, investigators gave the boys and girls more extended tests of such things as parental encouragement (did parents encourage boys more than girls?) and whether youngsters consider mathematics to be masculine domains, causing girls to be less motivated in those areas. After careful testing, they had to eliminate such environmental influences as a liking for math, encouragement given by parents, childhood toy preferences, social pressures, the number of courses taken, the perception of mathematics as masculine, and more. They could find nothing environmental to account for the differences in mathematical aptitude.

A follow-up study attempting to find environmental influences was made of a group of girls who were given special encouragement, special mathematical training, and female role models with high mathematical ability, but the difference between boys and girls remained the same. Interestingly, within their group of sixty-five thousand, Benbow and Stanley found no significant difference in verbal ability between boys and girls on verbal SAT scores. A similar search for verbally talented youth resulted in equal numbers of boys and girls among the high scorers.

Benbow now freely confesses, "After 15 years looking for an environmental explanation and getting zero results, I gave up." The evidence is clear, she says, that the difference between the sexes has a biological basis. "And, if so, then it's likely to be connected to the male's right-hemisphere superiority in visual-spatial tasks. We're just beginning to have evidence that when there are two equally valid approaches to a problem, via words or via images, females tend to choose the approach through words and males the approach through images. Now the approach through images—which are visual-spatial and right-hemisphere—just happens to be much more effective, especially in higher mathematics, than the approach through words. Look at the way mathematicians are forced to talk to one another, through symbols on a blackboard. . . . To be a good scientist, at all, in fact, seems to require a set of qualities more characteristic of men than of women—spatial ability, a low social interest and an absorption in things. Let's face it, human males like to manipulate *things*—from Tinkertoys to the cosmos."

WHY CAN'T YOUR HYPOTHALAMUS BE MORE LIKE MINE?

Neuroscientists with an interest in sexual behavior had long been fascinated by the hypothalamus. The small gland is deep in the limbic area of the brain, and it had been well established that the limbic system is the "emotional brain," generating and mediating all moods and emotions, as well as the physiological responses of the autonomic nervous system associated with emotions—the dilating blood vessels that make us blush, or flush with anger; the pounding heart of passion or terror. The hypothalamus, it became increasingly clear by the early 1970's, is the "master gland" of the limbic system, and thus the central organ of both emotion and motivation. It is in charge of regulating many vital functions, including sex, and it does so by means of triggering the release of a variety of neurochemicals that in turn regulate other glands of the limbic system, such as the pituitary, and sending neurohormones flowing throughout the body, stimulating the ovaries or the testes to produce their own hormones, such as testosterone and estrogen. The hypothalamus regulates what medical students call "the four f's": feeding, fighting, fleeing, and sexual activity.

As neuropsychologist Diane McGuinness stated it, "The hypothalamus is the ultimate controller of the body's flow of hormones. And it's responsible for the way sex and reproductive behavior are organized—the estrus or menstrual cycle in females, for example, and the quite different pattern we see in males. The hypothalamus is almost certainly differently stamped by sex hormones before birth. It's like a photographic plate that is exposed before birth and then developed by a fresh rush of hormones at puberty."

Then, in 1973, English researchers Geoffrey Raisman and Pat Field sent waves of astonishment through the neuroscientific community when they demonstrated that male and female rats had dramatic anatomical differences in the neurons of the hypothalamus: that those of the males had denser and more complex synaptic connections.

Raisman and Field's study also revealed that if males were castrated immediately after birth, they would have a female-brain pattern of synaptic organization in the hypothalamus; and if a female was injected with testosterone just after birth, she would have a male pattern of synaptic organization. The implications of this study were revolutionary: Here was the first irrefutable evidence that the brains of the sexes had important differences, and the differences were exactly where they should have been, in that region of the brain that controlled the sexual hormones.

Dominique Toran-Allerand of Columbia University studied the cells of the hypothalamus of mice and discovered that cells not exposed to testosterone grew at a normal rate, while those exposed to testosterone grew much more and grew far faster. The conclusion was inescapable: The hypothalamus of males had to be much different from that of females, since males had much higher levels of testosterone in their brains.

Other scientists began to focus on an area of the hypothalamus called the sexually dimorphic nucleus of the medial preoptic area (SDN-POA), an area that plays a key role in sexual hormone release and sexual behavior. They found that not only were the neurons in this area much more densely interconnected synaptically in males than in females, but it is actually much larger and contains far more brain cells.

Then Roger Gorski and colleagues from the UC School of Medicine in Los Angeles transplanted tissue from the SDN-POA from young male rats to young female rats. They were amazed to find that the females began to engage in male mating behaviors. That is, simply by adding brain cells from a male to a female, these scientists were able to elicit a variety of complex behavior patterns.

In 1985, Dutch scientists D. F. Swaab and E. Fliers of the Netherlands Institute for Brain Research in Amsterdam found a similar sex difference in human brains. In autopsies of the brains of thirteen men and eighteen women, they found the SDN-POA to be on the average more than two and a half times as large in men as in women, and to contain more than 2.2 times as many cells. The evidence was clear: There were very great differences in the part of the brain known to trigger or control a variety of complex sexual activities and reproductive behavior patterns.

As research continued, other anatomical differences in the brains of males and females were discovered. Neuropsychologist Marian

Diamond of the UC at Berkeley began comparing the thickness of the neocortex—the convoluted thinking cap, seat of our higher functions—in male and female rats, and found that the right cortex is thicker in males at virtually all times (the left cortex is thicker in females, but only at certain ages). Interestingly these patterns, Diamond has found, can be changed by manipulations of sex hormones delivered to the brain—early castration of the males, for example, causes their brain anatomy to become more like that of females (probably by cutting the flow of the male hormone testosterone). In more recent studies Diamond has found evidence that the right cortex in human males is larger than in females.

THE SEX CONTRACT BETWEEN THE EARS

The biological differences between the sexes, researchers believe, is a result of the selective pressures of evolution. Doreen Kimura concludes, "The fact seems inescapable that men and women do differ genetically, physiologically and in many important ways psychologically. This should not be surprising to us, since as a species we have a long biological history of having two sexual forms and have had a sexual division of labor dating back perhaps several million years."

Speaking more specifically, Kimura has said, "In a hunter-gatherer society there would be strong selective pressures on the males to be highly specialized, specialized as hunters. To hunt successfully—which meant survival, genetic and otherwise—they would need eye acuity, goal-directedness, good gross-motor control and the ability to calculate distance, direction and the essentials of a situation: exactly the sort of visual and spatial skills that scientists find in human males today. To achieve these skills, though, they would need to give up to them a good deal of brain capacity. . . . Females, meanwhile—let us imagine—were subject to *different* evolutionary pressures and were being selected for *different* qualities from the males. And these qualities—maternal, social and cultural ones, let's say—required different motor skills, a different brain organization and better hemispheric integration perhaps. When language and its uses were acquired, then, they fitted rather differently into the architecture of the female brain."

Jerre Levy also cites differing evolutionary pressures as the source of the differences between male and female brains. "The evidence, you see, is that the hemispheres of male brains are specialists—they speak different languages, verbal and visual-spatial. And it may be that they can communicate with each other only in a formal way. . . . The hemispheres of *female* brains, on the other hand, don't seem to be such specialists." Female brains seem far more likely to have verbal access to nonverbal information, and be able to integrate nonverbal and verbal more quickly and easily, whereas, says Levy, "because of the difficulty [males] may have in communicating between their two hemispheres, they may have restricted verbal access to their emotional world."

THOSE EMOTIONAL MALES

In fact, this may be at the root of what females have traditionally seen as a lack of emotional sensitivity by males, and an apparent unwillingness to "open up" and express their emotions verbally.

In a 1986 study Ohio State University psychologist Anthony Greenwald and fellow researchers set out to see if the notion that women are more emotional than men was true. They tested forty-eight men and women to see who remembered powerfully emotional words better. The subjects were also asked to rate the words for emotional intensity. Earlier research had shown that the more intensely emotional an event or word, the more likely it is to be remembered.

Greenwald was surprised to find that the men and women scored the same in remembering the emotional words, but that women rated the words much higher on emotional intensity. In other words, the scientists concluded, women are not more likely to respond to events emotionally; rather, they are more likely to describe their responses in emotional terms.

Another study, by psychologist Martin Safer of Catholic University in Washington, D.C., has revealed that women seem to have a small but significant edge over men in gaining access to the information necessary to understand emotion and express it verbally, and that this edge is a result of differences in the structure of the brains of men and women.

Safer conducted an experiment to measure how well emotional information presented to the right hemisphere was transferred over to the left. He showed his subjects slides depicting human faces expressing various emotions. Using a procedure that guaranteed that some slides could be seen by only one hemisphere of the brain, Safer found that women were more accurate in judging the emotions shown on the screen. The women's superiority seemed to come from the fact that they used both hemispheres of the brain to understand emotion, while men relied mainly on their right hemisphere.

These and other studies also indirectly suggest that when males do translate their emotions into words, they tend to express them directly, while women seem more capable of manipulating their verbal expression of emotions. One recent two-year study by communications researcher William Owen of Texas A&M, for example, was directed at the way men and women express emotions. "Men tend to have a one-on-one connection between felt and expressed emotion," Owen concluded, "and they tend to say what they mean. Women tend to have a cognitive break between felt and expressed emotion."

The male separation between verbal and emotional brain may explain certain male characteristics, such as the man of action who speaks few words—the laconic, tight-lipped Hemingway hero, for example, who, exploding with emotions, can only say, "It was very good." In such characters, and their descendents—the Clint Eastwood, Sylvester Stallone, Chuck Norris variations—you can almost see the two hemispheres at work, one seething with emotions, the other tightly in control, translating the emotions into formal, verbal abstractions.

Then, too, this may be a factor in the frequently noted tendency of females to want to talk about their emotions: Numerous males have noted how, after making love, females often want to talk, asking their men to "express their emotions," when the males have assumed that that is exactly what they had just finished doing.

In recent years women have criticized this "unwillingness to communicate" as a crucial failing of men. Studies like sex-pollster Shere Hite's survey of *Women and Love* demonstrate how critical women are of this "withholding" of emotion. Virtually all of the women who responded, according to Hite, complain that they must initiate "communication." Most claim that it is they who start fights, but they are forced to do so as a way of communicating; that males will do almost anything to avoid fights is, according to the women, simply a sign of their fear of communication. Overwhelmingly women feel that their male's avoidance of verbal communication is a problem.

WHY CAN'T A MAN BE MORE LIKE A WOMAN?

"It's not us," claims Hite, "it's men's attitudes toward women that are causing the problem." Hite's respondents make it clear that the apparent unwillingness of males to talk to women correctly is not only a "problem" but wrong—something akin to a nasty habit, or a stubborn and selfish refusal to act rationally. This tendency, they believe, is the result of cultural conditioning, of being taught to be macho, tough, unemotional—tough guys don't talk about their emotions. In this vision baby males, born with the capability of being just as verbally expressive about their emotions, are brutally twisted by society and turned into tight-lipped, unemotional brutes. Males, in this view, have the same need and eagerness as women do to express explicitly in words their feelings and emotions; and the fact that they refuse to do so is simply another sign of their hatred or contempt for women, or of their immaturity or sickness.

However, as the studies described above indicate, the differences between males and females in the way they express their response to emotions appear to spring in large part from innate differences in brain structure. Psychologist Carol Tavris, coauthor of *The Longest War*, a book reviewing sex differences, points out, "It's too easy to portray the expressive wife as good and the stoic husband as horrible; in fact, they are just different."

Humans have always seen the absurdity of the attitude satirized in the lyric "Why can't a woman be more like a man?" And yet in recent years, many cultural determinists, assuming all sex differences are caused by environmental influences and can be altered by reeducation, are seriously suggesting not only that men should be more like women, but also that it is *right* to be like a woman and *wrong* to be like a man.

THE GRADE SCHOOL CONSPIRACY

Psychologist Diane McGuinness believes that attitudes have become institutionalized in the nation's educational system, and provides strong evidence that such attitudes pose a danger to the entire culture. Grade school, McGuinness has concluded, is strongly biased against the natural skills and brain-functioning styles of boys. In the early years, virtually all the teaching focuses on reading and writing— verbal skills in which girls are clearly superior, due to the more diffuse organization of verbal activity in both hemispheres. As a result, McGuinness says, "boys fill remedial reading classes, don't learn to spell, and are classified as dyslexic or learning-disabled four times as often as girls." If these "punitive categories" had existed earlier, they would have included such geniuses as Faraday, Edison, and Einstein.

Over 95 percent of all students classified as suffering from the "disease" known as "hyperactivity" are boys. Citing this as just one example of the apparent educational conspiracy to ignore sex differences, McGuinness observes that "hiding the knowledge concerning sex-specific attitudes in learning has done far more harm than good." It has, in fact, caused an immense amount of suffering, says McGuinness, "in many boys who *normally* are slower to acquire reading skills when compared to girls. Even more pernicious is the spectacle of young boys on medication for a 'disease' that has no valid diagnosis."

A vision arises of Huck Finn, with his well-known distaste for schools and book learning, being "sivilized" by the Hannibal, Missouri, school system by being diagnosed as "hyperactive," turned into a brain-numbed zombie by his prescribed medication, spending his afternoons placidly attending his remedial reading class.

HORMONES IN THE BODY-MIND

So far we have seen evidence that, speaking in general, males and females seem to differ in the structure and organization of their brains, particularly in the operations of the brain's hemispheres. The question now arises, how are those differing behaviors and abilities maintained? What is the actual mechanism that influences those behaviors and abilities?

The answer, it is becoming increasingly clear, is the chemistry of the brain (or the "body-mind"). It has long been known that certain neurochemicals, known as *hormones*, play an important role in sexual behavior, and that the levels and activities of certain sex hormones have differed between males and females. For example, we all know that when certain hormones begin to flow into the bloodstream during puberty, boys and girls undergo dramatic changes. The same hormones (Gn–RH, or gonadotropin-releasing hormone, LH, or lutenizing hormone, and FSH, or follicle-stimulating hormone) produce different effects in males and females. In women, the hormones trigger the production of estrogen. In males, they signal the testes to produce testosterone. Under the influence of these hormones, males and females become physically different: Males develop facial hair, heavier bones, and muscles; females menstruate, develop breasts and wider hips, and so on.

The physical influences of the hormones continue throughout life. When a woman becomes pregnant, her body secretes more sex hormones than at any other time, triggering the complex series of physical transformations that take place during the growth of the fetus, such as increasing her blood volume to increase the flow of nutrients to the embryo, damping her immune system so she won't reject the fetus as foreign tissue, and triggering the production of mother's milk.

Testosterone causes males to develop strong, muscular bodies, and plays a part in male reproductive capabilities by triggering the production of sperm.

It has been noted that evolution seems to have provided women with an "edge" during their childbearing years, when more women than men are needed to perpetuate the species. Estrogen helps keep women's levels of cholesterol lower and makes their blood vessels more resilient to stress. Men, on the other hand, seem designed to protect women—their blood clots faster than women's, perhaps because of the greater likelihood that men would be injured, but this makes men more likely to suffer heart attacks. But after reproductive years are past, the female edge disappears: Female sex hormones such as estrogen subside, making women prone to heart disease and osteoporosis, as well as hot flashes and vaginal dryness. Males suffer reduced levels of testosterone with age, leading to some depression and lethargy, and to loss of some physical strength, but tend to remain healthier in their later years than do women. A study by Dr. Sidney Katz of the Brown University biology and medicine department, published in *The New England Journal of Medicine*, revealed that men sixty-five to sixty-nine years old spend an average of 71 percent of their remaining years in good health, while their female counterparts of the same age can expect to live only 54 percent of the rest of their lives in good health.

The fact that these neurochemicals called hormones have such dramatic physical influences has been known for so long that we accept it without question. Now, however, it is becoming increasingly clear that neurochemicals contribute not just to gross physical differences between the sexes but also to differences in other, more subtle types of behavior, including attitudes, emotions, and capabilities.

TAKING THE LEFT-HANDED APPROACH

Take, for example, the mysterious case of the left-handed dyslexic math prodigy. It's a mystery that was first explored by the late Norman Geschwind, a Harvard University neurologist. In the early 1980's, Geschwind noticed that there was a link of some sort between left-handedness and language disorders, such as dyslexia, which is characterized by difficulty in learning to read. Intrigued, Geschwind began investigating, and found that left-handers had a greater incidence not only of dyslexia but also of autoimmune diseases of all sorts. In his researches he found that learning disabilities were twelve times more frequent in left-handers than in right-handers, and at least three times more frequent in the left-handers' relatives. About 11 percent of left-handers suffered from autoimmune diseases, compared to only 4 percent of right-handers, while the incidence of autoimmune diseases in the relatives of left-handers was double what it was among relatives of right-handers.

Geschwind's conclusions at first seemed inexplicable, but finally he began to suspect that the learning and autoimmune disorders and the left-handedness resulted from excess production of or sensitivity to *testosterone* in the fetus.

It had already been established that fetal testes secreted large amounts of the hormone that affected the development of brain structures, and that brain anatomy could be influenced by altering levels of testosterone.

Geschwind concluded that testosterone actually slows the growth of the left hemisphere—where most verbal processing takes place. As a result of this slowing of growth in the left brain, the right brain—which has more control over visual-spatial and mathematical ability—takes up the slack. In effect, the testosterone causes the right hemisphere to grow larger, and left-handedness becomes more likely to result. "Consequently," Geschwind asserted, "males end up right-handed less often than females."

What Geschwind found was that left-handedness and immune-system disorders were not only linked to abnormalities such as autism, dyslexia, or stuttering, but were also linked to certain kinds of gift-edness, particularly artistic, musical, or mathematical talent. "The interesting thing," Geschwind remarked, "is that the pathology of these disorders is a pathology of superiority as well as inferiority, since you often find remarkable talents in the learning disabled." All of these characteristics were entangled in some sort of relationship that had to do with testosterone, and all of them were more common among males than among females.

The link with giftedness in math, music, and the arts occurs, Geschwind proposed, because genius for math, music, and art seems to depend heavily on right-hemisphere brain functions. "If you get the mechanism adjusted just right you get superior right hemisphere talents," said Geschwind. "But the mechanism is a bit treacherous. If you overdo it, you're going to get into trouble. It's a funny mechanism. At first, it looks like you have to deliberately produce damage to produce giftedness." He pointed out, "In principle, you might be able to prevent the learning disorders, but if you did, you would want to find a way that wouldn't reduce the superior talents."

Geschwind's findings, announced and published in 1982, rattled the seismographs in the world of the cultural determinists. But in support of his assertions came evidence from a study by Marian Annett of the Lanchester Polytechnic in Coventry, England, that a disproportionate number of artists, musicians, mathematicians, and engineers are left-handed.

Camilla Benbow and Julian Stanley were intrigued by Geschwind's ideas. They had already accumulated their huge body of data about youthful students with gifts in mathematics. Now they decided to contact those thousands of students to see if they were left-handed and had immune-system disorders. Their findings supported Geschwind's.

Fully 20 percent of the mathematically gifted youths were left-handed—making them more than twice as likely to be left-handed than the general population. Sixty percent of them had immune-system disorders—over five times the incidence in the general population (most of these immune disorders were allergies and asthma). And, as we have seen, fewer than 10 percent of their gifted mathematics students were girls: the ratio of mathematically gifted males to mathematically gifted females was 13 to 1.

As Benbow and Stanley moved from the high scorers to those who were less gifted, they found those were less likely to be left-handed or to have immune disorders. They were also less likely to be boys. As they reached those students who had made average scores on the math SAT, they found the incidence of left-handedness and immune disorders about the same as those in the general population. And they found the ratio of boys to girls about the same as in the general population.

Studies of the brains of dyslexics by Harvard neurologist Albert M. Galaburda proved what Geschwind had already surmised: In the brains of dyslexics, the language areas in the right hemispheres were as large as those in the left, and the right hemisphere also contained a greater than normal number of brain cells. (With the language center in the right hemisphere so well developed, the researchers theorized, it would rival the left hemisphere for control of the language function and the competition between hemispheres could hinder the reading process, causing the dyslexia.) One cause of this abnormal growth of the right hemisphere, Galaburda and colleagues believe, is high levels of the male hormone testosterone during the second trimester of pregnancy, when the fetal brain is forming the neocortex, where language skills and other higher functions reside. As we have noted, far more boys than girls are dyslexic.

Evidence came from another direction. Dr. Richard Held of the MIT Infant Development Laboratory found that for a critical period, in the early months of life, baby girls are distinctly ahead of baby boys in some areas of brain growth. By the age of about seven months, boys have caught up. The key to the differences, Held discovered, was the "masculinizing effect" of testosterone.

CAN YOU VISUALIZE THIS?

More evidence of the link between neurochemicals and sex differences came from neurologist Daniel Hier and endocrinologist William Crowley, who investigated the capacity of certain subjects to visualize and manipulate complex three-dimensional objects in visual space.

Hier and Crowley studied nineteen men who had suffered since birth or since childhood from a rare condition (idiopathic hypogonadotrophic hypogonadism) characterized by extremely small testes and —as a consequence—a scarcity of testosterone, and tested their visual-spatial abilities, along with the visual-spatial abilities of nineteen men with normal levels of testosterone. They found that the first group scored as well on verbal problems as the normal men, but they did much worse—as much as 25–30 percent worse—on tasks that measured visual-spatial ability. Significantly there was a direct correlation between testosterone levels and visual-spatial abilities: Those with lowest levels of testosterone had the poorest visual-spatial abilities.

Hier and Crowley also tested men who had idiopathic hypogonadotrophic hypogonadism but who, unlike the nineteen earlier subjects, had contracted it *after puberty*, and found that their visual-spatial abilities were as strong as the normal men's. And when they tried administering testosterone to the men who had contracted the disease before puberty, they found that it had no effect on their visual-spatial skills. Somehow, visual-spatial ability seemed to be fixed in the brain before puberty. The findings, according to Hier and Crowley, suggested that testosterone exerts "a permanent organizing influence on the brain before or at puberty in boys." In fact, they concluded, the presence of sufficient testosterone at or before puberty "is a critical factor in the development of spatial ability."

Shortly after that study, Columbia University researcher Anke Erhardt announced that she had found not only that spatial abilities were usually stronger in males than females, but that in both sexes, superior spatial skills were found in those who matured late. Males, as has been frequently noted, mature later than do females, and there is some evidence that this late maturity is a result of their prenatal exposure to high levels of testosterone. Erhardt noted that prenatal exposure of females to high levels of the male hormone might contribute to their late development and to their spatial skills.

In a separate study Erhardt found some evidence that this might be the case, and concluded that conversely, women whose mothers were taking *female* hormones in pregnancy showed more feminine behavior, while women who showed more "malelike" or tomboy behavior in youth actually had higher IQs than the group whose mothers were taking female hormones. Thus, like the findings of Galaburda, Erhardt's studies indicate that the presence and quantities of certain male or female hormones during pregnancy can exert apparently permanent influence over such things as spatial skills and IQ scores.

THE NEUROCHEMISTRY OF HOMOSEXUALITY

At about the same time as these findings were becoming known, another study showed that certain behaviors thought to be culturally determined had important biological components. Psychobiologist Brian Gladue and other researchers at State University of New York, Stony Brook, gave injections of the female hormone estrogen to a group made up of twenty-nine men who were heterosexual, fourteen men who were homosexual, and twelve heterosexual women. Estrogen is known to trigger a brief fall followed by a sharp rise to about double the baseline level of luteinizing hormone (LH) in women but not in heterosexual men (heterosexual males show a brief drop in LH followed by a gradual return to baseline). As expected, the heterosexual men's hormonal systems responded to the estrogen much differently than the women's. However, the homosexuals' pattern of LH secretion was similar to that of women—a brief fall followed by a steep rise (to a level about 38 percent higher than baseline, a less dramatic rise than that found in females). The study, concluded Gladue, illustrates "a biological aspect of homosexuality that is clear enough to alter the opinion that it is purely cultural." The study suggests, according to Gladue, "that biological markers for sexual orientation may exist."

Gladue's study confirmed those done earlier in East Germany by Gunter Dorner, director of the Institute for Experimental Endocrinology at Humboldt University in East Berlin. As early as 1964 Dorner began experimenting with giving rats injections of estrogen, and quickly found that homosexual male rats responded with the surge of LH characteristic of female rats. He then applied this technique to humans and found again that male homosexuals responded to estrogen with the flood LH, while heterosexuals did not.

While Dorner was performing his studies, other scientists, including Ingeborg Ward at Villanova University, were discovering that when pregnant female rats were subjected to stress, their male offspring showed extremely low levels of testosterone, and exhibited "feminized" and "demasculinized" behavior as adults, becoming homosexual or bisexual. Fascinated by the connection between stress during pregnancy and reduced levels of testosterone in offspring, Dorner began to search for connections between stress and male homosexuality in humans. He concluded that there was a significant relationship between maternal stress during pregnancy and male bisexuality and, in particular, male homosexuality. As Dorner has summed it up, "About a third of the homosexual men and their mothers reported having been exposed to severe maternal stress— such as bereavement, rape or severe anxiety. And about another third reported moderate stress. This wasn't true of the heterosexual men. None of them reported severe stress. And only ten percent reported even moderate stress."

As a result, Dorner has said, "I am forced to conclude that male homosexuality is the result of permanent neurochemical changes in the hypothalamus effected by reduced levels of testosterone during fetal life." Stress and other factors, Dorner has concluded, "permanently alter the neural circuitry of the brain, the nerve pathways that are controlled by the *local* hormones, the neurotransmitters—particularly serotonin, dopamine and norepinephrine."

Dorner's studies have led him to believe fetal neurochemical events influence a wide variety of behaviors, including mood, aggression, and use of energy. As he has said, the sex hormones "don't just suddenly appear out of nowhere at puberty. Nor do they just meander about the body. *They know where to go.* The cells that are their targets have already been primed, in the womb, to respond to the hormones that are now being produced. They've already—long before—been *organized*—by the early production of the sex hormones *themselves*, in a masculine or feminine way. This is true of the body, of the reproductive organs, heart, lungs, liver and kidney. But it is also true of the *brain*. The tissues, neural circuitry and chemistry of the brain have already been stamped during fetal life by the sex hormones. The foundations have already been laid, before birth, for the range of behaviors that will characterize the organism as male or female in adult life."

There are, then, differences in the anatomy and cell arrangements of the brain—in the size and number of cells in the sexually dimorphic nucleus of the preoptic area of the hypothalamus, in the size of the corpus callosum, in the size of the hemispheres and specific areas of the hemispheres. And these anatomical differences contribute to differences in such areas as visual-spatial skills, verbal abilities, communication, emotional expressiveness, susceptibility to autoimmune disorders, musical and mathematical talents, and more.

These anatomical differences, we found, seem to interact with neurochemical differences, and the neurochemical differences, like the anatomical ones, seem rooted in evolutionary biology. If, as scientists assert, we evolved through millions of years as hunters and gatherers, with males requiring keen visual-spatial abilities and high levels of aggressiveness, then it makes sense that those males with higher levels of testosterone, linked to visual-spatial skills, physical size, strength, and aggressiveness, would be more likely to reproduce and pass on their genetic tendencies to succeeding generations than would males with lower levels of testosterone. Females capable of communicating clearly and expressively would be more likely to produce offspring that would learn the skills of survival so that they could in turn produce offspring.

But the forces of evolution can be dramatically and permanently thwarted or twisted by means of alterations in certain neurochemicals during the nine months of fetal development, with stress and other environmental forces causing alterations in hormonal levels that can produce an infinite variety of human behaviors, including masculinized females and feminized males, hypermasculine males and hyperfeminine females, homosexuals, bisexuals, and heterosexuals—individuals whose behavior patterns are fixed before birth, and extraordinarily resistant to change.

These three types of influence on behavior—influences arising from anatomical differences in the brain, influences arising from genetic, evolutionary neurochemical differences, and influences arising from neurochemical events that take place while the fetus is developing—are keys to an enormous amount of sexual behavior and styles of interpersonal behavior, including aggressiveness, risk-taking, social dominance, adherence to moral standards, strength of attitude and belief systems, sense of control, sociability.

That is, these powerful, relatively permanent influences have a lot to do with how people act in the sex-power nexus.

12

WHO'S ON TOP?: BIOPOLITICS IN THE SEX-POWER NEXUS

· · · · · · · · · · · · · · · · · ·

Virility is proved by remaining in power.

—*General Manuel Antonio Noriega, ruler of Panama,*
responding to mass demonstrations seeking his ouster

THE BIOLOGY OF POWER

If the drives, impulses, emotions, ideas, and other things that we are
used to thinking of as products of "mind," and aspects of "psychology," are in fact products of the flow of neurochemicals, then, as
brain scientist Jerre Levy insists, "Not all biology is psychology, but
in my view, *all* psychology *is* biology."

Most of us need little convincing that human sexuality has a powerful biological component. But the relation between power and bi-

ology is less self-evident. After all, just what is power? It usually doesn't have the same palpable physicality that sex does. Is it possible that power—the desire that people have to possess it, use it—has biochemical roots as strong as those of sex, that the desire to exercise power springs from innate hormonal and neurochemical forces as urgent as the desire for sex, and produces ecstasies, frustrations, and satisfactions as sensual and erotic as those of sex? Is it possible that the drives and states of arousal, desires, and gratifications are governed by the very same neurochemicals, are in fact part of the same biological process?

THE T FACTOR: TESTOSTERONE

Testosterone is an anabolic steroid—that is, it promotes the synthesis of proteins from food and promotes the growth and regeneration of tissue (unlike estrogen, a catabolic steroid, which promotes the breakdown of proteins, slows down growth, and leads to the increased storage of fat on the body). Since males have far greater quantities of testosterone than females, males are generally larger than women. Their bodies are also different in their makeup: On the average the bodies of males comprise about 40 percent muscle and 15 percent fat, while the bodies of females are about 23 percent muscle and 25 percent fat. Men have wider shoulders and longer arms, they deliver oxygen to their muscles more efficiently, and, pound for pound, their upper body is two to three times more powerful than women's.

Annelise Korner has dedicated many years to studying the behavior of newborn infants, and has demonstrated that even at birth boys show far greater muscle strength (such as a greater head lift while in the prone position) than girls. As Bob Goy of the Regional Primate Research Center at the University of Wisconsin in Madison has said, testosterone and the other sex hormones are "important evolutionary agents, the agents of a very ancient evolutionary program. . . . The female has puberty earlier, for example, and her growth is slowed, because it's not to her reproductive advantage to invest too heavily in growth. She develops breasts and pubic hair to demonstrate that she has now reached sexual maturity. And she's given large fat deposits as a protection against the coming of lean times, so that she and any future breast-feeding offspring will survive when there's no food available." The male, on the other hand, has higher levels of testosterone; according to Goy, "he invests much more heavily in growth and muscular strength than the female does. This is likely to be part of his *separate* evolutionary legacy—of male-male competition and hunting."

Testosterone is most highly concentrated in the hypothalamus, and scientists have recently discovered that injection of testosterone has an arousing or excitatory influence on the hypothalamus and limbic system, which is to say on that part of the brain regulating emotions, sex, and aggression. Biological anthropologist and medical doctor Melvin Konner points out, "It is one thing to say that the hormone probably influences sex and aggression by acting on the brain; it is quite another to find a major nerve bundle deep in the brain, likely to be involved in sex and aggression, that can fire more easily when testosterone acts on it than when it does not. A key link in the story has been formed."

Perhaps the most intriguing fact about testosterone is that scientific evidence indicates that it is necessary for male sexual arousal and desire. Testosterone, recent studies have shown, is a genuine aphrodisiac. Physiologist Julian Davidson and colleagues at Stanford University performed a study of men suffering from extremely low levels of sexual desire as the result of underactive gonads. They found that doses of testosterone dramatically increased their frequency of sexual fantasies and restored their sexual desire. Said Davidson, "It's now very clear that testosterone is the biological substrate of desire, at least in men."

Testosterone is so essential to male sexual desire that one method now being used to treat male sexual offenders is to require them to take drugs (such as Depo-Provera) that sharply reduce their levels of testosterone. According to medical psychologist John Money of Johns Hopkins, the reduction in testosterone "suppresses or lessens the frequency of erection and ejaculation and also lessens the feeling of libido and the mental imagery of sexual arousal."

There is evidence that when males are anticipating sexual activity, their levels of testosterone increase. Another study indicates that testosterone levels in males increase both before and after sex. When testosterone is removed by means of castration, there is a dramatic decline in sexual activity, but when testosterone is administered to these males, the decline is reversed.

But even though it is a "male" hormone, testosterone also plays an important role in female sexual desire. Though females produce testosterone in smaller quantities than do males, that small amount has powerful effects: Scientists have found that females experience substantial decreases in sexual activity if they are no longer producing testosterone. On the other hand, if testosterone is administered to females, it increases both sexual desire and frequency of sexual activity. Doses of testosterone are now routinely used to treat the loss of desire in women who are postmenopausal or who have had their ovaries removed.

Studies by Harold Lief, emeritus professor of psychiatry at the University of Pennsylvania, show that in normal females those periods in the menstrual cycle when they are producing the greatest amounts of testosterone—just before and during ovulation—are apparently the periods of most intense sexual desire. As Jo Durden-Smith and Diane deSimone point out in their study *Sex and the Brain*, this period "*also* seems to coincide with a period when a woman is most sensitive to smell; when she is most *visually* sensitive; and, most fascinatingly, when she is at her most arithmetically able."

GATEKEEPERS AND SEEKERS

Given the facts that males have higher levels of testosterone than females, it's hard to escape the conclusion that males apparently, on the average, have a stronger drive or desire to engage in sexual activity than do females. A vast number of studies, including cross-cultural studies, support this conclusion. For example, males are far more likely to masturbate prior to adolescence than are females. (University of Wisconsin psychologist John DeLamater summarizes four separate recent researches into incidence of masturbation by age thirteen in his study "Gender Differences in Sexual Scenarios," and finds that even well after the sexual revolution and the women's liberation movement have altered the sexual behavior of females, two thirds of the male subjects had masturbated by age thirteen compared to one third of the female subjects.)

In a variety of large-scale surveys men and women were asked their reactions to their first intercourse experience. In all of the studies, males reported positive reactions. From 75 percent to over 90 percent of the men in these studies found the first experience "enjoyable and satisfying." Only 50 to 75 percent of females had a favorable reaction, and in addition, they were more likely than men to report feeling guilty after their first experience.

Much evidence indicates that for men, most women, including strangers, are perceived as potential sexual partners, while women are more likely to perceive as potential sexual partners only men whom they already know. Males tend to attribute more sexual meaning to a wide range of behaviors than do females: They expect that women who wear "sexy" clothing desire sex, and they are more likely to interpret female friendliness as sexual interest.

Psychologist Frank Saal, for example, had two hundred students watch a videotape of a male teacher and a female student talking together, and asked them about the professor and student's intentions toward each other. Saal found that men saw far more sexual innuendo in the conversation than women did, rating both people in the video as more sexy, seductive, and flirtatious, and were more likely to see attraction and interest between the two. Women viewed the conversation as merely friendly.

One researcher surveyed a large number of dating and newly married couples, asking whether they wished their partners were more or less predictable about when they wanted to have sex, more or less variable about where they had sex, and more or less "wild and sexy." The female respondents replied that their male partners were about right in each of these qualities. Men overwhelmingly said they wished their partners were less predictable about timing, more variable with regard to the location of sex, and more wild and sexy.

A 1988 survey of 289 sex therapists revealed that the most common complaint among couples was a discrepancy between partners in their desire for sex. In most cases the males' desire for sex was greater than that of the females. A survey of couples by Joseph LoPiccolo, a psychologist at the University of Missouri, and Jerry Friedman, a sex therapist in Stony Brook, New York, revealed that men generally expressed a greater desire for sex than did their wives, with, for example, more than 12 percent of the men saying they preferred intercourse more than once a day, while about 3 percent of women expressed the same preference.

In a 1982 study of receptivity to heterosexual invitations by strangers, males and females were approached and told by members of the opposite sex that "I've been noticing you around campus, and I find you to be very attractive." This statement was followed by one of three invitations: Would you go out on a date with me; would you come to my apartment; or, would you go to bed with me? Men and women were equally likely to accept the date: About 50 percent said yes. But about 70 percent of the men were willing to go to the woman's apartment, while only 6 percent of the women accepted that offer. And fully 75 percent of the men were quite willing to go to bed with the unknown woman, while none of the women accepted that offer. That is, males were far more eager to go to bed with a woman they had just met than they were to go out on a date with her!

A variety of studies seem to indicate that females are less sexually aroused than males by sexual stimuli. Females have been found to avoid sex stimuli more than males, and when questioned in surveys regarding their experiences with and reactions to explicit pictorial, verbal, or written depictions of sexual activity, males always exceed females in reported sexual arousal. A number of studies have found that females are less aroused by group-sex and oral-sex stimuli than are males. Also, in summarizing a number of studies, Kansas State University psychologist and sex researcher William Griffitt reports that "apparently sexual stimuli evoke stronger expectancies for sexual behavior in males than in females."

DISRUPTING COGNITIVE PROCESSES WITH SEX

It has been consistently found that females' reports of affective responses to and evaluations of sexual stimuli are much more negative than those of males. Studies have found these differences in responses to visual, auditory, and written sexual stimuli. A large number of studies indicate that, following exposure to a variety of sexual stimuli, females are likely to report feelings of repulsion, irritation, anger, nausea, and disgust. Exposed to the same stimuli, males more often report positive affective feelings such as curiosity, excitement, eagerness, entertainment. Griffitt reports, "When affective responses such as those described are factor analyzed and combined into orthogonal positive and negative dimensions . . . females generally respond more negatively and less positively to sexual stimuli than do males."

When given the Sexual Opinion Survey, which measures whether people respond to sexual cues with positive (erotophilic) or negative (erotophobic) emotions, female scores are significantly lower (more negative) than those of males. A Sex Anxiety Inventory shows that females report higher expectancies than males for negative feelings associated with sexual stimuli. On the Mosher Sex Guilt Scales, female scores indicate they have more guilt regarding sex than do males. And several studies, including a 1983 survey by Griffitt, have revealed that, in Griffitt's words, "females generally evaluate sexual stimuli less favorably and are more likely to judge erotica as pornographic and to favor its legal restriction than are males."

In this regard it is fascinating to note the findings of sex researcher Meg Gerrard of Iowa State University, who has spent the last fifteen years studying the relationship between attitudes toward sexuality, sexual activity, and contraceptive use. Noting that women tend to score higher on the Mosher Sex Guilt Scales, she observes that this reveals a "disposition manifested by resistance to sexual temptation, inhibited sexual behavior, and/or the disruption of cognitive processes in sex-related situations." In one study, high and low sex guilt subjects were read either sexually arousing (erotic) passages or neutral passages, and then listened to a lecture. The high sex guilt subjects, says Gerrard, "remembered less of the lecture information than did low guilt subjects." That is, high sex guilt can, in many situations, have a disruptive effect on a subject's ability to learn or to think effectively. Gerrard finds that "women who are high in sex guilt appear to be misinformed or confused about sexual matters."

Gerrard has also found evidence that like high sex guilt, erotophobia, as measured by the Sexual Opinion Survey, tends to interfere with cognitive processes. Erotophobes, Gerrard notes, also "react to erotic slides more negatively, are less interested in viewing erotica, and are more likely to favor restricting erotic materials than are erotophilics."

In the field of sexual fantasy, males are much more likely to have sex dreams (for over forty years studies have continued to report that about 80 percent of males and 40 percent of females have sex dreams that result in orgasm). Fewer females (69 percent) than males (84 percent) report having sexual fantasies. There is also continuing evidence emerging that the content of the sexual fantasies of males is different from that of females: Male fantasies more often have to do with sex with strangers, group sex, extraordinary sexual virility, sexual irresistibility, and forcing sex on their partners. Females are more likely to fantasize being submissive, being forced to have sex, feeling romance and affection, and being seduced or seducing others.

Even the most recent studies show that both men and women report that it is the male who usually initiates the sexual behaviors in which the couple engage, that it is usually the male who requests increased sexual intimacy, and that females are virtually always the ones to limit a couple's sexual activity. Sex researcher Griffitt summarizes the findings of a number of recent studies with the observation, "Part of being masculine for males is sexual success, and part of being feminine for females is limited sexual accessibility."

So despite the sex revolution, despite more than twenty years of feminists pursuing sexual equality, the ancient pattern endures: Males are the seekers and females the gatekeepers of sex.

THE EVOLUTION OF SEXUAL DESIRE

When looked at from an evolutionary viewpoint, in terms of differing reproductive strategies, this sex difference makes perfect sense. As neuroscientist Candace Pert puts it, "Of course men and women have entirely different attitudes toward sex, and those attitudes are hardwired in the brain, not learned. . . . The brain doesn't know the Pill was invented. Women are programmed since time immemorial to get that guy back to take care of any offspring that might ensue. After all, our mothers had babies, our grandmothers had babies: women alive today are the result of a long line of women who reproduced."

What Pert describes is the innate sex difference in parental investment or optimal mating strategy: Females can produce fewer offspring than can males, must invest more of their own life in each child, and thus must be more selective in their sexual partners. So in evolutionary terms, females with lower levels of testosterone would tend to be selected for, while those with high levels of testosterone would tend to produce fewer surviving offspring, and thus to disappear from the gene pool.

It's easy to see why this is so. Females with lower levels of testosterone would tend to have less intense sexual desire, and thus would be less likely to have sex impulsively and indiscriminately. They would be able to control their own sexual appetites more, and thus be able to choose their sexual partners more pragmatically, with an eye toward which would be the best providers and protectors of their offspring, and those who showed evidence of possessing genes that would contribute to the successful survival of their offspring. Also, since such a female would be less likely to seek other males for sex partners, the male she did mate with would be more certain that any offspring were his, and would be more likely to invest his time and energy in care of those offspring, thus increasing their chance of survival.

Females with high levels of testosterone, on the other hand, would have less evolutionary success for several reasons. First, since they would tend to mate more frequently and with a wider variety of males, they would be less selective in choosing their sexual partners, and more likely to become pregnant by an inappropriate male—one who was genetically less desirable, less capable of caring for offspring, or one who had no desire to care for any offspring.

Second, such females would be less desirable as mates to males, because males would be less likely to invest themselves in supporting and raising offspring with a female who was likely to be seeking out other sexual partners.

On the other hand, powerful sexual desire has clear reproductive advantages for males: Those males capable of being aroused quickly and frequently by females will be more likely to seek out sexual partners and be more capable of taking advantage of those mating opportunities that arise than will males with little or no sexual desire. As we have seen, testosterone level is strongly related to experienced sexual desire. Testosterone is essential for male sexual arousal, and higher levels of testosterone seem to produce males who are more easily aroused and arousable, and more likely to engage in sexual activities. So, in evolutionary terms, males with relatively high levels of this biochemical would tend to be selected for.

Yet we can speculate that males whose levels of sexual desire are too high could in some ways sabotage their own reproductive success: Since males must compete with each other for sexual access to females, those with extremely strong sex drives would be more likely to become involved in competition and potentially harmful or fatal conflict with other males, and would have such conflicts more frequently than would males with more controllable sexual desires. Also, males who were compelled to spread their seed widely and had little ability to control their sexual activities would be bound to find themselves in dangerous situations if and when they were caught having sex with the partners of other males.

Such dangerously high testosterone males are also dangerous to females and to society. For example, researchers at Clarke Institute of Psychiatry and Mt. Sinai Hospital, both in Toronto, measured hormone levels of twenty men convicted of rape or attempted rape and of twenty nonrapists. They found much higher levels of a precursor to testosterone among the sexually aggressive men. The scientists noted that "there may be a biological basis" to "sexually aggressive behavior."

Finally, such highly promiscuous males would be less likely to form pair-bonds or to invest time and energy in insuring the survival of their individual offspring. Thus, their offspring, and their high-testosterone genes, would have less chance of surviving than would the offspring of males with sufficient but not excessive levels of testosterone.

Since levels of testosterone are genetically determined, or heritable, and since testosterone is the biological substrate of the sex drive, it's logical to assume that the strength of the sex drive is heritable. Evidence that this is so has been provided by University of London psychologist Hans J. Eysenck, who tested a group of several generations of subjects to determine the strength of their sex drive and their age at first sexual intercourse. He found that these two characteristics were directly related and, most important, were passed on from generation to generation.

WHO'S GOT THE DIAMONDS, WHO'S GOT THE GOLD?

Sex, for both males and females, is the key to reproductive success. It is, like food and water, a natural resource. Without sex, as without water or food, the genes do not survive. Natural resources have value, and they become more valuable as they become scarcer. Groups or individuals who possess or control scarce natural resources such as food and water thereby have *power* over those seeking access to those resources, power that they can exercise in many ways, such as by demanding that the seekers pay or exchange other valuable resources, perform labor, or submit to other demands, such as following certain rules of conduct.

Of course, if the demands are too onerous, or if the need of those seeking access to the resources is too strong, the seekers can resort to another kind of power: the strength of arms. The history books are full of tales of wars, revolutions, uprisings, and competition among individuals, classes, clans, tribes, and nations about control over water rights, access to and control over fertile land, and over what those things represent: food, jobs, wealth, survival.

As an essential resource, sex represents power: the power to reproduce, to project one's genes into future generations. Since it is advantageous in evolutionary terms for males to produce as many offspring as possible, then for males, sexual access to fertile females is a source of power. And we have noted that among primates and humans dominant males have sexual access to disproportionate numbers of females, with some males maintaining large harems.

As we saw earlier, ethnographic surveys indicate that the vast majority of societies practice polygyny. Ethnographic surveys examining the practice of exchanging goods or services at marriage reveal that in the majority of societies, the male or his family gave goods and services to the female's family, while societies in which the female's family gave gifts to the male's family were exceedingly rare. As biological anthropologist Melvin Konner observes, "These data seem to suggest strongly that in most human matchmaking females are the scarce resource being competed and often paid for."

Social psychologist John DeLamater of the University of Wisconsin, Madison, has surveyed a vast amount of research and concludes, "Men initiate sexual behavior and women control it. . . . Thus, men possess and exercise proactive power and women possess and exercise reactive power in heterosexual relationships."

Whatever other cultural significances it may have, then, sex equals power. Like water rights, land, diamonds, or gold, it enables its possessor or controller to exercise power over others. And recent research indicates that even among the most "liberated" groups, sex remains something that males try to "get" and that females choose to "give." In every act of sex or sexual "conquest," a male is not only gaining the opportunity to exercise his power to reproduce, to propagate his genes, but is also demonstrating to himself and others his own powers or relative dominance in the social order and his dominance over other males who were in competition with him for the female.

Females, as the source of reproduction itself, possess within themselves the power that is so highly valued. It is in their selectiveness, their refusal to engage in indiscriminate sex, that they maintain and exercise it.

Thus, every aspect of sex is weighted with power. From the male's courtship of the female, which may involve giving gifts or otherwise displaying his own social dominance, to his more or less seductive attempts to persuade the female to have sex with him, he is exercising and seeking power. If he can persuade the female to give in to his advances, then he has succeeded in taking away from her some of her power over him, the power to deny him sex.

If the female has been extremely selective, that is, is a virgin, or has been (or is being) sought after by many men and has refused them sexual access, then the sex she possesses is scarce, its value is higher, and the power the male gains in the conquest is far greater than with a female known to be unselective and promiscuous in her choice of mates. And far greater is the power he gains over the other males who have been suitors—he has proven dominant where they were rejected.

To some degree, the more selective the female is, the greater is her power. And yet if she is too selective, if her standards are so impossibly high that the male has no hope of ever gaining her assent, then the male will be off in search of other potential partners. And so every aspect of the sexual mating dance, from the first coyly flirtatious glance to the sexual act itself, is part of a complex series of negotiations about power: social power, power over another individual, and, ultimately, the power to produce life, to extend one's own genetic self into the future. Beneath the surface of urgent desire, under the hearts and flowers of romance and sentimentality, lies raw politics, a struggle for survival, and, ultimately, in a very real sense, the power to survive death.

The power that both sexes bring to the negotiating table seems linked in part to the action of the same biochemical testosterone, and to the different levels of this hormone in their systems. A biochemical difference between the sexes has, the evidence strongly suggests, led men and women to different strategies for exercising power, and a clash of those strategies has contributed to what has been called the longest war—the one between the sexes.

Some feminists, confronted with this evidence, have rejected it, believing that the proactive power of males, their tendency to seek sex more actively, places them at an advantage over females. Other feminists, including anthropologists such as Sarah Blaffer Hrdy, have concluded that in fact the balance of power is weighted more heavily to females. After all, they point out, it is the females who make the ultimate choice of who their sex partners will be, who hold the power to decide which males will be chosen to project their genes into future generations. The females control the means of reproduction, and the males, no matter how actively they seek sex, must first pass the tests administered by the females. They must submit to being part of what is, in the words of anthropologist Irven DeVore, "a vast breeding experiment run by females."

TESTOSTERONE AND AGGRESSION

In the late 1970's June Reinisch, a young developmental psychobiologist at Rutgers, discovered that prenatal exposure to progestins—male hormones closely related to testosterone—exercised a powerful influence on whether children would respond to conflict with physical aggression. Reinisch had carefully set up the study to eliminate any possible sources of bias: Half the children had been exposed to the male hormones, while the other subjects were their brothers and sisters of the same sex who had not been exposed. The testers were not allowed to know which children had been exposed to the male hormones and which had not. In appearance, the children who had been exposed were no different from those who had not. Their mothers had forgotten or had never known they had been given the hormones—most of them believed they had been given vitamins. When Reinisch analyzed the findings, she said, "The results were so shocking that I actually sat on them for a year." In fact, she admits, "I was almost afraid to publish them."

For a year she analyzed and reanalyzed her data, submitting them to the scrutiny of respected colleagues, before she submitted her results for publication. "You don't expect effects like that," said Reinisch, who is now the director of the Kinsey Institute for Research in Sex, Gender, and Reproduction at Indiana University. "You expect delicate little effects that you need fancy-schmantzy statistics to bring out. Not this time. The simplest tests were all we needed."

The reason for her trepidation was simple: Her study revealed a clear biological basis for aggression. To the social scientific and academic establishment, such an idea was pure heresy. At that time the accepted truth of the cultural–determinist mainstream was that stated most clearly by behavioral genetics researcher John Paul Scott: "All research findings point to the fact that there is no physiological evidence of any internal need or spontaneous drive for fighting; that all stimulation for aggression eventually comes from forces present in the external environment."

Reinisch's findings proved this false. She discovered that boys who had been exposed prenatally to the testosteronelike hormone were *more than twice as likely* as their unexposed brothers to choose physical aggression in response to typical childhood conflicts, such as arguments over a game. Girls who had been exposed were also far more likely to choose aggression than were their unexposed sisters.

Her findings not only contradicted the accepted doctrine that aggression was purely a result of conditioning, but they also overthrew a second, fiercely held belief of the cultural-determinist mainstream, that humans are born free of hard-wired sexual differences, that differences between the sexes are confined to the anatomy, that differences in psychology and behavior—such as differing levels of aggression—are solely the result of conditioning or environmental influences. Reinisch found that those males who had not been exposed to the male hormone before birth still had mean physical-aggression scores higher than those of the females who *had* been exposed. The exposed boys had a mean physical aggression score of 9.75, the unexposed brothers had a mean score of 4.88; the exposed girls had a mean score of 4.0, while their unexposed sisters had a mean score of 2.6.

The evidence was clear: While both the males and females exposed to the male hormone before birth had higher levels of aggression than did their unexposed siblings, the innate differences between the sexes were even greater. On average, the *least* aggressive boys were still significantly more aggressive than the *most* aggressive "masculinized" girls.

Evidence of the influence of male hormones like testosterone on aggression and on the biological differences in levels of aggression between the sexes had been steadily accumulating for years. In 1974 the highly respected psychologist Eleanor Maccoby and her Stanford University associate Carol Jacklin published a classic work, *The Psychology of Sex Differences*. They found that the most overwhelming evidence for innate differences between the sexes was in the area of aggressive behavior: Boys were more aggressive than girls in virtually every culture studied and in specific measures of hitting, kicking, verbal aggression, hostility. This higher aggressiveness of boys carried over even into dreams and fantasies.

Other cross-cultural studies, such as the Beatrice and John Whiting six-cultures study, also show greater aggressive behavior among boys and men. In every culture there is murder, and in every culture most murderers are men. In one sample of 122 distinct societies around the world, men were the weapon-makers in all of them. As Melvin Konner observes in his examination of aggressiveness, "What we are dealing with, to be sure, is a difference in degree, but one so large that it may as well be qualitative. Men are more violent than women. . . . This is not to say anything, yet, about capacity; it is merely a statement of plain, observable fact: men are more violent than women and women are more nurturant, at least toward infants and children, than men. I am sorry if this is a cliche; that cannot make it less factual."

Cultural determinists insist that male aggressive behavior is the result of some sort of universal sex-role training rather than biology. Such a position is hard to defend, however, after studies, such as the research by Annelise Korner, showing that even newborn male infants, who cannot yet have been exposed to sex-role training, show greater aggressiveness. An experiment with rhesus monkeys—good experimental subjects because of their close similarities to humans— casts more light on the relative unimportance of sex-role training to aggression. Both male and female monkeys were raised in complete social isolation, with no opportunity to identify with the parent or any other monkeys of the same sex. When the monkeys were about three (corresponding to a human age of about ten years old), they were placed in a room with a rhesus infant. The scientists discovered dramatic sexual differences: Female juveniles took care of the infant more, and the males hit the infant more.

But the real death blow to the views of the cultural determinists comes not from observations of behavior patterns and not from psychological or anthropological studies, but from the studies of the relationship between biochemistry and behavior. Scientists have known for many years that injections of testosterone administered to female rats could cause them to become more aggressive; that castration of male rats reduces their aggressiveness, and testosterone restores it. Similar connections between testosterone and aggressiveness have been found in many animals, including apes and monkeys.

And humans. Among the many studies involving human levels of testosterone and aggression is that of L. Kreuz and R. Rose, whose investigation of male prison inmates revealed a direct correlation between adult testosterone levels and age of first arrest. Those with the highest levels had been arrested at the earliest ages. Another study of convicts revealed that those who were socially dominant and those who were chronically aggressive both had significantly higher levels of testosterone than did the convicts who were neither dominant nor aggressive. A study of testosterone levels among male juvenile delinquents showed that higher levels were linked to higher levels of observed aggressive behavior. Scientists have also found that juvenile boys who are administered testosterone become more aggressive. Another study revealed that hockey players who are more aggressive in response to perceived threats have higher levels of testosterone.

Since testosterone is an anabolic steroid, high levels of it can help stimulate muscle size and strength, but a side effect, widely known among athletes, is that steroids also increase aggressiveness. In a recent murder case the defense lawyer of a bodybuilder accused of brutally torturing and beating to death another man based an insanity plea on the fact that the bodybuilder's heavy use of steroids had turned him into a "seething volcano" of violence. And the lawyer produced a number of scientists to support his claim that the steroids had turned the body builder into "a powder keg."

Says neuroscientist Candace Pert, "Each sex has to grapple with its own hard-wired programming. . . . Women don't realize how much men have to struggle to control themselves. In their early teens, when testosterone starts to surge, young men feel angry. There is now a proven connection between violent behavior and elevated testosterone levels. A Y chromosome [i.e. being a male] is a real cross to bear. It's a predisposition toward angry, violent, competitive, macho behavior."

Levels of testosterone in human females have been found to influence their aggressiveness also. Perhaps the most impressive evidence of this has come from the work of Anke Ehrhardt of the Columbia College of Physicians and Surgeons and New York State Psychiatric Institute. Ehrhardt and her colleagues spent years studying women suffering from adrenogenital syndrome, a genetic defect that causes them to produce abnormally high levels of testosterone while they are still in the womb. This defect can be surgically corrected soon after birth, and hormone levels normalized with cortisone-replace-ment treatment, but no matter how soon after birth the condition is corrected, the females will differ from normal females both psychologically and behaviorally.

Females exposed to high levels of testosterone before birth, Ehrhardt discovered, are described by themselves, their parents, and their peers as significantly more "tomboyish" than normal females. They are highly energetic, choose boys rather than girls as playmates, and are much more likely than their female peers to be athletic and to participate in rough-and-tumble play and competitive team sports requiring aggressive behavior.

BRIDGING THE GAP BETWEEN INTENTION AND REALITY

To reproduce, males must not only be sexually attracted to females and desire to have sex with them, they must actually succeed in having sex with them. And in this regard, as all males quickly and painfully learn, there is a yawning gap between intention and reality. From the male's point of view there simply aren't enough females to go around, and so a male must compete for sexual success with other sexually seeking males. In many species this involves vicious battles between males.

It makes sense, in evolutionary terms, that the same biological factors that would cause males to seek sex—sexual desire and arousal—would also provide them with the capacity to attain sex— the capacity to compete, physically, if necessary, with other males for access to females. Since such competition can be dangerous, we would expect that the biological factor involved in seeking sex and in aggression would also be linked with danger and fear, or what scientists have called the "fight or flight" response. There is much evidence that testosterone is involved in that response. As Jo Durden-Smith and Diane deSimone point out, "It makes sense that the sex drive, aggression and testosterone should come together in men, along with intensity, quick reaction and visual-spatial skill, in one evolutionary package. For males in nature often have to fight to mate. And the hominid males from whom we are descended had, above all, to hunt, if they were to guarantee the success of their genetic investment—their offspring. For this they needed precisely the qualities that testosterone . . . seems to bring together in one bundle."

There's no doubt that, in Melvin Konner's words, "males have evolved a system in which aggressive and sexual tendencies are compatible if not mutually enhancing." The evidence is so strong that behavioral endocrinologists Bruce Svare and Craig Kinsley are led to exclaim, "Indeed, after literally thousands of research articles on the topic, it can be said quite definitively that dimorphisms in sex and aggression follow the same basic rules." In many species of birds and mammals, Konner points out, "male gestures of courtship and sexual invitation are similar or identical to those of . . . threat and dominance. . . . There is also evidence that some of the same conditions that might be expected to elicit fighting behavior can elicit male sexual behavior. For example, painful electric shock to a male rat will cause him to fight if he is in the presence of another male, but will enhance his sexual activity if he is in the presence of a female. Considering the many situations in nature in which males have to fight for the sex they want, this association is not surprising." According to psychologist Bernie Zilbergeld, author of *Male Sexuality*, the physiological signs of both anger and sexual arousal are almost identical, and it doesn't take much to transform one urge into the other. "It's as if," he says, "the body were saying, 'Am I fighting or mating?' "

SEX AND DOMINANCE

For males, the scientific evidence is clear, social dominance is closely related to sexual dominance; while their manifestations seem different, they are, biologically speaking, identical.

In an attempt to study the relationship between dominance and testosterone in humans, scientists tested male tennis players. The competitors were told that they would be rewarded with a hundred-dollar prize if they won their match. One hour after competition their testosterone was measured. In virtually every case the winners had elevated levels of testosterone while the losers showed reductions in their levels of the hormone. In a study of the members of a Harvard wrestling team, all the competitors produced elevated levels of testosterone during the match, but the winners exhibited greater elevations than did the losers, and those who wrestled to draws had levels of testosterone midway between the losers and the winners.

In other interesting studies relating dominance or status to testosterone, males receiving their medical degrees had elevations in testosterone within one day of the graduating ceremony. On the other hand, a study of young recruits during basic training showed clear reductions in testosterone.

For males, the sexual value of dominance is clear. In one study, scientists had subjects rate the sexual attractiveness of both males and females who exhibited nonverbal expressions of social dominance. The experimenters found that such dominance signs enormously enhanced the sexual attractiveness of a male being judged by a female, but social dominance signs exhibited by females had no effect on the ratings given them by males. A wealth of studies of this sort leave no doubt of the evolutionary value to males of being dominant: Simply stated, females prefer dominant males. As Henry Kissinger noted, "Power is the ultimate aphrodisiac."

Still, it's clear that too much testosterone can be as fatal for a male's genetic survival as too little. Studies linking high testosterone with violent criminals and other antisocial behavior provide evidence of how the simple *capacity* for aggression, the preference for dominance, can, propelled by too much testosterone, lead males into self-destructive behavior. Men who love war too much do not survive to reproduce, and males who spend their reproductive years behind bars are not winners in the reproductive sweepstakes.

Furthermore, highly or uncontrollably aggressive males are simply too dangerous for societies to have around. There is evidence that females are not sexually receptive to males who are too aggressive, since they threaten the females' own safety and reproductive success. Often it is the other males who, for their own safety and reproductive futures, will band together to weed out these berserkers.

UCLA psychiatrist Michael McGuire has spent some fifteen years studying patterns of behavior among monkeys, and points out an intriguing dynamic between violence and dominance. The dominant male monkey, he points out, is not "a big bully who pushes everybody around. He's just the opposite, really. It's the subordinate males who are nasty and grumpy; when a male becomes dominant, all of a sudden he becomes benevolent, sweet. He sits with the females and grooms them. . . . He's less aggressive when he's dominant. The fight is to get there, but once you're established and everybody acknowledges your power, you keep the peace."

The dominant male, McGuire points out, "does what he wants," and has "access to any resources, including the females." And yet, "If you watch closely, you see that the females select [a subordinate] male that they groom with. . . . Within two weeks the male favored by the females will be dominant. Now, do the females know something we don't know?"

The aggressive, "proactive" power is essential for a male's reproductive success, but it is constantly confronted with the female power, the power to attract and to select.

13

Land of the Free and Home of the Thrill-Seekers

. . . .

. . . something inside of me kept saying, There was the Sunday-school, you coulda gone to it; and if you'd a done it they'd a learnt you there that people that acts as I'd been acting about that nigger goes to the everlasting fire. . . .

I studied a minute, sort of holding my breath, and then says to myself: "All right, then, I'll go to Hell." . . . It was awful thoughts and awful words, but they was said. And I let them stay said; and never thought no more about reforming. I shoved the whole thing out of my head, and said I would take up wickedness again, which was in my line, being brung up to it, and the other warn't.

—*Mark Twain*, Huckleberry Finn

In exploring the nature of the links between biochemistry and such behavioral characteristics as sex drive, aggression, and dominance, we should be aware that, insofar as they are products of biology, they are heritable. Intriguingly psychologists are now synthesizing a wealth of research into personality and behavior, and are discovering that sex drive and aggressiveness are just components of a larger, interlinked network of behavioral characteristics—including social dominance, emotional volatility, and propensity for risk-taking—with strong genetic components.

BIG T AND LITTLE T

The key to this cluster of behavioral characteristics seems to be how individuals respond to or seek out stimulation. If we see the need for stimulation, or what psychologist Marvin Zuckerman calls "sensation seeking," as constituting a spectrum, then we quickly notice that certain individuals have very high needs for it, while others at the other end of the spectrum have very low desires for it. At the high end of the spectrum are those individuals who Frank Farley, a psychologist at the University of Wisconsin, Madison, has dubbed "Type T personalities," or "Big T's," with the T standing for both *thrill-seeking* and *testosterone*, since, Farley notes, a number of studies have shown "that men who are high in stimulation-seeking also have rather high testosterone levels." Correspondingly, at the other end of the scale are what Farley calls "Type t personalities" or "Little t's."

Says Farley, "I must emphasize that thrill seekers aren't stress seekers. I've spoken to many world-class adventurers—balloonists, sky-divers, rock climbers, round-the-world sailors—and I get the impression they're seeking fun, excitement, challenge and risk, but not stress. Sigmund Freud would have said these people have a death wish, but the opposite is true: They have a powerful *life* wish."

In Farley's words, "Big T's, as a group, tend to be more creative and more extroverted, take more risks, have more experimental artistic preferences and prefer more variety in their sex lives than do Little t's." For men, according to Farley, "the Type T personality is associated with strong sex drive and sexual interest. Type T men also are very confident of their sex roles. For women, the Type T personality is associated with a lack of sexual repression." Big-T men and women "report more partners and more variety in heterosexual activities than do Little t people. Big T's also seem to have greater interest in erotic material of many types, including pornography. . . . In a sample of never-married, heterosexual, young college men and women, matched on age and year in school, the greatest sexual satisfaction was usually reported by Big T men who primarily seek mental stimulation and by Big T women who seek physical and mental stimulation in about equal parts."

In addition, as we would expect, Big T's are far more aggressive than Little t's, and more dominant personalities as well. Big T's, Farley has found, "are risk-takers and adventurers who seek excitement and stimulation wherever they can find or create it. . . . I believe

that thrill-seeking can lead some Type T's to outstanding creativity
. . . but it can lead others to extremely destructive, even criminal,
behavior."

Farley cites studies showing that among adolescents both creativity
and delinquence are linked to Type-T personalities, with the socio-
economic status of the youths largely determining how the Type-T
characteristics will be expressed: "We found that creativity but not
delinquency was significantly predicted in the higher social group and
delinquency but not creativity in the lower social group."

Other studies have shown that stimulation-seeking and risk-taking
Big-T people have higher levels of such self-destructive behaviors as
alcoholism and smoking, and have almost twice as many driving
accidents as Little-t people.

The Little-t personality, on the other hand, is "someone who clings
to certainty and predictability, avoiding risks and the unfamiliar,"
according to Farley. "Such people are usually neither criminal nor
creative—they're gray compared with the bold red of the Type T
personality." As for dominance, Farley and others have noted that
virtually all political figures—indeed, virtually all public figures—are
Big T's, while, notes Farley, "People at the opposite end of the
personality spectrum (Type t or Little t) are rarely public figures." It
is for this reason Farley has focused his studies on Big-T personalities,
"because I believe these are the people who are likely to have enormous impact on our society's character—for good and ill."

Who are Big T's? "First," notes Farley, "it's more likely to be a
man than a woman." Farley's studies show that men usually score
higher on Type-T measures than do women. Many other studies
of sensation seeking, aggressiveness, and resistance to authority,
consistently show males higher in Big-T characteristics. Studies of
risk-taking, for example, ranging from game-players to Wall Street
investors, reveal that boys and men are significantly more willing to
take risks than girls and women. Since testosterone levels are linked
to Type-T behavior, the predominance of males makes sense.

"Second," Farley continues, "it's likely to be a young person."
Levels of testosterone are at their highest during the same years Farley
has found the strongest expression of Type-T behavior: late teens to
early twenties, with a decline into old age. It should also be noted
that the overwhelming majority of all crimes are committed by
people—usually males—in that age group. Farley points out, "We
have found juvenile delinquents to be much more Type T than non-

delinquents matched on age, gender, race and social class." When Farley and his associates tested female delinquents in prison, they found that "being a Type T person was significantly related to fighting, disobeying supervisors and attempting to escape."

Another characteristic of Big T's is higher creativity and a style of thought Farley calls "transmutative thinking," that is, "they are exceptionally facile at shifting from one cognitive process to another and at transforming one mode of mental representation into another. They may move with greater ease from the abstract to the concrete and back compared with Little t's. . . . Their tendency to seek the novel, unknown and uncertain, combined with their risk-taking characteristic, further enhances their likelihood of being creative. Conversely, Little t's, who usually don't have this cognitive style and avoid uncertainty, novelty and risk-taking, are unlikely to be highly creative."

THE GENETICS OF THRILLS

When the University of Minnesota researchers monitored their 350 pairs of twins, many of them separated soon after birth and reared by different families, they noted not only how important genetic factors were in determining personality traits, but that the trait the researchers found to be most strongly controlled by genes is the one they call "social potency." A person high in this trait is forceful, persuasive, masterful, likes to take charge and to be not only a leader but the center of attention. A second trait strongly under genetic control is emotionality—both positive and negative. A person high in positive emotionality is ready to feel optimism, while one high in negative emotionality is ready to feel anxiety and anger. Such people are emotionally volatile, with hair-trigger emotions.

A third trait that the statistics show is much more genetically than environmentally controlled is what the researchers call "absorption." A person high in this trait tends to think visually, has a vivid imagination, and easily becomes completely wrapped up in a task, aesthetic experience, or mental world.

A fourth trait with a large amount of genetic influence is aggression. A person high in this trait is physically aggressive, enjoys violence or conflict, has a taste for risk, danger, and excitement.

Clearly this cluster of largely inherited traits is similar to that we've been discussing as Big-T personalities: individuals who are aggressive, thrill-seeking, skilled at absorbed or "transmutative thinking," and with a need for dominance.

The findings from the University of Minnesota scientists revealed a second cluster of personality traits strongly determined or influenced by heredity. The most highly heritable trait in this cluster, as strongly genetic as the social potency of the first cluster, is "traditionalism." A person high in this trait is a conformist, respecting authority, following the rules, obedient, prudish.

A second trait in this cluster is "risk avoidance." People high in this trait are cautious, avoiding risks and dangers, willing to take a safe route even if that is more difficult or longer, shunning excitement and gravitating toward safe activities.

Clearly this cluster of hereditary traits is similar to what we have been calling the Little-t personality.

Not only are these personality characteristics heritable, but they appear to be powerfully resistant to change over the life span of an individual. In a recent study some ten thousand people ranging in age from twenty-five to seventy-four were followed for nine years and given periodic personality tests; in another study, three hundred couples were tested first back in 1935, and retested several times over the next fifty years. These and other studies have revealed that three basic aspects of an individual personality remain extremely stable throughout life: emotional volatility or anxiety, friendliness, and an eagerness for stimulation or novel experiences. Big T's and Little t's, it seems, are not only born that way, they tend to stay that way.

BIG T'S AND LITTLE T'S TOGETHER

Most of us, of course, are neither Big T's nor Little t's, but fall somewhere between the two extremes, neither as driven for risk and excitement as Big T's nor as dependent on certainty, clarity, rigidity, conformity, and safety as Little t's. Most of us will have inherited a mixture of these components, perhaps combining a taste for risk-taking, for example, with a strong sense of traditionalism. But the fact remains that, at least along the sex-power nexus, these two personality types represent opposite poles, to a very large degree influenced by heredity.

For a species like our relatively weak and defenseless but large-brained protohominid ancestors to survive and flourish, it would have been extremely valuable and perhaps necessary for each group to have a number of Big-T individuals. Their high levels of energy, creativity, and aggressiveness and their willingness to take risks and venture into the unknown would have benefited the entire group in situations such as hunting dangerous game, finding new sources of food and water, exploring new territories, defending the group in battles with other groups of protohominids, developing new weapons, tools, means of communicating with each other, and new ideas—ideas having to do with the importance of accumulating knowledge and wisdom through experience, and with the development of abstract concepts such as justice.

But those early protohominid bands would also have needed a number of individuals who avoided risk so they could remain at home to insure the stability of the group, individuals who were Little t's. With their distaste for conflict, and their preference for stability, structure, tradition, safety, cooperation, and respect for authority, they would have helped maintain order and relative peace within the band, and would have insured the transmission of certain types of knowledge and information through the creation and maintenance of traditions.

Big T's and Little t's would have functioned complementarily and cooperatively, giving the early human groups far more flexibility and a greater range of capabilities than groups made up of all one personality type. In fact, it may well be true that the social interactions necessary to maintain a band or group with sufficient structure, order, novelty, and resiliency to include within itself both Big T's and Little t's were a key to the flowering of a new type of protohominid grouping, something that could truly be called a culture.

MY COUNTRY, BIG T, OF THEE I SING

We can now begin to see how the sex-power nexus operates in a broader sociopolitical and sociohistorical context. We know humankind is made up of a variety of groups with clear genetic differences, ranging from size to skin color to facial features, and that these humans are scattered over the earth in a variety of groupings, from clan to tribe to nation.

Is it possible that some cultures or nations have traits or behavior patterns or "personalities" that are to some degree influenced by the genetic makeup of the people comprised by that culture or nation? What about, for example, the United States? Here we have a nation whose founders were men and women who refused to conform, who left behind what was thought to be civilization and set out at great risk to themselves on tiny wooden ships for a largely unknown, unexplored and "uncivilized" New World. Who with extraordinary energy set about exploring a mysterious and dangerous wilderness continent.

Just as a guess, one would say that these adventurers and their descendants were probably Big-T people. Certainly all the historical evidence would lead us to think so. From its inception, this nation has had a tendency to solve its problems through aggression and violence. The original settlers quickly concluded that the best way to handle the fact that the continent was already inhabited was to take the land away from those natives—historians have documented well the massacres and attacks on the Indians that began almost as soon as the settlers got off their boats.

Big T's are leaders and anti-authoritarians who do not like to be told what to do, and soon this nation's settlers decided to overthrow their government (controlled by more "civilized" and less Big-T bureaucrats from England) and did so not through diplomacy but through armed and extremely bloody revolution. Once their independence was secured, the Americans set about aggressively to push westward, continuing their eradication of the Indians. It was, they declared, their "manifest destiny" to control the entire continent, and so they launched into a war with Mexico, and forcefully took from that country virtually all of the southwestern United States.

Big T's do not find it easy to cooperate, and chafe under authority, and so the nation was divided into states and regions that tended to seek their own destiny. When these tendencies became too great, part of the nation sought its own independence, and the country was fragmented and convulsed by what historians believe was the most bloody civil war the world has known. When the wounds of that war had barely healed and the nation had become more secure in its own power, it undertook a series of aggressive wars all over the globe, uniting the nation with "glorious" exploits in tiny tropical places like the Philippines, Nicaragua, and Cuba (with Teddy Roosevelt becoming a national hero through his celebrated charge up San Juan Hill with the Rough Riders, and then as president formulating his excellent Big-T foreign policy—"Speak softly and carry a big stick").

Big-T foreign policy, expressed in such actions as the U.S. occupation of Nicaragua and installation of dictator Anastasio Somoza, its overthrow of the Guatemalan government in 1954, its attempted invasion of Cuba at the Bay of Pigs, and its invasion of the Dominican Republic, is still hugely in favor in this country, as shown by the extreme popularity of President Reagan's invasion of the island of Grenada, in which the big stick of U.S. military might was mobilized to overrun a tiny and virtually defenseless island said to be threatened by an evil communist menace.

The Cold War embodied the Big-T love of risk and aggression, mobilizing the passions of the American people in a sort of continuing high-noon showdown with the black-hatted Russian bad guys: Who would be the first to go for his gun, the ultimate big stick?

Big-T foreign policy is expressed in its most pure form by modern film heroes like Clint Eastwood's soft-speaking Dirty Harry, who sticks his .357 Magnum in the face of a psychopathic criminal (representing communism or some other hated foreign ideology) and whispers, "Make my day"; and by the equally tight-lipped Rambo, who splatters hordes of un-American creeps across the jungle with the big stick of his MAC-11 machine pistol.

Such paragons of Big T-ism are popular in large part because they are successful. But Big T foreign policy often matches its penchant for adventure and risk-taking with an extreme disregard for such Little-t virtues as caution and long-range planning, and thus we encounter such Big T's as those who blithely ignored warnings of impending disaster and sent in the marines to Beirut, "showing the flag," only to have hundreds of them blown up while sleeping; or Oliver North, valiantly carrying cakes to Iranian extremists and then selling arms to them and using the proceeds to buy arms for the Nicaraguan Contras (against the explicit law passed by the Little-t Congressional liberals), as well as supporting murderous cocaine dealers and assisting them in smuggling drugs into this country in a bold Big-T attempt to get more support for the Contras, who were themselves proving to be one of the most brutal groups of rapists, murderers, and torturers ever assembled in one small jungle.

The extraordinary popularity of violent, aggressive film heroes and the immense wave of popular support for Oliver North that arose during his testimony before Congress in the Iran-Contra hearings could give a visitor from another planet the impression that this nation had some extremely aggressive tendencies. And the statistics would support that impression. Against the four-hundred-year trend of declining personal violence in the Western world, which cultural historian Norbert Elias attributes to "the civilizing process," the United States stands out. Americans carry more guns, murder each other far more, and commit more violent crimes against each other than any other nation on earth.

MOVING WEST: THE BIOGEOGRAPHY OF T-ISM

Big-T personalities, as we know, are not only aggressive, but also restless, adventurous, eager for novelty, innovative, always ready to move into unknown territory. And again our nation's history seems to have been fueled by testosterone, with explorers, frontiersmen, gunslingers, cardsharps, prospectors, hungry entrepreneurs, and the whole horde of pioneers looking for a new life, new land, or simply something new, leaving behind the predictable, settled life of eastern towns and cities and moving west. Adding their energies to the westward movement after 1840 were successive waves of immigrants, Irish, Germans, Scandinavians, Italians. Immigrants are more often Big T's than those who remain in the old country. As University of Colorado political scientist Ted Robert Gurr points out in his study "Violence in America," each wave of immigrants "added disproportionately to crime and mayhem" in American life; "Many were rootless young men who indulged a penchant for drinking and street brawling."

We can assume from what we know about Big T's that life on the western frontier was violent, filled with risk-taking and stimulation-seeking, centered on the struggles of individuals rather than institutions. And the evidence historians of the Old West have been steadily accumulating from historical records indicates that this was indeed the case.

Since Big-T characteristics are heritable, we can also surmise that the modern American West is still more Big T than the East. And a recent study has shown this to be true. Using the latest census statistics and other evidence, sociologists and demographers have been able to focus on those areas of the West that are still based on traditional western modes of life: ranching, farming, mining, logging, small cities and towns, plains, desert, wilderness. They have found that these areas, which still include much of the land west of Kansas, and many of whose inhabitants are descendants of nineteenth-century westward-bound Big T's, remain as volatile, dangerous, and Big T as the Wild West of a century ago. Their statistics show, for example, that in comparison with the rest of the nation, people in these areas die at younger ages, are more likely to die of violence or misadventure, have higher levels of such self-destructive behaviors as smoking, drug abuse, and alcoholism, and have by far the highest rates of automobile accidents. At particular risk in this new Wild West are young males (whose testosterone levels are, of course, the highest).

But if America is indeed a Big-T nation, then its high rates of violence, crime, and aggressiveness should be balanced by the positive Big-T characteristics: We would expect it, to use Farley's definition, to be "enormously energetic and creative, with outstanding innovativeness in all domains." And it seems self-evident that America, with its trailblazing and energetic exploration of both the concept and the actuality of democracy and of human rights—particularly the novel belief in an "inalienable" human right to "liberty" or freedom—and in its extraordinary history of achievements in the arts and sciences, ranks very high among the nations of the world in those qualities. This creativity seems to be a by-product of the recalcitrant Big-T orneriness that America so admires. As writer James Fallows observes in his analysis of America's unique "talent for disorder," "Most of our national myths are about people who won't listen to others and end up doing what supposedly can't be done."

Interestingly the biogeography of T-ism we have been observing —the tendency of Big T's to move west—has also been documented in the realms of innovative thinking and doing what supposedly can't be done. California, for example, not only has more scientists than any other state in the union, it also has more Nobel Prize winners than all the other states combined (while the nation as a whole has more Nobel Prize winners than any other nation). Also, truly innovative thinking is often by definition viewed by the establishment as heresy (as Galileo's heliocentric view of the universe was condemned as heresy by the Catholic Church). With this in mind, Rodney Stark of the University of Washington undertook a survey of what he called "the geography of heresy." Using a wealth of demographic data, Stark found that most heretics live in the West. Among the facts Stark uncovered were that west of the Rockies there are more cults, more astrologers listed in the phone books of major cities, and a lower percentage of membership in the mainstream churches than in the rest of the country.

This makes perfect sense, since from the beginning the settlers of America were in a very real sense religious heretics. Edmund Burke said of early Americans that they were the products of "the dissidence of dissent and the Protestantism of the Protestants."

As philosopher-author Robert Anton Wilson points out, "Every heresy that left Europe produced newer, wilder heresies in the Eastern Seaboard, 1600–1800. Those that were 'too far out' had to move further West and produced the 1000 Utopian communities (anarchist, evangelical, free-love, etc.) that were attempted in the mid-West during the 19th Century. Those who were even further 'out'—out of the traditional mode—moved further Westward in the last 30–70 years."

Even in the realm of business, the Big-T mythos of the Wild West continues to transfix the nation. Once we mythologized the lone cowboy, seeing heroic virtues in the self-reliant man who could ride into a corrupt frontier town and risk his life to overcome the black-hatted villains. Today, the myth of the lone cowboy has been replaced by the myth of the lone entrepreneur, and we see heroic virtues in the individual who can push boldly into the unknown and succeed in turning risk into wealth. In the popular imagination, Shane has given way to H. Ross Perot, Billy the Kid to Donald Trump.

IN SEARCH OF DUSKY MAIDENS: SUBVERSIVE SEX AROUND THE CAMPFIRE

Many literary scholars have observed that the finest American writers have expressed what they have variously called rebellious, anarchistic, antinomian, romantic, transcendental, visionary, and erotic energies, with their heroes and heroines rebelling against tradition and cultural expectations, running away from home, going to war, going to sea, exploring the frontiers, seeking stimulation, adventure, risk, exposing themselves to danger in search of some intensely personal sense of satisfaction that can be gained not through fulfilling the culture's expectations or fitting into social roles but only through an individual fulfillment or through a personal redemption through decisive action, often violent and bloody. This "mainstream of American literature" we can now see is a mainstream of Big-T characteristics.

In their works (and often in their lives as well), these mainstream American authors have exemplified how Big-T characteristics, such as aggression, risk-taking, danger, violence, novelty, unpredictability, defiance of authority, and sublime creativity, are inseparably fused with sex. To think of great American fiction is to recall Nathaniel Hawthorne's dark tales of the dangers of sexual repression (as in *The Scarlet Letter, The House of Seven Gables,* and "Young Goodman Brown"), Poe's eerie erotic fantasies mingling blood and beauty, sex and death; Whitman's lusty singing out of the ecstasy of free sexuality and the beauties of the human body; Melville's vision of a sexual paradise where young American sailors can jump ship and make love with naked dark-skinned South Sea Island maidens in a dream of irrevocably lost sexual innocence; Hemingway's heroes, initiated into the ecstasies of free sexuality by sweet-smelling dusky Indian maidens, or discovering the fusion of sex and death as in *A Farewell to Arms,* or finding, like Jake Barnes, emasculated by a war wound, that without physical sexuality true creativity and productivity is impossible; Thomas Pynchon's vision of *V*, the eternal and mysterious female sexual power that emerges everywhere and in all times to shape history and define reality. And on and on.

Sex to these classic American writers was not a mere social or physical matter, not a means of "relating" with other people, of reproduction, or release of animal urgings, but rather an essential aspect of creativity, a key to the mysteries, a means of access or approach to that ineffable experience or knowing toward which the Big T seems driven—that ultimate transcendent connection that is at the root of all the stimulation-seeking and risk-taking. Often these writers have expressed their Gnostic sexuality in forms that did not have social approval or could even be called perverse.

In *Love and Death in the American Novel,* literary critic Leslie Fiedler revealed how much of America's great literature is founded on subversive and often homoerotic sexuality, telling of white males who flee respectability and the norms of society to find some deeper satisfaction in undergoing danger together with another male—often a male of another race, and therefore not a representative of the society being fled—and experiencing an indescribable but sexually tinged sense of safety and love with that other male. And so we have such scenes as Fenimore Cooper's intrepid Natty Bumppo with his noble Indian friends around a wilderness campfire, Melville's Ishmael sleeping with his arms wrapped around the Polynesian cannibal harpooner Queequeg, Huck and Jim at peace together on the raft floating down the Mississippi, Jack Kerouac's alter ego Sal Paradise riding joyously through the American night with his car-thief buddy Dean Moriarty at the wheel manically discoursing on love, death, sex, and the meaning of life, and Ken Kesey's hero McMurphy finding companionship in the insane asylum with the big Indian Chief Broom.

This homoerotic companionship beyond the boundaries of society continued to be the subtext of popular novels, films, and TV shows, from the smoldering "kemo sabe" connection between the Lone Ranger and Tonto to the intergalactic odd-couple chemistry of Commander Kirk and Spock, to the good-buddyism-to-the-death of Butch Cassidy and the Sundance Kid; and continues in the flood of recent films and TV shows, like *Lethal Weapon, Miami Vice,* and *Beverly Hills Cop,* portraying a black and a white male joined together as cops or private eyes or escaped convicts.

POWER TO THE PEOPLE: LITTLE T RULES

Big T's may be excellent individuals to explore a dangerous new land, but they are not well equipped to join together in harmony with each other and form a stable, peaceful society in that new land.

Little t's, on the other hand, are perfectly equipped to do just that: Their greatest goals in life are exactly those things Big T's abhor— predictability, low risk, clarity, rigidity, structure, affiliation, absence of conflict. They not only enjoy making rules, they enjoy following them. And so what appears to have happened in America is that the Big T's were temporarily forced to band together and create a revolution, after which they were forced to hammer together a revolutionary political and legal system—a system with a distinctly Big-T flavor, with great emphasis on individual liberties, personal freedoms, and with a carefully crafted system of checks and balances to insure that the government they were creating would remain unpredictable, ambiguous, flexible, intrinsically based on conflict, and thus free from tendencies toward centralization of authority.

After they had done that, like all Big T's, they broke apart and set out on their own adventurous searches for stimulation (some of which, of course, would involve energetically seeking power and dominance within that political system). Meanwhile, the Little t's took over the enterprise and began to run it.

14

THE FEMINIZATION OF
AMERICAN CULTURE

· ·

*Like lightning, she shoved her weapon over the banisters and into
the startled bearded face. Before he could even fumble at his belt,
she pulled the trigger. . . . The man crashed backwards to the
floor. . . . Scarlett ran down the stairs and stood over him,
gazing down into what was left of the face above the beard, a
bloody pit where the nose had been, glazing eyes burned with
powder. . . . Her eyes went to the stubby hairy hand on the floor
so close to the sewing box and suddenly she was vitally alive
again, vitally glad with a cool tigerish joy. She could have
ground her heel into the gaping wound which had been his nose
and taken sweet pleasure in the feel of his warm blood on her bare
feet. She had struck a blow for Tara—and for Ellen.*

—*Margaret Mitchell,* Gone With the Wind

"The Lord Himself wrote it!"

—*Harriet Beecher Stowe, describing* Uncle Tom's Cabin

It's clear that while many Big T's are men, many Little t's are
women. And while Big T's tend to exercise power and seek fulfillment as individuals, through mental or physical stimulation and risk-
taking, Little t's tend to exercise power and seek fulfillment through
cooperation with others, through allying themselves in structured
groups, through being part of something larger than themselves that

will offer them rules to follow, traditions to maintain, a sense of order.

One example of the sex differences in T-levels seen in American politics is the gaping "gender gap" noted in recent presidential elections. Polls showed that Ronald Reagan and George Bush had much greater support from male voters than from females, while Jimmy Carter, Walter Mondale, and Michael Dukakis drew far more of their votes from females than from males. Reagan and Bush both emphasized such Big-T issues as military might, rugged individualism, and the need to "kick ass," while their opponents represented many Little-t values, such as the need for arms control, and greater government support for such domestic issues as education, child care, and so on.

The dichotomy may shed some light on a phenomenon of American history noted by many historians and elucidated most straightforwardly by feminist historian Ann Douglas in her book *The Feminization of American Culture*. This is the fact that very rapidly after the Revolution and the establishment of the United States, the nation began to establish a distinctly American culture, and that the institutions, ideals, and leadership of this culture were determined by women (in alliance with the Protestant churches).

The alliance between women and church was a natural one. Women brought their men to church on Sunday (there's a wealth of evidence that throughout American history many men have attended church mainly because their wives have urged them to), and in doing so assured that the church would become the most important social institution. In cities and towns across America, one's social respectability or even acceptability became dependent upon and was maintained by weekly church attendance. And under the umbrella of the churches, the women of the community formed a variety of "women's groups" that allowed them the opportunity to join together for socializing and exercising power.

In return, the church offered American women a Protestant Christianity that emphasized not the hellfire-and-brimstone messages of the older Puritan ministers such as Cotton Mather and Jonathan Edwards, but a more social and Little-t message in which Jesus was a befriender and protector of little children, urging his followers to turn the other cheek, blessing the meek and mild, proclaiming that a soft answer turneth away wrath, and in general expecting good Christians to behave properly and respectably, maintaining order, following rules, respecting elders, protecting the weak, giving to the poor, taming any thirst for the pleasures of the flesh, and protecting the family. What the church did, that is, was provide an unshakable moral authority for a remarkably pure Little-t system of values.

Out of this alliance of women and the church came some of the most powerful movements of the nineteenth century, including abolitionism, temperance, early feminism, and a variety of social reform movements (including struggles against urban poverty, child labor, and prostitution). The Women's Christian Temperance Union, or WCTU, for example, was founded in 1874, and by the turn of the century had a membership of over one million women. Its founders came from church organizations like the Ladies' and Pastors' Christian Union, and emphasized the need for women to move "from prayers to politics." The WCTU helped form such groups as PTA and Travelers Aid, established some of the first day-care centers, and fought for women's rights and child labor laws. From its inception, the WCTU was in the forefront of the fight for prohibition. Often bands of WCTU members would go to local saloons, where they would kneel and pray to persuade tavern owners to curtail their business. Their moral and political power was so great that they ultimately succeeded in forcing the government to enact a constitutional amendment prohibiting liquor sales. The eighteenth amendment was enacted by Congress in 1920.

Women also became the arbiters, creators, and consumers of American secular "culture." To a large degree, this culture was transmitted through the written word. By the mid-nineteenth century the magazines with the highest circulations were women's magazines, like *Godey's Lady's Book*, and the best-selling authors of novels were women. Creators of classic Big-T fiction struggled to support themselves, turning out novels that were commercial flops (Melville's *Moby Dick*, for example, sold few copies, and eventually he was forced to support himself as a customs house inspector; Whitman published successive versions of his *Leaves of Grass* by himself in small editions and never gained wide readership; Hawthorne became a diplomat; Poe worked as an editor for women's magazines like *Godey's Lady's Book* and drank himself into an early grave). Meanwhile, year after year, Harriet Beecher Stowe, Lydia Sigourney, Fanny Fern (Sara Payson Willis), and other women turned out sentimental romances that topped the best-seller lists and sold extraordinary numbers of copies.

Very early on in American history, then, we can see the emergence of a conflict that has continued to this day. the genetically influenced, biological differences between Big T's and Little t's formulated itself as a conflict between, on the one hand, the proponents of "culture," morality, and social order, and, on the other hand, the "barbaric," "vulgar," seekers of stimulation. It was, and remains, a conflict between cultural establishments such as the church, the family, and "society," and individuals who thrive on the frontiers of life, both the actual frontier of the West and the other frontiers such as the skid rows, red-light districts, barrooms, barracks, boxing arenas, in the smoke-filled rooms of power politics, and in the wheeling and dealing of big business.

It is a conflict expressed most clearly in American fiction. In the Big-T fiction written by males, it emerges as a strong distaste for women and the things women represent.

No Good Men: The Defamiliarization of Masculinity

In classic women's novels, on the other hand, the authors describe in glowing terms the pleasures of domesticity, simplicity, structure, clarity, the values of friendship, love, family life, a network of complex and enduring relationships. Often the novels portray these as lost or destroyed, and generally the cause of the destruction is the aggressive, dangerous, wilful, evil, and, at root, childishly incomprehensible acts of males, who seem bent on disrupting all that is good by going off on absurd impulses—going to war, leaving wife and family for another woman, destroying themselves through drink, foolish financial dealings, gambling and other risky, self-destructive, and classically Big-T behavior.

In such novels the search for self-expansion or growth, fulfillment, or wisdom—the key to Big-T novels—is not seen as a search that must be undertaken through conflict, risk, adventure, into the unknown, but rather as a search in which growth must be experienced, the self ultimately found, in *relationships*. As psychologist Alexandra G. Kaplan of Wellesley College puts it, "For women, growth isn't equated with increasing proportions of separation, but with increasing the complexity of one's relational matrix—adding numbers of people, and greater depth, sophistication, and quality of relationship . . . a

big part of who you are as a woman is who you are with others."
So novels by women often are "celebrations" of relationships: of the
family, the primal bond between females (particularly between mothers and daughters), friends, community, romantic love—as well as
celebrations of vengeance against males who would disrupt the network of relationships.

Even when a heroine in these novels goes into the unknown, it is
often not with the exhilaration and sense of freedom of Big-T heroes,
but with dread, because she is cast out, carried away against her will
to distant foreign lands, as in Susan Warner's powerful *The Wide Wide
World*, a nineteenth-century novel recently "rediscovered" and highly
acclaimed by academic feminist literary critics. The novel tells the
story of a young woman orphaned and exiled to dour and unbearable
relatives in bleak Scotland, and is filled with a sense of lost home,
family, community, self.

It is as if in these women's novels we are seeing the heroes of the
classic Big-T novels through Little-t eyes, not as heroes but as villains,
creeps, dolts. In novels such as Alice Walker's *The Color Purple*, for
example, we re-vision Jim of *Huckleberry Finn*, and find him no longer
brave and noble. Quite the contrary, all the black males in Walker's
novel are seen as shiftless ne'er-do-wells, ignorant thugs, violent
woman-beaters, and moral cretins, while women bravely carry on,
lovingly, maintaining the family, the network of relationships, the
tradition, doing the real work.

Through the eyes of these writers we see Ishmael, Natty Bumppo,
Huck Finn, Hemingway's heroes, Kerouac's alter egos, not as spiritual
seekers but as posturing bullies, selfish children who refuse to grow
up, settle down, raise a family, become part of the community, and
learn to open up emotionally and communicate. The fact that males
seem unwilling to do this is the cause of one theme that seems to run
through many women's novels: resentment.

In *Terrorists and Novelists*, novelist and critic Diane Johnson writes,
"Men recount disillusion and depression, followed by recovery and
action," while "in writing, as in mourning, it sometimes appears that
women have reserved or been assigned the duty of expressing human
resentment, leaving men to fashion the consolations."

This tone of resentment in novels by women can arouse counter-
resentment in many of their male readers. As one male writer complained to me, "I can see a novel by a woman about Mary the mother
of Jesus. There goes young Jesus off to spend forty days and nights

agonizing in the wilderness while Mary shakes her head and commiserates with her sisters and friends and they're all saying, Well, what do you expect, he's a man! They're all just reckless little boys. Ah, but Mary says, when will he grow up and settle down? Why's he want to go do these crazy things?"

In part this mutual resentment springs from the ancient misperception we have discussed so often, the belief that men and women are in essence, or could be, or ideally *should* be the same: that there is a single human nature. In these novels we see women wondering why men can't be more like them, while men wonder why women can't be more like men. Throughout the 1960's and 1970's feminist literary critics and social scientists made it an article of faith that men and women were basically the same, that differences in psychology, behavior, such as those expressed in their fiction, were the result of role-training. In the last decade, however, as the accumulation of evidence has become overwhelming that there are clear biological sex differences, that there is a "female nature" that is different from "male nature," there has emerged a new understanding by feminists that they must clearly address these differences.

In literature, this has led to the flowering of "gynocriticism": academic feminist studies of women's literature as distinctly different from or Other than men's literature. As Princeton literary critic Elaine Showalter puts it, what is in progress is a "defamiliarization of masculinity," or a "poetics of the Other," in which women's literature can be approached not from the same critical perspectives as literature by men but in a way that values that literature for its distinct femaleness.

A DIFFERENT VOICE

A key to this movement has been the growing understanding that men and women operate on what are in essence different standards of morality—an insight made more credible and clear by the work of Harvard psychologist and professor of education Carole Gilligan in her acclaimed and influential 1982 book, *In a Different Voice: Psychological Theory and Women's Development*. Gilligan's research revealed that historically our culture has been working on the assumption that there is a single standard of morality, which could be defined as *the* moral perspective, a morality based on the abstract concept of justice.

This view defined the process of human moral development as one of increasing independence or separation from others (individuation or differentiation), with the goal of human growth being to attain the ability to recognize and respect universal rights. The most widely accepted measures of moral development, based on these theories, were devised by psychologist Lawrence Kohlberg. In study after study girls and women were found to lag far behind boys and men in attaining them.

But Gilligan contended that the reason for this sex difference was that males and females speak and operate morally in "different voices": that female moral values are "care-focused" rather than "justice-focused," that females place "an ethic of responsibility as the center of women's moral concern, anchoring the self in a world of relationships and giving rise to activities of care." The male "morality of rights," she observed, "differs from the morality of responsibility in its consideration of the individual rather than the relationship as primary."

Gilligan has pointed out that there is a biological basis for these differences, which "arise in a social context where factors of social status and power combine with reproductive biology." The influence of natural selection on the development of different moral "voices" by males and females can be understood when we remember that the evolutionary task of both males and females is to transmit copies of their genes to future generations, but that the strategies that are most likely to be successful for one sex are quite different from those of the other. In evolutionary terms, it is the task of boys to separate themselves, physically and emotionally, from their mother and to become another thing entirely, a man and a father. Girls, however, attain biological success when they model themselves after their mothers, orienting themselves within a network of relationships. In Gilligan's words, "Since masculinity is defined through separation while femininity is defined through attachment, male gender identity is threatened by intimacy while female gender identity is threatened by separation."

"Male success is typically achieved by effective competition; female success, by relationship, especially with their own offspring and other relatives," points out psychologist David Barash. "Thus, for boys and men, morality is at its most ideal and alluring when it is a morality of justice, of theoretical principles that place restraints upon aggressive, competitive, self-serving tendencies; for girls and women, on the other hand, morality is suffused with images of relationship, of caring, and of taking care of others. Male morality, as Gilligan describes it, is an ethic of *inhibiting* one's nasty self; female morality, in contrast, emphasizes *releasing* the caring self." Or, to return to the terms we've been using, male morality seems to consist to a large degree in restraining the potentially destructive Big-T aspects of the self (while still encouraging the constructive Big-T characteristics, such as the energetic, even risk-taking pursuit of direct experience of "higher" wisdom, i.e., justice, truth, freedom, God). Female morality, on the other hand, seems to consist to a large degree in expressing freely the constructive Little-t aspects of the self while discouraging potentially destructive Little-t characteristics (avoidance of risk, overreliance on structure, predictability, boredom, unthinking submission to authority).

To recognize these sex differences is not to claim that one sex is superior or inferior in its thinking or morality. But Gilligan's work initially received considerable criticism from some feminists who, according to Gilligan, "thought to talk about differences was to invite oppression."

THE HIERARCHY AND THE WEB: THE POLITICS OF THRILLS AND COMPASSION

Far from inviting oppression, Gilligan's ideas provide us with fresh evidence of the historical inevitability that women will continue to gain greater political power in the United States.

When we observe the history of the exercise of political power in the United States, it becomes evident that there has been a rapidly increasing trend toward interrelationship and interdependency among political institutions. This is a change that was not anticipated by the individuals who set up the political structures of this country some two hundred years ago. Built in to that Big-T political system was a tendency toward separation of powers and toward separateness in general: The federal government was divided into the executive, legislative, and judicial branches, each with its carefully parceled-out powers; the individual states maintained their own sovereignty, and had their own executive, legislative, and judicial bodies; within the states, various counties, cities, and towns had their own governing arms and political systems. The whole was set up as a hierarchy, with each level of the hierarchy jealously guarding its own powers, patrolling its own turf, so to speak. This structure allowed Big-T males (and they were almost always males) the opportunity to struggle to the "top" of one level of the hierarchy, where they could then exercise their dominance and retain their independence and individuality without feeling they were subservient to other Big-T politicians. County sheriffs and county commissioners, for example, while certainly not as powerful as a state governor or U. S. senator, could still exercise enormous power in their own localities—even today, there are still cases of sheriffs or county commissioners who, through their powers to appoint people to jobs, to award road building contracts, and so on, have secured themselves what amount to lifetime sinecures, where they rule like pocket dictators.

For those Big-T individuals with sufficient energy, ambition, desire for stimulation, appetite for conflict, and love of power, the leadership of one fiefdom could serve as a springboard for his attempt to jump up to higher levels in the hierarchy: from precinct captain to commissioner to mayor to governor to senator to president.

In recent decades, however, this hierarchy of separate parts has begun to break down. In part this is a result of the nation's growth —once separate towns have grown so large they have fused into an urban sprawl that may cover an entire county, or parts of two or three counties, or two or three states. Thus fiefdoms are now inextricably interlocked with other fiefdoms, as six or eight different police departments, several county sheriffs' departments, and the state police of several different states, for example, or a number of mayors, town councils, city commissions, county commissions, the port authority, and interstate advisory boards, must all function together in an attempt to govern or serve what is in effect one big city.

A second and more important reason for the breakdown of the Big-T hierarchy has been the explosive growth of information technology, including the proliferation of computers and the ascendance of television journalism. No longer are the political events in individual towns and cities of interest only to the residents of those towns and cities—political scandals, economic developments, strikes, new voter initiatives, fresh political faces and ideas, all are communicated instantly to the entire nation and become events of direct concern to the entire populace. A female fire fighter suspended for breast-feeding her baby on duty in Iowa City becomes overnight a rallying cause for feminists throughout the country; the uncovering of racism or corruption in the police department of one city gives impetus to antiracism and anticorruption movements in scores of cities; the confessed adultery or homosexuality of one congressman immediately brings the sexual proclivities of all politicians under popular scrutiny, and so on. And through the vast information-storage and communication capacities of corporate and governmental computer networks, information about individuals, economic trends, corporate finance, the workings of local governments immediately are available to all. The country is no longer a vast patchwork of separate fiefdoms but a single, though rather poorly woven, fabric.

Another, related reason for the breakdown of the Big-T political hierarchy is that as the nation has grown, so has the rest of the world grown, and our economy can no longer be seen as separate from the rest of the world but rather must be recognized as an interwoven element of an interdependent world economy: Developments in Japanese technology become of great importance to steelworkers in Pittsburgh, autoworkers in Detroit, electronics workers in San Jose and Boston, real estate developers in Honolulu. So those cities, and all of the towns, cities, counties, and states of America, are no longer politically autonomous, but are locked into a nationwide and worldwide network, and the politics of those cities are of importance to the entire nation. And the politicians are forced into a network of relatedness to a huge network

And because the media have made people so aware of this worldwide interrelatedness, people have realized that the traditional forms of relationships with foreign countries, in which the United States acted as an independent, powerful, monolithic nation, attempting to work its will, whether through diplomacy or military strength, upon other independent nations, can no longer work. The nations are inextricably bound up in each other's politics and economy.

Which leads to another truth made so evident by the media: the U.S. government can no longer pursue saber-rattling, aggressive, Big-T foreign policy unless it can convince the nation that there is an overriding reason for it to do so. When the national newsmagazines and network television news shows began showing color images of the war in Vietnam, and galleries of portraits of young American boys and men who had been killed in Vietnam that week, the war became not just a confusing skirmish in some isolated little jungle country but a matter of immediate personal knowledge and concern to all Americans. And they moved to put an end to that war. The same thing took place when the marine barracks was exploded in Lebanon. And it took place again when the media showed what was happening in the jungles of Honduras and Nicaragua, and people decided that there was no clear reason why our government should be funding what appeared to be murderous terrorists, and certainly no reason at all why American soldiers should become involved in what might turn into another Vietnam.

A final effect of the media explosion is that people have concluded from their own observation that nuclear war is not a viable option, that it is a threat to all life on this planet. Among other things, the unforgettable televised images of Americans fleeing for their lives from the nuclear accident at Three Mile Island, of Russians dying from nuclear poisoning in the aftermath of the Chernobyl disaster, of well-known authorities like Carl Sagan talking about the nuclear winter that would follow a nuclear war, have convinced masses of Americans that there would be no escaping a nuclear war.

One upshot of this transformation of American life is that the electorate is more willing both to participate themselves and to elect leaders or representatives who they feel are capable of working well in a network of power-sharing and interconnection. And because of the increased amount of information available to them through the media, they are better informed about the capabilities and personalities of the people who are seeking their votes. This means first of all that people are no longer so willing to unquestioningly support a candidate simply because of that person's Big-T characteristics: Charisma, high energy, an aura of power and dominance, fiery oratory, are still assets, but no longer prerequisites. And because people are better informed about the candidates, it is no longer so easy for the parties or local political machines to handpick a candidate and engineer his or her election.

It also means that politics has become a less attractive career choice for many Big-T personalities, since they are keenly aware that the very things that draw them into politics might be the things that destroy their career. Events like Watergate, the Iran-Contra scandal, Abscam (in which various congressmen were videotaped by the FBI in the act of accepting bribe money from bogus Arabs), the destruction of Gary Hart because of his apparent affair with a young model and of John Tower because of his alleged fondness for wine and women (as well as dozens of other local political scandals that have burst into the headlines since Watergate gave investigative journalism a good name and made it possible for journalists to write about aspects of politics and politicians that were formerly taboo), have demonstrated that politicians can come to harm for doing those very things that Big-T politicians have been doing ever since the nation was established: peddling influence, playing dirty tricks on each other, conducting secret missions, trying to overthrow foreign governments, and reaping the sexual benefits of the ultimate aphrodisiac, power.

All of which brings us back to Carole Gilligan's "different voices." She writes, "The images of hierarchy and web . . . convey different ways of structuring relationships and are associated with different views of morality and self . . . As the top of the hierarchy becomes the edge of the web and as the center of a network of connection becomes the middle of a hierarchical progression, each image marks as dangerous the place which the other defines as safe."

In the past, politics has been a game of hierarchies; but in recent years, as we have seen, it has become a web. It seems self-evident, then, that those who function most effectively within a web of relationships and responsibilities will play a larger role in the direct exercise of power within that web. What that means, I believe, is that women will continue to be elected into political offices in greater and greater numbers, and will continue to exercise more and more influence over who is elected into political offices. And the reason this will be so is not, as some feminists have asserted, *despite* their female natures but *because* of their female natures. As biological anthropologist Melvin Konner writes, it is "extremely difficult for an informed, objective observer to discard the hypothesis that the genders differ in their degree of violent behavior for reasons that are in part physiological." This being so, Konner concludes, "Then it seems to me that one policy implication is plausible: Serious disarmament may ultimately necessitate an increase in the proportion of women in government."

The violent records of past and present female rulers such as Indira Gandhi and Margaret Thatcher, and the violent notions of such modern Attilas as Jeane Kirkpatrick, have no real relevance here, since, in Konner's words, "Such women have invariably been embedded in and bound by an almost totally masculine power structure, and have gotten where they were by being unrepresentative of their gender. Some women are, of course, as violent as almost any man. But speaking of averages—central tendencies, as the statisticians call them—we can have little doubt that we would all be safer if the world's weapons systems were controlled by average women instead of by average men."

This does not mean, however, that Big-T personalities will disappear from leadership positions. For such personalities not only thrive on the exercise of power, they have unique capabilities that make them extremely valuable as leaders. As psychologist Frank Farley points out, "The Big T personality has less fear and anxiety relative to other people and would experience less stress in unavoidable crises. That enables them to keep their cool and make the right decision under pressure." In addition, as Farley's research has revealed, Big T's are highly creative, and, says Farley, "one major facet of creativity is embracing novelty and uncertainty. So they do well in unprecedented situations that require creative solutions." As long as we must face situations that require clearheaded action and decision-making under pressure and the ability to come up with creative solutions to unprecedented problems, it will be to our advantage to have Big-T individuals in positions of power. Just as long as they're not the only ones there.

PART III

THE

TRANSFORMATION

. . . .

Now I a fourfold vision see,
And a fourfold vision is given to me;
'Tis fourfold in my supreme delight
And threefold in soft Beulah's night
And twofold always. May God us keep
From Single vision & Newton's sleep!

—William Blake

You . . . You said,
"There are many truths,
but they are not parts of a truth."
Then the tree, at night, began to change . . .

It was when you said,
"The idols have seen lots of poverty,
Snakes and gold and lice,
But not the truth",

It was at that time, that the silence was largest
And longest, the night was roundest,
The fragrance of the autumn warmest,
Closest and strongest.

—Wallace Stevens, "On the Road Home"

15

FEAR OF SEX

· ·

What overwhelmed him in that instant was admiration for the gesture with which she had thrown her clothes aside. With its grace and carelessness it seemed to annihilate a whole culture, a whole system of thought, as though Big Brother and the Party and the Thought Police could all be swept into nothingness by a single splendid movement of the arm. . . . The Party was trying to kill the sex instinct, or, if it could not be killed, then to distort it and dirty it. . . . In the old days, he thought, a man looked at a girl's body and saw that it was desirable and that was the end of the story. But you could not have pure love or lust nowadays. No emotion was pure because everything was mixed up with fear and hatred. Their embrace had been a battle, the climax a victory. It was a blow struck against the Party. It was a political act.

—George Orwell, 1984

The society Orwell described is fictional. But when it comes to nonfictional societies, there is probably more "fear and hatred" mixed up with matters of sex in America today than in any other society or period in history. You could cite the sexual repression of Victorian England or late nineteenth-century Vienna, but those times were remarkably tame and reserved in comparison with today. This is a time, after all, when ordinarily law-abiding citizens have banded together to firebomb medical clinics that provide abortions, outlets for information about birth control, and bookstores that carry sexually oriented materials. A time when a Harvard biology professor is physically assaulted by other Harvard intellectuals and students in the midst of a public address, simply because his work deals with biological differences between the sexes. A time when writers of intellect can earnestly proclaim in best-selling books that all males, without exception, are rapists. A time when political leaders and theorists can arouse cheering multitudes by asserting that heterosexual sex is an act of war by men against women, that "coitus is punishment." A time when scientists and academics are fired, denied tenure, and denied publication in professional journals, simply because their work deals with sex differences. A time when large numbers of educated citizens are insisting that the freedom of expression guaranteed by the Constitution should be denied to those expressions having to do with sex. A time when individuals are relentlessly reminded that every act of sex outside of a long-term monogamous relationship might, because of AIDS, lead to their death.

This is the battleground, the blood-drenched patch of earth over which crazed and battered combatants struggle, howling in fear and hatred. It is the bitter fight we observed in Part I from our observers' perch in the tree. But then we climbed down from the tree and went off in search of facts, information that might cast some light on the origins of the war. Throughout Part II we explored some of the latest findings in the field of evolutionary biology.

We have come quite a distance, knocked on a lot of doors, stuck our heads into quite a few laboratories and scientists' offices and listened to what they have discovered about the sexual nature of domesticated primates (i.e., humans). Now, here we are, back at the sex-power nexus, and the battle is still raging. It seems like a good time to climb back up to our observation point in the tree and try to apply the insights we've gained from evolutionary biology to the battles we see taking place below. Why are these people fighting?

THE HERESY-HUNTING PARTY

Our first observation is that while they are fighting under a number of banners—End Abortion, No Sex Education, Reproductive Freedom, Ban Porn, Protect the First Amendment, Coitus Is Punishment, Defend the Family, All Males Are Rapists, Sex Is Fun—they fall into two opposing forces. One, an alliance of Christian fundamentalists, political and cultural conservatives, and antipornography radical feminists, is united in its desire to set strict limitations on sexual activities. The other, a patchwork, heterogeneous band, is not so much "pro-sex" as it is united around its support for freedom of expression, particularly as that freedom is protected by the Constitution.

We have already noted the seeming incongruity of the alliance between radical feminists and right-wing Christians. But now, when we focus on their psychological characteristics, we quickly see that whatever their surface differences, the individuals in these groups are in many ways psychologically identical. Not only do they share the same hostility toward most types of sex, but that hostility is a result of the same underlying conceptual structure.

There is evidence that both groups are erotophobic (defined by the Sexual Opinion Survey as "a persistent and general tendency to respond to sexual cues with negative emotions"). Erotophobics have been found to masturbate less, have fewer premarital sexual partners, react to erotic pictures more negatively, have less interest in viewing erotica, and be more likely to favor restricting erotic materials than are erotophilics.

There is also evidence that both erotophobic groups have high levels of sex guilt, defined by Mosher as "a personality disposition characterized by a generalized expectance of self-monitored punishment for violating or anticipating violating standards of proper sexual conduct." The phrase "standards of proper sexual conduct" is important, for it offers a key to the underlying authoritarian structure that unites these superficially different groups: They base their opposition on standards that have been established by a Higher Authority. For the right-wing Christians, that higher authority is God. For the radical feminists, the higher authority is the "truth" of feminism itself.

Both of these groups have had the truth revealed to them that sexual behavior is of two types: "normal" (or, as in the definition of sex guilt above, "proper") and "abnormal" (or "perverted," "evil," or "obscene"). Both groups are absolutely certain about what is normal or proper sex, and their beliefs are quite simple, clear, and rigid. For the Christian conservatives, normal sex is the sex that takes place between husband and wife. Those who are not married have but one sexual option: total abstinence. Anything else is sinful, sacrilege, evil. For the censorial feminists, normal sex is that which is "politically correct": initiated by women, controlled by women, and without the slightest hint of male dominance. Anything else is rape, according to Robin Morgan; and Andrea Dworkin asserts that "Coitus is punishment," and "Sexual relations between a man and a woman are politically acceptable only when the man has a limp penis."

These groups do not doubt that their truth is The Truth. All proponents of alternative truths are by definition purveyors of lies. As writer-philosopher Robert Anton Wilson points out, "This is the best rhetorical stance for a heresy-hunter, since it is rooted deeply in primate psychology. It is much easier to rile up a herd of primates by hollering 'That gang over there are sneaks, cheats and liars' than by the Liberal path of saying 'That gang has an honest difference of opinion with us.' Hitler pointed this out in *Mein Kampf,* every demagogue knows it." Thus, author Marilyn French: "All men are rapists and that's all they are."

These groups have no hesitation in attempting to impose their beliefs on everyone else on the planet—it is doing them a service, after all, to force them to see the truth. So when civil libertarians tell the antisex forces that if they do not approve of birth-control clinics they do not have to use them, that if they feel erotic materials are bad, they do not have to purchase them, and so on, they are not satisfied: They want to make sure that *no one else* can have access to them either. They're not worried about themselves being harmed by perverted sex, for they've seen the truth—it's everyone else who needs to be saved.

As we enumerate the psychological characteristics and underlying belief systems that unite these antisex groups, it becomes apparent that we are encountering a cluster of characteristics we have discussed earlier. Both in their beliefs and in their sex, these individuals demand stability, low risk, little variety, simplicity, clarity, rigidity, structure, and authority. They fear and condemn sex that involves conflict, dominance, high intensity, high levels of arousal, novelty, unpredictability, creativity, ambiguity, and little or no structure. They gain their power and are most comfortable acting not as individuals but as members of a group. In other words, these individuals are classic examples of Little t's.

But interestingly these groups of Little-t individuals derive much of their power from the dynamism of their leaders: Virtually all of them energetic, high-intensity, charismatic, dominant, aggressive individuals who seem to be Big T's. As Big T's, they tend to have higher sex drive and sexual interest, and so we can understand more clearly why such leaders are so often found to be involved in sexual and other high-risk escapades, like the flamboyant preacher Jimmy Swaggart, who admitted to committing "pornographic" acts with prostitutes, and Jim Bakker, who confessed to having sex with a young church secretary in what was allegedly only one of many sexual episodes involving not only young women but young men as well.

Charismatic antiporn leader Andrea Dworkin, too, while condemning virtually all erotic literature, has published her own novel *Fire and Ice* that has been described by literary critics as comparable to the steamiest, raunchiest pornography ever written. And like the flamboyant televangelists, Dworkin aggressively promotes herself and her books through television appearances and mass rallies, where she preaches with all the impassioned flair of a gospel tent–show revivalist.

Why do Little t's become followers of such individuals? Research indicates that this is the way Little t's gain strength and feel powerful. Psychologist David Winter, for example, performed research to measure what he termed "the power motive." In one study, he had a group of business-school students observe a film of the inaugural address of John F. Kennedy (who had only recently been assassinated and was a charismatic leader for the subjects of the study). Winter performed psychological measurements of these subjects, and contrasted them with the results produced after watching a neutral film about architecture. He had expected the subjects exposed to the Kennedy film to experience feelings of submission, following, obedience, or loyalty. Instead, he was surprised to find the Kennedy film had enormously increased the subjects' feelings of strength, power, and confidence. As Harvard personality psychologist David C. McClelland observed of this and subsequent studies, "It was apparent that charismatic leaders are effective because they arouse power motivation in their followers."

McClelland went on to conduct research in the power motive, and found that individuals who have a high power motivation have a single goal, which is "*to feel powerful.*" His research revealed that individuals can fulfill this power motivation in a variety of ways. These "power strategies" include finding a source of power within the self or outside the self, serving others, influencing others, controlling the self. For the people we are describing as Little t's, McClelland found, "the source of power comes from outside the self but its object is strengthening the self." People of this sort, Mc-

Clelland notes, are often described as "dependent." And, in fact, he says, "they are dependent. They may depend on alcohol, an admired leader, or God. But it is a mistake to think of them as being dependent because they like to feel dependent. Quite the contrary: They are dependent because it makes them feel strong to be near a source of strength. . . . There is no such thing as a need for dependency, a need to feel weak and dependent; what is sometimes described as a need for dependency is the act of being dependent or weak, which has as its goal feeling strong."

ON THE ODD RELATIONSHIP BETWEEN THE BRAIN AND PENIS

I have noted that these Little-t individuals are what psychologists call erotophobics, and from the intensity of their hostility toward most types of sex it's clear that there is something about sex that is extremely frightening to them: Possibly that it can lead to experiences of intense stimulation and arousal, ambiguity, unpredictability, novelty, absence of authority or structure. And so, to avoid these distasteful and frightening experiences, Little t's erect a variety of barriers between themselves and the experiential free-fall of high-intensity sex.

The fundamentalist Christians do so by enforcing sexual abstinence, and by restricting the experience of sex to those who are married. The feminists do so by limiting sex to certain "politically correct" forms. But as anthropologist Muriel Dimen points out, "Sexuality is by its nature an experience that benefits from a stance that anything goes, that any avenue may (but not must) be explored. Erotic pleasure mushrooms when there are no musts. But this accessibility means that sexual experience can be affected by anything. Sexual intimacy is too generous an experience to exclude anything, including the forces of the unconscious and the forces of hierarchy. . . . Sexual intimacy is therefore particularly resistant to rules of political correctness—or, rather, when it succumbs to rules, passion disappears."

During sex, the self is no longer experienced as stable and unchanging. As philosopher Murray Davis observes, "the self seems to become more malleable, more open to alteration, during sexual arousal. . . . The psychological energy that normally sustains identity boundaries through internal integration and external defenses is suspended. . . . By turning off the defenses that normally preserve the integrity of the identity, sexual arousal temporarily opens the identity to essential change—whether for better or for worse."

While these erotophobics often explain their hostility to sex as based in their desire to turn away from "worldly" desires, the reality is quite different. As Davis explains, "Sex, in short, is not so much a worldly as an other-worldly desire, drawing consciousness away from both the mundane world of everyday life and its traditional spiritual rival."

Neurologist Robert Heath of Tulane University inserted minute electrodes into the limbic septal region (or "pleasure center") of a subject's brain and monitored what happened during orgasm. Heath found "the most dramatic kind of electrical discharge. The intensity at this local site was equivalent to what the whole brain experiences during epileptic seizure."

Heath notes that once sexual activity has begun, one's perceptions alter dramatically, because, as he points out, "The part of the brain that's so powerfully affected—the pleasure center—is the part that controls awareness." As a result, various perceptual and cognitive distortions, such as a distortion of the sense of time, are a primary feature of sexual experience.

A recent study casts more light on the mind-altering effects of orgasm. A group of men, some of whom had difficulties in reaching orgasm, were wired up to a device that monitored their brain-wave activity while they were having sex. The researchers discovered that in the men who reached orgasm, their brain-wave activity altered dramatically, with the dominance shifting to the right hemisphere. Those men who did not have this shift to right-hemisphere dominance were those who could not reach orgasm. The researchers concluded that activation of the right hemisphere was a key to orgasm. For those individuals who are strongly left-hemisphere dominant, a sudden shift to right hemisphere dominance, with its spontaneous upwelling of vivid imagery, powerful emotions, and unpredictable, even seemingly irrational ideas, can be a disorienting and even frightening experience.

Julian Davidson, a reproductive neuroendocrinologist at Stanford, defines orgasm as "stress, bringing on a very sudden, intense neurological and endocrinological shift," virtually identical to other

spontaneous altered states of consciousness induced by dramatic physiological changes, like the hysterical reactions at teen rock concerts
and the fundamentalist born-again experience.

Perhaps the most succinct description of the relation between sexual
experience and "normal" mental function is the old Italian adage:
"When the penis rises to the sky, the brains fall to the ground."

ALTERED STATES OF CONSCIOUSNESS AND THE YELLOW OCTOPUS FROM ALPHA CENTAURI

Little t's do not like having their brains fall to the ground. With their
need for stability, clarity, predictability, and structure, they are disturbed and frightened by altered states of consciousness. Thus, many
fundamentalist sects not only forbid sex (outside of marriage and, in
some strict sects, even among married people) but also forbid the use
of alcohol, tobacco, and even such mild mood-altering substances as
coffee and soft drinks that contain caffeine.

The only time Little t's permit themselves to let go of their tight
grasp on "normal" consciousness is when the dissolving of the self
takes place within the "safety" of the group. Christian fundamentalists
going through a born-again experience, falling into seizures of ecstasy,
speaking in tongues, handling snakes, and rolling in the aisles are
experiencing "a very sudden, intense neurological and endocrinological shift" that is comparable to orgasm, but they are doing so along
with scores of their fellow believers, in a way that has been actively
encouraged by the group and by the example of thousands of brothers
and sisters who have preceded them along the path. Should they let
go in a way that takes them beyond the boundaries established by
authority, and, for example, begin shouting Marxist slogans, masturbating in the aisle, or expounding upon their vision of yellow
octopuses from Alpha Centauri, they will quickly find themselves
the object of fear and revulsion from the other members of the group.
The experience is an altered state, and has the power of an orgasm,
but it must take the socially approved form—that is, even in their
experiences of letting go, Little t's require the same predictability,
low risk, and high structure that they demand in their normal states
of consciousness.

But intense sexual experience does not permit this kind of predictability and control. As Davis points out, "Intercourse reveals

individuals to be not the closed container they imagined but rather an open sieve." Sexual experience tends to draw consciousness into a world in which the body and the self are open and mutable. "This discontinuity between everyday reality and erotic reality deeply disturbs" such individuals, Davis emphasizes, "by making them painfully aware that the world is not all of a piece. They have tried to restore its wholeness by constricting erotic reality as much as possible—compartmentalizing the times and places it may occur (e.g., at night in bed), obscuring its activities (e.g., by turning out the lights), and repressing the very words that describe it."

Often the groups seeking to constrict erotic reality claim their goal is not to suppress sexuality itself but only to discourage "unhealthy" or abnormal sex. Thus, opponents of abortion rights claim they are most concerned with protecting the lives of the unborn, and those hostile to sex education contend they simply believe that sex education should take place within the family. But in fact, surveys show that anti-abortion forces are most concerned that easy access to abortions encourages abnormal sex (i.e., sexual activity by women who aren't married) by allowing promiscuous women to use abortion as a method of birth control: They want everyone to fear the consequences of unmarried sex as much as they do, and believe those who have sinned by engaging in sex and becoming pregnant should be made to suffer for their sins by being forced to give birth and bear the responsibility for their child, however unwanted that child may be. It's also evident that those opposed to sex education in the schools do not truly believe sex education should take place within the family, since surveys clearly show that there is far *less* discussion of sexual issues in the homes of those people than in the homes of people who support sex education. The fact is that these people simply do not want young people to deal with sexual issues at all.

Similarly in recent years these groups have consistently opposed public funding for AIDS research and education on the grounds that such research should come from the private sector, and that education about AIDS should take place in the home. In fact, they believe that AIDS is simply divine punishment of individuals who have engaged in abnormal sex (the 1988 convention of the Southern Baptists, for example, unanimously adopted a resolution that homosexuality is "an abomination in the eyes of God," declaring that "the Bible is very clear in its teaching that homosexuality is a manifestation of a depraved nature . . . a perversion of divine standards and a violation of nature and of natural affections"). Abnormal sex, in other words, may lead to death, and those who engage in it deserve the consequences.

Antiporn feminists claim that they are not opposed to sex itself, but only to images of sexual activity that are harmful to women. But in their most unguarded and passionate statements they reveal their beliefs that what is harmful to women are virtually all forms of heterosexual sex. Writer Robin Morgan asserts in *The Demon Lover: On the Sexuality of Terrorism* (1989) that males are "demons," and their sexual desire is demonic terrorism against women. Susan Brownmiller compares sexual imagery to Nazi propaganda. Political scientist Jean Bethke Elshtain, author of *Public Man, Private Woman: Women in Social and Political Thought*, observes that this "raises the verbal ante and defines pornography as the most urgent of all contemporary feminist concerns. Something else is going on here, a hidden issue, the serpent in the Garden of Eden for many leading anti-pornography feminists: heterosexual sexuality itself."

As feminist writer Pat Califia declares in her essay "The New Puritans," "Only if one thinks of sex itself as a degrading act can one believe that all pornography degrades and harms women."

DIFFERENT VOICES, DIFFERENT CHOICES

As we observe the contending forces in the sex-power nexus and listen to their slogans and battle cries, we can detect a curious contrast. On the one hand, we find the antisex forces claiming to act out of a concern for relationships and social connections: They speak of the sisterhood of all women, protecting the family, defending the community, affirming the Christian fellowship of all believers. On the other hand, the supporters of sexual freedom seem to base their actions on more abstract principles: They speak of protecting constitutional rights, the First Amendment, the principles of democracy, the separation of church and state, the rights to privacy, the rights of individuals.

What we are witnessing, it seems, is a confrontation of differing moralities. If the confrontation seems familiar, it's because the contending moralities are precisely those outlined by psychologist Carole Gilligan: the "morality of rights," with its concern for justice, abstract laws, and ethical principles, and its "consideration of the individual rather than the relationship as primary"; and the "morality of responsibility," with its "anchoring [of] the self in a world of relationship and giving rise to activities of care," and its primary concern for attachment, intimacy, and the welfare of the group.

Simply by using the information that the core of the antisex forces is made up of individuals with Little-t personality characteristics and with care- and responsibility-centered moralities, we can make some predictions about those individuals. The first is that a very large number of them must be women. The morality of responsibility is, as Gilligan demonstrates so convincingly, a female morality. And research indicates that disproportionate numbers of Little t's tend to be women. Actually we don't need to make that a prediction, since surveys of anti-abortion, anti-sex education, anti–birth control, and antipornography forces reveal that the overwhelming majority of them are women (though these groups sometimes have leaders who are males). For example, a recent *New York Times*-CBS News poll reveals that while a majority of men favor abortion rights for women, a majority of women oppose legalized abortions and would favor more restrictive laws.

We also know, from the evidence of psychological studies cited earlier, that women in general tend to have higher levels of erotophobia. (In an exhaustive survey of the research, Kansas State University psychologist William Griffitt found that females had more sex-negative scores than males on such tests as the Sexual Opinion Survey, the Sex Anxiety Inventory, and the Mosher Sex Guilt Scales. He concludes that "females are disposed to respond more negatively than are males to a wide array of sexual stimuli . . . and are more likely to judge erotica as pornographic and to favor its legal restriction than are males.")

Biological anthropologist Melvin Konner examines the roots of the female tendency to view sex with a greater amount of fear than males. "It has been said that a basic response of women to sex is fear," he observes. "This should not be surprising, since one basic response of any creature to the approach of any other is fear; especially if (as may be the case with sex) the other is not yet the object of intimate trust. . . . However, one must go beyond the general antagonism of sex and fear to suggest that women have special reason to respond to the former with the latter. In our species . . . males are better equipped to inflict damage than females. And women are of course risking much more in any act of sex than men are, even taking only the reproductive consequences." But beyond this, Konner asserts, females are aware "that males have evolved a system in which aggressive and sexual tendencies are compatible if not mutually enhancing." Konner points out that, as we have noted, in many species the male gestures of courtship and sexual invitation are like those of threat and dominance, and that the area of the brain that controls sex is also the locus of aggression, so that one activity can quickly overflow or be transformed into the other. And while males often show a meek or submissive side in their courtship of females, to demonstrate what good fathers they would make, there are many other sexual situations in which, Konner points out, "swagger, bluff, threat, and even force may edge out the romantic gestures of courtship." Konner also observes that testosterone appears from the latest research to be "facilitating to aggression but antagonistic to fear." If in fact testosterone does counteract fear, the fact that males secrete greater amounts of testosterone than do females could partly explain the different levels of fear of sex between males and females.

The second prediction or assumption we can make from the information linking Little-t characteristics and responsibility-centered moralities with the forces seeking to restrict sexual activity is that to a significant degree these tendencies are determined genetically. (As we have seen, the University of Minnesota study of identical twins separated shortly after birth revealed that one of the traits found to be most strongly determined by heredity was "traditionalism," or the tendency to follow rules and authority, to endorse high moral standards and strict discipline, and to be prudish in sexual matters.) And we also know from studies cited earlier that such genetically influenced personality characteristics tend to remain remarkably stable over the lifetime of an individual and are highly resistant to change.

This leads us to our third prediction about the forces seeking restrictions on sexuality: These individuals, strongly influenced by tendencies or preferences that are hard-wired into their brains, will not be persuaded to alter their views by "rational" arguments based on abstract concepts such as justice, and the rights of individuals.

RENEGOTIATING THE SEX CONTRACT: OR, WHO'S SUING WHOM?

All of this leads us back to the forces of evolutionary biology, and the observation that in terms of the differing reproductive strategies of males and females this tendency for more females than males to be involved in the struggle to restrict sexuality makes perfect sense. While males derive an evolutionary advantage from spreading their seed as widely as possible, females derive an evolutionary advantage from being highly selective in their choice of sexual partners. It is an essential part of the sex contract: Females agree to "give" sex on a regular basis to males, who agree in turn to support and protect them and their offspring.

What the struggle in the sex-power nexus indicates is that the same evolutionary forces that have caused individual women to value "limited sexual accessibility" hold true on a wider, sociopolitical level. If sex becomes widely available and easy to obtain for males, then sex becomes devalued and the power individual females derive from it is diminished: If a woman is too selective, males can simply go elsewhere. Thus it is to the advantage of females to be sure that the rule of limited sexual accessibility is enforced throughout the entire society.

The sexual revolution of the 1960's that resulted from the development of the Pill as well as from other cultural forces had the effect of making sex much easier for males to obtain. Though feminists initially saw the revolution as beneficial to women, by allowing them to expand and explore their own sexual natures, over the years, many of them felt that by devaluing sex and disrupting the basis of the sex contract, the sexual revolution posed a severe threat to their own power.

Thus, while in 1974 Andrea Dworkin wrote about a pornographic newspaper called *Suck* that it "has made positive contributions. Sucking is approached in a new way. Sucking cock, sucking cunt, how to, how good. Sperm tastes good, so does cunt. In particular, the emphasis on sucking cunt serves to demystify cunt in a spectacular way . . . it is a source of pleasure, a beautiful part of female physiology, to be seen, touched, tasted," by 1983, she was writing that pornography is an evil, "one cannot be a feminist and support" it, and anyone who defends it is showing "anti-feminist contempt for women."

Alan Soble, a professor of philosophy at St. John's University, discusses the concerns about female power that produced this shift in attitudes in his study *Pornography: Marxism, Feminism, and the Future of Sexuality:*

> *The radical feminist protest against pornography thereby revives the old battle of the sexes. Pornography becomes the central*

*feminist issue in the same way that prostitution was the central
issue in the late nineteenth century. Those earlier feminists exaggerated the extent and the coerciveness of prostitution; they
opposed contraception and divorce as dangerous to the economic
security and sexual values of women; and they saw as the root
of their problems a male sexuality that had to be tamed or restrained. Similarly, radical feminists often exaggerate the extent
of abusive depictions in pornography, and they usually think that
the coercion suffered by women who are pornographic prostitutes
goes beyond the economic coercion of capitalism. . . . Pornography, they think, puts pressure on women to accommodate to
male sexuality (like contraception). . . . Pornography not only
provides men with an alternative to sexual activity with women,
but threatens to pull men away from women altogether. Like
abortion, divorce, and prostitution, which can make some women
useless, superfluous, and powerless by undermining their value
as lovers, wives, and mothers, pornography is dangerous to wom-
en's values and economic survival. And men's interest in pornography comes from the same reprehensible male sexuality that
the earlier feminists had wanted to tame.*

Radical feminists talk about the evils of male dominance; right-
wing Christian women speak of the threat to the home and family
posed by sexual freedoms; but we see that these superficially different
groups are pursuing a single underlying goal: power. Both radical
feminists and right-wing Christian women are united in a concern
that transcends mere politics—the threat that pornography, and all
types of sexual freedoms, pose to the power of women, to their value
as lovers, wives, and mothers, and to their economic survival. As
Soble observes, "This unified women's movement, in which 'political
persuasion' is irrelevant, threatens to become merely the female side
of the war between the sexes, grounded ultimately in women's dislike
of male sexuality."

WINNING THE HEARTS AND MINDS OF THE MASSES

*In women's groups, the political clones, the Dworkinites . . .
are the high priestesses of feminism, conjuring up the "wimmin's"
revolution. As I understand it, after the wimmin's revolution,. sex*

will consist of wimmin holding hands, taking their shirts off and dancing in a circle. Then we will fall asleep at exactly the same moment. If we didn't all fall asleep, something else might happen —something male-identified, objectifying, pornographic, noisy, and undignified. Something like an orgasm.

—Pat Califia, "A Secret Side of Lesbian Sexuality"

The great mass of humanity falls somewhere in between the Little t's and the Big T's: We are ranged along a bell-shaped curve, with some of us having tendencies toward the t-end of the curve, others toward the T-end, and the greatest numbers found toward the center of the curve.

This majority, which we might call Medium t's, does not share the erotophobic Little t's hostility toward sexuality. After all, over half of the individuals who now rent pornographic videotapes are females. And there is the extraordinary popularity of sexually arousing women's romance novels. And as Pat Califia's raspberry to "Dworkinites" indicates, many feminists have little sympathy for the sexually repressive aspects of the "wimmin's revolution."

If the goal of the antisex forces is to gain sufficient political power to "enforce" their views of sexuality, then somehow they must reach out to the great mass of Medium t's, both male and female, and convince them that it is in their best interest, or morally right, to join with the antisex forces. To do this, they must talk in terms that Medium t's can understand.

As countless missionaries, politicians, preachers, advertising executives, and propagandists have discovered, it is not easy to win hearts and minds, but it can be done.

16

Mind Wars:
The Germ Theory
of Ideas

In the beginning was the Word.
—*The Gospel According to John*

The word is a virus.
—*William Burroughs*

The essence of biology is information. Each individual life form has its own genetic structure, which is a complex set of instructions, or *information*, coded into its DNA. This bundle of protein-coated information determines how that life form will grow—whether it will become an azalea or a grizzly bear—and, to a large degree, how it will behave, how it will live. Science has advanced to a point where it is now possible to decode genetic information, to print it out on paper or store it and analyze it in computers, and to insert new information into the genetic structure, producing a variety of entirely new life forms. Genetic engineering, that is, is a way of manipulating information.

The essence of evolutionary biology is the communication or transmission of genetic information. Through reproduction, a life form can pass along to future generations its own bundle of genetic information or messages. This information is subject to adaptive evolutionary forces: As a result of environmental pressures, or competition with other forms of genetic information—the evolutionary struggle for survival—some bundles of genetic information will be more adaptive or "fit" to survive than others. That information will be selected for; that is, it will continue to be transmitted to succeeding generations, and will become more common in the genetic information pool, while the information that is less adaptive will be selected against, and will tend to become less common or disappear altogether. Natural selection, in other words, is a process of *information selection*.

The life forms that carry the bundles of genetic information are simple messengers, like relay runners who carry the baton (or bundle of information) a certain distance and then, having passed it on to another runner, can collapse by the roadside, their mission accomplished. It is the message, not the runner, that is important.

Perhaps the most highly adaptive bundle of information is the one that has to do with self-replication or reproduction. It is such a highly adaptive message, in fact—has such high survival value—that the genetic material of all life forms on the planet today carries it.

THE ATTACK OF THE MIND PARASITES

Over the course of evolutionary history it proved highly adaptive for life forms to develop ways to transmit information nongenetically. This type of communication can take many forms, from the releasing of certain molecules or pheromones that are carried in the air to other members of the species, to the complex dance patterns that honey bees fly to tell other bees the location of pollen, to the songs of birds and whales, to the subtle resonances of human speech, writing, music, and art.

As scientists have studied the nongenetic transmission of information in recent years, they have come to realize that certain information patterns seem to carry within them self-replication messages: When the information pattern is received by an individual, that individual then has not only the capacity but also a tendency to transmit that information pattern to other individuals. It is almost as if these packets of information carry with them a hidden command: "Pass me along!" Or, in a more highly evolved form: "It is your duty to spread this information."

Anthropologists and evolutionary biologists have been struck by the similarity between genes, which are molecular bundles of self-replicating information, and these other, apparently nonmolecular bundles of self-replicating information. Seeking an analogy to the word "gene," British biologist Richard Dawkins in 1976 coined the term "meme" (to rhyme with theme), which he defined as a self-replicating information pattern that uses *minds* to get itself reproduced. According to Dawkins, "Examples of memes are tunes, ideas, catch-phrases, clothes fashions, ways of making pots or of building arches. Just as genes propagate themselves in the gene pool by leaping from body to body via sperms or eggs, so memes propagate themselves in the meme pool by leaping from brain to brain via a process which, in the broad sense, can be called imitation. If a scientist hears, or reads about, a good idea, he passes it on to his colleagues and students. He mentions it in his articles and his lectures. If the idea catches on, it can be said to propagate itself, spreading from brain to brain."

As N. K. Humphrey, a colleague of Dawkins, summed it up, "memes should be regarded as living structures, not just metaphor-ically but technically. When you plant a fertile meme in my mind, you literally parasitize my brain, turning it into a vehicle for the meme's propagation in just the way that a virus may parasitize the genetic mechanism of a host cell."

The evolutionary value of memes is clear—the ability to pass on complex bundles of information, such as the right way to chip a tool out of a piece of rock, make pottery, hunt down different types of animals, or find water or edible plants, was an enormous advance over the potentially lethal method of trial and error. Since the capacity to transmit memes has such a high survival value, individuals with that capacity would tend to become commoner in the gene pool, while those whose brains did not have that capacity would tend to disappear. The result is that our brains have been molded by the forces of natural selection to insure that we have a highly developed receptivity to memes.

Compared to the slow transmission of genetic information over generations, memes can carry information virtually instantaneously.

As a result, cultural or meme-mediated evolution can take place with extraordinary speed. Already, Dawkins observes, memes are "achieving evolutionary change at a rate that leaves the old gene panting far behind."

In an early approach to meme-theory, neurophysiologist and Nobel laureate Roger Sperry observed in a 1965 article, "Ideas cause ideas and help evolve new ideas. They interact with each other and with other mental forces in the same brain, in neighboring brains, and, thanks to global communication, in far distant, foreign brains. And they also interact with the external surroundings to produce in toto a burstwise advance in evolution that is far beyond anything to hit the evolutionary scene yet, including the emergence of the living cell."

Not all ideas or information are memes. A momentary thought or idea that is not transmitted to others, or does not take hold in the minds of others, does not become a meme.

As genes can only propagate themselves by leaping from body to body via sperms or eggs, memes survive only by leaping from mind to mind. This they can do, like genes, by finding a willing recipient, or by somehow slipping past or overpowering the defenses of a recipient. And just as genes are subject to the forces of natural selection, memes too must prove their "fitness" to survive in the environment of the human mind, and in competition or cooperation with the huge assortment of other memes that are circulating, migrating, and reproducing themselves in human culture.

Molecular biologist Jacques Monod cast light on the important distinction between memes and other types of information with his observation, in his 1970 book *Chance and Necessity*, that memes (or what he, like Sperry, called "ideas") are imbued with power—their own "spreading power," and the "power to perform" and "power to expand" that they confer upon their recipients:

> *The performance value of an idea depends upon the change it brings to the behavior of the person or the group that adopts it. The human group upon which a given idea confers greater cohesiveness, greater ambition, and greater self-confidence thereby receives from it an added power to expand which will insure the promotion of the idea itself. Its capacity to "take," the extent*

*to which it can be "put over," has little to do with the amount
of objective truth the idea may contain. The important thing about
the stout armature a religious ideology constitutes for a society is
not what goes into its structure, but the fact that this structure is
accepted, that it gains sway. So one cannot well separate such an
idea's power to spread from its power to perform. The "spreading
power"—the infectivity, as it were—of ideas . . . depends upon
preexisting structures in the mind, among them ideas already
implanted by culture, but also undoubtedly upon certain innate
structures. . . . What is very plain, however, is that the ideas
having the highest invading potential are those that explain man
by assigning him his place in an immanent destiny, in whose
bosom his anxiety dissolves.*

INFECTIOUS INFORMATION, AND LENIN'S SEALED TRUCK

When viruses were first discovered, scientists were fascinated and
appalled by their devious and pernicious reproductive strategy: The
tiny organisms actually entered their larger and more self-sufficient
host organisms and "hijacked" or "enslaved" them, comandeering
the facilities of the host and tricking them into carrying out a sequence
of replicating operations that created new copies of the virus, which
could then go off and hijack more hosts to replicate themselves further, and so on.

Many have been struck by the similarity between viruses and
memes. Like viruses, memes are *infectious*. While viruses use cells to
get themselves copied so that they can infect other cells, memes use
minds to get themselves copied: They are "infectious information."
For this reason students of memetics speak of it as "the germ theory
of ideas."

As one student of memetics, H. Keith Henson, points out, "The
analogy is remarkably close. For example, genes in cold viruses that
cause sneezes by irritating noses spread themselves by this route to
new hosts and become more common in the gene pool of a cold virus.
Memes cause those they have successfuly infected to spread the meme
by both direct methods (proselytizing) and indirect methods (such as
writing). Such memes become more common in the culture pool."

Just as some germs are benign while others are harmful, so memes can increase human knowledge, wealth, and well-being or cause sicknesses of the mind that have lethal consequences. And just as the unchecked spread of some viruses can result in epidemics of disease, so the spread of memes can cause dangerous epidemics of mass social movements. We are all aware of this quality of memes on some level as we speak of the "virulent" nature of racism and the "contagion" of hatred that can spark riots and pogroms. Winston Churchill, for example, in *The Aftermath*, his post–World War II look at the global consequences of the war, condemns the Germans for having "transported Lenin in a sealed truck like a plague bacillus from Switzerland to Russia." It was not the physical germs that Lenin carried with him that Churchill saw as dangerous, but the memes that occupied his mind.

The discoveries of Pasteur and Koch that led to the widespread acceptance of the germ theory of disease brought about an enormous reduction in human suffering and death as a result of disease. Once society was able to reject the longstanding memes that disease was a result of bad air or demonic influences, the meme about microorganisms called germs enabled them to pinpoint and eliminate causes of diseases, such as contaminated water supplies; to determine modes of transmission and work to eliminate them through such techniques as quarantines and sanitary practices; and, most wonderful, to heighten people's resistance to infection by immunization—inoculating them with less virulent forms of the germs.

In the same way, proponents of memetics now contend, the application of meme theory to some of the nonbiological epidemics sweeping our planet can bring about an enormous reduction in human suffering. As examples, these meme theorists (should we call them memeticians or memeticists?) point to the diseaselike spread of drug use in recent years. Despite the expenditure of billions of dollars and the passage of Draconian laws that have filled the nation's prisons to overflowing, the spread of drug use continues unchecked. Perhaps, argue the memeticists, this is because the authorities are as misguided in their attempts to stamp out the epidemic as were the efforts of European authorities to eradicate the Black Plague by saying masses or blaming Jews. As Keith Henson writes, if the spread of drug use "were formally considered as an epidemic with memes as the infecting agents, the ways by which behavior spreads might get more attention. . . . Some efforts in the past, especially those which wildly exaggerated the dangers of a drug such as marijuana, may have *in-*

creased the behavior of taking other drugs. These efforts may have immunized those exposed against believing any official pronouncements about drugs."

KAMIKAZE THOUGHTS, KILLER MEMES, AND MUTANT IDEAS

One odd characteristic of some viruses is that their self-replication messages are so strong that they will ultimately destroy themselves by killing their host. Similarly there are memes that have such a powerful grip on their host they can cause the host's destruction. One colorful example is the odd politico-messianic-conspiracy meme that infected Jim Jones and his disciples and caused Jones and over nine hundred followers to commit suicide with poisoned Kool-Aid. Such self-destruct memes are thankfully self-limiting, since their carriers are not likely to be around long enough to continue to spread them.

Far more dangerous are the memes that instruct their carriers to kill not only themselves, but others. These include those memes that inspired Japanese kamikaze pilots, and that persuade young Shiite Muslims to transport themselves into paradise by strolling across minefields or driving cars packed with high explosives into selected infidel targets.

And more dangerous still are those sinister memes that instruct their carriers to kill others who might hinder the replication of the meme, such as the ayatollah Khomeini, who put out a murder contract on an author whose book he claimed is harmful to the Muslim religion. And since these lethal memes induce their carriers to remain alive and spread the infection as widely as possible, the social movements or epidemics they produce can be monstrous.

One such epidemic social movement, the Inquisition, was spread by memes having to do with the Devil and his influence over humans. It lasted about three hundred years, and historians estimate that it resulted in the torture and execution of between 5 million and 6 million people—far more deaths than were caused by all the wars waged during those centuries.

Many of us, carriers of more sophisticated memes about human psychology and neuroscience, are no longer susceptible to infection by the Inquisition memes (though memes about demonic possession, devil worship, human sacrifice, witches, and warlocks continue to severely infect millions).

This points up another interesting characteristic of memes. Just as genes, and the life forms that carry them, have, in the course of their evolution over millions of years developed increasing variety and complexity (take for example, the enormous growth in the size and complexity of the human brain), so memes have undergone a remarkable evolution in variety, complexity, and sophistication. The relatively simple meme that the earth was the center of the universe, for example, has now virtually disappeared and been replaced by a much more complex cosmological meme involving a primordial Big Bang, an expanding universe, and black holes (though this set of memes may appear just as primitive to our descendants as the earth-centered meme does to us).

The memes that have survived from the relatively distant past, such as religions and astrology, are extraordinarily effective in causing those who are infected by them to spread and defend them (as Monod points out, they have the "highest invading potential" because they "explain man by assigning him his place in an immanent destiny, in whose bosom his anxiety dissolves"). And since memes have increased enormously in variety in recent history, the ones that have thrived in the expanded new marketplace of memes are also highly infectious (which is to say they can confer upon their recipients enormous "power to expand").

THE ARMS RACE IN THE BRAIN

"It is also plausible," Keith Henson observes, "that in the tens of millennia since memetic evolution became a major factor there has been a biological counterrevolution. The parts of our brains that hold our belief systems have probably undergone biological adaptation to be better at detecting dangerous memes and more skeptical about memes that result in death or seriously interfere with reproductive success."

This would lead us to suspect that in a sort of evolutionary arms race, as we have become more resistant to dangerous memes, they have responded with mutation into forms that are even more effective in infecting us, like a flu virus that keeps one step ahead of our development of antiflu vaccines.

Technological advances have been a part of the environment in which memes have evolved, so there has been a clear survival value for memes in developing into forms that make effective use of technology. In fact, there are some memes whose effectiveness has *depended* on making innovative uses of new technology. The germ-theory-of-disease meme, for example, simmered for ages without infecting many people until advances in technology, such as the development of reliable microscopes and other laboratory equipment, allowed it to quickly infect the finest scientific minds of the day.

The rise of Adolf Hitler and the Nazi movement coincided with the development of radio and films with soundtracks. Before radio, even a demagogue with the oratorical powers of Hitler would have been able to speak to—and infect with his virulent memes—at most a few thousand people at a time. Radio enabled him to speak live to millions of people at once. And since radio was still new, people were still largely unexposed to its powers, and listened transfixed, transported, and moved by this technological wonder, which seemed to make the words pouring out of it more powerful and remarkable (unlike today, when people have developed so much immunity to the memes pouring over the radio waves that they can study or work with a radio talk-show yammering unheard in the background).

Similarly the advent of sound-film made it possible for the huge numbers of citizens who packed the German cinemas to both hear and see Hitler in the high-quality film footage that accompanied the features, in close-up shots that seemed to put them right there on the podium with him.

As Henson observes, "Had plague struck Germany in the '30s instead of Nazism, we would have understood it in terms of susceptibility, vectors, and disease organisms. What did happen may soon be modeled and understood in terms of the social and economic disruptions of the time increasing the number of people susceptible to fanatical beliefs, just as poor diet is known to increase the number of those susceptible to tuberculosis. For vectors, we have personal contact, the written word, radio, and amplified voices substituting for rats, lice, mosquitoes, and coughed out droplets."

There are many other examples of meme outbreaks in recent years that were made possible by technological advances. The advent of the 45-rpm record—light, thin, made of virtually unbreakable plastic, perfect for brief and pungent musical compositions—was a primary mode of transmission for the rock-and-roll meme that revolutionized

Western cultures. The proliferation of television combined with portable videotape cameras made possible the kind of on-the-scene network news coverage of events like the Vietnam War that sparked outbreaks of antiwar memes in the United States. And the outbreak of the taking of hostages from Western nations by Middle-Eastern terrorists as a method of transmitting memes is directly related to the same minicam technology that insures that the terrorists will be able to broadcast on prime-time television.

INTOLERANCE AND THE GOLDEN MEME

One key trait of memes, and one that can make them exceedingly dangerous, is their intolerance of competing memes. In evolutionary terms, tolerance of competing memes could be fatal, since memes inducing tolerance would be eradicated or suppressed by memes inducing intolerance. This holds true of even the most apparently innocuous memes. I have observed personally the mutual intolerance of two individuals who were infected with conflicting right-way-to-iron-a-shirt memes. While each of them ultimately professed resigned (but scornful) tolerance for the other's shirt-ironing meme, it was apparent that deep in their hearts they remained absolutely certain that theirs was the one true shirt-ironing meme, and that given the opportunity, they would dearly love to stamp out the offending and heretical false shirt-ironing meme. And anyone who believes that tolerance plays any part in the science meme has never observed the fierce conflicts, hostility, attempts at suppression, and character assassination among contending camps of, just for example, microbiologists, physicists, or anthropologists.

Nevertheless, it has become clear over the last few hundred years that, given the vast, confused, rapidly changing, and growing marketplace of memes, it is advantageous for competing memes to develop a limited tolerance for each other. This recognition by memes that there are other memes, that the carriers of these other memes are not scoundrels, liars, or the minions of the Devil but simply other meme-infected humans, and that the competing memes will have to coexist, is what may be called the meme about memes, or the meta-meme. It can be seen as a mutated version of a meme that entered our culture from the body of Judeo-Christian memes, the admirable but generally ignored Golden Rule. In its present form, which I'll call the Golden Meme, it infects its carriers with the message: Do not impose yours on others, as you would not want others to impose theirs on you.

DEVELOPING MEME IMMUNITY

Just as inoculation with weak or inactive microorganisms can enable us to develop resistance or immunity to the diseases caused by those microorganisms, exposure to weak or inactive memes—memes that still contain their basic structure and information but with their self-replication and intolerance messages inactivated—may increase our immunity or resistance to the more virulent forms of those memes.

This suggests a general strategy to avoid outbreaks of dangerous memes: Expose yourself to as many memes as possible while maintaining a high level of meme-immunity or resistance. One way to maintain meme-immunity appears to be total skepticism: Doubt everything. But this is itself a nasty sort of meme that condemns its carrier to a dour and cranky life. And besides, all memes carry information (or a special type of information called misinformation), much of it quite valuable, some of it wonderful, and a bit of it, somewhere, if only you can find it, the Big Stuff.

A happier policy seems to be to make use of the meme about memes: Be conscious that all these schools of thought, ideologies, bodies of knowledge, belief systems, expressions of The Truth, paradigms, ideas, and so-called facts are simply memes; expose yourself to as many as possible, take whatever information is valuable, and discard the rest.

"In the area of meme tolerance the western world may be unique," Henson points out. "We think of censorship as evil; where but in an advanced ecosystem of memes could such a strange idea have emerged?"

THE UNPREDICTABILITY OF INFORMATION

In discussing memes as carriers of information, author-philosopher Robert Anton Wilson asserts that ours is an information society, that in a very real sense information equals wealth, and that the explosion of information that has taken place in the last century has caused a parallel explosion in the "real wealth" of the world. This being so, he argues, "then the increase in empirical memes is a goal to be sought by all, except for hard-core masochists and sadists who think it is good to have a large portion of the population living in misery." But as Wilson points out, "Such wealth-producing empirical memes only increase rapidly in what Sir Karl Popper calls 'an Open Society,' and an Open Society is one in which memes of all sorts migrate rapidly —i.e. a society based on Justice Holmes's 'free marketplace of ideas,' where, as Justice Black argued so passionately, 'no laws' abridging the circulation of memes is understood literally to mean 'no laws.' I believe we all get 'richer'—both materially and 'mentally' or 'psychologically'—in such an Open Society."

What is information? To answer this question, Wilson directs us to the work of Claude Shannon, the father of information theory, who in 1948 defined a message (or what we're calling a meme) as a sequence of signals, each of which has a certain predictability. Shannon found that it was possible to determine mathematically how much information a given message carried. His formula revealed that, in Wilson's words, "the information in a message is the reverse of your ability to predict the message before you receive it. As Professor Norbert Weiner magnificently expressed it, what this equation implies is that there is more information in great poetry than in political speeches."

Since information is valuable and makes you a "richer" person, and since information increases as unpredictability increases, then, Wilson contends, "almost any meme that is new to you is good for you, whether you like it or not. Of course, some memes can be lethal (We Remember Jonestown) but we can still extract information from them if we do not allow them to hypnotize us. To say it otherwise, *the only dangerous memes are Fundamentalist memes,* and even they are only dangerous to those who accept them Fundamentalistically. Even dogmatic memes are harmless to us, if we use them as glosses instead of worshipping them as Idols."

This kind of immunity to memes, Wilson points out, is only possible if we discard the two-valued, Yes or No, True or False Aristotelian logic that is, unfortunately, one of the memes that has shaped the Western mind. Wilson argues, "Since art has long functioned without Aristotelian logic— only a few pixillated critics ever argue on the basis, 'Beethoven is True, so Wagner is False' or 'Western Art is True, so African Art is False'—we merely have to recognize that all glosses or models are works of art in order to liberate ourselves from dogmatism, fanaticism and Fundamentalism of all sorts. We can then take what is good or useful out of any meme, and not allow any meme to become a virus that 'possesses' us and makes us intellectual slaves."

MEME WARFARE IN THE SEX-POWER NEXUS

With this background in mind, the first thing we notice is that the sex–power nexus is a veritable hotbed of memes. Some of the forces are firing sizzling meme-bombs, such as: All Males Are Rapists! Abortion Is Murder! Pornography Is the Theory, Rape Is the Practice! Homosexuality Is an Abomination and Perversion in the Eyes of the Lord! Rock Music Is the Work of the Devil! Burn Dirty Books! Sex Is Dirty! Sex Equals Death!

The opposing forces are shooting off some heavy-caliber memes as well, including memes having to do with Justice, Freedom of Expression, the Right to Privacy, Liberty, and the Pursuit of Happiness. Most of these memes are variants of the metameme of tolerance, even (or especially) if this means tolerance of memes we despise, such as allowing Nazis to demonstrate (if they do so peacefully).

The antisex forces have aroused strong resistance even from individuals and groups who have no strong memes about various sexual freedoms. Many people can have sympathy with some of the memes that infect the antisex forces, such as being disgusted with porn, being personally opposed to having an abortion themselves, and having absolutely no desire to pursue "perverse" sexual practices. These forces would be quite willing to allow the antisex forces to hold their own memes. It is the intolerance of the antisex groups, their attempts to force the rest of society to be infected by their memes, that arouses resistance. As Henson points out, "Western culture is a vast ecosystem where memes of many classes engage in 'fair' competition with each other. Attempts to subvert fair competition by changing laws or education (such as introducing 'creation science' into schools) draw opposition from defenders of a wide variety of memes which have evolved within this environnment."

The conflict in the sex-power nexus, then, is in many ways a conflict over tolerance. It is also a serious struggle for power. As we noted earlier, memes not only *possess* power but *confer* it: the "power to expand," in Monod's terms, produced by the "greater cohesiveness, greater ambition, and greater self-confidence" the memes provide to their carriers. In a head-to-head confrontation between a virulently intolerant meme and a tolerant meme (or even an intolerant meme held in check by the metameme of tolerance) the intolerant meme will have an enormous advantage. It is like a confrontation between one person, who says, "Well, I don't agree with you, but I will turn my other cheek," and another, who says, "I don't agree with you, and I will rip out your liver and burn you alive because you're a heretic and a tool of the Devil."

It is this passionate intolerance that can make even tiny splinter groups so dangerous in a society that professes to value the Golden Meme: A few emotionally explosive memoids can impose their meme on vast numbers of people who are not infected with any meme strong enough to make them resist the virulent meme carriers.

Instead of gaining immunity by exposing themselves to as many memes as possible, such individuals seem compelled to give themselves wholly to only a single overriding meme and to deny any validity whatsoever to any competing memes. As Richard Dawkins observes, "The truly appalling thing all such people have in common, whether they are incited to murder by ayatollahs or to less violent observances by television evangelists, is that they know, for certain, that their particular brand of revealed truth is absolute and needs no reasoned defense."

I have suggested above that many of the forces seeking to limit sexuality are motivated by genetic predispositions. Is it possible that such genetically predisposed Little-t individuals also have a tendency to become infected with intolerant memes, and to hold on to those memes tenaciously?

Is it possible that some brains are genetically more receptive to intolerance memes, or, stated in a different way, that some brains, once infected with memes, are less open to new memes that might cause them to modify their own?

HOW BRAINS ARE LIKE BUSY FREEWAYS

One insight into the question comes out of the theories of an extraordinary Russian-born Belgian Nobel Prize-winning theoretical

chemist, Ilya Prigogine, who has spent the last half-century attempting to understand the dynamics of evolution, or growth, or increasing
order. If classical physics and the Second Law of Thermodynamics
are correct, and the universe is tending toward ever-increasing ran-
domness (a process called entropy), how is it possible that life forms
can evolve? Life, it seems, moves toward ever-increasing order, but
the Second Law of Thermodynamics demands that it should gain
entropy, decaying into the state of equilibrium known as "heat
death."

The secret of this process, Prigogine discovered, was that order
arises *because* of disorder, life emerges *out of* entropy, not *against* it.
Entropy, Prigogine found, only applies to closed systems, systems
that are totally self-contained, with no flow of matter or energy between the system and its environment. However, Prigogine pointed
out, living systems are always *open systems*, always exchanging matter
and energy with the outside environment. The open system known
as a human being, for example, is always taking in energy and matter
in the form of food, light, oxygen, information, and is always sending
matter and energy back into the environment (or dissipating entropy)
in the form of carbon dioxide, waste, heat, art, and other excretions.

A key factor about open systems is that they are what Prigogine
calls *far from equilibrium*: They are extremely unstable, constantly adjust to all kinds of unpredictable outside forces, grow in unexpected
ways, reproduce, fix themselves when they get out of whack, learn
to operate in new ways when part of the system is lost or altered.
Prigogine focused his studies on a number of physical and chemical
systems that somehow spontaneously developed ordered structures,
on certain mixtures that, when heated, begin to "self-organize" into
structures of extraordinary complexity and beauty, at times taking
on patterns that resemble living cells. In his studies of these chemical
reactions and his mathematical analysis of the processes, Prigogine
obtained the experimental evidence he needed that ordered structures
are an *inevitable* product of far-from-equilibrium situations. It was a
process Prigogine called "order through fluctuation," and the structures that emerged he called *dissipative structures*, and for this startling
theory he was awarded the Nobel Prize.

Prigogine, and other scientists, quickly saw that his theory had
relevance to all open systems in which a structure exchanges energy
with its environment: a seed, a society, a town, a living body, an

ecosystem, a highway network. All such systems take in energy from the surroundings, the energy is used to maintain or alter the structure of the system, and the entropy produced is expelled to the environment. This process constitutes a sort of "metabolism" (from the Greek words *meta*, beyond, and *ballein*, to throw.) A word usually applied to zoology and biology, metabolism refers to the sum of all the processes involved in the building up, maintaining, and destruction of protoplasm: that is, it is a process of *life*.

What's so exciting about Prigogine's insight is that it offers new ways of understanding the dynamics—or life—of such systems.

ESCAPE TO A HIGHER ORDER, OR: NO WHIRLPOOLS IN ROCKS

According to Prigogine, dissipative structures need a continuous energy flow from outside. And, in fact, such structures are largely *formed by* the energy and matter flowing through them, just as our bodies are not simply preexistent structures that pass energy and matter through them in the form of food, water, oxygen, and so on—they literally *are* the energy and matter that flow through them. Dissipative structures, that is, are *flow*.

Dissipative structures are created by and thrive in a far-from-equilibrium environment—you can't imagine a whirlpool forming in, say, a stone, or a cup of cold coffee. Since dissipative structures must remain open to an exchange with the environment, the structures must pass fluctuating amounts and kinds of energy through themselves, which causes the structure itself to fluctuate. Up to a certain point, the structure can absorb these fluctuations, dissipate the entropy, and still maintain its internal organization. For example, the human body can suffer certain damages and still heal itself through its self-organizing capacity. A society is able to absorb the disruptions and instability caused by a minor war; it can suffer a moderate famine or drought and still "heal" itself.

At a certain point, though, the fluctuation begins to grow too great to be absorbed and healed, and the structure becomes more and more unstable. As the fluctuations increase, the structure reaches a critical point and becomes highly unstable: Perturbed by fluctuations, the elements of the system are brought into contact with other elements of the system in new ways. Now, the system has the potential to move in an almost infinite variety of unpredictable directions, like an unstable society on the verge of revolution.

At this point, which Prigogine calls the "bifurcation point," even a small fluctuation can be sufficient to push the elements of the system beyond where they can heal themselves. Then suddenly the entire system seems to shudder and fall apart. In some cases the system may be destroyed. But if the system survives, it does so by emerging into a new pattern. The elements of the system, having increased their interactions with each other and been brought into contact with each other in novel ways, reorganize in a different form, create a new organization: The nation that has undergone a revolution, with different levels of the society having been brought into contact with one another in new ways, creates a new government that is somehow able to absorb and dissipate the energy that had created the revolution; the human body creates new antibodies that are able to overcome a disease—out of chaos emerges a transformed system. The dissipative structure has, in Prigogine's words, "escaped into a higher order."

Prigogine's vision of a universe of dissipative structures replaces the mechanistic view of a cosmos of "things" with a cosmos of "process." The entire process, with structures transforming themselves into new structures of greater complexity and diversification, is unpredictable, self-organizing, and evolutionary.

Prigogine's ideas have had an impact in virtually every field of human inquiry, and the concept of dissipative structures has been fruitfully applied to such phenomena as the moment an audience breaks into applause, the growth of plants, the economic patterns of human culture, the psychology of altered states of consciousness, the origin and development of cancer cells, and artistic inspiration. The U.S. Department of Transportation has even used it to analyze and predict traffic-flow patterns (crowded freeways turn out to be a fine example of dissipative structures).

In many ways, Prigogine's ideas are profoundly optimistic. By demonstrating that periods of instability, perturbation, upheaval, and collapse and chaos are not to be seen as evils but as necessities, as phases through which every structure must pass in order to evolve to higher levels of complexity, the theory of dissipative structures clarifies how out of political and economic upheavals we can evolve new social orders, how the volatile and disordered process of artistic creation can lead to new artistic forms and visions, how psychological suffering, anxiety, and collapse can lead to new emotional, intellectual, and spiritual strengths, and how confusion and doubt can lead to new scientific ideas.

Prigogine himself at times supports this optimistic view. "Now," he says, "looking at biology, social behavior, ecology, and economics, we begin to have a meeting point between the various concepts of evolution. . . . Near equilibrium you always go to the most banal, the most uniform state. The general idea of classical physics is that we progress toward the running down of the universe. What we see here on Earth, on the other hand, is just the opposite of that. Instead of going to heat death, we see successive diversification. . . . With the paradigm of self-organization we see a transition from disorder to order. In the field of psychological activity this is perhaps the main experience we have—every artistic or scientific creation implies a transition from disorder to order."

THE MEME-POWERED LIGHT BULB IN THE BRAIN

Prigogine's insights provide us with important information about how the brain operates, and in particular about how the brain receives, responds to, and is transformed by energy flowing through it, by which I mean *information*, or memes. Prigogine's insights give us compelling reasons to believe that, given the appropriate influx of energy, the brain as dissipative structure can be destabilized, made subject to internal fluctuations, and that these fluctuations can be amplified until the structure spontaneously and unpredictably shifts, like a kaleidoscope falling into a new pattern, and the brain transforms itself into a new state, more ordered, more coherent, more complex, more interconnected, more *highly evolved* than before. In the brain this "escape to a higher order" is experienced as having a new idea: the Eureka event, the Aha! moment, the light bulb going on in the brain. This movement or "leap" to a higher level of complexity and connectedness is what we mean by "learning."

It also is what we are talking about when we say that someone is infected by a meme. The brain is able to accept certain amounts of energy input (such as memes) and assimilate them without any serious challenge to the internal organization of the brain. "Yes, all right," we say in response to certain memes, "this all makes sense." However, at a certain level of intensity, the brain's fluctuations become too great to be damped, and the brain will escape from its old pattern into a new structure. First, things no longer make "sense," i.e., the old memes are insufficient to explain things; then, with a shock of recognition, they make a new type of sense, sense of a sort we have never before imagined.

We have all had the experience of having our brain structure (which we might call our preconceptions or our rational minds or our vision of reality) challenged by new memes, new ways of looking at life, events that somehow don't fit into our ordered way of seeing things or that challenge our sense of ethics. Often we resist these challenges completely; often we can fit them into the dissipative structure of our brain without causing fluctuations or perturbations that are too violent. And sometimes the whole house of cards comes falling down and we see things afresh, with what Blake called a cleansing of our doors of perception.

Some people are infected with the meme that things like mental transformation, evolution, and growth are good things. Perhaps they are genetically predisposed to accept such a meme: actually enjoy allowing new types of information or energy to flow through their brains, causing fluctuations and escape to a higher order.

Big T's believe, to paraphrase Robert Anton Wilson, that any meme that is new is good for you. A necessary characteristic of these individuals is that their minds are quite flexible and mobile: As with well-oiled wheels, it doesn't take much force to get them spinning. The greater the flexibility of the system, the greater the number of interactions among its various parts, the greater its susceptibility to fluctuations, and the greater its potential for evolution, transformation, diversification, evolution, and wisdom.

Thus, the theory of dissipative structures supports the long-standing assumption that artists, creative thinkers, and others who are constantly seeking to open themselves up to new ideas or memes are on the whole more mentally fluid, more susceptible to turmoil or perturbations in the brain. Farley notes that one of the primary Big-T characteristics is what he calls "transmutative thinking," noting that such individuals are "exceptionally facile at shifting from one cognitive process to another and at transforming one mode of mental representation into another," and concludes that this mental fluidity is "related to the high degree of creativity" seen in Big T's. This kind of mental mobility can, as Farley emphasizes, lead to various kinds of instability, anxiety, and turmoil, including self-destructive behavior. But as Prigogine emphasizes, it is out of the instability that higher levels of mental connectedness emerge.

Creative minds, those open to all memes, have experienced the escape to a higher order frequently· They know that out of instability, uncertainty, and even chaos can come creativity and wisdom. So they are able to go through such experiences with ease and even pleasure—the anxiety of disorder is experienced by them as the excitement of new ideas, the fear of loss-of-self is experienced as the heightening of awareness and intensifying of senses that accompanies risk and adventure.

TURNING OFF THE LIGHT BULB

There are also individuals who are infected with the meme that things like mental transformation, perturbation, and growth are bad things. They dislike very much the feelings of anxiety, novelty, risk, and unpredictability that accompany increased mental fluctuations and instability. Like wheels that have not turned much, they become rusted, resistant to movement, and it can take tremendous force to get them spinning. Such people, who resist new ideas and experiences, who refer every idea or experience to their past, who are always sure they are right, never experience self-doubt, and are intolerant of novelty—these people are trying to eliminate the influx of new energy and matter into their brains. That is, they are trying to turn their brains into closed systems, like a cup of coffee gone cold, a stone, a rusted wheel. To cause such rigid personality structures to escape to a higher order requires an enormous amount of energy input. And the process of transformation can be a terrifying ordeal for such people, a descent into chaos.

For those rigid personalities who have never gone through such transformation since childhood, the descent into chaos can appear to have no exit. To give up their grasp on their reassuring and stable memes can seem very much like death. Thus, they hold on to their stabilizing memes with all their strength, clinging with teeth and fingernails, convinced that those who are challenging their memes are vicious, crazy, and most of all *immoral* destroyers of all that is good, solid, stable, reliable.

Such individuals can justify almost any action to hold on to those memes, to transmit and even impose those memes on the rest of society, since they know they are doing what is morally right. To the torturers and executioners of the Inquisition, the terrible human suffering they caused was the work of God, and was not only justified but necessary to counter the insidious influences of the Devil. As Alvin Gouldner observes in his *For Sociology*, "It is when man is at his most purely moral that he may be most dangerous to the interests, and most callously indifferent to the needs, of others. Social systems know no fury like the man of moral absolutism aroused."

What we are seeing in the sex-power nexus is the fury of aroused men and women of moral absolutism, individuals who are desperately trying to maintain the stable structures within their brains in the face of increasing perturbations and fluctuations that seem to threaten them with chaos. What we are seeing is meme warfare.

17

Putting on the Armor: Sexual Imprints and the Emotional Plague

• •

What is repressed in sexual life will reappear [in distorted form]
in daily life.

—Sigmund Freud

As the caterpillar chooses the fairest leaves to lay her eggs on, so
the priest lays his curse on the fairest joys.

—William Blake, "The Marriage of Heaven and Hell"

The interrelationship between rigid personality structures and physical rigidity has been studied by scientists for a long time, but I had an opportunity to witness it firsthand while gathering research for a book I was writing about recent developments in neuroscience. Over a period of several years I interviewed a large number of people as they were experiencing the effects of a variety of "brain machines," devices to increase the flow of information and energy to the brain. These devices seemed to increase fluctuations in, or to destabilize, certain brain-mind structures and to trigger experiences: Many of the users experienced vivid images, intense memories, altered states of consciousness, and creative ideas that they found entertaining and quite valuable.

Many of the subjects commented on the extraordinarily deep levels of physical relaxation they experienced while using the devices. And that relaxation was verified by electroencephalographs that monitored brain-wave activity and electromyographs that measured muscle tension.

A small minority of the subjects, however, had quite different responses. As the brain machines began sending increased information and energy to their brains, and as they began experiencing novel feelings, ideas, sensations, and emotions, their bodies became increasingly rigid. They actually stiffened, their muscles grew tense, their hands began to tremble—you could see the veins bulging in their necks. It was as if they were desperately clinging to that state of consciousness they believed was "normal." Often when they were removed from the device, they exclaimed that nothing had happened. In many cases they stated that the experience was simply "boring." By successfully turning their brains and bodies into rigid, tight, impenetrable objects, they had been able to resist or deflect the increased information input.

A psychiatrist who had observed this phenomenon in his clients guided me to a rereading of the works of a psychiatrist who had spent his entire career investigating the relationship between mental and bodily rigidity. Dr. Wilhelm Reich was an original member of Freud's inner circle in Vienna who had gone beyond Freud. Reich asserted that the cause of all illness, mental and physical, was the inability to achieve fully satisfying sexuality. By repressing natural sexual energies, Reich claimed, individuals create energy blockages, and their bodies take on a rigidity, or what Reich called "armor." Physical and emotional traumas can also cause body and character rigidity or armoring, and this armoring in turn blocks the free flow and expression of healthy sexual energies—the very energies that are necessary to "heal" the traumas. Thus, Reich concluded, both "mental" illnesses— neurosis, psychosis, depression, anxiety, and sociopathic or borderline personalities—and physical illnesses, ranging from asthma to cancer, are the result of character armor resulting from sexual repression or the blockage of sexual energies. The rigidity becomes "anchored" in the individual's muscles and respiratory system.

This armoring, Reich claimed, is not a metaphor, not a psychological construct, but a very real disease, which is spread or transmitted by a bundle of information, or what we are calling a meme, having to do with sexual repression. Most often it is transmitted from one generation to the next: As young children begin to express their natural sexual energies and interests, they are punished or reprimanded by their parents, who convey the information or meme that sex is "bad." As a result, young people become frightened of their own sexuality and try to hold it back; this holding back requires real physical effort, manifested by muscular tension, rigidity, and respiratory blockages.

MOTHER JEEPS AND PING-PONG BALLS AS SEX OBJECTS

Ethologists tell the story of a baby giraffe whose mother was hit and killed by a Jeep. The giraffe, confused and traumatized, needed to find a mother substitute, and the only thing comparable was the Jeep. Thereafter, the giraffe followed the Jeep everywhere, attempted to suckle from it, and when the giraffe became an adult even tried to mate with the Jeep. No matter how much the giraffe was chased away, it always returned, and always retained its attachment to the Jeep. The giraffe had become what scientists call *imprinted* with the Jeep.

The literature is full of similar tales of odd imprints. Ethologist Konrad Lorenz observed baby geese who, when their mothers were removed, became imprinted to him, to the patterns on the walls of their cages—one gosling even became imprinted to a Ping-Pong ball, and when the animal matured, it had no sexual attraction to female geese, but faithfully attempted to mate with the Ping-Pong ball.

Humans, too, receive imprints, often in infancy, and these imprints stay with us the rest of our lives. Imprints are a remarkable type of learning that takes place when the brain is in an exceedingly vulnerable, malleable, open, and receptive state. Though the content of imprints is the result of experiences, the ability to take imprints, scientists have discovered, is hard-wired into the brain. It is as if we are born with a roll of unexposed photographic film in our brains. At some point the lens of our mind opens, and mysteriously but very rapidly, the film is exposed. The image that becomes imprinted on that film can be just about anything. Only the accidents of our life experiences will determine whether we become imprinted with an image of a loving human mother, a Jeep, or a Ping-Pong ball.

The process of imprinting consists of transmitting a bundle of information into someone's brain. Imprints are, then, what we have been calling memes, but they are a very special, tenacious type of meme. Throughout our lives, we are constantly exposed to new memes in the process we call learning. Memes must compete in the open marketplace of memes, and those that prove useful we keep, while those that are not useful can be discarded with little difficulty. At one point in our lives we might be firm believers in the meme that Santa Claus visits our house on Christmas Eve, that storks deliver babies, or that the moon is made of green cheese. When we are confronted with memes that contradict those beliefs, we can leave the old memes behind, like clothes we have outgrown.

Imprints, however, cannot be so easily discarded. They are so deeply imbedded within our brains that they often cannot be uprooted even when the imprinted person is confronted with convincing evidence that the imprinted meme is absolutely neither true or useful, is in fact stupid, harmful, or dangerous. Indeed, in many cases, as psychologists and ethologists have carefully shown, the more you threaten or contradict an individual's imprint, the more strongly does the individual cling to it. Lorenz and others have repeatedly demonstrated that even negative reinforcement, i.e., punishing an individual for acting on (or "believing") its imprint, doesn't discourage that belief. Quite the contrary, punishing an individual for following its imprint actually tends to increase the strength of the imprint. Once the giraffe became imprinted to the Jeep, and the goose to its Ping-Pong ball, there was no way for them to "unlearn" the imprint, and they remained attached to their imprinted objects for the rest of their lives.

One reason for this is, as we have seen, that imprints take place when the brain is in a peculiarly open, highly receptive state. Scientists who have investigated imprinting have found that during the brief period when the imprint is being made, it produces very definite anatomical and neurochemical changes, becoming stamped indelibly upon the neurons of the brain.

A second reason imprints are so resistant to change is that the individuals who have been imprinted are generally not aware that they have. Imprints are, in other words, unconscious. Individuals may act in ways that are, to an observer, clearly abnormal, such as attempting to mate with a Jeep or a Ping-Pong ball. But to the individual, this behavior seems right and normal. The imprint has not only been forgotten, it has never been remembered.

STATE-BOUND LEARNING

In one of Charlie Chaplin's funniest scenes, his bowler-hatted little tramp is befriended by a drunken rich man, who takes him in, wines and dines him, professes his great affection for Charlie, and invites him to stay in his mansion. The next morning, the rich man, now sober, is astonished to find this unknown tramp in his mansion, and tosses poor Charlie out. That evening, drunk again, the rich man encounters Charlie and once again professes his great friendship, wondering where Charlie has been. Charlie is befuddled, but we viewers get the joke: What the rich man experiences when he is drunk can only be remembered when he is in the same state.

In recent years a large number of scientific studies have been made of this phenomenon, and they have proven that *all* memories are to a greater or lesser degree "state dependent" or "state-bound." That is, we remember something best when we are in the same mental or physical state we were in when we first learned it. In one study, subjects were divided into two groups: One group consumed several drinks of alcohol, the other drank water. Then each was given the same material to learn. When tested later to see how well they recalled the material, the subjects who had been slightly tipsy when they learned the material did not remember it well when they were sober, but when given several drinks again, their recall soared. The subjects in the other group remembered best when stone sober, but when given a few drinks their recall deteriorated.

Other studies have found that things learned when one is happy are remembered best when one is happy, what we learn when cold is remembered best when we are cold, and so on. Recent experiments with rats at Kent State University demonstrated that rats who were administered stress, such as electrical shocks, had amnesia for the learning until they were shocked again, at which point the learning was recalled.

This concept of state-dependent learning offers us another clue to the nature of imprints, and to why imprints are so difficult to alter. We can see that one thing that makes these imprints unconscious or difficult to bring into consciousness (or remember) is that they are state-bound.

Most of our deepest imprints take place in infancy or early childhood, including those having to do with the expression of sexual energies. And often these imprints are quite negative. As medical psychologist John Money of Johns Hopkins notes, "Perfectly nice, reasonable mothers and fathers go berserk when they encounter the first appearance of normal sexual rehearsal play in their children." Perhaps the infant or child begins to do something that is perfectly natural, like playing with his (we will imagine this example is a boy) genitals, enjoying and exploring the sensations he can produce. A parent notices his sex play and immediately threatens him by shouting "Bad!" or "Naughty!" in an angry voice, or punishes him by slapping his hands or shaking him. At that point an imprint is created. At that point the child's feelings about sex are altered in a way that will influence his behavior for the rest of his life.

SEX AND TRAUMA IN THE TWILIGHT ZONE

One reason for the profound effect of such childhood experiences is the curious type of electrical activity that is taking place in the child's brain. Using electroencephalographs, scientists have found that the human brain produces electrical activity (brain waves) of four distinct varieties. The most rapid brain waves, called *beta* waves, are produced when we are in ordinary waking states of consciousness. When we close our eyes and become relaxed or unfocused, brain-wave activity slows down, and we produce *alpha* waves.

As we become even more profoundly relaxed, we enter a trancelike state in which we produce very slow brain waves called *theta* waves. And slowest of all are *delta* waves, produced in states of unconsciousness, like deep sleep or coma.

Much recent research has focused on the third, or theta, state. When the brain produces large quantities of theta activity, there results a mysterious, dreamlike state of consciousness that some scientists have called "the twilight state." Most adults experience this elusive state rarely—often only in the brief moments between waking and sleep, when vivid, spontaneous images (called hypnagogic images), memories from childhood, or surprising ideas flit across their mind. Scientists investigating theta have found that this trancelike state is the key to memory, learning, and creativity.

Biofeedback expert Thomas Budzynski of the University of Colorado Medical Center has done extensive research into the properties of the theta state, and has found that it is the state in which the brain can learn enormous amounts very quickly; it is, in fact, the state in which "superlearning" takes place. One reason this is possible is that the normal "critical" or rational consciousness associated with rapid beta activity, which filters out most of the information coming into the brain, and "edits" reality, is suspended, allowing virtually everything to go directly into memory. Says Budzynski, "The hypnagogic state, the twilight state, between waking and sleep, has these properties *of uncritical acceptance of verbal material, or almost any material it can process.*" It is in this "altered" or trancelike state of consciousness, Budzynski says, that "*a lot of work gets done very quickly.*"

Biofeedback researchers Elmer and Alyce Green of the Menninger Foundation taught subjects to enter the theta state and found it "to be associated with a deeply internalized state and with a quieting of the body, emotions, and thoughts, thus allowing usually 'unheard or unseen things' to come to the consciousness in the form of hypnagogic memory." They discovered that the subjects frequently reported vivid memories of long-forgotten childhood events: "They were not like going through a memory in one's mind," write the Greens, "but rather like an experience, a reliving." They also found that those producing theta waves frequently had "new and valid ideas or syntheses of ideas, not primarily by deduction, but springing by intuition from unconscious sources." Finally they discovered that the subjects they taught to enter the theta state reported that they had life-altering insights, or what the Greens called "integrative experiences." Also, the Greens were surprised to note that those taught to enter the theta state became very healthy; while the control group (the one not producing theta) continued to have its normal number of illnesses, the theta group had almost no illness whatsoever.

Psychobiologist James McGaugh of UC at Irvine conducted a series of experiments to investigate learning and memory in rats, and found that theta waves were essential for the formation of memory. In fact, the best predictor of memory, McGaugh found, was the quantity of theta waves produced in the rat's brain. Theta waves, he believes, are an indication that the brain is in the right state to process and store information, whether it is new information to be learned or old information emerging in the form of memories.

Scientists investigating memory have now determined that for memories to be formed, the brain must undergo a process called Long Term Potentiation (LTP). Recently Gary Lynch and John Larson, also of UC at Irvine, discovered that LTP is especially effective when the brain is producing theta waves. "We have found the magic rhythm," says Dr. Lynch, "the theta rhythm."

Significantly the theta rhythm is what Lynch calls "the natural, indigenous rhythm" of a part of the brain called the hippocampus, which is essential for the formation and storage of new memories and the calling up of old memories. The hippocampus is a part of the limbic system, that part of the brain that evolved long before the development of the neocortex.

Most of us are aware of the value of the theta state, though we may know it by other names. We have only to remember all the tales of great ideas and seminal discoveries—and even our own flashes of insight—that occur as feelings, images, or a sudden "knowing" as the thinker is staring drowsily into a fire, walking alone upon a beach, gazing pensively into the distance: in other words, in theta.

How nice it would be if we could enter this beneficial, productive brain-wave state at will. Unfortunately, for most adults it occurs only fleetingly, in those brief moments between waking and sleep. Even if you intentionally try to produce theta waves, you will in most cases quickly fall asleep. Studies of the brain waves of experienced meditators show that when they are in that state they know as deep meditation, *samadhi*, illumination, or bliss, they are producing large quantities of theta waves. But to be able to produce these trancelike theta states at will is not easy to learn: A study of Zen monks showed that those who produced theta most readily were those with more than twenty years of meditation experience.

Scientists have also discovered that the theta state is produced by emotional or physical trauma. Research indicates that when people experience a sudden shocking event, their brain-wave activity shifts into theta. Anyone who has been in a car accident, for example, will be familiar with the extraordinary alteration in consciousness that takes place: Everything seems to slow down, you notice details with uncanny clarity and vividness, you are separated from the external world, sudden memories appear (some people have the experience that their life, or parts of it, is flashing before their eyes). Anyone who has observed the survivors of a disaster will have noticed their trancelike behavior, as they sit wide-eyed, passive, benumbed, lost in some other world.

In many cases, these trancelike or "hypnoidal" states result in amnesia—the victims will find that they cannot remember part or all of the traumatic event. It is as if the mind, having had such powerful and painful information pierced into its deepest, most sensitive areas, buries the memories away, in an attempt to spare the victim further pain. The imprint becomes hidden, or, as Reich would say, it becomes armored.

But nevertheless one of the characteristics of the theta state is a spontaneous upwelling of vivid memories from childhood. I have observed people using brain-altering devices that draw the subject into the theta state, and many of them emerge from the experience speaking of having experienced events from their childhood that they had long forgotten. One man, for example, described to me with awe his feeling of being back on the front porch of his childhood home, playing Parcheesi: He recalled the exact configuration of tooth-marks on the yellow Parcheesi marker, the smell of the asphalt from the street, the voice on the radio announcing that Edmund Hillary and Tenzing Norgay had conquered Mount Everest—something that had happened over thirty years earlier. "It was like I was right there," he said, "living it!"

One intriguing finding that has emerged from brain research is that, while adults rarely produce theta, children are in a theta state most of the time—up to the age of twelve or thirteen, children produce mostly theta waves, and then the amount of theta progressively decreases as the child grows into adulthood. In other words, children spend most of their time in what we adults would call a trancelike, altered state of consciousness, and one that is extremely open and receptive, highly conducive to the learning of new information and the formation of memories.

So, let's return to the infant or child who has been exploring its sexuality and is suddenly punished or reprimanded by its parent. The infant, already in an altered and highly receptive state of consciousness (the theta state), is confused, shocked, and terrified. Like the victim of a car accident or some other trauma, the child is thrust even deeper into an altered state of consciousness. In this trancelike state, the child's mind is totally exposed, open, receptive, suggestible. It is in that state in which, as Dr. Budzynski says, there is "uncritical ac-

ceptance of verbal material, or almost any material it can process."
What is "learned" during that state is learned in the most direct and
intense way possible, and, as a result of Long Term Potentiation,
what is learned becomes a permanent part of the child's memory.

What the child learns is that what it was doing is somehow "bad,"
so bad that it has threatened the child's security and caused the parent
to punish it and (apparently) stop loving it. It learns that it should
not engage in such behavior again, since that might cause another
traumatic punishment from its parents. It learns to associate sex with
fear. The information is routed through the emotional or limbic system and becomes a permanent part of the child's mind: The child
becomes imprinted. But the imprint itself, and the experience that
produced the imprint, are buried away in a sort of posttrauma amnesia. The imprint, that is, becomes unconscious.

Since the infant is often still in a preverbal state when it is imprinted,
when it grows up it cannot approach or remember this experience
or imprint verbally—and so it is only a feeling. It is also inaccessible
to the conscious mind because it has been coded into memory via the
limbic system, and thus cannot be approached through logical, verbal,
or intellectual analysis, or through the other "higher" mental faculties
of the neocortex, but only through the preverbal, emotional, primitive awareness of the limbic brain. (No "talk therapy" can deal with
such early experiences—how can one talk about something for which
one has no words?) The imprint is also unconscious because it is not
simply a memory but rather a state of being—something that happens
all over the body simultaneously: It is imprinted not just as certain
words, images, emotions, or ideas, but as a whole-body state of
muscular tightness and rigidity, and respiratory tension.

Most important, the imprint is unconscious because it is state-
dependent. The imprinting took place when the child was in an altered
state of consciousness—a state of shock, fear, total dependency, extraordinary mental openness, heightened sensitivity, and sexual
arousal. Therefore, like the drunk who when he is sober can't remember befriending Charlie Chaplin, the adult living in what society
calls a "normal" state of consciousness (i.e., the one dominated by
beta-wave activity) cannot gain access to the imprint experience.

Furthermore, the adult has learned to avoid like the plague any
experience that might thrust him or her back into that terrifying
infantile state of total dependency, helplessness, fear, and openness.
Whatever it was that happened back then, the brain has tried to heal

the wound by burying it. The adult continues to act on the imprint received decades ago, that certain types of experience are bad, and has no more knowledge he or she is acting in response to an imprint than a fish has knowledge that it is swimming in water, or that there is something else up there above the surface called air.

There can be no doubt that early imprints are extremely hard to alter. "Give us a child until he is six, and he'll be ours forever." Søren Kierkegaard said this, quoting the Jesuits. It is, of course, just as true of the children of Baptists, Buddhists, television-watchers, or blood-drinkers. It is a simple, observable fact that most children in most societies grow up to be very much like the preceding generation, with its same loves, hates, fears, desires. This is a testament to the powers of imprinting.

THE MIND-GENE CONNECTION

With recent breakthroughs in neuroscience and in our knowledge of how neurochemicals and their receptors function at the molecular level, scientists are beginning to understand how what were once thought to be purely "mental" events can become imprinted in the body on the cellular level as chronic conditions, thus allowing state-dependent learning, which is centered in the emotional brain or limbic system, to become the mechanism of human disease.

Psychologist Ernest Rossi explores this "mind-gene connection" in his recent book *The Psychobiology of Mind-Body Healing*, and points out how "languages of the mind," such as words, ideas, sensations, are integrated in the limbic system, which can also speak the "languages of the body," communicating with the organs and cells by means of neurochemical messengers.

Says Rossi, "Under 'mental' stress, the limbic-hypothalamic system in the brain converts the neural messages of mind into the neurohormonal 'messenger molecules' of the body. These, in turn, can direct the endocrine system to produce steroid hormones that can reach into the nucleus of different cells of the body to modulate the expression of genes. These genes then direct the cells to produce the various molecules that will regulate metabolism, growth, activity level, sexuality, and the immune response in sickness and health. . . . Mind ultimately does modulate the creation and expression of the molecules of life!"

Through these recent discoveries, says Rossi, "we're at last building the bridge between biochemistry and psychoanalysis." According
to Rossi, "We can reconceptualize a lot of classical physiology by
seeing nerves, blood vessels and bones as channels for the mind-
molecule connection."

The mind-gene connection provides us with a neurobiological explanation of how, as Reich contended, traumatic events and imprints
can become anchored as chronic physical conditions, or armoring.
What we see and experience can enter us via our limbic brain and
transform our bodies permanently.

Traumas or negative imprints enter the limbic-hypothalamic system and influence the body on a cellular level while the individual is
in a highly charged (or altered) state of consciousness, a state Rossi
says is very much like a hypnotic trance. Since this is a state in which
the mind is uniquely receptive to new information, the response to
the trauma or imprint takes place and is "learned," i.e., becomes a
habitual pattern, on a cellular (and unconscious) level.

Theoretically we could detect our own unwanted habitual patterns,
and intentionally try to alter them. But the "learning" that has created
the patterns is very much state-dependent. The only way to correct
or undo the negative pattern is to enter a mental state like that in
which the original learning (or mislearning) took place. This explains
how many body-centered or holistic psychotherapeutic techniques
(such as Rolfing, rebirthing, Bioenergetics, hypnotherapy, confrontational therapy) work: They encourage the subject to become deeply
relaxed, or highly charged emotionally, so that theta-wave activity
increases, allowing the subject to reenter or reaccess the original mental state, where the trauma or imprint can be experienced, articulated,
and replaced by new learning or imprints.

This also explains why when adults enter the theta state, they are
so frequently overwhelmed by memories from childhood: Those
memories are, as we have noted, state-dependent memories; they
took place when the child was in an altered state—the theta state.

These early traumatic imprints, according to Reich, are anchored
in the body in the form of muscular tightness and rigidity and respiratory blocks; these blocks in turn, through the constant tension
and stress they place on the body, are manifested throughout life by
physical ailments ranging from asthma to high blood pressure to
cancer. By learning to return frequently to the childlike theta state,
we can surmise, adults like those studied by the Greens are able to

release many of the rigidities and blockages that are the root cause of their long-standing illnesses, and thus become more physically healthy.

BAPTISM, BOOT CAMP, AND THE PRISONER IN THE CLOSET

Imprints are hard to change. And yet such changes happen all the time. The human brain has enormous plasticity—it has the capacity to reorganize itself, forge new neural pathways, undergo a Prigoginian escape to a higher order. But seldom accidentally. To be reimprinted, the individual must be returned to the state in which the imprinting first took place. In general, as we have seen, this means a return to the experience of infancy—which means an experience of dependency, and an altered state of consciousness (whether it be bliss, terror, love, rage, or all of these).

Virtually all successful cults, religions, or organizations have developed highly effective reimprinting techniques. Think of being submerged, unable to breathe, held under water in the arms of someone else, and then think of baptism (as practiced by fundamentalist Christians), and the experience of being "born again" it is intended to produce. Think of going to boot camp, being cut off from the family and community, being exhausted, confused, and systematically terrorized by your drill sergeant, and you can easily see why recruits soon come to "love" their sergeants and their rifles, and make the step from believing that killing is wrong to believing, as the marine slogan says, "Kill 'em all and let God sort them out." Think of going away on a religious "retreat," where the social bonds are cut and the brain enters a theta state and the presence of God is everywhere.

Or consider the Stockholm Syndrome, in which individuals who are kidnapped and held hostage by terrorists come to identify with their kidnappers and to side with them against their would-be rescuers. These hostages have been forced into a state of infancy: isolated from any previous bonds, thrown into an altered state of consciousness by terror, totally dependent for food, protection, and life itself on the kidnappers. Little wonder that they become so open and receptive to the ideas and the human warmth (real or imagined) of their captors. Day after day Patty Hearst sat imprisoned in a cramped, lightless closet, terrified and alone, her only human contacts coming in conversations with her captors, who described to her their political vision of armed revolution against a fascist capitalist state. Like a baby giraffe quickly switching its mother-love imprint from its dead mother to the Jeep that killed her, Patty was soon eager to emerge from her closet as Comrade Tania, a bank-robbing, gun-slinging revolutionary filled with disgust for fascist pigs like her mother and father.

Many other common experiences are capable of causing us to become reimprinted. Think of being a teenager and going to a rock concert where the loud music is playing everywhere, so loud your whole body is resonating to it, and there is nothing but the music and the musicians and all the other bodies and you can scream and hyperventilate and allow your body to writhe and unleash.

Think of making love with someone and having an orgasm that is so astonishing you think your soul is going to fly out of your body, while a voice in your ear is crying, "God, oh God, I love you!"

FASCISM, CONNIPTION FITS, AND THE GREAT AMERICAN HAIR SHIRT

Reich was not concerned solely with how what he called armoring affected individuals. From his research and his observations he concluded that this "character armoring" is reflected in the culture as a whole. Freud had pointed out that repressed sexual energies will return or reappear in distorted form, and Reich found that in heavily armored individuals and societies the "return" of the repressed energies is likely to take the form of fascist social and political behaviors, such as the persecution of scapegoats, outbreaks of mass violence, fanaticism, nationalism, intolerance, sadism, masochism, rape, war. Reich called this problem the Emotional Plague of Mankind.

This "plague" is so deeply entrenched, according to Reich, that any attempt to root it out can lead to an eruption of hysteria or fascist violence.

Reich himself is a good example of what can happen to someone who attempts to puncture the character armor of society. He was expelled from the Communist and Socialist parties and the International Psychoanalytical Society, and driven out of Germany and Austria by the Nazis. At various points in his career he was branded a sex maniac. In the United States he was accused of being a Nazi agent, harassed by the FBI and the FDA, denounced by the AMA, persecuted and jailed, and in 1957 all his scientific books and papers were seized and burned in an incinerator in New York City by the U.S. government. Shortly thereafter, he died in jail. Philosopher Robert Anton Wilson observes, "From Reich's point of view, all of this harassment and slander happened because those who have the Emotional Plague are terrified and furious whenever anybody threatens to make them aware, even for a second, of just how sick they are. *Any* attempt to alleviate the Character Armor without great subtlety and caution unleashes terror, violence and what my grandfather called conniption fits."

To return to the sex-power nexus, we can now understand more clearly the source of the fanaticism and conniption fits of the antisex forces, and the true nature of the "armor" and rigidity they carry with them into the battle.

Normal, healthy humans have a natural interest in sex. According to Reich, we *need* to express our sexual energies fully and freely through unrestrained whole-body orgasms to remain physically and mentally healthy. But because of childhood imprints, many Americans feel ashamed and guilty of their sexuality. Because of our guilt, shame, and fear, we attempt to suppress our sexual energies. We do this by holding back, which causes muscular tensions resulting in energy blockages, respiratory tightness, and armoring. As a result of our armor, our bodies are not loose and "flowing" enough to permit true whole-body orgasms: What we experience as orgasm is but a pinched, partial, tension-racked and unsatisfactory version of the real thing.

But no matter how much we armor ourselves, the sexual energies cannot be totally eradicated. The repressed energies express themselves in a different form. They are invested in things, possessions, and invested in others, experienced vicariously—thus our obsession with the accumulation of wealth and material objects, thus the enormous interest in the sex lives and romances of television and movie stars, politicians, rock stars; thus the mass consumption by women of romance novels; thus the huge sales of sexually oriented magazines like *Playboy*, *Penthouse*, *Hustler*, *Playgirl*, and *Cosmopolitan*.

This constitutes the double bind of the American spirit, the nagging itching of the Great American Hair Shirt. We have sexual energies and needs, but we have been imprinted to believe they are bad, so to punish ourselves we put on the scratchy hair shirt of guilt. Sex is forbidden, or dirty, so we make certain that all our sexual experiences are frustrating and unsatisfying. Sex is bad or something to be hidden away, but everywhere we look in our culture, there is sex: sexual images in advertising, in the media, in the arts. There is sex everywhere, of course, because we have put it there ourselves, because we need it and because at the same time we need to feel guilty about it —and so we have developed a culture filled with sexual imagery, a culture based on secondhand sex, which we are obsessed with and despise.

Since there is sex everywhere we look, we are constantly feeling guilty: The hair shirt continues to itch. And even as the hair shirt makes us feel guilty, it also reminds us constantly of what is being denied, of our true needs that are never truly fulfilled. Why else would we be aroused by tacky subway advertisements or television characters or mindless movie stars or predictable romance novels?

Sex makes us feel guilty or frightened, and yet it's impossible for most people to stop being interested in sex. How can we express our interest in sex without feeling guilty? One way is to pretend that our interest is in something other than sex. Let's ask the candidate if he has ever committed adultery. Let's ask his wife what she thinks about adultery. . . . This is not prurient interest in sex, something to feel guilty about: This is interest in politics. This does not make the hair shirt itch. And so it goes: We express our sexual interests with obsessive frequency, and yet, as long as we can convince ourselves we are really interested in something else—news, health, religion, stamping out abortion, censoring pornography—we can remain free of guilt. And as long as we can do that, we can continue to believe that sex is something dirty, bad, forbidden, other. As, of course, we have been imprinted to do.

18

Meme Warfare in the Sex-Power Nexus

. . . .

Violence has come to be regarded by ever larger sectors of the population . . . as a legitimate instrument, indeed as the only instrument to change reality and achieve progress and development. This, to put it simply, is madness. A good part of this violence proceeds from a political fiction, from the idea that through a system and a body of ideas you can capture reality in its entirety and express it, organize it and reform it in a perfectly logical way. Every ideology leads ultimately to fanaticism, and fanaticism is fiction trying to impose itself on reality in the name of science.

—Mario Vargas Llosa, "Fictions that Breed Violence"

It was when I said,
"There is no such thing as the truth,"
That the grapes seemed fatter.
The fox ran out of his hole. . . .

—Wallace Stevens, "On the Road Home"

In the last few chapters I have been using a variety of approaches—among them Big-T/Little-t analysis; meme theory; dissipative structure theory; information theory; Reichian psychobiology; and psycho-neurology—to try to get a clear picture of the antisex forces. It is a bit like taking photographs of something from a number of different angles, and using several different lenses.

But when we combine the images from all the different angles, the once-blurry picture springs into focus. What once appeared to be a number of different groups, we now see, is in fact a single force, composed of individuals who are very much the same in many essential ways. Whether they are opposed to abortion, pornography, birth-control clinics, sex education, erotic art, miniskirts, expressions of youthful sexual energies, rock music, or extramarital sex, they all seem to be heavily armored, tight, resistant to change, stamped from early childhood with an imprint emphasizing the negative qualities of human sexuality, and maintained in their views by a constant barrage of antisex memes.

The content of the common imprint is well described by feminist writer Lisa Duggan: "Americans have been reared and educated in a cultural environment which insists upon the link between sex and aggression, sex and chaos, sex and death. From earliest childhood, we all learn to fear sex. These deeply imbedded, unconscious fears are echoed and elaborated in nearly all our major sources of ideology, from the Bible to psychoanalysis to popular cultural forms such as the National Enquirer and the evening news. Nearly all of us share certain assumptions about sex: It arouses antisocial impulses, primarily masculine, which must be contained by marriage and women; if overstimulated, sexual energy can shatter family life and set in motion a destructive spree of exploitative promiscuity, rape, child abuse, and murder."

Imprinted and infected with virulent sexual-repression memes, these individuals are rigidly and desperately holding back their own sexual energies, energies that are being rechanneled and expressed in their zealous and obsessive struggle to keep everyone else sexually repressed.

THE MEME ABOUT SEX

We have discussed in a general way the memes that unite these seemingly disparate groups and individuals. Now, it's time to look more closely at them.

The first of them is that sex is dangerous. Not only dangerous but potentially deadly. No matter how they protest that they are only opposed to "abnormal" sex, the evidence provided by psychologists, scientists, and by their own behavior and statements makes it clear that sex itself is deeply threatening to the antisex crusaders. The act of sex, by thrusting the individual into an altered state of consciousness, threatens to permit the individual to return to the infantile, open state in which he or she was first imprinted against sex, and potentially to be reimprinted in a more sexually open way. Such mental states are to be avoided at all costs, and anything that tends to produce them, ranging from sex to art to new ideas to high-intensity music to mind-altering drugs, must be declared immoral, illegal, politically incorrect, sinful, antisocial, subversive, bad, or taboo.

For individuals who need to be rigidly in control, a return to this state of powerless openness is very much like an experience of death. So it's no wonder that they see uncontrolled sex as not only dangerous but even deadly, leading to "a destructive spree of exploitative promiscuity, rape, child abuse, and murder." These individuals, observes Lisa Duggan, live in a "hermetic world in which the leap from sex to death and destruction seems inevitable."

THE MEME ABOUT THE SEXES

The second meme that unites these groups is that females are superior to males. This meme is expressed by the right-wing fundamentalists, both male and female, in their belief that women are "pure" and more "moral" than men. Women are seen as the repositories of goodness and all the positive values and virtues that make family life possible, and as the moral anchor of the family.

Related to this Pure Woman on a Pedestal meme is the Virgin and Whore meme. Since women are purer and better than men, they are not allowed to sully that purity; if they do, they are no longer good but "bad." Once fallen from the pedestal, such women can never climb back onto it again. There is no middle ground between faithful wife and fallen women, between good girl and bad. Bad women are seen as especially dangerous, because, since men are so flawed by nature, they can very easily be led astray, tempted down the path of wickedness by bad women.

While the antisex radical feminists profess to believe that the Woman on a Pedestal and the Virgin/Whore are simply sexist myths created to oppress women, they actually share the meme of innate female superiority that gave birth to these memes. In their demands for a new society based on female values, they consistently characterize as female all the things they consider to be "good," such as peace, love, emotional openness, nurturance, and cooperation, while classifying as male values all those things they consider bad, including aggression, violence, war, and competitiveness.

This leads us to a variant of the meme about female superiority, which is the meme that males are innately bad and dangerous. Among the Christian fundamentalists this meme is convenient for both males and females. Males can use it to excuse their failings: If they indulge in sinful sex or other bad behavior, well, that's just the way men are, poor driven creatures, until they are forgiven or saved by the love of a good woman. Fundamentalist women also find this meme convenient, since it places them at the center of the redemption drama: Men may be lustful brutes, but that after all is just their nature, and the only way they can be redeemed and welcomed back into the fold of the family is by being "civilized" and restrained through the forgiveness and love and patient guidance of a female. In this view sex is something base that naturally appeals to the base nature of males, but kept strictly within the boundaries of a marriage, it can be used by a woman as a tool to keep the man from straying from the home and family.

In the antisex radical feminist version of this meme, the prospects for male redemption are less sanguine: Men are rapists or aggressive, sex-crazed beasts. The only way they can be admitted into decent feminist society, and even then only conditionally and warily, is by totally accepting superior female values. Or, looked at another way, the only hope for salvation is to "impose a female standard" upon our culture.

WHAT ALL THIS HAS TO DO WITH POWER

As we have often noted, sex and power tend to be opposite sides of the same coin, and the meme that sex is bad and dangerous provides its carriers with an enormously powerful tool to control behavior. Johns Hopkins medical psychologist John Money observes, "It's a pretty simple piece of psychology that if you terrorize small children, making them afraid of doing something the human organism normally does in healthy development, then you've put in place a lever of guilt and shame. All you need to do after that is pull the lever and they jump to attention and do whatever you tell them. So taboos are extremely widespread, the most common by far being the taboo against sex."

The sex taboo is imprinted in an experience of guilt and fear, and this guilt and fear remain in place—however deeply concealed—throughout life. Fear, of course, is perhaps our most powerful and primitive emotion. As scientists have discovered, when people are placed in a state of fear, there is a marked deterioration in their higher, more rational capabilities: Fear triggers the fight-or-flight response through those preverbal levels of the brain that evolved earliest, the so-called reptile brain and the emotional brain of the limbic system, while leaving our rational, verbal cerebral cortex in a state of disarray. We have all experienced firsthand how when we are in a state of fear or anxiety we simply don't think very well. Robert Anton Wilson points out, *"Throughout human life, when the bio-survival circuit senses danger, all other mental activity ceases."*

In a variety of studies, individuals with high levels of erotophobia or sex guilt were exposed to sexual stimuli (such as reading an erotic passage) and then given a lecture or something to learn. Subsequent tests show that the ability of the individuals to think logically or to remember correctly is damaged. Exposure to sexual stimuli, in effect, turns certain seemingly intelligent people into numbskulls.

This could be predicted, of course, since it is already well known that fear disrupts cognition. For erotophobics and people with high levels of sex guilt, the stimulus that triggers the fear response is sex itself: The bio-survival circuit senses danger (sex), and other mental activity ceases.

SPREADING FEAR TO SELL SALVATION

Because fear so effectively disrupts cognition, it can be used to implant ideas, information, or automatic responses into someone's mind and body: Fear is not just a lever to make people jump to attention and do whatever you tell them, it is a highly effective tool for spreading memes.

As we have noted, individuals with high levels of sex guilt and sex anxiety suffer cognitive disruptions in "sex-related situations." For them, sexual stimuli produce fear or a perception of danger; as a result, cognition is disrupted. And during this period of cognitive disruption, they are in an extremely open and receptive state: Their resistance to meme infection is very low.

All of which provides an insight into the proselytizing (or meme-spreading) strategies and oratorical techniques of the antisex forces. In their speeches, sermons, interviews, and articles, these crusaders do not simply state their ideas, tell what they are opposed to and why. Instead, they describe or present graphically, with vivid details, the most shocking example of the thing they oppose.

In the case of the anti-abortion forces, this might include color films or slides of bloody fetuses, accompanied by chants of "Abortion Is Murder!" and "Baby Killers!" In the case of opponents of sex education, this might include the telling of a tale about a young girl who, having taken a sex-education course, quickly became promiscuous and within months was out working the streets as a prostitute and drug addict, accompanied by repetitive incantations such as "Sex education should take place in the home, not the school," and "Sex education causes sex participation!" In the case of the antipornography forces, this might include films or slides or descriptions of the most violent and scabrous types of graphic sexual images, or cautionary tales of young women who took off their clothes for a camera, rocketed to porn stardom, and committed suicide in deranged shame, accompanied by cries that "pornography is the theory, rape is the practice!" and "coitus is punishment!"

Since the antisex leaders *want* the people they are addressing to suffer cognitive disruption, they must make sure that the situation is a "sex-related" situation, to produce the needed fear/danger response. Since the situation they are addressing people in—whether speaking in a lecture hall, on a television talk show, from a pulpit, or writing in a book or magazine—is not by its nature a sex-related situation, the antisex leader must do everything possible to turn it into one. That means telling vivid, sexually loaded tales of promiscuous, sperm-drenched high school girls, describing or showing shocking erotic images, and so on.

The listeners and watchers are presented with highly charged sexual stimuli; the sexual stimuli disrupt their cognitive processes, causing them to go into a highly charged mental state; they become extremely suggestible and open to new information or memes, and accept fully, unquestioningly, the ideas that the speaker is presenting to them in the form of chants or slogans. The transmission of the memes has taken place. All you need to do after that, in the words of John Money, "is pull the lever and they jump to attention and do whatever you tell them."

Robert Anton Wilson points out that, "Whoever can scare people enough . . . can sell them quickly on any verbal map that seems to give them relief, i.e., cure the anxiety. By frightening people with Hell and then offering them Salvation, the most ignorant or crooked individuals can 'sell' a whole system of thought that cannot bear two minutes of rational analysis."

To control people's fear and guilt about sexuality is, in a very real sense, to possess power over them, to rule them. Seen in this light, it becomes apparent that the antisex forces are engaged in a struggle that is not moral but political. The true purpose of the sexual taboos (or memes) they spread is not so much to stop people from engaging in sexual activities that are truly dangerous, but to "pull the lever" and make them "jump to attention and do whatever you tell them."

BLACK-HATTED THUGS IN PREACHER'S GARB: THE NOT-SO-SECRET AGENDA

Thus, we can see the large-scale political agenda of the right-wing fundamentalist antisex forces: Their political ambitions go far beyond the sexual realm. The same groups that are struggling to keep books that mention sex out of school libraries and to end sex education in public schools are also actively engaged in eliminating from the curriculum of public schools such things as discussions of values or morals, alcohol or drugs, nuclear war, feminism, population or population control, ecology, and evolution, as well as any guided fantasy or imagery techniques, the writing of autobiographies, diaries, or log books for assignments, role-playing games, and anything that smacks of a "psychological approach to life." One such group, mentioned earlier, recently won a federal court decision against the Greenville, Tennessee, school system, based on its opposition to the mention in public schools of the Renaissance, Leonardo da Vinci, the diary of Anne Frank, any texts that attempt to stimulate the imagination of young readers, *The Wizard of Oz*, and all references to feminism and to pacifism.

This group was provided financial support and lawyers from the staff of Concerned Women of America, the Washington-based organization led by Beverly LeHaye, and by a right-wing lawyers' group founded by television evangelist and politician Pat Robertson.

The same groups that are so passionately pushing for sexually restrictive laws have also been actively engaged in funding the activities of the Contra guerrillas in Central America, in providing financial support for right-wing military dictatorships around the world, in pushing for a greater use of the death penalty, in attempting to force the United States to withdraw from the United Nations, in demanding a more conservative Supreme Court that would take a more restrictive view of First Amendment rights, in attempting to establish daily prayers in public schools, in supporting political candidates who vow to eliminate the separation of church and state and turn the nation into a "Christian state." The true goal of these groups, then, is "law and order": the law that they establish (through divine guidance) and the order that results from the suppression of any opposition to their rule.

There is a good reason for this attempt to disguise an extremist political agenda as a moral crusade. America is, as we have observed, a nation with a strong traditional admiration for Big-T values: Even the most Little-t of Americans learn to voice their respect for such Big-T values as aggressiveness, adventurousness, individualism, liberty, and so on. With a strong Big-T heritage, many Americans have a congenital suspicion of ideologies and authoritarianism: Both communism and fascism are "un-American" not so much because of the ideas and ideals they represent, but because in practical terms they threaten to limit the freewheeling and cantankerous individualism Americans so admire. Authoritarian ideologies represent, in the American Wild West mythos, the faceless, remorseless, impersonal, powerful forces from the East, whose policies are enforced by well-armed, unshaven, black-hatted thugs—they want to put up barbed-wire fences all over the great prairies and ranges of the West and turn us self-sufficient cowboys into hired hands.

Americans, that is, have little sympathy for authoritarian political programs. While polls show they strongly support such socialist enterprises as Social Security, compulsory public education, and a national health-care program, they would never support a mainstream political candidate they suspected of being a socialist, or tinged with socialist (or radical, or even strongly "liberal") ideas. Similarly, while many Americans may have sympathy for some of the ideas expressed by the far right, including racism, religious intolerance, anticommunism, and nationalism, no mainstream political candidate can win running on an overtly fascist, extremist platform. Politicians with even relatively mild leanings to the right and the left generally go the way of George McGovern and Barry Goldwater, while true ideologues, such as long-time Communist party leader Gus Hall, American Nazi leader George Lincoln Rockwell, and black Islam leader Louis Farrakhan are scornfully dismissed by most as freaks, oddballs, weirdos, and whackos.

For extremist ideas to get the support of the American mainstream, they must be disguised as something else, as Ronald Reagan disguised himself as a benevolent old fuddy-duddy and his vicious and economically disastrous right-wing program as a simple, down-home attempt to balance the budget and strengthen our defense.

Aware that their political goals, if stated outright, would be rejected by most Americans, the forces of the far right have needed some sort of disguise; they have had to dress the black-hatted thugs in some costume that would make them appear less sinister, more trustworthy. And what better disguise than the garb of a preacher, the saver of souls, whose apparent interest is morality, God's will, and not politics.

Similarly, what better way to disguise a political program than as a compassionate moral concern with sex? Our national sexual ambivalence presented the forces of the far right with an ideal means of entry into the national political arena. The politicians pretended that they were not politicians at all, but simple moral crusaders against rape, child molestation, adolescent promiscuity, sexual violence against women, and ugly sexual perversions—why, these are things that all citizens of goodwill agree are harmful, aren't they?

And the preachers and moral crusaders delivered their message in terms guaranteed to capture the attention and arouse the fears of sexually obsessed Americans. They spoke of "danger" in terms that would arouse anxiety, fright, guilt, and shame in the breasts of all who had been imprinted against sex.

And so, for example, in speeches condemning the 7-Eleven chain of stores for carrying *Playboy* magazine, Jerry Falwell accused the stores of "poisoning" the minds of America. Evangelist Bob Tilton told the crowd that if America allowed 7-Eleven stores to sell magazines like *Playboy*, "she will fall, like all other countries that have been attacked by communism and indecency!" And Beverly LeHaye of Concerned Women for America proclaimed that a boycott of the store chain would be "the greatest thing we could do to improve family life in America!"

And so what purported to be a discussion of morals becomes pure politics, the discomfort with looking at pictures of naked women turns into an assertion of patriotism; the preference for chastity and monogamy becomes a defense of the American family; the struggle against shameless sexuality becomes the struggle against Godless communism; and all who disagree, such as anticensorship groups, become "un-American," bent on poisoning the minds of America, which is to say, traitors.

TOWARD MATRIARCHY, OR, WHAT IS LIBERTY IN THE FACE OF DEATH?

Like the forces of the far right, the antiporn radical feminists have political ambitions that go far beyond the mere eradication of pornography. These same groups who decree that only "politically correct" sex can be allowed are also struggling against the free spread of any *information* they declare to be politically incorrect (that is, any information they decide may be "harmful to women"). They are also convinced that, since no male can be truly sympathetic with women, and since males are by nature aggressors and rapists, they must use a sexist standard, and decree that the only acceptable political leaders are females. They present themselves as that most sympathetic figure, Mom, filled with compassion for victims of sexual crimes, protecting the weaker children on the playground from the nasty and aggressive bad boys, and attempting to make this world safer for us all. The only hope for the future of humankind, they assert, is the imposition of a matriarchy.

Before scoffing at the possibility of imposing a matriarchy, or female standard, upon the nation, it should be remembered that scientists have determined that the key to the major differences between males and females is "prenatal androgenization": A slight increase in the amount of testosterone a fetus receives during a very brief period during the eighth week of pregnancy can cause males to become more aggressive, have higher mathematical and visual-spatial abilities, and so on, and can cause females to become more "malelike." Conversely, decreased amounts of testosterone during that crucial period can cause males to become less aggressive and more like females, and make females "hyperfeminine." Scientists already have the ability to alter prenatal testosterone levels in this way, in fact have been doing so unintentionally for years by prescribing certain hormones to pregnant women. As we have also seen, many sex offenders are now being "chemically emasculated" by doses of anti-androgens, chemicals that lower their testosterone levels (and eliminate their sex drives as well as their aggressiveness).

Now, many feminists are speaking quite frankly of the need to use this available scientific technology to make males more like females. As one radical feminist biochemist remarked to science writer Howard Rheingold, a logical next step might be to "promote a more peaceful humanity by altering prenatal androgenization or readjusting hormone levels at puberty." It would not take much: just a little dollop of certain hormones during a brief period of pregnancy, and we could have an entire generation of peaceful, unaggressive, nurturing boys.

Extraordinary steps, you might say. But that is the point of the rhetoric of the antisex forces, the message of the memes they are spreading: The dangers of unfettered sexuality are so great that extraordinary steps are demanded; particularly those leading to greater political repression (and to a greater consolidation of power in the hands of those leading the fight against dangerous sexuality). Theirs is, as Lisa Duggan writes, a world in which unapproved types of sexuality are spoken of in apocalyptic terms, as contributing to the " 'decline of western civilization' in which love and trust give way to sex and murder. In this environment, the objections of civil libertarians, anti-censorship feminists, and publishers, and the qualifications and cautions of dissenting social scientists sound feeble. What is Liberty in the face of Death?"

HOW INFORMATION BECOMES PORNOGRAPHY

For the people who wish to maintain their power, it is not just sex, but information itself that is dangerous. Information, as we have seen, is by its very definition unpredictable. What cannot be predicted cannot be controlled. What cannot be controlled can erupt at any time into the state that is most feared both by Little t's and by the individuals who are driven to exercise power over the masses: the state of chaos, anarchy. To these wielders or seekers of power, the free spread and dissemination of new ideas—memes that are different from their own—represents a threat not only to their power, but to the very stability and orderliness of society. And so their true political agenda is to do everything possible to restrict the free flow of information. To do this, they will use all the moral and political suasion available to them to label such information and experiences "immoral," "sexist," "sinful," "obscene," "blasphemous," or "politically incorrect."

Just how tight the link is between the control of sex and the control of power (and how conscious of this link the antisex forces are) can be seen in the response of President Richard Nixon, upon receiving the *Report on the Commission on Obscenity and Pornography* in 1970. The report, as we have noted, concluded that sexual materials posed no dangers, recommended that all laws prohibiting the distribution of sexual materials to consenting adults be repealed, and asserted, "Governmental regulation of moral choice can deprive the individual of the responsibility for personal decision which is essential to the formation of genuine moral standards."

Nixon immediately condemned the report as "morally bankrupt," and went on to assert that "if an attitude of permissiveness were to be adopted regarding pornography, this would contribute to an atmosphere condoning anarchy in every other field—and would increase the threat to our social order as well as to our moral principles."

Fordham professor Walter Kendrick, author of *The Secret Museum: Pornography in Modern Culture*, observes that Nixon's words express "the true reasons why pornography has always inspired anxiety in the wielders of power. It is indeed a symbol for anarchy. . . . On the surface, pornography threatens nothing but the unleashing of sexuality; but that unleashing, as Nixon said, turns immediately into wantonness of every other kind, including the promiscuous redistribution of property. The fear that this will follow, that sex will become self-conscious and recognize its own political nature, constituted 'pornography' at its origin and fuels it now."

The goal of the antisex forces, as Kendrick points out, is, above all, to "regulate the behavior of those who seem to threaten the social order."

19

THE BIG PAYOFF

. . . .

*So perhaps we must make up our minds to the idea that
altogether it is not possible for the claims of the sexual instinct to
be reconciled with the demands of culture. . . . This very
incapacity in the sexual instinct to yield full satisfaction as soon as
it submits to the first demands of culture becomes the source,
however, of the grandest cultural achievements, which are brought
to birth by ever greater sublimation of the components of the
sexual instinct. For what motive would induce man to put his
sexual energy to other uses if by any disposal of it he could obtain
fully satisfying pleasure? He would never let go of this pleasure
and would make no further progress.*

—*Sigmund Freud, "The Most Prevalent Form of Degradation in
Erotic Life"*

SEX AND THE POWER TO BE

In a very real way, sex *is* power. In one sense, sex offers an individual
power over the sexual partner. This is clearly the case in situations
in which one individual is sexually dominant. But in all sexual relations between two people, each of the participants enjoys power
over the other: the power that comes from knowing that one is capable
of sexually arousing one's partner, that one is physically desired by

one's partner, that one can intensify and then satisfy the partner's sexual desire, that one can be the vehicle for guiding one's partner to a precious experience of ecstasy, release from pain, mundane concerns, loneliness, or stress. Numerous studies and surveys reveal that for many people it is this aspect of sex that provides them with the greatest pleasure. The power to give pleasure and excitement to one's partner can be seen as a manifestation of love, affection, and caring.

But even more important, sex offers each of us a simple affirmation of self, of our existence. We are all, in the final analysis, single, isolated creatures, moving through our lives toward death, in a complex world over which we have little control. In the act of sex, we assert in the most direct way possible that we are alive, that there is great joy in being alive, that we are possessed of marvelous energy and power, that at least for this brief period we are at the center of the universe.

And when we are engaged in sex, we are not only asserting the reality and sweetness of our own existence, but are engaged in an act that can produce new life, that can project our own genes into future generations, that can, in a real sense, allow part of us to live even beyond our own individual death. Even in sex in which we use contraceptives or in which there is no possibility of actual reproduction, our bodies still feel the life-giving reproductive potential of the act: Biologically every act of sex carries with it that life-creating charge. In sex, we are alive, and we assert that there is a value in our life. Sex, that is, offers the individual a power that is complete in itself: the "power to be."

THE ULTIMATE APHRODISIAC

As Freud and so many others have noted, sexual energies that are repressed do not disappear but return in other forms. And since sex and power are, in many ways, opposite sides of the same coin, the most logical form in which repressed sexual energies can return is in the form of power. By exercising power over others, individuals can assert the power to be that has been denied them in sexual terms.

We have all heard of and, to some degree experienced, the erotic, seductive, sensual nature of power. Military officers formulating battle plans, ordering those plans to be executed, and controlling the movements of their forces on the field of battle write in their memoirs of experiencing an almost orgasmic feeling of exhilaration and ecstasy, unmatched by any other experience. The halfback who threads his way through the opposition and streaks ninety yards into the end zone falls to his knees, leaps, and writhes in an explosion of sensual euphoria. Business moguls describe how the moments when they succeed in making a big deal provide them with a rush of orgasmic pleasure. In interviews and autobiographies, actors and performers speak of how their moments on stage before an audience were the most "real" moments of their lives, and provided them with a feeling of power and ecstasy that was "better than sex."

When Henry Kissinger asserted that "power is the ultimate aphrodisiac," he was apparently referring to his ability as a powerful man to attract beautiful women. But in another sense, power is the ultimate aphrodisiac by intensifying the sexual pleasure of life itself. It provides its possessor a sort of King Midas touch, in which everything he or she touches (or experiences) is transformed into erotic gratification. We have spent a great deal of time discussing how sex equals power. But when we flip the coin over, we can now see, the equation still holds: Power equals sex.

THE REWARDS OF SEXUAL REPRESSION

As with sex, the acquisition and maintenance of power is not easily accomplished. One obvious technique is to use brute force: Do as I say or I will shoot you, or rape you, or put you in jail. This technique has its drawbacks. The individual or groups being forced will feel powerless, and in an assertion of their own power to be, they will resist. Even if they acquiesce, they will do so grudgingly, and rebel at the first good opportunity. No, a far more effective technique for acquiring and maintaining power is to gain control not only over their bodies but also over their hearts and minds. In the realm of sex, this technique is called seduction. In the realm of power, it is what we have called the spreading of memes.

Though the general on the battlefield has the power to force his soldiers to follow his orders, even that power is less effective than that of the memes with which the soldiers have been infected, through an arduous, well-planned training regimen—memes proclaiming the values of patriotism, courage, loyalty to one's fellow soldiers, obedience, and the utter shame of giving in to cowardice.

Similarly religious leaders, ranging from the pope to the ayatollah to a Christian fundamentalist evangelistic preacher, can use types of force to maintain power over their followers—the history of most religions is full of bloody holy wars, heretics burned at the stake, or, as with the early American Puritans, sinners locked publicly into stocks. But this type of power has been far less effective in creating true believers than that of the memes religious leaders are able to implant in the brains of their followers.

These memes can provide power through the force of fear—such as terrifying descriptions of the eternal hellfire that awaits those who are disobedient or sinful—or through positive incentives to individuals to be obedient—the promise of heaven, eternal life, or the indescribable pleasures of paradise that await martyrs who die for the cause of Allah. It is the power of memes, not brute force, that causes young Shiite believers to blow themselves to smithereens by driving trucks loaded with high explosives into the encampments of infidels. It is the power of memes, not brute force, that enabled early Christians to face the lions in the Coliseum, that sent Christian missionaries off to face the dangers of life among hostile African tribes.

All of the world's religions, in fact, have survived and flourished —have acquired and maintained their power—because they have developed highly sophisticated techniques for transmitting and implanting powerful self-replicating memes. In most cases this meme implantation begins in early childhood.

What is most intriguing is that in virtually all religions, those individuals who take the most active role in the spreading of these sexual-repression memes are either sexually celibate or expected to restrict severely their own sexual activities. This is the reason that the sexual failings of priests, nuns, or preachers like Jim Bakker and Jimmy Swaggart are so much more horrifying to their followers than similar sexual activities by friends and neighbors.

If the most active spreaders of memes about sex are those who are the least active sexually (or who must suppress their own sexual energies most vigorously), then there is an interesting dynamic at work here. Is it possible that there is some connection between sexual energy and the spreading of memes?

MEME EROTICS

Memes are the nonmaterial counterpart of genes. Both genes and memes are packets of information that have the purpose of reproducing or replicating themselves. Genes propagate themselves in a physical way; in the words of anthropologist Richard Dawkins, they do so "by leaping from body to body via sperms or eggs."

Since sex is the key to the whole process of gene propagation, it is essential, in evolutionary terms, that humans engage in sex. Thus, the forces of evolution have insured that humans would want to engage in this activity by providing them with a reward for doing so. The reward (or at least one reward) is pleasure. As neuroscientist Candace Pert of the NIMH puts it, "If you were designing a robot vehicle to walk into the future and survive, as God was when he was designing human beings, you'd wire it up so that the kinds of behavior that would ensure the survival of that species—sex and eating, for instance—are naturally reinforcing. Behavior is modifiable, and it is controlled by the anticipation of pain or pleasure, punishment or reward. And the anticipation of pain or pleasure has to be coded in the brain." When humans have sex, neuroscientists have discovered, their brain and nervous system rewards them for doing so (or "reinforces" that behavior) by releasing large quantities of extremely pleasurable neurochemicals. Among these neurochemicals are the euphoria-producing *endorphins*, known as the body's own opiates.

Memes, too, seek to replicate or propagate themselves—by leaping from brain to brain. Though their process of reproduction is non-molecular, it remains nonetheless extremely similar to sex: The activity of implanting a meme in people's brains is a lot like having sex with them.

The similarity is one humans have long recognized, at least unconsciously. It's no linguistic coincidence that we speak of "seminal" ideas and "disseminating" information, that teachers speak of their students as "fertile" minds, that certain ideas are spoken of as being "seductive" and others as "barren" or "sterile," that "propaganda" derives from the same root as "propagate," that we speak of being "pregnant" with a new idea, that we say someone who is not getting his message across to others effectively is "just jerking off," that we describe certain highly successful cult leaders as being "mind-fuckers" and speak of certain ideas as "really fucking up my brain."

And just as there is enormous evolutionary value in having humans capable of having sex, so there is a clear evolutionary value in being able to receive and pass on complex bundles of information. Being able to transmit the best way to hunt down a woolly mammoth, find water and nonpoisonous plants, and make pottery, for example, offers a great evolutionary advantage over having to learn such things by trial and error. Individuals who had this capacity to receive and propagate such memes would tend to become more common in the gene pool, while those whose brains were not so receptive would tend to disappear. The result is that our brains have been molded by the forces of natural selection to insure that we have a highly developed receptivity to memes.

THE BIG PAYOFF

Just as evolution insured that humans would actually engage in sexual activity by giving them a reward for doing so, evolution also seems to have insured that humans would engage in meme transmission by giving them a similar reward: pleasure.

Neuroscientists have recently discovered that the places in the human brain that produce the most endorphins and that contain the largest concentration of endorphin receptors are those involved most intimately with learning, which is to say, with receiving new information. The scientists have even mapped what they call the "reward pathways" or "pleasure centers" of the brain, and found them tightly connected with the learning centers and pathways. According to neuroscientist Aryeh Routtenberg of Northwestern University, "The evidence clearly shows that the brain-reward pathways play an important role in learning and memory." And Routtenberg explains, "The pathways of brain reward may function as the pathways of memory consolidation. By this I mean that when something is learned, activity in the brain-reward pathways facilitates the formation of memory."

It's a truth we have all experienced: We are presented with new information, a new idea, that somehow doesn't quite make sense, doesn't quite fit into our brain. We resist it or we play around with it. Then, suddenly, with a thrill, it slips in; we understand. The light bulb goes on in the brain. Aha! The new idea or information makes sense, and we are filled with a flood of pleasure, a sensual feeling of satisfaction as our body flows with warmth. We have just received a new meme, and our brain is rewarding us by releasing large quantities of endorphins and other pleasure-producing neurochemicals. A classic example is the rapture and ecstasy experienced by born-again Christians at the moment their brains are fertilized by the fundamentalist meme.

And after we have received the meme, what happens next? We want to spread the meme. And so we go out in search of other brains that seem to us to be fertile; that is, that have the potential of receiving the meme. If we are nuclear physicists and have just received a new meme about physics, we will not attempt to spread it to someone with no knowledge of physics, but will seek out someone with enough knowledge of the subject to be capable of being fertilized with the new meme.

And again the reward is pleasure. We have all experienced something that seems tremendously important to us—that we must eliminate nuclear weapons, or that a Beethoven piano sonata must be played in a specific way to communicate the meme of that sonata most effectively, or that abortion is murder, or that pictures of naked bodies produce crime. We become alert, looking for likely individuals around us to whom we can transmit this crucial meme. When we find one—or a whole crowd of them, perhaps—we transmit the bundle of information to them. If their minds are fertile, which is to say susceptible or receptive, they are inseminated by the meme. They cry Aha!, they cheer, they agree with us, they are infected by the meme and immediately want to transmit it to others, or help us transmit it to others by contributing to our cause, signing petitions, attending demonstrations, purchasing our record or book. The meme has been propagated. We are filled with a rush of pleasure, satisfaction, a sense of having fulfilled a mission, as our brain pours out rewarding neurochemicals.

It is this sense of mission and its sensual reward that compels ideologues, preachers, actors, artists, entertainers, writers, to devote enormous energies to speaking or performing from every soapbox, stage, pulpit, and podium they can find. This is the reward that keeps many schoolteachers passionately engaged in what are otherwise pitifully underpaid and difficult jobs. This is the erotic reward so many people find to be better than sex. This is the Big Payoff.

TRADING OFF: THE COMPENSATIONS OF MONKDOM

We asked earlier: Is it possible that there is some connection between sexual energy and the spreading of memes? We can see now a part of the answer. The act of spreading memes is, itself, a quasisexual act. The act of spreading memes can be so rewarding, in fact, that it can actually replace sex as a means of expressing innate energies. We have probably all known individuals so devoted to certain causes or ideologies that they have no time left for a personal life or sexual activities: They have become monks to their cause.

There is good reason to believe that this is exactly the case with those priests, monks, nuns, and other religious authorities who must remain celibate, or who must suppress their natural sexual instincts. We must wonder, in fact, if that is not the fundamental reason why religions have required that their most dedicated followers be celibate— so that they would redirect their sexual energies into the spreading of the religion's memes, and gain their pleasure from memetic metasex rather than genetic reproduction.

One of the most satisfying ways to acquire and exercise power, it is clear, is by spreading powerful memes. Transmitting memes not only gives us power over others, it allows us to assert our power to be. Just as sex can affirm that power by making us part of the ongoing, infinite network of life, placing us momentarily at the center of a universe that has meaning, so transmitting memes affirms our power to be by giving us an integral role in the transmission or propagation— in the life, so to speak—of something that has deep meaning, that is larger than ourselves.

The transmission of memes even compensates us for the loss of sexual pleasure by rewarding us with a similar erotic gratification.

It's no wonder, then, that the followers of religions and other meme systems that suppress or deny human sexual energies are so energetic and dedicated in their attempts to proselytize: By the very intensity of their meme-spreading activities, they are gaining power and pleasure —thereby compensating themselves for their loss of the power and pleasure of sex.

And it's no wonder that ideologies and organizations that seek to control and mobilize the energies of their followers incorporate strong sexual-repression memes into their fundamental body of memes: After all, as Freud noted, if individuals were free to find satisfaction through the free expression of their sexual instincts, they would have no reason to seek satisfaction through other means.

As Wilhelm Reich and many others have pointed out, sexual freedom is by its very nature incompatible with authoritarianism.

The Catholic Church is a splendid example. From its earliest period, in the writings of Paul and the early church fathers, the church demanded that its followers severely restrict their sexual appetites and activities ("To fornicate is to sin against your own body," wrote Paul in his first letter to the Corinthians; the body is the "temple of God," and he who destroys that temple through fornication, "God will destroy him"). During the Inquisition many of those who were burned as witches or heretics were guilty only of unapproved sexual practices. Many of the heretical movements the church attempted to stamp out most fiercely were those based on sexual practices the church condemned, such as free love. Today, with its opposition to contraception, abortion, masturbation, premarital sex, and so on, the church continues to attempt to maintain its authority and power by suppressing the sexual energies of its members.

The total sexual suppression of Big Brother and the Anti-Sex League in George Orwell's *1984* offers a clear picture of how an authoritarian government maintains control over its subjects by criminalizing sexual activities. But there are a wealth of examples from real life. Among Hitler's first acts was the outlawing of pornography and homosexuality, and the Nazis attempted to exercise control over the sexual energies of the German people by setting up breeding systems that determined which individuals were sufficiently Aryan to reproduce, and with whom they should engage in sex. Among the first acts of the ayatollah Khomeini upon seizing power in Iran was the banning of such "pornography" as American movies and the institution of a variety of fundamentalist Islamic sexual restrictions. Among these restrictions was the requirement that women cover themselves in public by wearing the *chador*, thus simultaneously suppressing female sexuality and insuring that males would not be sexually aroused by the sight of a woman's body. The ayatollah's demand that writer Salman Rushdie be put to death for his "obscene" book *The Satanic Verses* was, according to Islamic scholars, partly based on the book's attribution of unacceptable sexual acts to the Prophet.

Suppressing sexual freedom is an essential step in gaining power and control. In this country, the forces of the far right describe their efforts to suppress most types of sexual activity as an effort to restore America's strength, as a return to the values that made our nation mighty. In their view, most sexual activity, by contributing to the nation's decline, is unpatriotic and un-American. But behind their professions of simple patriotism lies a clear political agenda for establishing a highly authoritarian political system in this nation.

The forces of Christian fundamentalism describe their efforts to suppress sexual activity as a simple desire to follow the word of God. But their campaigns to keep sex education out of schools are just one example of the way they would like to gain control over everything that children are taught.

The antiporn feminists portray themselves as benevolent protectors of women, trying to eradicate materials that are, they claim, incitements to commit crimes against women. But in their attempts to pass clearly unconstitutional laws that would, for example, make it a crime to print or publish anything that portrays a woman in an inferior position to a man, we can see the desire to establish an authoritarian system that would allow them to impose not only their sexual standards but also their social and political standards. And to suppress other feminists who do not agree with them. Feminist writer Phyllis Chesler has noted this intolerance with concern: "Instead of tolerating and even celebrating the differences among us, women are policing each other's actions, trying to keep one another in line." She points out that this type of police action is only a first step toward an authoritarian state that would keep us all "safe from rebels."

And so it becomes clear that sexual suppression is not an end in itself but rather a means to an end. By such suppression, these groups insure that their members will be passionate, tireless, dedicated carriers of their meme.

SAMURAI AND SOLDIER OF FORTUNE: THE CONTROLLED-THRILLS FACTOR

Sex is, in the words of Susan Sontag, "among the extreme rather than the ordinary experiences of humanity. Tamed as it may be, sexuality remains one of the demonic forces in human consciousness— pushing us at intervals close to taboo and dangerous desires." Sex, that is, can be unpredictable and cause us to act in unpredictable ways.

It is interesting that these characteristics of sex—high intensity, unpredictability, individualism, creativity, resistance to authority—are the very characteristics that define the Big-T personality. And it has always been Big-T individuals—both the positive Big T's, such as creative thinkers, risk-takers, adventurers, and the negative Big T's, such as criminals and drug addicts—who have proven most difficult for authoritarian movements, from the Catholic Church to the Nazis to the modern fundamentalists, to control.

There seems to be something in the Big-T personality that makes such individuals less susceptible to infection by authoritarian memes. Perhaps it is because authoritarian memes are intolerant of other, competing memes. These self-replicating memes, as Robert Anton Wilson points out, "contain an internal command that whoever receives them should go and transmit them to as many other people as possible. Each of these memes is intended to reach every human eventually and totally transform the world in the process." Such memes cannot simply be accepted as true, they must be accepted as The Whole Truth. Thus, other competing memes cannot be accepted as just another sort of truth, they must be lies, or, The Big Lie.

But Big-T personalities, with their intense curiosity, their driving need for novelty and new experiences, their suspicion of accepted truths, seem by nature incapable of fully accepting any meme as The Whole Truth. Are those memes in competition? ask the Big T's. Great! We love competition. Let's put them in the ring together and see what happens!

When Big T's do support authoritarian movements, it is because those movements offer them the thrills, the risks, the ability to lead and to gain victory in competition that they require. Authoritarian movements recognize the value of having such energetic, aggressive, cool-under-pressure, and forceful individuals support them, so they make accommodations and provide special roles for Big T's.

Medieval Japan, for example, was a highly structured society anchored by a group of authoritarian feudal memes having to do with obedience, loyalty, and accepting one's proper place in the hierarchy. But as in all societies, there were certain aggressive, Big-T individuals who could not accept the role into which they had been born. It would not do to have these aggressive individuals roaming free, disrupting the social structure. So a place was made for them within the structure that would harness their unique talents and energies: They were permitted to become members of a group of noble warriors called Samurai. These men swore oaths of obedience to one or another of the feudal warlords, and thus nominally accepted the dominant authoritarian memes. But within that overriding structure they were able to act as Big-T individuals, following the code of *Bushido* ("military-knight ways," or "the way of the sword"), a code requiring its followers to live every moment in the existential awareness of their own mortality. Thus, the Samurai were able to turn such Big-T characteristics as aggressiveness, daring, risk-taking, fierce individualism, and stimulation-seeking into noble ideals.

Virtually all movements guided by authoritarian memes have their Samurai, or Big-T individuals who act not because they have been truly infected by the memes but to satisfy their own need for risk, adventure, stimulation, and dominance. At times, as with mercenaries or soldiers of fortune, they do not even profess to believe in the memes they are fighting for. Since they are not truly infected by the memes, they feel free to ignore the rules of conduct that guide the behavior of the true believers: Their standards are different, guided by Big-T impulses. Thus, police are supposedly defenders of law and order, but often act with a disregard for laws and often feel a greater sense of identification with criminals—fellow Big T's—than they do with ordinary, law-abiding, and (to them) boring citizens. As frequent news stories attest, the same is true of many spies and intelligence agents.

It often happens, however, that because of their innate qualities— great energy, creativity, aggressiveness, charisma, desire for dominance —Big-T individuals rise into leadership positions in these social, political, or religious movements. At that point a conflict arises: As leaders, they are expected to embody and exemplify the memes that guide the movement, while in truth they are not actually infected with those memes. As public figures, they must profess to believe the memes, must use all their skills and energies to spread the memes as widely as possible, and they undertake the challenge with gusto, fully enjoying the acclaim and the power that comes with being a leader. In their private lives, however, they feel no need to limit their impulses by the memes they have been spreading in public. Those memes apply to the followers, the masses, the true believers, not to them.

Thus, we have the examples of history—the popes of ages past who publicly professed celibacy while maintaining stables of mistresses and fathering armies of bastards, the communist leaders who spoke publicly of the equal distribution of wealth but who lived in luxury, the president who vows never to deal with terrorists while covertly trading shiploads of arms to Iran for the return of hostages, the conservative politicians and television commentators who cry out publicly for life sentences for drug dealers while sniffing cocaine at dinner parties.

And thus we have Bible-banging evangelist preachers, like Jim Bakker, Jimmy Swaggart, and a whole choirloft full of others of lesser renown, calling down the wrath of God on sexual sinners, while hopping on church secretaries, choirboys, or prostitutes after the TV lights are out and the congregation has gone home. We have crusaders against sex like the member of Attorney General Meese's Commission on Pornography who publicly declared his belief that masturbation can lead to sexual disorders and loudly proclaimed that he hated erotic materials because they were harmful to women, while declaring in private, "Of course, none of this would happen if women learned how to give a really good blow job." We have antiporn vigilante Andrea Dworkin, declaring that the essence of pornography is "the eroticization of murder," and then churning out fiction that is by any standards flagrantly pornographic. We have conservative politicians who cry out against homosexuality and then are discovered to be homosexual themselves. We have the right-wing leader who declares that sexual promiscuity is destroying the family, who is later discovered to have participated in a stag party in which prostitutes provided him with oral sex. And on and on.

Seen through the lenses of meme theory and Big-T personality analysis, these occurrences, and the fierce dedication the antisex forces bring to the struggle in the sex-power nexus, begin to make sense. The vast majority of the forces, the foot soldiers, are true believers. Heavily armored by sexual-repression imprints and fully infected with memes having to do with the evils of "perverse" or "sinful" sex, they firmly believe they are engaged in a noble or holy battle to save the world. Through the very intensity of their commitment they regain and assert the "power to be" that they have been denied by the repression of their natural sexual energies. In their enthusiastic spreading of memes, they are rewarded with the pleasure of power, and with the erotic joys of spreading powerful memes.

These foot soldiers are led by energetic generals who are fre-

quently Big T's. While some of these leaders seem to be true ideologues, firmly in the grip of the memes they are committed to
spreading, for many of them the antisex memes and issues are convenient opportunities for the acquisition and exercise of political
power, the power to control not only human sexuality, but every
aspect of human life.

20

THE WILD MAN, THE SACRED PROSTITUTE, AND THE QUEST FOR POWER

· ·

The ancient tradition that the world will be consumed in fire at the end of six thousand years is true . . . the whole creation will be consumed and appear infinite and holy, whereas it now appears finite and corrupt.

This will come to pass by an improvement of sensual enjoyment.

—*William Blake "The Marriage of Heaven and Hell"*

TURNCOATS AND TRAITORS IN THE HYSTERICAL SUPERNOVA

The sexual pendulum, which swept from the conservatism of the 1950's to the sexual revolution and the outburst of Gnosticism of the 1960's and early 1970's, has for the last decade been swinging back toward greater and greater sexual conservatism. But there are signs that the pendulum is reaching the end of its arc. As historian William Irwin Thompson points out, "We're now seeing a return of religious warfare, which for me as a historian is prima facie evidence that the Age of Religion is over, that this is its hysterical supernova, its sunset effect, its swan song . . . whatever way you want to identify this phenomenon of passing away with intensity.

"It passes away," Thompson says, "for several reasons: It exhausts itself because of violence. And it tends to be entropic: Fundamentalisms always define themselves by narrower and narrower, purer systems of ideology, so that the right-wing people pointing the finger at Reagan and saying he's not right-wing enough, or Shiites, will split among themselves."

Even now we are seeing this splitting, entropic process at work among the movements for sexual restriction. Among the Christian right, for example, there are bitter battles going on for control of the church leadership. In the most recent convention of the 14.7-million-member Southern Baptist Church, there was a fierce struggle, in which the church leaders were accused of not being sufficiently fundamentalist. They were ousted and replaced by a more rigidly fundamentalist group, who pledged to fire the less fundamentalist teachers at their seminaries and replace them with more "purely" fundamentalist teachers.

Another example of the struggles taking place is the conflict between Christian fundamentalists, with their belief in the total inerrancy of the Bible and more reserved forms of worship, and evangelicals, who prefer a more flamboyant, ecstatic form of worship. This struggle came to the attention of many when fundamentalist leader Jerry Falwell attempted to gain control of evangelical leader Jim Bakker's PTL (Praise The Lord) organization in the aftermath of Bakker's sexual scandal and resignation. The PTL evangelicals reacted furiously, and Falwell was quickly ejected.

The same sort of splitting is taking place among the antisex feminists. Some groups are simply opposed to certain types of pornography, but refuse to advocate outright censorship, arguing that the best strategy is to educate the public about the assumed dangers of pornography. Other groups struggle for the passage of laws like the Dworkin-MacKinnon Act that would, in effect, censor all words and pictures that they objected to. The latter group condemns those feminist groups that are opposed to censorship as not being "true" feminists, and engage in "purges" of those who are not sufficiently ideologically pure. As feminist writer Gayle Rubin observes, "I have never seen a position become dogma with so little debate, with so little examination of its possible ramifications or of other perspectives. . . . Anyone who has tried to raise other issues and who has questioned this analysis has been trashed very quickly as an anti-feminist or personally attacked." Splitting off from these groups are even "purer" feminists, who have themselves begun to fragment into a variety of warring factions.

What this fragmentation of fundamentalist groups leads toward, as William Irwin Thompson observes, is the "total entropy of a war of individuals against individuals, until everything just goes into total destruction, and survivors, or the people who are elsewhere, turn away in loathing and rejection of that as a cultural form, and they look for another level of order higher up that can be visionary or integrative. Ideology, therefore, begins to be useless as a form of connective tissue among different cultures. . . . So I don't think the fundamentalists are going to stop anything. They can't, in fact, because fundamentalists tend to encourage their opposites."

It is as if, out there on the sex-power nexus, all the fundamentalist forces that once seemed to present such a united front have begun to turn upon themselves, swinging their axes and cudgels at each other as much as at the original enemy. Their crusade remains as urgent as ever, but now they are becoming convinced that many of their fellow crusaders are themselves traitors, turncoats, or heretics.

The battle to control sex has always been a battle for power. And now, as it appears that real power is almost within their grasp, the fundamentalists, the evangelicals, the right-to-lifers, the campus censors, the book-burners, the abortion-clinic bombers, the right-wing politicos, the antiporn feminists, begin to look around themselves and wonder, Who are the true crusaders? Who are the real allies? Who deserves to carry the banner? And who, when the battle is won, will gain control of the power?

MAD DANCERS ON THE BATTLEFIELD

The crusaders are keenly aware of the open channel linking sex and power: They relish the sexuality of power, but are disturbed by the power of sexuality. For them the power of sex is so great and terrifying that they fear that if it were released it would lead, in Richard

Nixon's words, "to an atmosphere condoning anarchy in every other field." Sex, that is, is so powerful it can tear apart the cosmos.

In general, the forces they are fighting have pooh-poohed their view of the explosive, disruptive power of sex. To these others, sex is a natural function that rational people can make an important but not uncontrollable part of their lives. Their resistance to the antisex forces springs not from an opposing desire to unleash the explosive powers of sex, but from a more abstract assertion of the value of human freedom and an interest in maintaining public health.

So in a sense the conflict in the sex-power nexus has been taking place on two different planes, one group engaged in a holy war against a monstrous power that threatens to throw the world into chaos, the other rationally defending the First Amendment and freedom, and wondering what all the fuss is about, since sex is, after all, just a natural, pleasant, and generally innocuous human function.

But there is another, rapidly growing movement that is in complete agreement with the antisex forces about the power of sex to unleash enormous forces that can disrupt the social order: It simply disagrees that this is something to be feared. Yes, say the members of this movement, sex can tear us out of our ordinary states of consciousness; yes, it can shatter our carefully constructed personalities; yes, it can propel us beyond the limits of human experience accepted by society; yes, it can thrust us into experiences that are uncontrollable and inexplicable. Great! This is not only the greatest value but also the true meaning of sex. And it is through sex that humans find their own value and true meaning. For sex is not, as the antisex forces contend, a demonic power, but a power that can link humans to the divine, and initiate them into spiritual knowledge and reveal to them the secrets of existence.

It is as if, while the battle rages on in the sex-power nexus, a motley cheering band of men and women clad in the colorful costumes of hairy wild men, goddesses, Sumerian temple prostitutes, and Taoist priests, has pitched tents right in the middle of the battlefield. And there, ignoring the combat going on around them, they have thrown off their clothes and begun banging on drums, dancing madly, and engaging in an extraordinary variety of odd and ecstatic sexual acts. Make love, they cry to the contending forces beyond their encampment, not war!

THE WILD MAN, THE WARRIOR, AND THE EAGLE'S POWER

Around the flickering campfire the group of men growl, cry, howl like wild animals. We are males, they shout, and we have male energies, we are fierce, bold, ecstatic, sensitive! We are one with the hairy wild man of our ancient, collective past, and we can now fully feel our male pain, male joy, male sexuality, male power.

They are a group of typical late-1980's American men—dentists, lawyers, politicians, ranchers, mailmen, business executives, who have taken five days off from their busy lives to gather together at a retreat and explore their sexual identities. They are attending a Wild Man Workshop.

The Wild Man Workshops were begun in the mid-1980's by National Book Award–winning poet Robert Bly, and emerged from the tremendous response Bly received from a widely discussed magazine interview in which he analyzed the state of males and their relationship with women. "The step of the male bringing forth his own feminine consciousness is an important one," he observed, "and yet I have the sense there is something wrong. The male in the last twenty years has become more thoughtful, more gentle. But by this process, he has not become more free. He's a nice boy who not only pleases his mother but also the young woman he is living with."

"What I'm proposing," Bly went on, "is that every modern male has, lying at the bottom of his psyche, a large, primitive man covered with hair down to his feet. Making contact with this wildman . . . is the process that still hasn't taken place in contemporary culture." This wild man, Bly contends, is not a poetic image or intellectual construct, but biological, the genetic legacy of thousands of generations of male hunters: It is a pure expression of "instinctive, sexually primitive, even frightening [but] nourishing male energy." All great cultures, according to Bly, have lived with images of this energy, except ours. Says Bly, "In our culture now, the young male, being parted from positive masculine values by the collapse of mythology, and separated physically from his father by the Industrial Revolution, is often, in this new age, full of feminine values. Many of these values are marvelous, but their presence in his psyche are not well balanced by positive male values." Making contact with the wild man is a primary task for today's males, says Bly, and those who do so have "true strength." This strength is not only physical, but spiritual. Says

Bly, "Getting in touch with the wildman means religious life for a man in the broadest sense of the phrase."

The response to Bly's ideas was enormous, and he began leading Wild Man Workshops in wilderness retreats around the country. As news of these workshops spread by word of mouth, thousands of males sought to enroll, far more than could be accommodated. Soon a variety of men who had learned from Bly began leading their own Wild Man Workshops. Today, there usually are a number of such workshops going on every week around the country, and they have spawned scores of ongoing male groups that meet regularly to discover their male sexual identities and explore the meaning of maleness through the telling and retelling of myths, and by chanting, dancing, drumming, hunting and tracking, mock battles, and exploration of their true wild-man sexual desires.

Often, upon opening themselves to their wild man, these men find that they are full of astounding amounts of grief and anguish as a result of trouble in their marriages or relationships. They find that in their sex lives they are what Bly calls "nice boys," not expressing true male sexual energy, but the sort of sexual energy they have been taught by females—their mothers, wives, lovers. They discover that male sexual energy is something different, something "fierce," ecstatic, energetic; that if they can learn to tap this sexual energy, they can attain spiritual and physical joys and satisfactions they have never known before. And that in the act of sex that fully expresses their male energies, they can gain not only spiritual wisdom, but power.

In their search to regain forgotten male powers, these seekers also find guidance in the writings of Carlos Castaneda, whose "tales of power" describe his attempts to learn "the way of the warrior" from the teachings of the Mexican Indian sorcerer Don Juan. As Don Juan emphasizes, "It is the Eagle's command that sexual energy be used for creating life. Through sexual energy, the Eagle bestows awareness. . . . All I know is what it means to warriors. They know that the only real energy we possess is life-bestowing sexual energy. This knowledge makes them permanently conscious of that responsibility."

THE JAGUAR WOMAN, THE HOLY WHORE, AND VAGINAL WEIGHT LIFTING

Increasing numbers of women, too, are exploring a more mystical, spiritual view of sex, calling upon ancient fertility goddesses and the teachings of female shamans and sorceresses, convinced that female sexuality can be a link to sacred, divine powers. Around the country thousands of women gather each weekend for "transformative" workshops and seminars with such titles as "Reclaiming Female Sexual Power," or "Reclaiming the Goddess," that claim to assist women in "locating the source of sexual power within you," or "opening your sexual chakras."

One of the leaders of this movement is also, like Bly, a poet. Deena Metzger delivered an influential paper to a feminist conference on art and culture that was widely reprinted, photocopied, and passed from hand to hand among groups of feminists. In "Re-vamping the World: On the Return of the Holy Prostitute," Metzger, like Bly, argued for a rediscovery of ancient sexual powers that have been suppressed by our Judeo-Christian culture. She observed that in ancient Sumeria, Mesopotamia, Egypt, Greece, among the holiest spots were the temples of the sacred prostitutes. "In these temples," she claimed, "men were cleansed, not sullied, morality was restored, not desecrated, sexuality was not perverted but divine.

"The original whore," she continued, "was a priestess, the conduit to the divine, the one through whose body one entered the sacred arena and was restored. Warriors, soldiers, soiled by combat within the world of men, came to the Holy Prostitute . . . in order to be cleansed and reunited with the gods."

Through their bodies, these temple prostitutes, associated with such goddesses as Hathor, Ishtar, Anath, Astarte, and Asherah, offered access to the divine, a pathway to wholeness and unity with the One. "As the body was the means," observed Metzger, "so inevitably pleasure was an accompaniment, but the essential attribute of sexuality, in this context, was prayer."

The question that Metzger posed was: "How do we relate to this today, as women, as feminists? Is there a way we can resanctify society, become the priestesses again, put ourselves in the service of the gods and eros?" The answer, she argued, was that "if we utilize the feminine it is possible that the planet will survive, and also the species, and that eventually we will thrive, and without the feminine and eros everything is irretrievably lost. . . . And so women must all become Holy Prostitutes again."

To do this, Metzger claimed, "we must engage in two heresies. The second is to re-sanctify the body; the first even more difficult task is to return to the very early, neolithic, pagan, matriarchal perception of the sacred universe itself. But to overthrow secular thought may be the heretical act of the century. . . . The task is to accept the body as spiritual, and sexuality and erotic love as spiritual disciplines, to believe that eros is pragmatic."

Thousands of women have responded to Metzger's call to seek spiritual wisdom and power by rediscovering their links with the forces represented by the ancient fertility goddesses and sex deities. One influential figure in this movement has been Lynn Andrews, who has overseen the production of a series of enormously popular (and supposedly nonfiction) books (*Medicine Woman, Jaguar Woman, Star Woman, Crystal Woman*), and led mass workshops around the nation teaching women how to gain power through sexual practices she claims to have learned from a number of female shamans or sorceresses from traditional cultures, such as Australian aborigines and Native American Indians. The lesson these traditional shamans have to teach, she says, is, "Power is female. That's always the first lesson of shamanistic training." By proper use of the unique female sexual power, she claims, women can "heal the feminine consciousness within men and within women." This healing, she believes, will result in a "sacred androgyny."

Many men and women are seeking this integration of sexuality with spirituality through the study and practice of ancient esoteric sexual techniques derived from Taoism, Tantric yoga, Kundalini, witchcraft, and Sufism. Taoist Master Mantak Chia, for example, has gained a worldwide following among both men and women through his best-selling books on Taoist sexual techniques, and has established centers to teach "sexual kung fu" throughout the United States, Canada, Europe, Australia, and the Far East. He also travels widely, conducting immensely popular workshops, in which he teaches men and women how to transform sexual energy through an "alchemical transmutation of body, mind and spirit" in which sexual essence, or "ching," is used to propel individuals into a state of "pure consciousness" in which they are united with "we chi, the nothingness from which the oneness of the Tao emerges." To help humans learn to use their sexual energy for spiritual goals, Chia teaches such arcane practices as Testicle Breathing, the Nine Shallow/One Deep Thrusting Method, Learning to Circulate Your Chi in the Microcosmic Orbit, the Big Draw, Cultivating the Valley Orgasm, Cultivating Ovarian Energy, Ovarian Breathing, the Orgasmic Upward Draw, and Vaginal Weight Lifting.

THOSE IN THE KNOW: THE REEMERGENCE OF THE HERESY

The hundreds of thousands of men and women unleashing their sexual Wild Man, Holy Prostitute, and Jaguar Woman, and assiduously practicing breathing through their testicles and lifting weights with their vaginas are just a small part of a larger movement of Americans seeking to gain spiritual wisdom and power through sex. This "New Age movement," made up of postfeminist women and men who have been influenced by the psychological self-help and human-potential movements as well as by Eastern mystical and Western occult thinking, represent what Carl A. Raschke, professor of religious studies at the University of Denver, calls "the most powerful social force in the country today."

But "New Age" appears to be something of a misnomer, since, as social critic Christopher Lasch points out, its proponents "believe that the way to a better world may lie in ideas from the past rather than in new ideas. The intuition underlying New Age movements, the bedrock feeling . . . [is] that mankind has lost the collective knowledge of how to live with dignity and grace . . . that man's future depends on a renewal of prematurely discarded traditions of thought and practice."

The most important of those prematurely discarded traditions is the belief that, in Lasch's words, "[Human] salvation lies in the knowledge that his spiritual nature links him to the divine realm to which he is destined to return. Those already initiated into the secrets of existence—those in the know, to refer to the literal meaning of *gnosis*—understand that man is divine, that his divine origin and destiny set him apart from the rest of creation, and there is no limit to his powers."

No limit to human powers for those in the know! And those who are in the know know that the pathway to those unlimited powers is through the divine ecstasy of sex, that proper sexual practice is a

direct channel to the essences of the universe, the divine spark within
us all. They know that sexual pleasure is a form of worship, a gift
from the divinity, and a means of reconnecting with the divine.

What we are seeing, in other words, is a rebirth of gnosticism,
that heresy so monstrous and frightening to the church that it has
been ruthlessly suppressed wherever it emerged, whether as the thir-
teenth-century Albigensian heresy, the fourteenth-century Brethren
of the Free Spirit, or the Rosicrucian movement of the late nineteenth
century. Certainly by now, with our awareness of the relationship
between sex and power, we can understand the reason for the church's
hatred and fear of gnosticism.

SEX BEYOND SPACE AND TIME

Many now are rejecting not only the authoritarianism and the ideology of the antisex forces that sex is something evil, dangerous, or
dirty, but also the memes of many of those who are battling against
the antisex forces, that sex is something innocuous and ordinary,
simply a natural human function like eating, breathing, and excreting.

These sexual gnostics are rejecting not just sexual repression, but
also the trivialization or secularization of sex that took place as a result
of the sexual revolution. They believe that sexuality, used as a sacred
rather than a secular practice, can provide a way to mend the separation between mind and body, erase the dualism of good and evil,
right and wrong, true or false, shatter normal, ordinary reality, break
through the limits of consciousness and reunite the human spark of
energy with the infinite light of the divine.

Perhaps the most eloquent proponent of this New Age gnosticism
is writer George Leonard, whose book *The End of Sex* argues that
sex—sex as something trivial, ordinary, good for you—"is an idea
whose time has passed." Instead, Leonard insists, sex must be replaced
by what he calls "erotic love." "For me," he writes, "the erotic
encounter is ecstatic in the dictionary sense of the word. It takes me
out of my set position, my stasis. It permits me the unique freedom
of stripping away every mask, every facade that I usually present to
the world, and of existing for a while in that state of pure being. . . .
I am not male, my love is not female. We are one, one entity. Through
the tumult of love, we have arrived at a radiant stillness, the center
of the dance."

At this point, writes Leonard, one can "travel beyond even space and time and enter a sublime darkness. Seeing nothing, hearing nothing, I am totally connected with my love and, through her, with all of existence. That which was veiled is unveiled, that which was hidden is revealed: Beneath all appearance, beyond all customary distinctions, there is a deeper self that wears no mask. In the darkness, there is an illumination. In love, I have found nothing and all things."

Harking back to the ancient Taoist belief that sexual energy can propel individuals into a state of "pure consciousness," Leonard proclaims, "It is the glory and the grace of erotic love that it offers each of us the opportunity of passionate connection with another and, through that, of a larger connectiveness. The erotic urge draws us toward creation, toward the condition of potent nothingness from which all existence unfolds."

THE PRAGMATISM OF EROS

In their writings, in the advertisements and catalog descriptions of their workshops, seminars, retreats, courses, and transformational weekends, the sexual gnostics speak frequently and emphatically of how their esoteric sex practices can lead to "self-empowerment," "regaining personal power," "locating the source of power within" "reclaiming the power of the feminine," "freeing the god and goddess power within us," and "getting in touch with male power." As Christopher Lasch describes gnosticism, "Those in the know . . . understand that man is divine, that . . . there is no limit to his powers."

This promise of limitless powers gained through mystical, often secret, often sexual practices forms the core teaching of gnostic practices throughout history. The alchemists, for example, left cryptic texts describing the ritualistic refining of chemicals to produce the Philosophers' Stone—the magical substance that would confer on its possessor limitless powers—writings that were in fact metaphoric descriptions of techniques for uniting male energies with female energies.

Throughout history, the methods for acquiring powers through esoteric sexual practices have been jealously guarded secrets, revealed only to a select few. In part, secrecy was maintained to protect them from being misused. According to Taoist master Mantak Chia, the ancient masters "felt bound to reveal their potent secrets to only the most select disciples, those who had proven their devotion to the Master's ideals by years of arduous self-sacrifice and service. . . . To guarantee that the formulae not be used for selfish purposes, these Masters often transmitted to each disciple only a part of the doctrine. Thus, only if the disciples banded together and shared their learning could the supreme potencies be unleashed. If anyone selfishly withheld his learning, they would never receive the whole doctrine."

Self-protection also played a part in the desire to keep the doctrines secret, since in virtually every authoritarian society the teachings would have been seen by those in power as subversive and heretical, and violently suppressed. The medieval alchemists, for example, would have been burned at the stake as sorcerers by the church authorities. So they protected their secrets by disguising them as arcane chemical experiments and recording them in journals containing only mystifying and apparently unrelated fragments.

THE MORNING OF THE MAGICIANS

But now, apparently, something has changed; the sorcerers have come out of their closet and begun to teach the "secret doctrines" to anyone willing to listen and learn. Why the sudden revelation of these long-protected secrets? Because, say the new gnostics, the human species has reached the end of one era and is poised on the brink of a new one, is on the verge of an "evolutionary leap of consciousness" that can transform the human species and the entire world. And because if humans do not make this evolutionary leap, they are doomed.

"The historic moment is already late," writes Mantak Chia. "The human condition is too desperate to deprive our species of a potentially great infusion of vital energy. If the human race is not quickly infused with a new life energy to render it more harmonious . . . we are all, earthly Masters and mortals, threatened with an untenably harsh existence, if not extinction."

The sexual gnostics proclaim that all of the forces doing battle on the nexus—Christian fundamentalists, civil-liberties lawyers, anti-porn feminists, *Playboy* readers, right-to-lifers, protectors of abortion rights—all are part of the old order that will be destroyed forever in the cataclysm that is approaching. It is as if two armies are struggling over possession of some small patch of earth, so involved in the skirmish that they don't even notice the immense hurricane that is sweeping down on them. Wake up, cry the gnostics, and see what is approaching. It is possible we may still survive!

Possible but not certain. Perhaps the whole structure may collapse into chaos. For in the view of these New Age gnostics, the entire planet is a Prigoginian dissipative structure.

In evolutionary terms, when the amount of energy flowing through a system becomes too great, the fluctuations in the system become so powerful that they begin to destabilize the entire system. At that "bifurcation point," the entire system faces two possibilities: It can either fall apart, or it can escape to a higher order by restructuring itself so that it can accommodate the increased influx of energy.

The New Age gnostics point out that today more than ever before, humans seem to be at a crucial and potentially cataclysmic bifurcation point. Our global dissipative structure is experiencing an enormously increased flow-through of energy and matter, as we consume fuels, food, natural resources, and other materials at a skyrocketing rate. The amount of pure information flowing through the system is increasing exponentially, so much of it that no one seems quite sure what to do with it all. At the same time, we are experiencing increasing entropy, as general disorder, conflict, social disintegration, and environmental depletion send perturbations through the fragile human-earth ecosystem. We seem to be nearing the point at which the fluctuations will be too powerful to be damped, the bifurcation point that will, in Prigogine's words, "lead us to the best or to the worst." The outcome is not yet clear.

And so the sexual gnostics, who wandered onto the scene looking like a band of apolitical mystics, turn out to be making the biggest political move of all the forces contending on the nexus. For the power they are after is not about who will control a political party, who will run a school board or a nation, but about what will become of the world. As George Leonard contends, "The erotic urge draws us toward creation, toward the condition of potent nothingness from which all existence unfolds." And what greater power than to be one with the source from which all existence unfolds? In sexual love, says Deena Metzger, we surrender our uniqueness and "become world." And, she argues, "If we become world reaching to the gods, then love is essentially a spiritual act which redeems the world." The task, she observes, "is to accept the body as spiritual, and sexuality and erotic love as spiritual disciplines, to believe that eros is pragmatic."

21

RENEGOTIATING THE SEX CONTRACT

. . . .

*The state of being grasped by the God beyond God . . . is the
situation on the boundary of man's possibilities. It is this
boundary. It is not a place where one can live, it is without the
safety of words and concepts, it is without a name, a church, a
cult, a theology. But it is moving in the depth of all of them. It is
the* power *of being . . . of which they are fragmentary
expressions. . . .* The courage to be is rooted in the God
who appears when God has disappeared in the anxiety of
doubt.

—*Paul Tillich,* The Courage to Be

LIFE GOES ON

I've become so involved in the battle on the nexus I've almost forgotten that other life goes on. The combatants out there are the
committed ones, the True Believers, the ones who have been strongly
infected by certain memes. Most of us aren't out there. We may
observe with great interest, we may have strong sympathies for some
of the contending forces, but for the most part we continue about
our daily lives, taking no active role in the sexual wars, not particularly

frightened that *Playboy* magazine or *Debbie Does Dallas* represents the decline of Western civilization, not really convinced that the fundamentalists' demands for chastity and the censorship of school texts will lead us into a totalitarian church-state, somewhat skeptical that if we unleash our hairy wild man or turn ourselves into sacred sex goddesses we can gain access to divine powers and transform the planet.

To a great degree the conflict on the nexus is dominated by Big T's and Little t's. The Big T's seek power: the power of dominating others through aggression and the strength of the individual will; the power of affirming the self through acts of creativity, energy, spontaneity, and the power to transcend ordinary reality through high-risk life lived without rules, beyond the boundaries. For them, sex can be one route toward this power. Little t's also seek power: the power of establishing and maintaining structure and order; the power of being part of a network of relationships or of an ideological structure that can give order to reality. For them, sex in its most unrestricted, unpredictable forms is a threat; but they can substitute for the satisfactions of sex the pleasures of accepting and transmitting powerful memes.

But most of us, neither Big T's nor Little t's, seek transcendence and pleasure, and affirm our own power to be, through that mysterious fusion of sex and power called romantic love. It is comforting to think that this capacity has evolved through natural selection: that love has a high survival value. In ancient evolutionary history, the capacity for two individuals to form a bond based on some sort of affection would have been adaptive, by insuring that the male would stay around to protect and provide for his mate and their offspring. Certainly evolution has provided us with rewards for such behavior: The rush of euphoria we experience in "falling in love" is produced by the release in our brain of large quantities of the very same neurochemicals that are involved in the ecstasy of a cocaine high; and the warm glow of pleasure and security we experience in a long-term love relationship is produced by the release of endorphins, the body's natural anxiety-relieving pleasure neurochemicals. And so most of us Medium T's find in romantic love a mingling of the benefits and rewards sought by both Big T's and Little t's. We experience risk, adventure, and thrills, unpredictability, arousal, and intense physical sensation, at levels that, while perhaps not high enough to satisfy sensation-hungry Big T's, are high enough to challenge and reward

us. We experience also the Little-t pleasure and security in being part
of a larger whole, a network of relatedness. And so, while the battle
rages on the nexus, most of us continue to lead our lives in the
experience of work and love.

Life goes on. Nevertheless, life goes on in a different way than it
did only a few years ago. Our ideas about sex, and power, and the
relationships between men and women, have changed. The constant
barrage of information we receive from the mass media about the
ongoing struggle in the nexus—stories about the AIDS epidemic, the
confrontations over abortion rights, the debates about pornography,
the scandals involving politicians and religious leaders, the book-
burnings and record-burnings, the changing role of women—have
made us all more aware of our own sexual energies, attitudes, and
behavior. Most of us have been personally affected by the issues at
stake in the nexus, whether we have lost friends to AIDS, been forced
to deal with new sexual confrontations in the workplace, seen friends
torn apart by bitter divorces and battles over child custody.

This immense, historical restructuring and rearrangement of sex
and power has been gathering force for thousands of years—perhaps
ever since our prehistoric ancestors changed their style of life from
that of free-roving hunters and gatherers to tillers of the soil and
urban dwellers.

EVOLUTION BY LEAPS AND BOUNDS

Evolutionary *time* generally seems very slow. But anthropologists
and evolutionary biologists now believe, and fossil evidence indicates,
that when evolutionary *changes* take place, they can do so with extraordinary speed. In what is called the "punctuated equilibrium"
theory of evolution, species seem to remain stable for long ages, and
then, usually as a result of rapid environmental changes, they alter
rapidly: Mutant genes with high survival value become more prevalent in the gene pool through natural selection. In the view of these
scientists, evolution is characterized by a series of leaps and bounds,
rather than a gradual, incremental, eons-long progression.

In some ways evolutionary changes are like geological changes—
the surface of the earth seems to remain stable for centuries, but
beneath the surface seismic pressures build, huge masses of rock grind
against each other, molten rocks increase in temperature and expand,

and suddenly the forces become too great, layers of rock buckle, fault lines slip, volcanic eruptions of molten rock burst out of the ground and in a few moments the surface of the earth has changed; where once there was level ground are now gaping crevasses or tilted cliff faces, where there were cities are now heaps of rubble.

Perhaps what we are seeing now is one of those times when evolutionary equilibrium is being "punctuated," when seismic pressures that have been building are being released, and fault lines slip, causing cultural earthquakes and eruptions. The townspeople go about their lives, unaware or too busy to notice that the ground is about to open beneath their feet.

For millions of years our prehistoric ancestors evolved through a process of natural selection, and found their niche in the planet's ecosystem as skillful hunters and gatherers. Those who functioned well survived to pass on their genes, and the species evolved with those characteristics. Part of that evolutionary process involved the establishment of what has been called "the sex contract"—males and females developed differing but complementary capacities and worked together to insure the survival of their offspring.

But then suddenly, almost overnight in terms of evolutionary history, everything changed. Over a period of a few thousand years humans had created a new environment for themselves called "civilization" and they were no longer running around as hunter-gatherers, but raising crops and inhabiting cities, no longer part of a small clan, but a tiny part of a huge nation-state. In that evolutionary instant when cultural evolution overtook physical evolution, many of the skills, physical capacities, and behavior patterns hard-wired into the human brain became obsolete.

Virtually overnight, the human cultural and physical environment changed. But human bodies and brains did not change. Today, we know from the evidence of ancient skeletons unearthed in the Middle East, our bodies and brains are anatomically identical to those of our ancestors one hundred thousand years ago.

Fortunately the human brain has an enormous capacity to override hard-wired patterns. Indeed, this capacity may be the crucial one that sets us apart from our primate ancestors. Still, many hard-wired patterns remain, and continue to influence our behavior. And many of the patterns that seem particularly resistant to change have to do with sexuality.

One of these is the genetically carried command to reproduce.

Even in the face of disastrous overpopulation, humans still respond to this internal command, and many authorities still encourage it. Ernst Mayr points out, "The worst problem is the population explosion. A stable global population would be the first step in the salvation of mankind. But as long as we have church authorities, especially the popes, who proclaim, 'Go out and breed as much as you can,' there is no hope for mankind." Still, in many areas of the world increased education, sex-education, and birth-control campaigns have succeeded in stabilizing, and in some cases even reducing, population.

Another sexual pattern that we have retained virtually intact from the days when we were chasing the woolly mammoth across the savannas is the sex contract. For centuries now its basic terms have had little to do with the actual environmental pressures faced by men and women. In the industrial and technological era, women are just as capable as men of going out and doing the "hunting"—performing the jobs—necessary to provide for themselves and their offspring. Increasingly, the work that must be done has nothing to do with the sex of the hunter or worker.

And yet even today, when recent surveys show that over 50 percent of the jobs in America classified as "the professions" are held by women, and over half of all adult women are employed outside the home, that pattern persists. Men are still largely viewed as being the providers, the defenders, "stronger" somehow, and responsible for the support and the protection of the family, while women are viewed as the nurturers, providing the male with sex and succor, caring for the young, and maintaining a stable home environment. Even among individuals who have consciously tried to override this program, the ancient hard-wired programs persist, bursting into the open now and then as, for example, when women bemoan the severe conflicts they face between motherhood and work, and males confess their difficulties in suppressing their sexual drives and dealing with women coworkers as their equals or their superiors.

JUST BEFORE THE EARTHQUAKE, THE DOGS HOWL

Yet now, it seems, something has changed. Throughout the entire culture large numbers of people seem to have stopped suddenly, taken a look at the sex contract, fine print and all, and said, "Hey, this contract doesn't work. Let's renegotiate the terms."

Perhaps it's a case of punctuated-equilibrium evolution—over thousands of years, as the environment changed dramatically, the sex contract remained stable, inviolate, even as its terms became increasingly outdated, painful, and untenable. But finally the stresses have grown too great. It is as if two immense rock faces have been pressed up against each other at a fault line, with pressures building almost undetectably over the centuries, until finally the earth begins to tremble, the rock faces buckle, and with a huge groaning and grinding noise, it all breaks loose. The result is a cultural earthquake.

Seen in this way, the upheavals of the last thirty years—the sexual revolution, the women's movement, the antisex crusade, the entire battle taking place on the sex-power nexus—are revealed not as causes of the earthquake, but as preliminary tremors, indicators that vast forces that have been building up for centuries are about to break loose. The real earthquake, or as Californians say, the Big One, hasn't happened yet. But it now seems inevitable. And as dogs are able to detect an earthquake just before it occurs, so a lot of humans have felt the tremors and have begun to howl.

What is taking place is a breaking down of the old sex contract. For many people, this severing of sex from its ancient contractual bonds has been a fact of life for years. As a result of widely available birth-control devices, sex is no longer linked by necessity to reproduction. In fact, scientific breakthroughs such as *in vitro* fertilization—test-tube babies—have made it possible to eliminate sex from reproduction.

Men and women can approach sexual relations in a new way, not as a transaction in which each party exchanges something the other wants in return for something else, but as something that can be shared equally, as something ruled not by contractual rights and duties, but by mutual respect, affection, and love. Many men and women see the breakdown of the old contract as an event to be celebrated, an opportunity to create a new order of society, in which men and women can interact with each other as equals, sharers, partners, lovers.

But for many people, the possibility that the sex contract may be dissolved is cause for dread and terror, and breeds visions of impending anarchy and sexual license. For them the sex contract is, as it has been for most humans for hundreds of thousands of years, the single most solid, unshakable, unquestionable ordering principle of human existence. Ideologies are abstract and intangible. God, too, often seems remote and separate from ordinary day-to-day existence. But the sex contract, and all it involves—man the hunter and warrior, father, husband, patriarch, protector, and provider; woman the pure, the fertile and receptive one, mother, wife, matriarch, nurturer, provider of sex, loyalty, and love—is the structure on which everything else rests: the meme within which other memes exist.

For them, the threat of the dissolution of the sex contract produces horror. They see it, like Satan himself, as having the potential to taint all of existence, taking on any disguise it wishes, in fact taking on a multitude of disguises at once, appearing here as the right to unrestricted abortions, there as a proliferation of vile pornography, here as an assertion that there are biological components to differences between the sexes, over there as sex education in the schools, here again as the distribution of contraceptives.

THE SLIPPERY SLOPE FROM MASTURBATION TO CHAOS

The fundamentalists, as we have seen, have high levels of anxiety and guilt regarding sex. Their fear of sex is largely based on the fact that the sexual experience can shatter the individual's rigidly maintained sense of identity, making the self vulnerable and open to change. Their fear is stamped upon them, in most cases, by imprints laid down in infancy and childhood, and is constantly reinforced by religious teachings that emphasize the sinfulness and dirtiness of sex. These groups insist that sex must only take place within the bounds of the "holy" institution of marriage.

Whatever forces threaten the sex contract, then, must be zealously destroyed. Legalized abortions, they believe, encourage sexual promiscuity by removing the threat of danger from sexual activity. The "right to life" that they are so eager to protect is, in truth, a disguise for the "right to restrict sexual intercourse." Similarly their opposition to sex education, the dissemination of birth-control information and devices, pornography and erotica, and so on, on what are purportedly "moral" grounds, are in fact campaigns to stamp out anything that they believe would increase sexual activity that is outside the bounds dictated by the sex contract.

Like the religious fundamentalists, the feminist fundamentalists fear sex, seeing it as a power that unleashes forces that are especially dangerous for women. They claim to oppose erotic materials on the ground that they are intrinsically "harmful" to women. But as Columbia University anthropologist Carole S. Vance observes, their efforts to restrict erotic materials are in fact a way of attempting to thwart the male sex drive. "In the end," she says, "the fight against pornography is a campaign against male masturbation, in that pornography is used for that purpose. It's a slippery slope. One thing leads to another: so masturbation leads to pornography, pornography causes violence, and all of a sudden, we've gone from masturbation to rape. We've posited this kind of male monster. . . ."

And to limit the perceived dangers of sex, the feminist fundamentalists, just like the religious fundamentalists, insist that it only take place under the terms of the sex contract. In their interpretation of that contract they emphasize the ancient role of women as controllers of sex—sex is something that women may choose to give to males, but only when males meet certain criteria.

Sex, in their view, is an aspect of female power. It is part of the power guaranteed to them by the sex contract. And any type of sex that does not meet their standards, and over which they do not have control—such as male masturbation, pornography, sexual fantasies, sex with prostitutes, sex that takes place on the male's terms—threatens their power, as well as the sanctity of the sex contract. As such it is dangerous and must be suppressed.

The second aspect of the sex contract that these crusaders insist must continue to be enforced is that women are somehow weaker than men, and therefore deserve special protection. This view is especially evident in their efforts to enact ordinances, such as the Dworkin-MacKinnon Act. The idea that women are in need of special protection is indeed very old. It was a key factor that led to the forging of the sex contract several million years ago when our protohominid hunter-gatherer ancestors were evolving in a dangerous environment in which women, burdened with offspring, were truly in need of special protection.

For both the religious and feminist fundamentalists, then, the ancient sex contract must be defended at all costs, for it serves not only as the strongest barrier against the anarchic dangers of human sexual energies, but as the means whereby they can continue to acquire and exercise power. Ostensibly the power the sex contract provides these groups is only the power to control sexual activities. But the power to control human sexuality provides direct access to a far greater power—the power to control virtually all aspects of human behavior and human thought. As Dr. John Money observes, once you have taught people to fear "something the human organism normally does in healthy development, then you've put in place a lever of guilt and shame. All you need to do after that is pull the lever and they jump to attention and do whatever you tell them."

SEX AS INFORMATION AND EARTHQUAKE

I began this book by wondering why some friends of mine became so perturbed by certain ideas. I thought at first their perturbations had something to do with sex itself. I now see the threat was not sex so much as information. There is certain information, they were saying, that is dangerous and should be suppressed. Not because it has to do with sex, but because it has to do with the meaning of reality.

Information, as I have learned, is energy that is transmitted. The amount of information contained in a transmission of energy is related to its unpredictability. Sex, too, is energy. At its best, when it is a real transmission of energy between two people, sex leads inexorably into the realm of unpredictability. Sex, that is, is a form of information.

When energy, such as information, flows into an open system, it challenges that structure, producing fluctuations, until, if the energy is strong enough, the structure becomes destabilized, falls apart, and—perhaps—reintegrates itself in an unpredictable way at a higher level of complexity. This is what is called evolution, learning, or acquiring wisdom.

So, too, when sex/information/energy flows freely through the dissipative structure of the human brain and body, the structure reaches a point at which it has the potential to escape to a higher order. But certain people, because of sexual imprints, because of the heavy armor they wear as physical and mental rigidity, because of the vested interest they have in maintaining the old order, will do whatever they can to limit the flow of energy through the system. On a physical level, that means limiting the flow of unpredictable sensory energy, such as sex. On a mental, social, spiritual, or political level, that means limiting the flow of information. So the struggle by these forces to suppress information, and thereby to control behavior, can be seen as a determination to insure social, political, spiritual, and psychological stability and predictability and suppress change and unpredictability.

Seen in this light, the struggle in the nexus takes on not just historical but evolutionary significance.

AGAINST INSTABILITY: SELFISH GENES, INTOLERANT MEMES

In evolutionary biology, stability is a crucial ordering principle. As Richard Dawkins observes, "Darwin's 'survival of the fittest' is really a special case of a more general law of survival of the stable." Genes insure their survival—their stability over time—by making copies of themselves. But as a result of unpredictable copying mistakes, or genetic mutations, the process of biological evolution occurs.

Here is an intriguing paradox: Natural selection favors stability and predictability, but an essential prerequisite for evolution is instability and unpredictability. As Dawkins points out, "Nothing actually 'wants' to evolve. Evolution is something that happens, willy-nilly, in spite of all the efforts of the replicators (and . . . of the genes) to prevent it happening."

The central law of meme evolution, too, is survival of the stable. Our intellectual universe is populated by memes that have survived, or maintained their stability, through their power to make copies of themselves by leaping from mind to mind. This power is related to their intolerance for competing memes.

In addition, the survival of memes depends on their ability to replicate themselves without copying errors, that is, on their predictability. Memes that generated incorrect copies of themselves— that got "misunderstood" each time they leaped from mind to mind—would, like the message passed along in the child's game of "telephone," tend to degenerate rapidly, and would disappear from the meme pool.

Earlier I suggested that what sets humans apart from our genetic ancestors is the capacity to override hard-wired programs. That capacity is a direct result of the enormous and rapid increase in size of the human cerebral cortex—the seat of our higher functions, and the source of our extraordinary proficiency in receiving and transmitting complex patterns of information, or memes.

I also suggested that developing this proficiency with memes represented an enormous evolutionary advance for our primate ancestors, and that our brains have been molded by natural selection to insure that we have a high receptivity to memes. This unique capacity to receive, manipulate, and transmit memes, to "learn," is in fact the key to our ability to override hard-wired programs.

But there is a curious irony here. For the very same evolutionary breakthrough that liberated us from slavery to our genetic programs—our development of sophisticated information-manipulation skills—simultaneously shackled us to another master. In freeing ourselves from the domination of our genes, we became subject to the domination of memes.

And while the instinctual drive of genes toward self-replication can seem ruthless and brutal—"Nature red in tooth and claw"—the innate intolerance of memes can generate ruthlessness and brutality unimaginable in gene-driven nature. Human history is a fabric of butchery, carnage, and cruelty spurred not by genetic imperatives but by memes.

THE CIVILIZING MEME AND THE FAUSTIAN PACT

Anxiety is the state in which a being is aware of its possible nonbeing.

—*Paul Tillich,* The Courage to Be

But memes also evolve. And one meme that has emerged and played an increasingly important role in human history is the metameme of tolerance. As cultural evolution accelerates, the spread of this meme has also increased. Using new techniques for compiling and analyzing data, historians have discovered that there has been a trend of declining personal violence in Western society—a trend they attribute to what cultural historian Norbert Elias calls "the civilizing process": the increasing ability of humans to restrain their aggressive impulses and the widespread acceptance of humanistic values.

Clearly a key to the civilizing process is the meme of tolerance. Whenever and wherever this metameme has been ignored, or overwhelmed by infectious intolerance memes, the civilizing process has broken down, and masses of humans have hurled themselves into wars, and been butchered, enslaved, and marched off to death camps. Historians have found that there are certain conditions, ranging from economic collapse to plagues and epidemics, that almost inevitably cause a weakening or collapse of the civilizing process. Invariably the element common to all of these decivilizing conditions is that large numbers of the people who live through them experience feelings of powerlessness and anxiety.

In his researches into "power motivation," Harvard psychologist David C. McClelland found that individuals who feel weak and powerless seek to gain power by submitting or attaching themselves to some powerful force outside themselves; they are, says McClelland, "oriented towards 'intake,' towards obtaining a sense of power and strength from outside."

There is a clear formula here, one that we have noticed before: the greater the powerlessness or anxiety, the greater the susceptibility to memes.

Unquestionably the enormous increase in the size of the human cerebral cortex was accompanied by an enormous expansion of our capacity for existential anxiety: The higher functions that emerge from the cortex are the very capacities that endow humans with an awareness of the passage of time, the contingency of existence, life, death, personal mortality, and nonbeing.

The emergence of consciousness, then, was inevitably linked with the experience of anxiety, and, equally inevitably, by the spread of those handy anxiety remedies called memes.

There is a neurochemical explanation for this. As we noted earlier, humans have evolved a system to reward behaviors that have a high survival value by providing the "reinforcement" of pleasurable brain chemicals such as endorphins. On the other hand, behaviors that pose a threat to our genetic survival are "negatively reinforced" by a painful lack of comforting neurochemicals and a flood of intensely agitating neurochemicals, producing a state we know as fear or anxiety. Fear and anxiety have high survival value in appropriate situations—when we confront a wild animal, for example—by triggering our fight-or-flight response.

But in situations in which there is no clear object of fear, and in which there can be no quick fight-or-flight response—such as social upheaval, despair, powerlessness, dread—there is no survival value in continuing to experience unremitting anxiety. Responding to anxiety with decisive action, on the other hand, has a high survival value. The anxiety, or threat of nonbeing, is alleviated by an assertion of being. And so natural selection has insured that humans are programmed with a strong escape-from-anxiety mechanism: When in such a state, we become extremely receptive to memes.

Memes quickly relieve our anxiety by "explaining" us, assigning us our place in an immanent destiny, providing us with the power to be, offering a secure haven from social, economic, or spiritual instability and unpredictability. And by linking us with a larger entity, they alleviate our sense of powerlessness and meaninglessness. The mechanism by which memes provide such benefits, scientists are now coming to understand, is neurochemical: the ability to receive memes, to learn, had a high survival value for our ancestors, so such learning was rewarded by a release of pleasurable neurochemicals. And so when humans experiencing anxiety suddenly accept or "learn" a powerful life-explaining meme, they are rewarded with a flood of neurochemical bliss: They "see the light," or are "born again."

But it's a Faustian bargain: To gain the benefits of a meme, one must become its servant, undertaking to transmit it to others accurately (without allowing copying errors) and without tolerance for competing memes. In essence, to become infected with a meme means to become intolerant of information—since information is unpredictable and "new," it is by definition different from the meme. Since the sole purpose of the meme is self-replication (stability), both copying errors and competing memes must be ruthlessly suppressed.

THE JEALOUS GOD, THE GOLDEN MEME, AND THE BUDDHA MIND

The adoption of memes to reduce the anxieties of increasing intelligence had a high survival value as long as humans lived as hunter-gatherers, in bands small and cohesive enough that everyone could share the same memes, and scattered so widely that they would rarely be forced to interact with bands carrying conflicting memes.

But with the emergence of cities came increasing conflict among the carriers of competing memes. Meme intolerance (such as "Thou shalt have no other Gods before Me") interacted with increasing anxiety and insecurity in a positive-feedback loop that contributed to increasingly disruptive wars, conquests, mass migrations, and religious persecutions. Many of these memes, as a result of their own rigid intolerance for other memes, led their carriers into self-destructive behaviors, such as continuous warfare, and thus eliminated themselves from the meme pool. High levels of meme intolerance, it began to appear, could sabotage the reproductive success of their carriers in an environment that was becoming ever more densely populated with a variety of intolerant competing memes.

On the other hand, memes that could *suppress* or limit their intolerance of competing memes sufficiently to coexist with them in the marketplace of memes had a high survival value. As a result, such memes began to increase in the meme-pool, in what historians have called the "civilizing process."

In the last eighty years, scientific breakthroughs such as Einstein's insights into relativity, Heisenberg's demonstration of the pervasive nature of uncertainty and indeterminacy, and other advances in quantum mechanics have led many to accept the meme about memes: that "reality" is an ultimately indeterminate matrix of energy upon which we superimpose a structure that is a product of our own mind; that all memes are simply memes, and can never be accepted as absolute truth or descriptions of what "really exists," but only as aspects of the interaction of our own brains with the universe, as "ways of seeing" or metaphor systems; that memes can be useful only as long as we remember that they are interpretations or models of reality, constantly subject to revision (or evolution) as new information is received. And that as long as we remain conscious of the process of creating our reality by superimposing structure, we will remain free from infection by intolerant memes and will continue learning, or evolving.

In many ways modern science has arrived at a vision of the nature of reality similar to the ancient wisdom of the East, that reality is maya or "illusory" in the sense that it is a product of our own minds. "All that we are is the result of all that we have thought," the Buddha observed in the Dhammapada. "It is founded on thought. It is based on thought."

WE HAVE ALWAYS LIVED IN THE TREES

Today, as a result of a variety of forces, including uncontrolled population growth, impending global ecological disaster, economic confusion, metastasizing poverty, and the proliferation of nuclear weapons, our instability, disorientation, powerlessness, and anxiety seem to have reached all-time high levels. It follows that our global susceptibility to infection by virulently intolerant memes is also at an all-time high. Certainly the appalling events in Africa, the Middle East, Northern Ireland, and Latin America suggest that the world is undergoing an unprecedented plague of violent extremism. Cultural historians have described a global "rebirth of fundamentalism" in the last decade, analyzing it in terms of politics or religion, but I think it makes more sense to see it in epidemiological terms. As a result of severe stress and anxiety, our conceptual immune systems have been damaged. The outbursts of violence around the world—religious bigotry, racism, nationalism, xenophobia, torture, terrorism—can be seen as a series of opportunistic meme infections. We are experiencing a sort of spiritual AIDS epidemic. Everywhere, to escape the terrors of instability and to acquire a power to be, individuals dissolve their anxiety in the bosom of the Absolute Truth revealed to them by one or another explanation meme.

This provides us with an opportunity to step back and see the conflict on the sex-power nexus in a broader perspective—not just in terms of personal (particularly sexual) freedom, but as an evolutionary struggle for survival.

I am struck by an image, a fable of our tree-dwelling primate ancestors, threatened by the receding of the African forests caused by climatic changes. Some of them have come down from the trees and begun to go out onto the savannas in search of game, tentatively rising onto their hind legs. Don't be fools, come back, cry their brothers and sisters in the trees—our people have always lived in trees, and always will; we are meant to be tree-dwellers. Beyond the trees lies madness!

Evolution happens despite the best efforts of the forces of stability to prevent its happening. In the realm of memes, one example of this is the evolution of the tolerance meme. Increasingly memes that permitted their carriers at least a limited amount of tolerance for other memes flourished in the meme pool, despite being vigorously suppressed as heresy by the established systems of intolerance memes.

Slowly, as people came into contact with foreign, heretical, or competing memes, like individuals inoculated with vaccines, they began to develop resistance or immunity to meme infection. In recent centuries, these tolerance-carriers have spread and increased at a rapidly accelerating rate.

However, in recent years this trend appears to have been reversed in much of the world. A key cause has been the enormous increase in anxiety and powerlessness being experienced everywhere. And our lowered resistance to meme infection has been aggravated by a quantum leap in the speed and effectiveness of meme vectors or means of transmission—virtually every person on the globe can now be exposed, directly, quickly, and repeatedly, to virulent memes by radio and television. Computer networks, telephones, portable audiocassette players, FAX machines, photocopiers, VCRs, automobiles, vast highway networks, and jet travel also contribute to the spreading potential of memes. Nothing in evolutionary history has equipped humans to deal with the sheer quantity of infective memes they are exposed to each day: In some ways it is like a long-isolated tribe suddenly exposed to invaders carrying a huge assortment of virulent germs to which the natives have no resistance.

THE AYATOLLAH ON CAMPUS

The nexus, then, is everywhere. The battle I have been describing is not just some limited intellectual struggle pitting antisex extremists against civil liberties lawyers, but an evolutionary struggle for survival that threatens the lives and the freedom of us all. I don't think it's too melodramatic to say the future of civilization is at stake.

When the ayatollah Khomeini offered millions of dollars in rewards and guaranteed entry to paradise to anyone who murdered Salman Rushdie, the author of an "obscene" and "blasphemous" book, thousands of the ayatollah's followers around the world rioted in support, bombed bookstores, hung effigies of the hated author with his eyes poked out, burned Rushdie's books, and assassinated at least one Islamic leader who had urged more tolerance.

Antisex feminist and Christian fundamentalist leaders—who have been performing their own public condemnations of "enemies" and book-burnings—reacted indignantly, stating that these events were the work of "Muslim extremists and madmen," implying that these "crazy Arabs" had nothing in common with their decent (Christian or humanist) Western methods.

But what is striking is not the differences between the ayatollah and the television evangelists and antisex crusaders, but what they have in common. All of them know, with total certainty, that their particular revealed truth is absolute.

Some argue that this outbreak of Western fundamentalism is relatively innocuous: After all, the antisex forces aren't putting out murder contracts on people. This is like arguing that the early manifestations of Nazism were innocuous—only a few brown-shirted bullies in the street. Already, the antisex forces have bombed or burned scores of abortion clinics and bookstores, have made physical attacks on campus speakers and patrons of bookstores and clinics, have made death threats to individuals who have supported sex education and abortion rights or opposed censorship in the schools.

We have noted how in universities and research centers scientists have been attacked, denied tenure, grants, and publication, because critics claim their work "should not be done." Such censorship is now becoming increasingly widespread and given the imprimatur of respected academic institutions. A growing number of universities, including Stanford University, Smith, Emory University, the University of Michigan, and the state universities of Wisconsin, are taking steps to amend the universities' fundamental guarantee of free speech by passing rules to suppress forms of expression they consider "offensive." At Stanford, for example, a new rule would punish expressions that "degrade, victimize, stigmatize or pejoratively characterize" individuals on the basis of sex, race, national origin, or sexual preference.

As critics point out, it does not take a stretch of the imagination to see such restrictions severely limiting the freedom of discourse and research. Already opponents of research into biological sex differences claim that any such research that suggests innate differences between the sexes by its very nature "stigmatizes" or "pejoratively characterizes" females. The new university rules could be used not only to suppress this or any other type of "offensive" research, but to prohibit faculty members or students from even discussing it, or expressing any ideas that are not approved by those in power.

Such attempts to punish expression of unpopular ideas have emerged directly from the efforts we discussed earlier to pass laws prohibiting "offensive" erotic expression on the grounds that it degraded, victimized, stigmatized, pejoratively characterized, or otherwise harmed women. As Gerald Gunther, a professor of constitutional law at Stanford, points out, "In each case, perfectly bright, sophisticated people will come around saying, 'This speech causes harm to me or someone that I value, and we ought to suppress it.' "

MEME EPIDEMIOLOGY

Today, we face greater threats to our species than ever before. These threats fill us with anxiety, and make us susceptible to reassuring memes that promise order, meaning, safety. The plague seems all around us, and the threat of the plague lowers our resistance to the plague virus. In our urgent desire to eradicate this threat to civilization, it is tempting to attack the carriers of intolerance memes. But that is to mistake the victims of the disease for the disease itself.

In our opposition to intolerance it is too easy to fall into the warfare model, itself a product of intolerance memes. The way to eliminate the threat of meme warfare is not through more war, but through treatment and prevention.

Smallpox was once one of the deadliest and most contagious diseases known to humans, but in recent years has been totally eradicated. This was accomplished not by directly attacking the virus itself, but by raising human immunity to the smallpox virus. Our attack on deadly memes can follow a similar strategy.

One important step in the prevention process is elimination of the forces that weaken the immune system. This means a concerted attack on those elements that increase human susceptibility to memes: anxiety, poverty, fear, violence, inequality, despair, alienation. A worldwide effort to "clean up" those breeding grounds of virulent memes would dramatically reduce their incidence.

But the key step is inoculation—injecting healthy individuals with a form of the virus so that their body learns the nature of the virus and can build up a permanent resistance or immunity to it. And so with memes, in exposing ourselves to them while our immune system is healthy—while we are not in a state of anxiety, or hatred, and are fully conscious of the fact that all memes are superimpositions of structure on the indeterminate matrix of reality—we allow our mind to learn their nature and develop a lasting resistance to their harmful elements. By exposing ourselves to as many memes as possible, we can enhance our tolerance. The free circulation of memes, then, is our most essential defense against infection. As Stanford constitutional law professor Gerald Gunther observes of that university's recent efforts to silence the expression of unpopular ideas, "More speech, not less, is the proper cure for offensive speech."

RISING TOWARD POWER

The struggle on the nexus, it has become clear, is the process of human evolution. The direction of human evolution has been toward higher intelligence, increased freedom from hard-wired responses, greater wisdom: more information. This intensification of energy flow through the human system has created unprecedented fluctuations and perturbations. The earth seems to tremble beneath our feet. The human system appears to be approaching a bifurcation point, to be about to collapse into chaos or reintegrate at a higher level of complexity, interrelatedness, and order. In the midst of the upheaval, and contributing to it, humans are divided by a struggle for survival that has taken the form of a battle for power.

Those who fear the unpredictable, who have nothing to learn because they already know The Truth, grow increasingly terrified as the tremors increase and the structure begins to break apart. Desperately they attempt to hold the structure together by brute force. Events are moving too rapidly, there are forces at work beyond their control. Their only hope is to make the fluctuations stop; the only way to do that is to decrease the amount of energy flowing into the system, to damp the influx of what is unpredictable, to suppress the flow of information. And thus they must have power, for only power can insure them control over those who would act unpredictably. They struggle to maintain the stability of the structure at all costs, for it embodies the meme that "explains" them and provides them with the power to be.

But evolution is impossible to control or suppress. It happens, willy-nilly. As always, the old species, predictable, rigid, is threatened by the pressures of a changed environment, and by the emergence of a new or mutated form better adapted to that environment. In this case, the old species consists of humans who cannot or will not override their hard-wiring, particularly the hard-wiring that caused them to respond to anxiety or uncertainty by enslaving themselves to intolerance memes. Their struggle for survival is against a new species, which appeared first as isolated individuals several thousand years ago, increased in numbers over the centuries, and is now spreading at an enormously accelerating rate. These beings are more intelligent and flexible, more capable of overriding hard-wired behaviors, aware of the provisional nature of all memes. All over the world, these are the humans who are climbing down from the trees of the shrinking forest and making exploratory treks on two legs out across the savannas, while the dwellers in the trees condemn them as heretics and traitors.

These new beings, molded by evolutionary pressures of which they are not even aware, accept change. When energy passes through their system, whether in the form of sex, information, or insight, they do not resist it but experience it as pleasure. And it is in this experience of themselves as participants in a constant unfolding, evolving, and creating of reality that they obtain their power to be.

They affirm their self in the process of leaving the self behind to become transformed by life; and in leaving the old self, they experience not only the power to be but also the Power of Being.

They live not to control or attain power over others, but to fully experience the means and process by which they transcend and transform themselves. This means and process is energy. And as William Blake pointed out, energy is eternal delight.

So let the earthquake come, they say, for when the earth has settled and the pieces of the human cultural structure have been reorganized, we may find that we have escaped to a higher order. Who knows?

BIBLIOGRAPHY

Abbey, A. "Sex differences in attributions for friendly behavior: Do males misperceive females' friendliness?" *Journal of Personality and Social Psychology*, 42 (1982) 830–838.

"Adult Bookstore Burns While Spectators Cheer." *New York Times*, October 31, 1986.

Anderson, Duncan. "The Delicate Sex: How Females Threaten, Starve and Abuse One Another." *Science 86*, April 1986, 42–48.

"Are male hormones key to mathematics skills?" *Brain/Mind Bulletin*, August 2, 1982, p. 1.

Bancroft, J. "The relationship between hormones and sexual behavior in humans." In ed. J. B. Hutchison, *Biological Determinants of Sexual Behavior*. Chichester, England: John Wiley and Sons, 1978.

Barash, David. *The Whisperings Within*. New York: Harper & Row, 1979.

——. *The Hare and the Tortoise: Culture, Biology, and Human Nature*. New York: Viking, 1986.

Barbach, Lonnie Garfield. *For Yourself: The Fulfillment of Female Sexuality*. New York: Signet, 1975.

——. ed. *Pleasures: Women Write Erotica*. Garden City, NY: Doubleday, 1984.

Barclay, A. M. "Information as a defensive control of sexual arousal." *Journal of Personality and Social Psychology*, 17 (1971) 244–249.

Baron, R. A. "Sexual arousal and physical aggression: The inhibiting influence of 'cheesecake' and nudes." *Bulletin of the Psychonomic Society*, 3 (1974) 337–339.

Barringer, Felicity. "Free Speech and Insults on Campus." *New York Times*, April 25, 1989.

Bateson, Patrick, S. Rose, and G. Horn. "Imprinting: Lasting Effects on Uracil Incorporation into Chick Brain." *Science*, 181 (1973) 576–578.

Baum, M. J., and J.T.M. Vreeburg. "Copulation in castrated male rats following combined treatment with estradiol and dihydrotestosterone." *Science*, 182 (1973) 283–285.

Becker, M. A., and D. Byrne. "Self-regulated exposure to erotica, recall errors, and subjective reasons as a function of erotophobia and Type A coronary-prone behavior." *Journal of Personality and Social Psychology*, 48 (1985) 760–767.

Beeman, E. A. "The effect of male hormone on aggressive behavior in mice." *Physiological Zoology*, 20 (1947) 373–405.

Bell, R. "Hormone influences on human aggression." *Irish Journal of Medical Science*, 147, Suppl. 1 (1978) 5–9.

Benbow, Camilla Persson, and Julian C. Stanley. "Sex Differences in Mathematical Ability: Fact or Artifact?" *Science*, December (1980).

Berman, G. "Sexual Behavior: Hard Times with the Coolidge Effect." In eds. M. H. Siegel and H. P. Ziegler, *Psychological Research: The Inside Story*. New York: Harper & Row, 1976.

———, and J. Davidson. *Biological Bases of Sexual Behavior*. New York: Harper & Row, 1974.

Bernstein, I. S., T. P. Gordon, and R. M. Rose. "The interaction of hormones, behavior, and social context in nonhuman primates." In ed. B. Svare, *Hormones and Aggressive Behavior*. New York: Plenum Press, 1983.

"Biological Basis of Homosexuality." *Brain/Mind Bulletin*, November 19, 1984.

Blake, Randolph. "Neurohormones and Sexual Preference." *Psychology Today*, January 1985.

Blakely, Mary. "Is One Woman's Sexuality Another Woman's Pornography?" *Ms.*, April 1985.

Blank, Robert H. "The Infertility Epidemic." *UTNE Reader*, April/May 1985, p. 31.

Bloom, Floyd. "Neuropeptides and other mediators in the central nervous system." *The Journal of Immunology*, 132:2 (1985) 766–768.

Bly, Robert. "Interview." *New Age Journal*, August 1982.

———. "Men's Initiation Rites." *UTNE Reader* April–May 1986, pp. 42–49.

Booth, J. E. "Sexual behavior of neonatally castrated rats injected during infancy with oestrogen and dihydrotestosterone." *Journal of Endocrinology*, 72 (1977) 135–141.

Bowden, N. G., and P. F. Brain. "Blockade of testosterone-maintained intermale fighting in albino laboratory mice by an aromatization inhibitor." *Physiology and Behavior*, 20 (1978) 543–546.

Bower, B. "The left hand of math and verbal talent." *Science News*, April 27, 1985, p. 263.

———. "The 'math gap': Puzzling sex differences." *Science News*, December 6, 1986, p. 357.

Bozzi, Vincent. "Sex and the Romance Reader." *Psychology Today*, November 1985.

"Brain Research Enjoying an Explosion of Interest." *Los Angeles Times*, January 25, 1984.

Breedlove, S. M., and A. P. Arnold. "Hormone accumulation in a sexually dimorphic motor nucleus in the rat spinal cord." *Science*, 210 (1980) 564–566.

Brodie, H. K. H., et al. "Plasma testosterone levels in heterosexual and homosexual men." *American Journal of Psychiatry* 131 (1974) 82–83.

Brody, Jane E. "Homosexual Study Cites Hormone Link." *New York Times*, September 21, 1989.

Bronson, F. H., and C. Desjardins. "Neonatal androgen administration and adult aggressiveness in female mice." *General and Comparative Endocrinology*, 15 (1970) 320–325.

Brown, Norman O. *Life Against Death*. New York: Random House, 1959.

Brown, W., and G. Davis. "Serum testosterone and irritability in man." *Psychosomatic Medicine*, 37 (1975) 87–97.

Brownmiller, Susan. *Against Our Will: Men, Women, and Rape*. New York: Simon and Schuster, 1975.

———. *Femininity*. New York: Linden Press, 1984.

Budzynski, Thomas. "Biofeedback and the Twilight States of Consciousness." In G. E. Schwartz and D. Shapiro, eds., *Consciousness and Self-Regulation*, Vol. 1. New York: Plenum, 1976.

———. "Tuning in on the Twilight Zone." *Psychology Today*, August 1977.

———. "A Brain Lateralization Model for REST." Paper delivered at International Conference on REST and Self-Regulation, Denver, CO, March 18, 1983.

Burstyn, Varda. "Censoring who [*sic*]: Why state censorship backfires." *Our Times*, November 1984, pp. 27–44.

———, ed., *Women Against Censorship*, Vancouver, BC: Douglas & McIntyre, 1985.

Byette, Beverly. "The Battle of the Sexes, Continued: Communiqués From the Trenches—Interview with Carole Gilligan." *Los Angeles Times*, September 25, 1985.

Califia, Pat. "Feminism vs. Sex. A New Conservative Wave?" *The Advocate*, February 21, 1980, pp. 4–6.

———. "The New Puritans." *The Advocate*, April 17, 1980.

———. "A Secret Side of Lesbian Sexuality." In eds. T. Weinberg and G. W. Levi Kamel, *S & M*. Buffalo, NY: Prometheus, 1983.

Calvin, William, and George Ojemann. *Inside the Brain*. New York: New American Library, 1980.

Campbell, D. T. "On the conflicts between biological and social evolution and between psychology and moral tradition." *American Psychologist*, 30 (1975) 1103–1126.

Carson, L. M. Kit. "Robert Bly wants to make a man of you." *UTNE Reader*, December 1984/January 1985.

Casteneda, Carlos. *Tales of Power*. New York: Simon and Schuster, 1974.

Chagnon, Napoleon A., and William Irons, eds. *Evolutionary Biology and Social Behavior: An Anthropological Perspective*. North Scituate, MA: Duxbury Press, 1979.

Chambless, D. L., and J. L. Lifshitz. Self-reported sexual anxiety and arousal: The expanded Sexual Arousability Inventory. *Journal of Sex Research*, 20 (1984) 241–254.

Chamove, Arnold, Harry Harlow, and Gary Mitchell. "Sex Differences in the Infant-Directed Behavior of Preadolescent Rhesus Monkeys." *Child Development*, 38 (1967) 329–335.

Chia, Mantak, and Maneewan Chia. *Healing Love Through the Tao: Cultivating Female Sexual Energy*. Huntington, NY: Healing Tao Books, 1986.

————, and Michael Winn. *Taoist Secrets of Love: Cultivating Male Sexual Energy.* New York: Aurora Press, 1984.

Christon, Lawrence. "Imperiled Masculinity and Screen Warriors." *Los Angeles Times,* June 22, 1986.

Ciaccio, L. A., R. D. Lisk, and L. A. Reuter. "Prelordotic behavior in the hamster: A hormonally modulated transition from aggression to sexual receptivity." *Journal of Comparative and Physiological Psychology,* 93 (1979) 771–780.

Clark, R., and E. Hatfield. "Gender differences in receptivity to sexual offers." In E. R. Allgeier and N. B. McCormick, eds., *Gender Roles and Sexual Behavior: The Changing Boundaries.* Palo Alto, CA: Mayfield, 1982.

Clendinen, Dudley. "Fundamentalists Win a Federal Suit Over Schoolbooks." *New York Times,* Oct. 25, 1987.

Clutton-Brock, T., and P. Harvey, eds. *Readings in Sociobiology.* San Francisco: W. H. Freeman, 1978.

Cohn, Norman. *The Pursuit of the Millennium: Revolutionary Millenarians and Mystical Anarchists of the Middle Ages.* London: Paladin, 1970.

Coles, C. D., and M. J. Shamp. "Some sexual, personality, and demographic characteristics of women readers of erotic romances." *Archives of Sexual Behavior,* 13: 3 (1984), 187–209.

Commission on Obscenity and Pornography. *The Report of the Commission on Obscenity and Pornography.* Washington, D.C.: U.S. Government Printing Office, 1970.

Cooper, Jack R., Floyd E. Bloom, and Robert H. Roth. *The Biochemical Basis of Neuropharmacology,* 3rd edition. New York: Oxford University Press, 1978.

Cowley, Geoffrey. "How the Mind Was Designed." *Newsweek,* March 13, 1989, pp. 56–58.

Crowley, W. R., and F. P. Zemlan. "The neurochemical control of mating behavior." In ed. N. T. Adler, *Neuroendocrinology of Reproduction.* New York: Plenum, 1981.

Dahlberg, Frances, ed. *Woman the Gatherer.* New Haven: Yale University Press, 1981.

Daly, Mary. *Gyn/Ecology: The Metaethics of Radical Feminism.* Boston: Beacon Press, 1978.

Damassa, D. A., E. R., Smith and J. Davidson. "The relationship between circulating testosterone levels and sexual behavior." *Hormones and Behavior,* 8 (1977) 275–286.

Darwin, Charles. *The Origin of Species.* London: John Murray, 1859.

————. *The Descent of Man and the Selection in Relation to Sex.* London: John Murray, 1871.

D'Augelli, J. F., and H. Cross. "Relationship of sex guilt and moral reasoning to premarital sex in college women and in couples." *Journal of Consulting and Clinical Psychology,* 43 (1975) 40–47.

Davidson, J. M. "Activation of the male rat's sexual behavior by intracerebral implantation of androgen." *Endocrinology,* 79 (1966) 783–794.

Davis, Lisa. "The Personality Genes." *Hippocrates.* May/June 1987.

Davis, Murray, S. *Smut: Erotic Reality/Obscene Ideology*. Chicago: University of Chicago Press, 1983.

Dawkins, Richard. *The Selfish Gene*. New York: Oxford University Press, 1976.

———. "Put Your Money on Evolution." *New York Times Book Review*, April 16, 1989.

DeCrow, Karen. "Strange Bedfellows." *Penthouse*, May 1985, pp. 96–97.

"Defense in Slaying Case Cites Steroid Addiction." *New York Times*, May 29, 1988.

de Lacoste-Utamsing, Christine, and Ralph Holloway. "Sexual Dimorphism in the Human Corpus Callosum." *Science*, June 25 (1982).

DeLamater, John. "Gender Differences in Sexual Scenarios." In ed. Kathryn Kelley, *Females, Males, and Sexuality: Theories and Research*. Albany, NY. State University of New York Press, 1987.

Denenberg, Victor, H., et al. "Infantile Stimulation Induces Brain Lateralization in Rats." *Science*, 201 (1980) 1150–52.

Dershowitz, Alan M. "A 20th Century Inquisition." *Penthouse*, July 1986.

———. "Partners Against Porn." *Harper's*, May 1985.

DeVore, Irven, ed. *Primate Behavior: Field Studies of Monkeys and Apes*. New York: Holt, Rinehart & Winston, 1965.

Diamant, Anita. "The hairy question of how gender affects therapy." *The Boston Phoenix*, January 11, 1983, p. 8.

Diamond, Irene. "Pornography and Repression: A Reconsideration." *Signs*, 5: 4 (1980) 686–701.

Diamond, Marian, et al. "Differences in Occipital Cortical Synapses from Environmentally Enriched, Impoverished, and Standard Colony Rats." *Journal of Neuroscience Research*, Vol. 1, pp. 109–119.

Dimen, Muriel. *Surviving Sexual Contradictions*. New York: Macmillan, 1988.

Dinnerstein, Dorothy. *The Mermaid and the Minotaur: Sexual Arrangements and Human Malaise*. New York: Harper & Row, 1977.

Dixon, A. F. "Androgen and Aggressive Behavior in Primates: A Review." *Aggressive Behavior*, 6, 37–68.

Doering, C., et al. "Negative affect and plasma testosterone: A longitudinal human study." *Psychosomatic Medicine*, 37 (1975) 484–491.

Donnerstein, Edward. "Pornography and sexual violence." *Medical Aspects of Human Sexuality*, 13 (1979) 103.

———. Interview in "Sex, Violence & Values: Changing Images." An *ABC News Special*, April 6, 1986.

———. "Erotica and human aggression." In eds. R. Geen and E. Donnerstein, *Aggression: Theoretical and Empirical Reviews*. New York: Academic Press, 1983.

———, and Daniel G. Linz. "The Question of Pornography." *Psychology Today*, December 1986, pp. 56-59.

———, Daniel Linz, and Steven Penrod. *The Question of Pornography: Research Findings and Policy Implications*. New York: Free Press, 1987.

Dorner, Gunter. *Hormones and Brain Differentiation*. New York: Elsevier, 1976.

———. "Sexual Differentiation of the Brain." *Vitamins and Hormones*, 38 (1980).

Douglas, Ann. *The Feminization of American Culture*. New York: Alfred A. Knopf, 1977.

Duggan, L. "Censorship in the name of feminism." *Village Voice*, pp. 11–12, 16–17, and 42.

———. "Of Meese and Women: Porn Panic's New Face." *Village Voice*, December 3, 1985, pp. 33–39.

———. "History Between the Sheets: Politics Go Under Cover." *Village Voice/Literary Supplement*, September 24 1986, pp. 13-14.

Durden-Smith, Jo, and Diane deSimone. *Sex and the Brain: Is Biology Destiny?* New York: Warner Books, 1983.

Dworkin, A. *Woman Hating*. New York: Dutton, 1974.

———. "Pornography: The new terrorism." *New York University Review of Law and Social Change*, 8 (1979) 215–255.

———. *Pornography: Men Possessing Women*. New York: Perigee, 1981.

———. *Right-Wing Women*. New York: Perigee, 1983.

———. "Against the male flood: Censorship, pornography, and equality." *Harvard Women's Law Journal*, 8 (1985) 1–29.

Echols, Alice. "Cultural Feminism: Feminist Capitalism and the Anti-Pornography Movement." *Social Text*, 7 (1983) 34–53.

Edwards, D. A. "Early androgen stimulation and aggressive behavior in male and female mice." *Physiology and Behavior*, 4 (1969) 333–338.

———, and K. G. Burge. "Early androgen treatment and male and female sexual behavior in mice." *Hormones and Behavior*, 2 (1971) 49–58.

Ehrenkranz, J., E. Bliss, and M. Sheard. "Plasma testosterone: Correlation with aggressive behavior and social dominance in man." *Psychosomatic Medicine*, 36 (1974) 469–475.

Ehrenreich, Barbara. *The Hearts of Men: American Dreams and the Flight from Commitment*. Garden City, NY: Anchor Press, 1983.

———, Elizabeth Hess and Gloria Jacobs. *Re-Making Love: The Feminization of Sex*. New York: Doubleday, 1986.

Ehrhardt, Anke A., "Prenatal Hormonal Exposure and Psychosexual Differentiation." In ed. Edward Sachar, *Topics in Psychoendocrinology*. New York: Grune and Stratton, 1975.

———. "Behavioral effects of estrogen in the human female." *Pediatrics*, 62, Supplement, (1978) 1166–1170.

———, and S. W. Baker, "Fetal androgens, human central nervous system differentiation, and behavior sex differences." In eds. R. C. Friedman, R. M. Richart, and R. L. Vande Wiele. *Sex Differences in Behavior*. New York: John Wiley & Sons, 1974.

———, and H.F.L. Meyer-Bahlburg. "Effects of parental sex hormones on gender-related behavior." *Science*, 211 (1981) 1312–1318.

Eibl-Eibesfeldt, I. *Ethology: The Biology of Behavior*. New York: Holt, Rinehart & Winston, 1975.

Einsiedel, E. "Social and behavior science research analysis." In *Attorney*

General's Commission on Pornography Final Report. Washington, D.C.: U.S. Government Printing Office, 1986.

Elias, Michael. "Serum Cortisol, Testosterone, and Testosterone-Binding Globulin Responses to Competitive Fighting in Human Males," *Aggressive Behavior*, 7:3 (1981) 215–224.

Ellul, Jacques, *The Technological Society.* New York: Alfred A. Knopf, 1964.

Elshtain, Jean Bethke. "The New Porn Wars," *New Republic*, June 25, 1984.

Ember, Carol. "A Cross-Cultural Perspective on Sex Differences." In eds. Robert L. Monroe, Ruth H. Monroe, and Beatrice B. Whiting, *Handbook of Cross-Cultural Development.* New York: Garland Press, 1981.

English, Deirdre. "The Politics of Porn." *Mother Jones*, April 1980.

———, Amber Hollibaugh and Gayle Rubin, "Talking Sex: A Conversation on Sexuality and Feminism." *Socialist Review*, 11: 4 (1981) 43–62.

Eysenck. H. J. *Sex and personality.* London: Open Books, 1976.

———, and G. D. Wilson, *The Psychology of Sex.* London: Dent, 1979.

Farley, Frank. "The Big T in Personality." *Psychology Today*, May 1986, pp. 44–52.

———. "Risk-Taking." In Sharon Faelten, David Diamond, *Take Control of Your Life: A Complete Guide to Stress Relief,* Emmaus, PA.: Rodale Press, 1988.

Ferguson, A. "Sex war: The debate between radical and libertarian feminists." *Signs*, 10 (1984) 106–112.

Fiedler, Leslie. *Love and Death in the American Novel.* New York: Stein & Day, 1960.

Fisher, Helen E. *The Sex Contract: The Evolution of Human Behavior.* New York: William Morrow, 1982.

Fisher, W. A., and D. Byrne. "Sex differences in response to erotica? Love versus lust." *Journal of Personality and Social Psychology*, 36 (1978) 117–125.

Flor-Henry, Pierre. "Gender, Hemispheric Specialization and Psychopathology." *Social Science and Medicine*, 12 (1987).

———. "Cerebral Aspects of the Orgasmic Response: Normal and Deviational." In eds. Romano Forlee and Willy Pasini, *Medical Sexology: The Third International Congress.* Amsterdam and New York: Elsevier, 1980.

Franklin, Jon. *Molecules of the Mind: The Brave New Science of Molecular Psychology.* New York: Atheneum, 1987.

Freedman, Samuel, G. "Of History and Politics: Bitter Feminist Debate." *New York Times*, June 6, 1986.

Freud, S. "Three Essays on the Theory of Sexuality." In ed. A. A. Brill, *The Basic Writings of Sigmund Freud.* New York: Modern Library, 1938.

———. *The Standard Edition of the Complete Psychological Works of Sigmund Freud,* trans. and ed. James Strachey. London: Hogarth Press, 1953–64.

Friday, Nancy. *My Secret Garden: Women's Sexual Fantasies.* New York: Pocket Books, 1974.

Friedan, Betty. "How to Get the Women's Movement Moving Again." *New York Times Magazine*, November 3, 1985, pp. 26 and 108.

————. Interview in "Currents: The Porning of America." WNET-TV, n.d.

Frodi, A., J. Macauley, and P. R. Thome. "Are women always less aggressive than men? A review of the experimental literature." *Psychological Bulletin*, 84 (1977) 634–660.

Gallagher, Winifred. "The Etiology of Orgasm." *Discover*, February 1986.

Garcia, L. T., et al. "Sex differences in sexual arousal to different erotic stories." *Journal of Sex Research*, 20 (1984) 391–402.

Gerall, A. A., et al. "Effects of early castration in male rats on adult sexual behavior." *Journal of Comparative and Physiological Psychology*, 64 (1967) 206–212.

Gerrard, Meg. "Sex, sex guilt, and contraceptive use." *Journal of Personality and Social Psychology*, 42 (1982) 153–158.

————. "Emotional and Cognitive Barriers to Effective Contraception: Are Males and Females Really Different?" In ed. Kathryn Kelley, *Females, Males, and Sexuality: Theories and Research*. Albany, NY: State University of New York Press, 1987.

————, and F. X. Gibbons, "Sexual experience, sex guilt, and sexual moral reasoning." *Journal of Personality*, 50 (1982) 345–359.

Geschwind, Norman, and Peter Behan. "Lefthandedness: Association with Immune Disease, Migraine and Developmental Learning Disorder," *Proceedings of the National Academy of Sciences*, August 1982.

Gilbert, F. S., and M.P. Gamache, "The Sexual Opinion Survey: Structure and Use." *Journal of Sex Research*, 20 (1984) 293–309.

Gilligan, Carol. *In a Different Voice: Psychological Theory and Women's Development*. Cambridge, MA: Harvard University Press, 1982.

Glass, S. P., and T. L. Wright "The Relationship of Extramarital Sex, Length of Marriage and Sex Differences on Marital Satisfaction and Romanticism: Athanasio's Data Reanalyzed." *Journal of Marriage and the Family*, 39 (1977) 691–703.

Goldberg, Steven. "Numbers Don't Lie: Men Do Better Than Women— S.A.T. scores accurately reflect male superiority in math. *New York Times*, July 2, 1989.

Goldfoot, D. A., and J. J. van der Werff ten Bosch. "Mounting behavior of female guinea pigs after prenatal and adult administration of the propionates of testosterone, dihydrotestosterone, and androstanediol." *Hormones and Behavior*, 6 (1975) 139–148.

Goleman, Daniel. "Two Views of Marriage Explored: His and Hers." *New York Times*, April 1, 1986.

————. "Major Personality Study Finds That Traits Are Mostly Inherited." *New York Times*, December 2, 1986.

————. "Personality: Major Traits Found Stable Throughout Life." *New York Times*, June 9, 1987.

————. "The Experience of Touch: Research Points to a Critical Role." *New York Times*. February 2, 1988.

————. "Chemistry of Sexual Desire Yields Its Elusive Secrets." *New York Times*, October 18, 1988.

————. "Subtle but Intriguing Differences Found in the Brain Anatomy of Men and Women." *New York Times*, April 11, 1989.

————. "What Bothers Women About Men, and Vice Versa." *New York Times*, May 15, 1989.

Gorski, R., et al. "Evidence for a Morphological Sex Difference Within the Medial Preoptic Area of the Rat Brain," *Brain Research*, 148 (1978) 333–346.

Goy, R. "Early hormonal influences on the development of sexual and sex-related behavior." In eds. F. Schmitt, et al. *The Neurosciences: Second Study Program*. New York: Rockefeller University Press, 1970.

————, and Bruce McEwen, *Sexual Differentiation of the Brain*. Cambridge, MA: MIT Press, 1980.

Green, Elmer, and Alyce Green. *Beyond Biofeedback*. New York: Delacorte, 1977.

Greenhouse, Linda. "New Poll Finds Wide Support for Abortion Rights." *New York Times*, January 21, 1988.

Greenough, W. T., et al. "Sex differences in dendritic patterns in hamster preoptic area." *Brain Research*, 126 (1977) 63–72

Greer, William R. "The Changing Women's Marriage Market." *New York Times*, February 22, 1986.

Griffin, Susan. *Pornography and Silence: Culture's Revenge Against Nature*. New York: Harper & Row, 1981.

Griffitt, William. "Sexual experience and sexual responsiveness: Sex differences." *Archives of Sexual Behavior*, 4 (1975) 232–235.

————. "Females, Males, and Sexual Responses." In ed. Kathryn Kelley, *Females, Males, and Sexuality*. Albany, NY: State University of New York Press, 1987.

————, and D. L. Kaiser. "Affect, sex guilt, gender, and the rewarding-punishing effects of erotic stimuli." *Journal of Personality and Social Psychology*, 36 (1978) 850–858.

Gurr, Ted Robert. "Drowning in a Crime Wave." *New York Times*, April 13, 1989.

Hall, Elizabeth. "June Reinisch: Profile—New Directions for the Kinsey Institute." *Psychology Today*, June 1986.

Harding, C., and H. H. Feder. "Relation between individual differences in sexual behavior and plasma testosterone levels in the guinea pig." *Endocrinology*, 98 (1976) 1198–1205.

Hare, R., et al. "Autonomic responses to affective visual stimulation: Sex differences." *Journal of Experimental Research in Personality*, 5 (1971) 14–22.

Heath, Robert. "Interview." *Omni*, April 1984.

Heimer, L., and K. Larsson. "Impairment of mating behavior in male rats following lesions in the preoptic-anterior hypothalamic continuum." *Brain Research*, 3 (1966/67) 248–263.

Henson, H. Keith. "Memetics and the Modular Mind—Modeling the Development of Social Movements," *Analog Science Fiction/Science Fact*, August 1987, pp. 29–43.

————. "The Science of Information Viruses." In ed. Kevin Kelly, *Signal:*

Communication Tools for the Information Age. New York: Harmony Books, 1988.

Herrenkohl, Lorraine. "Prenatal Stress Reduces Fertility and Fecundity in Female Offspring." *Science*, 206 (1979).

Hertzberg, Hendrik. "Sluicegate." *New Republic*, June 1, 1987.

Hess, Eckhardt. *Imprinting*. Chicago: University of Chicago Press, 1974.

Hier, Daniel, and William Crowley. "Spatial Ability in Androgen-Deficient Men." *New England Journal of Medicine*, May 20, 1982.

Hite, Shere. *The Hite Report: Women In Love*. New York: Knopf, 1987.

Hofstadter, Douglas. "On Viral Sentences and Self-Replicating Structures." In *Metamagical Themas*. New York: Basic Books, 1985.

Holloway, Ralph. *Primate Aggression, Territoriality and Xenophobia*. New York: Academic Press, 1975.

Hoon, P. W., J. P. Wincze, and E. F. Hoon. "A test of reciprocal inhibition: Are anxiety and sexual arousal in women mutually inhibitory." *Journal of Abnormal Psychology*, 86 (1977) 65–74.

Hooper, Judith. "Feminism and the Brain." *Omni*, July 1981.

———, and Dick Teresi. *The Three-Pound Universe*. New York: Simon and Schuster, 1986.

Horn, Jack C. "Blood and Power." *Psychology Today*, January 1986.

Hougan, Jim. *Decadence: Radical Nostalgia, Narcissism, and Decline in the Seventies*. New York: William Morrow, 1975.

Hoyenga, Katherine Blick, and Kermit T. Hoyenga. "Gender and Energy Balance: Sex Differences in Adaptations for Feast and Famine." *Physiology and Behavior*, 28 (1982).

Hrdy, Sarah Blaffer. *The Woman That Never Evolved*. Cambridge, MA: Harvard University Press, 1981.

———. "Interview, *Omni*, June 1988.

Humes, Alison. "Fear of Porn—What's Really Behind It?—An Interview with Carol S. Vance." *Vogue*, September 1985.

Hutchison, J. B., ed. *Biological Determinants of Sexual Behavior*. New York: John Wiley and Sons, 1978.

Hutchison, Michael. *The Book of Floating*. New York: William Morrow, 1984.

———.*Megabrain*. New York: William Morrow, 1986.

Jacobson, C. D., and R. A. Gorski. "Neurogenesis of the sexually dimorphic nucleus of the preoptic area in the rat." *Journal of Comparative Neurology*, 196 (1981) 519–529.

Janda, L. H., and K. E. O'Grady. "Development of a sex anxiety inventory." *Journal of Consulting and Clinical Psychology*, 48 (1980) 169–175.

Johnson, Hillary. "Violence Against Women—Is Porn to Blame?" *Vogue*, September 1985.

Jolly, C. J. "A Suggested Case of Evolution by Sexual Selection in Primates." *Man*, 63 (1963).

Jonas, Hans. *The Gnostic Religion*. Boston: Beacon, 1963.

Jong, Erica. *Fear of Flying*. New York: Signet, 1973.

Kaplan, Helen Singer. "Interview." *Omni*, August 1981, pp. 73–92.

Kelley, Kathryn. "Sex, sex guilt, and authoritarianism: Differences in responses to explicit heterosexual and masturbatory slides." *Journal of Sex Research*, 21 (1985) 68–85.

———, ed. *Females, Males, and Sexuality: Theories and Research*. Albany, NY: State University of New York Press, 1987.

Kendrick, K. M., and R. F. Drewett. "Testosterone Reduces Refractory Period of Stria Terminalis Neurons in the Rat Brain." *Science*, 204 (1979) 877–790.

Kendrick, Walter. *The Secret Museum: Pornography in Modern Culture*. New York: Viking, 1987.

Kenrick, Douglas T., and Melanie R. Trost. "A Biosocial Theory of Heterosexual Relationships." In ed. Kathryn Kelley, *Females, Males, and Sexuality: Theories and Research*. Albany, NY: State University of New York Press, 1987.

Kimura, Doreen. "Male Brain, Female Brain: The Hidden Difference." *Psychology Today*, November 1985, pp. 51–58.

Klemesrud, Judy. "Joining Hands in the Fight Against Pornography." *New York Times*, August 26, 1985.

Koedt, Ann. "The Myth of the Vaginal Orgasm." In eds. D. Babcox and M. Belkin, *Liberation Now*. New York: Dell, pp. 311–320.

Kohlberg, Lawrence. *The Philosophy of Moral Development: Moral Stages and the Idea of Justice*. New York: Harper & Row, 1981.

Kolata, Gina. "Math Genius May Have Hormonal Basis." *Science*, 222 (1985) 1312.

Kolbert, Elizabeth. "Literary Feminism Comes of Age." *New York Times Magazine*, December 6, 1987.

Konner, Melvin. *The Tangled Wing*. New York: Holt, Rinehart & Winston, 1982.

Korner, Annelise. "Neonatal Startles, Smiles, Erections and Reflex Sucks as Related to State, Sex and Individuality." *Child Development*, 40 (1969) 1039–53.

———. "Sex Differences in Newborns with Special Reference to Differences in the Organization of Oral Behavior." *Journal of Child Psychology and Psychiatry*, 14 (1973) 19–29.

Koss, M. F., & K. E. Leonard. "Sexually aggressive men: Empirical findings and theoretical implications." In eds. N. M. Malamuth & E. Donnerstein, *Pornography and Sexual Aggression*. Orlando, FL: Academic Press, 1984.

Kreuz, Leo, and Robert Rose. "Assessment of Aggressive Behavior and Plasma Testosterone in a Young Criminal Population." *Psychosomatic Medicine*, 34 (1972) 321–332.

——— and J. Jennings. "Suppression of plasma testosterone levels and psychological stress." *Archives of General Psychiatry*, 26 (1972) 479–482.

Lasch, Christopher. *The Culture of Narcissism*. New York: W. W. Norton, 1979.

———. "Soul of a New Age." *Omni*, October, 1987.

Leary, Timothy. *The Politics of Ecstasy*. London: Granada Publishing, 1973.

Lederer, L. *Take Back the Night: Women on Pornography*. New York: William Morrow, 1980.

Lee, Richard. B., and Irven DeVore, eds. *Man the Hunter.* Chicago: Aldine, 1968.

Leonard, George. "The End of Sex," *Esquire,* December 1982.

Levy, Jerre. "Lateral Differences in the Human Brain in Cognition and Behavioral Control." In ed. P. Busei, *Cerebral Correlates of Conscious Experience.* New York: North Holland Publishing Company, 1978.

———. "Review of *Sexual Differentiation of the Brain* by Robert Goy and Bruce McEwen." *The Sciences,* March 1981.

———. "Interview." *Omni,* January 1985.

Lewin, Roger. "How Did Humans Evolve Big Brains?" *Science,* 216 (1982).

Loehlin, John C., and Robert C. Nichols. *Heredity, Environment and Personality: A Study of 850 Sets of Twins.* Austin: University of Texas Press, 1976.

Lorenz, Konrad. *On Aggression.* New York: Harcourt Brace Jovanovich, 1966.

———. *Foundations of Ethology.* New York: Springer-Verlag, 1981.

Love, R. E., L. R. Sloan, and J. J. Schmidt. "Viewing pornography and sex guilt: The priggish, the prudent, and the profligate." *Journal of Consulting and Clinical Psychology,* 44 (1976) 624–629.

Lovejoy, C. Owen. "The Origin of Man." *Science,* 211, (1981).

Lumsden, C. J., and E. O. Wilson. *Genes, Mind, and Culture: The Coevolutionary Process.* Cambridge, MA: Harvard University Press, 1981.

———. *Promethean Fire.* Cambridge, MA: Harvard University Press, 1983.

McCauley, C., and C. P. Swann. "Male-female differences in sexual fantasy." *Journal of Research in Personality,* 12 (1978) 76–86.

McClelland, David, C. *Power: The Inner Experience.* New York: Irvington Publishers, 1975.

Maccoby, Eleanor, and Carol Jacklin. *The Psychology of Sex Differences.* Palo Alto: Stanford University Press, 1974.

McGill, Thomas E., and G. Richard Tucker. "Genotype and Sex Drive in Intact and Castrated Mice." *Science,* 145 (1964) 514–515.

McGlone, J. "Sex differences in human brain asymmetry: A critical survey." *Behavioral and Brain Sciences,* 3 (1980) 215–263.

McGuinness, Diane. *When Children Don't Learn.* New York: Basic Books, 1985.

———, and Karl Pribram. "Auditory and Motor Aspects of Language Development in Males and Females." In eds. A. Ansara et al., *The Significance of Sex Differences in Dyslexia.*Towson, MD: The Orton Society, 1981.

MacKinnon, Catherine. Interview in "Sex, Violence & Values: Changing Images." An *ABC News Special,* April 6, 1986.

———. "Not a Moral Issue." *Yale Law and Policy Review,* 2 (1984) 321–345.

———. "Pornography, Civil Rights, and Speech: Commentary." *Harvard Civil Rights-Civil Liberties Law Review,* 20 (1985), 1–70.

MacLean, Paul D. *A Triune Concept of Brain and Behavior.* Toronto: University of Toronto Press, 1973.

Malamuth, N. M. "Aggression Against Women: Cultural and Individual

Causes." In eds. N. M. Malamuth and E. Donnerstein, *Pornography and Sexual Aggression*. New York: Academic Press, 1984.

Mann, M. A., and B. Svare. "Prenatal testosterone exposure elevates maternal aggression in mice." *Physiology and Behavior*, 30 (1983) 503–507.

Marcus, Steven. *The Other Victorians*. New York: Bantam, 1967.

Marcuse, Herbert. *Eros and Civilization*. New York: Vintage, 1962.

———. *One-Dimensional Man*. Boston: Beacon, 1964.

Martin, N. G., L. J. Eaves, and H. J. Eysenck. "Genetical, environmental, and personality factors influencing the age of first sexual intercourse in twins." *Journal of Biosocial Science*, 9 (1977) 91–97.

Marx, Jean L. "Autoimmunity in Left-Handers." *Science*, 217 (1982), 141–144.

May, Robert. *Sex and Fantasy: Patterns of Male and Female Development*. New York: W. W. Norton, 1980.

Mayr, Ernst. *Animal Species and Evolution*. Cambridge, MA: Harvard University Press, 1963.

———. "Interview." *Omni*, February 1983, pp. 73–119.

Mazur, A., and T. Lamb. "Testosterone, status, and mood in human males." *Hormones and Behavior*, 14 (1980) 236–246.

Mead, Margaret. *Male and Female*, 4th ed. New York: William Morrow, 1974.

Mendelsohn, M. J., and D. L. Mosher. "Effects of sex guilt and premarital sexual permissiveness on role-played sex education and moral attitudes." *Journal of Sex Research*, 15 (1979) 174–183.

Metzger, Deena. "Re-vamping the World: On the Return of the Holy Prostitute." *UTNE Reader*, August/September 1985, pp. 120–124.

Meyer, John A., et al. "Stress During Pregnancy: Effect on Catecholamines in Discrete Brain Regions of Offspring and Adults." *Brain Research*, 144 (1978)

Meyer-Bahlburg, H.F.L. "Sex hormones and male homosexuality in comparative perspective." *Archives of Sexual Behavior*, 6 (1977) 297–325.

———, et al. "Aggressiveness and testosterone measures in man." *Psychosomatic Medicine*, 35 (1973) 453.

———. "Aggressiveness and testosterone measures in man." *Psychosomatic Medicine*, 36 (1974) 269–274.

Moir, Anne, and David Jessel. *Brain Sex: The Real Difference Between Men and Women*. London: Michael Joseph, 1989.

Money, John. "Use of an androgen-depleting hormone in the treatment of male sex offenders." *Journal of Sex Research*, 6 (1970):165–172.

———. *Man and Woman, Boy and Girl: The Differentiation and Dimorphism of Gender Identity from Conception to Maturity*. Baltimore, MD: Johns Hopkins University Press, 1972.

———. *"Love & Love Sickness: The Science of Sex, Gender Difference, and Pair-bonding."* Baltimore, MD: Johns Hopkins University Press, 1980.

———. "Interview." In ed. Pamela Weintraub, *The Omni Interviews*. New York: Ticknor & Fields, 1984.

———, and A. A. Ehrhardt. "Prenatal hormonal exposure: Possible effects on behavior in man." In ed. R. P. Michael, *Endocrinology and Human Behavior*. London: Oxford University Press, 1968.

Monod, Jacques. *Chance and Necessity*. London: Collins, 1972.

Morgan, Robin. *Sisterhood Is Powerful*. New York: Vintage, 1970.

———. *The Demon Lover: On the Sexuality of Terrorism*. New York: W. W. Norton, 1989.

Mosher, D. L. "Measurement of guilt in females by self-report inventories." *Journal of Consulting and Clinical Psychology*, 32, (1968) 690–695.

———. "Sex differences, sex experience, sex guilt, and explicitly sexual films." *Journal of Social Issues*, 29 (1973) 95–112.

———. "Sex guilt and sex myths in college men and women." *Journal of Sex Research*, 15 (1979) 224–234.

———, and I. Greenberg. "Females' affective responses to reading erotic literature." *Journal of Consulting and Clinical Psychology*, 33 (1969) 472–477.

———, and K. E. O'Grady. "Sex guilt, trait anxiety, and females' subjective sexual arousal to erotica." *Motivation and Emotion*, 3 (1979) 235–250.

Moss, R. L., and S. M. McCann. "Induction of mating behavior in rats by LHRF." *Science*, 181 (1973) 177–179.

Murdock, George Peter. *Ethnographic Atlas*. Pittsburgh: University of Pittsburgh Press, 1967.

Murray, Thomas. "The Language of Singles Bars." *American Speech*, Spring 1985.

Nemy, Enid. "Woman and Investment: An Expert Says They Are Too Fearful of Risks." *New York Times*, December 18, 1983.

Nicholson, John. *Men & Women: How Different Are They?* Oxford: Oxford University Press, 1984.

O'Grady, K. E. "Affect, sex guilt, gender and the rewarding-punishing effects of erotic stimuli: A reanalysis and reinterpretation." *Journal of Personality and Social Psychology*, 43 (1982) 618–622.

Olds, James. "Behavioral Studies of Hypothalamic Functions: Drives and Reinforcements." In eds. R. G. Grenell and S. Gabay. *Biological Foundations of Psychiatry*, Vol. 1. New York: Raven, 1976.

Overton, D. "Major theories of state-dependent learning." In eds. B. Ho, D. Richards, and D. Chute, *Drug Discrimination and State-Dependent Learning*. New York: Academic Press, 1978.

Pally, Marcia. "Ban sexism, not pornography." *The Nation*, 240 (1985) 784–813.

———. Interview in "Currents: The Porning of America." WNET-TV, n.d.

———. "The Quick Fix." *Playboy*, December 1988, pp. 56–57.

Persky, H., K. Smith, and B. Basu. "Relation of psychologic measures of aggression and hostility to testosterone production in man." *Psychosomatic Medicine*, 33 (1971) 265–277.

Pert, Candace. "Interview." *Omni*. February 1982, pp. 62–112.

———, et al. "Neuropeptides and their receptors: A psychosomatic network." *The Journal of Immunology*, 135:2 (1985) 820s–826s.

Petersen, James R. "Politically Correct Sex." *Playboy*, October 1986.

Phoenix, C. H. "Prenatal Testosterone in the Nonhuman Primate and Its Consequences for Behavior." In eds. R. C. Friedman, R. M. Richart, and

R. L. Vande Wiele, *Sex Differences in Behavior*. New York: John Wiley and Sons, 1974.

Pilpel, Harriet. "Porn Vigilantes—Are they Confusing Feminism with Censorship?" *Vogue*, September 1985, 1129–1139.

"The Place of Pornography," a discussion among Susan Brownmiller, Erica Jong, Midge Decter, Aryeh Neier, Jean Bethke Elshtain, Al Goldstein, and Lewis H. Lapham. *Harper's*, November 1984, pp. 31–45.

Popp, Joseph L., and Irven DeVore. "Aggressive Competition and Social Dominance Theory: Synopsis." In eds. David A. Hamburg and Elizabeth R. McCown, *The Great Apes*. Reading, Mass.: Benjamin/Cummings, 1979.

Prigogine, Ilya. *From Being to Becoming*. San Francisco: Freeman, 1980.

———. "Interview." In Pamela Weintraub, ed. *The Omni Interviews*, New York: Ticknor & Fields, 1984.

———, and Isabelle Stengers. *Order Out of Chaos: Man's New Dialogue with Nature*. New York: Bantam, 1984.

Raisman, G., and P. M. Field. "Sexual Dimorphism in the Neurophil of the Preoptic Area of the Rat and Its Dependence on Neonatal Androgen." *Brain Research*, 54 (1973) 1–29.

Rathbone, M. P., P. A. Stewart, and F. Vetrano. "Strange Females Increase Plasma Testosterone Levels in Male Mice." *Science*, 189 (1982) 1104–1106.

Reich, Wilhelm. *The Sexual Revolution: Toward a Self-Regulating Character Structure*. New York: Farrar, Straus & Giroux, 1945.

———. *The Mass Psychology of Fascism*. New York: Farrar, Straus & Giroux, 1970.

———. *Character Analysis*. New York: Farrar, Straus & Giroux, 1972.

———. *The Function of the Orgasm*. New York: Farrar, Straus & Giroux, 1973.

Reinisch, June Mackover. "Fetal Hormones, the Brain, and Sex Differences: A Heuristic Integrative Review of the Literature." *Archives of Sexual Behavior*, 3 (1974) 51–90.

———. "Prenatal Exposure of Human Fetuses to Synthetic Progestin and Estrogen Affects Personality." *Nature*, 226 (1977) 561–562.

———. "Fetal Hormones, the Brain and Human Sex Differences." *Archives of Sexual Behavior*, 3 (1981).

———. "Prenatal exposure to synthetic progestins increases potential for aggression in humans." *Science*, 211 (1981) 1171–1173.

———. "Early Barbiturate Exposure: The Brain, Sexually Dimorphic Behavior and Learning." *Neuroscience and Biobehavioral Reviews*, 6 (1982).

Restak, Richard. *The Brain: The Last Frontier*. New York: Doubleday, 1979.

Rheingold, Howard. *Excursions to the Far Side of the Mind: A Book of Memes*. New York: William Morrow, 1988.

Rich, B. Ruby. "Anti-porn: Soft Issue, Hard World." *Village Voice*, July 20, 1977.

Richards, Janet. *The Sceptical Feminist*. Boston: Routledge and Kegan Paul, 1980.

Roberts, Leslie. "Sex and Cancer." *Science 86*, July/August, 1986.

Rose, Robert M. "Testosterone, aggression and homosexuality: A review of the literature and implications for future research." In ed. E. J. Sachar, *Topics in Psychoendocrinology*. New York: Grune and Stratton, 1975.

———, J. W. Holaday, and I. Bernstein. "Plasma testosterone, dominance rank, and aggressive behavior in male rhesus monkeys." *Nature*, 231 (1971) 366–368.

———, Thomas P. Gordon, and Irwin S. Bernstein. "Plasma Testosterone Levels in the Male Rhesus: Influences of Sexual and Social Stimuli." *Science* 178 (1972) 643–645.

———, et al. "Androgens and Aggression: A Review of Recent Findings in Primates." In ed. Ralph L. Holloway. *Aggression, Territoriality and Xenophobia. Primate*, New York: Academic Press, 1975.

———, I. S. Bernstein and T. P. Gordon. "Consequences of Social Conflict on Plasma Testosterone Levels in Rhesus Monkeys." *Psychosomatic Medicine*, 37 (1975) 50–61.

Rosenzweig, Mark R. "Effects of Environment on Development of Brain and Behavior." In eds. E. Tobach, L. R. Aronson, and E. Shaw. *The Biopsychology of Development*, New York: Academic Press, 1971.

———, Edward Bennett, and Marian C. Diamond. "Brain Changes in Response to Experience." *Scientific American*, 226 (1981), 22–29.

Rossi, Ernest Lawrence. *The Psychobiology of Mind-Body Healing, New Concepts of Therapeutic Hypnosis*. New York: W. W. Norton, 1986.

Routtenberg, Aryeh. "The Reward System of the Brain." *Scientific American*, November 1978.

———. *Biology of Reinforcement: Facets of Brain-Stimulation Reward*. New York: Academic Press, 1980.

Sachs, Benjamin D., and Ronald J. Barfield. "Copulatory Behavior of Male Rats Given Intermittent Electric Shocks." *Journal of Comparative and Physiological Psychology*, 86 (1974) 607–615.

Sade, Donald S. "Determinants of Dominance in a Group of Free-Ranging Rhesus Monkeys." In ed. S. Altmann, *Social Communication Among Primates*. Chicago: University of Chicago Press, 1967.

Sapolsky, B. S. "Arousal, affect, and the aggression-moderating effect of erotica." In eds. N. M. Malamuth and E. Donnerstein, *Pornography and Sexual Aggression*. New York: Academic Press, 1984.

Schecter, D., and R. Gandelman, "Intermale aggression in mice: Influence of gonadectomy and prior fighting experience." *Aggressive Behavior*, 7 (1981) 187–237.

———, S. M. Howard, and R. Gandelman. "Dihydrotestosterone promotes fighting behavior in female mice." *Hormones and Behavior*, 15 (1981) 233–237.

Scheer, Robert. "Inside the Meese Commission." *Playboy*, August 1986.

Schmidt, G. "Male-female differences in sexual arousal and behavior during and after exposure to sexually explicit stimuli." *Archives of Sexual Behavior*, 4 (1975) 353–364.

———, V. Sigusch and S. Schafer. "Responses to reading erotic stories: Male-female differences." *Archives of Sexual Behavior*, 2 (1973) 181–199.

Schwartz, S. "Effects of sex guilt and sexual arousal on the retention of birth control information." *Journal of Consulting and Clinical Psychology*, 41 (1973) 61–64.

Scott, John Paul, and John L. Fuller. *Genetics and the Social Behavior of the Dog*. Chicago: University of Chicago Press, 1965.

Selmanoff, M. K., B. D. Goldman, and B. E. Ginsburg. "Serum testosterone, agonistic behavior, and dominance in inbred strains of mice." *Hormones and Behavior*, 8 (1977) 107–119.

Shapiro, B. H., D. C. Levine, and N. T. Adler. "The testicular feminized rat: A naturally occurring model of androgen independent brain masculinization." *Science*, 209 (1980) 418–420.

Silberner, J. "Sex differences in the brain: Coming out of the closet." *Science News*, July 14, 1984.

———. "Hormone markers for homosexuality?" *Science News*, September 29, 1984.

Skinner, B. F. *The Behavior of Organisms*. New York: Appleton-Century-Crofts, 1938.

———. *Beyond Freedom and Dignity*. New York, Alfred A. Knopf, 1972.

Smith, Lynn. "The Battle of the Sexes, Continued: Communiqués from the Trenches—An Interview with Robert Bly." *Los Angeles Times*, September 25, 1985.

Snitow, Ann B. "Mass Market Romance: Pornography for Women Is Different." *Radical History Review*, 20 (1979) 141–161.

Soble, Alan. *Pornography: Marxism, Feminism, and the Future of Sexuality*. New Haven: Yale University Press, 1986.

Sontag, Susan. "The Pornographic Imagination." In *Styles of Radical Will*. New York: Dell, 1970.

———. *On Pornography*. New York: Farrar, Straus & Giroux, 1973.

———. "Notes on Art, Sex and Politics." *New York Times*, February 8, 1976.

Sperry, R. W. In ed. J. C. Eccles, *Brain and Conscious Experience*. New York: Springer, 1966.

———. "A modified concept of consciousness." *Psychological Review*, 76 (1969) 532–536.

Springer, Sally P., and Georg Deutsch. *Left Brain, Right Brain*. San Francisco: W. H. Freeman, 1981.

Starr, Douglas. "Brain Drugs." *Omni*, February 1983.

Stein, Kathleen. "The Biology of Power Plays." *Omni*, July 1985, pp. 68–114.

Steinem, Gloria. "Erotica and Pornography: A Clear and Present Difference." *Ms.*, November 1978.

Steinman, D., et al. "A comparison of male and female patterns of sexual arousal." *Archives of Sexual Behavior*, 10 (1981) 529–547.

Stevens, Jay. *LSD and the American Dream: Storming Heaven*. New York: Harper & Row, 1988.

Stiga, Richard G. "A Study of Erotic Film Performances—A Group of Occupational Exhibitionists." Ph.D. Thesis, School of Human Behavior, United States International University, San Diego, 1984.

Stone, G. R. "Antipornography legislation as viewpoint discrimination." *Harvard Journal of Law and Public Policy*, 9 (1986) 701.

Svare, B., ed. *Hormones and Aggressive Behavior.* New York: Plenum, 1983.

——, and Craig H. Kinsley. "Hormones and Sex-Related Behavior: A Comparative Analysis." In ed. Kathryn Kelley, *Females, Males, and Sexuality: Theories and Research.* Albany, NY: State University of New York Press, 1987.

Swaab, D. F. and E. Fliers. "A Sexually Dimorphic Nucleus in the Human Brain." *Science*, 228 (1985) 1112–1116.

Symons, Donald. *The Evolution of Human Sexuality.* New York: Oxford University Press, 1979.

——. "Interview." *Psychology Today*, February 1981, pp. 53–61.

Tavris, C., and C. Wade. *The Longest War: Sex Differences in Perspective*, 2nd ed. San Diego, CA, 1984.

"Testosterone implicated in male dyslexia, math achievement." *Brain/Mind Bulletin*, July 30, 1984.

Thompson, William Irwin. *At the Edge of History: Speculations on the Transformation of Culture.* New York: Harper & Row, 1972.

——. "Interview." *UTNE Reader*, July-August 1986.

Toran-Allerand, Dominique. "Sex Steroids and the Development of the Newborn Mouse Hypothalamus and Preoptic Area in Vitro: Implications for Sexual Differentiation." *Brain Research*, 106 (1976) 407–412.

——. "Sex steroids and the development of the newborn mouse hypothalamus and preoptic area in vitro: II. Morphological correlates and hormonal specificity." *Brain Research*, 189 (1980) 413–427.

Trivers, Robert L. "Parental Investment and Sexual Selection." In ed. Bernard G. Campbell, *Sexual Selection and the Descent of Man*, 1871–1971. Chicago: Aldine, 1974.

Ursin, H., E. Baade, and S. Levine, *Psychobiology of Stress: A Study of Coping Men.* New York: Academic Press, 1978.

"U.S. Court Rejects an Anti-Smut Law." *New York Times*, August 28, 1985.

"User's Guide to Hormones, A." *Newsweek*, January 12, 1987.

Vance, Carole S., ed. *Pleasure and Danger: Exploring Female Sexuality.* Boston: Routledge and Kegan Paul, 1984.

vom Saal, F. S. "Prenatal exposure to androgen influences morphology and aggressive behavior of male and female mice." *Hormones and Behavior*, 12 (1979) 1–11.

——, and F. H. Bronson. "Sexual characteristics of adult female mice are correlated with their blood testosterone levels during prenatal development." *Science*, 208 (1980) 597–599.

——, R. Gandelman, and B. Svare. "Aggression in male and female mice: Evidence for changed neural sensitivity in response to neonatal but not adult androgen exposure." *Physiology and Behavior*, 17 (1976) 53–57.

Walker, Alice. *The Temple of My Familiar.* New York: Harcourt, Brace, Jovanovich, 1989.

Ward, I. L. "Prenatal stress feminizes and demasculinizes the behavior of males." *Science*, 175 (1972) 82–84.

———, and J. Weisz. "Maternal stress alters plasma testosterone in fetal males." *Science*, 207 (1980) 328–329.

Washburn, Sherwood L. "Tools and Human Evolution." *Scientific American*, 203 (1960) 3–15.

Whiting, Beatrice Blyth. "Sex identity conflict and physical violence: A comparative study." *American Anthropologist*, 67 (1965) 123–140.

———, and Carolyn Pope Edwards. "A Cross-Cultural Analysis of Sex Differences in the Behavior of Children Aged Three Through Eleven." *Journal of Social Psychology*, 91 (1968) 171–188.

———, and John W. M. Whiting. *Children of Six Cultures: A Psychocultural Analysis*. Cambridge: Harvard University Press, 1975.

"Why Men Don't Speak Their Minds." *Science Digest*, November 1983.

Wilder, Rachel. "The Polygamous Majority." *Science Digest*, July 1982.

———. "The Coolidge Effect, or Cal Counts His Chickens." *Science Digest*, July 1982.

Will, George F. "Porn Rock Make You Blush? It Should." *Los Angeles Times*, September 16, 1985.

Wilson, E. O. *Sociobiology: The New Synthesis*. Cambridge, MA: Harvard University Press, 1975.

———. *On Human Nature*. Cambridge, MA: Harvard University Press, 1978.

Wilson, Glenn. *Love and Instinct*. New York: William Morrow, 1981.

Wilson, Robert Anton. *Prometheus Rising*. Phoenix, AZ: Falcon Press, 1983.

———. *Wilhelm Reich in Hell*. Phoenix, AZ: Falcon Press, 1987.

Winter, D. G. *The Power Motive*. New York: The Free Press, 1973.

Witelson, Sandra. "Sex and the Single Hemisphere: Specialization of the Right Hemisphere for Spatial Processing." *Science*, 193 (1976).

———. "Developmental Dyslexia: Two Right Hemispheres and None Left." *Science*, 195 (1976).

———. "Sex Differences in the Neurology of Cognition: Psychological, Social, Educational and Political Implications." In ed. E. Sulleret, *Le Fait Feminin*. Paris, France: Fayard, 1978.

"Women Now the Majority in Professions." *New York Times*, March 19, 1986.

Yerkes, R. M. "Social behavior of chimpanzees: Dominance between mates in relation to sexual status." *Journal of Comparative Psychology*, 30 (1940) 147–186.

Zarrow, M. X., P. Samuel Campbell, and Victor H. Denenberg. "Handling in Infancy: Increased Levels of the Hypothalamic Corticotropin Releasing Factor (CRF) Following Exposure to a Novel Situation." *Proceedings of the Society for Experimental Biology and Medicine*, 141 (1983) 356–358.

Zuckerman, Marvin. *Research on Pornography: Sex and the Life Cycle*. New York: Grune and Stratton, 1976.

———. *Sensation Seeking: Beyond the Optimal Level of Arousal*. Hillsdale, NJ: Lawrence Elbaum Associates, 1979.

INDEX

abortions, 17, 49–50, 58, 64, 122, 133, 235, 243, 245, 292, 328, 332
adultery, 117, 131–132, 133
advertising, 52–53, 56, 65
Against Our Will: Women and Rape (Brownmiller), 59–60, 122
aggression, 74, 92, 209, 212
  male sexuality linked with, 145, 202–203, 246
  skin sensitivity in, 105
  testosterone in, 188, 198–203, 246
  see also violence; warfare
AIDS (Acquired Immune Deficiency Syndrome), 75–76, 131, 162, 236, 243–244, 328, 340
anarchy, 297–298, 316, 331, 334
Andrews, Lynn, 320
Annett, Marian, 180
anxiety, 43, 298, 332, 337–339, 341, 343, 344–345
apes, 90, 95, 100, 101, 104
aphrodisiacs, 155, 189, 204, 300–301
artifacts, physical, 147
Attorney General, U.S., National Commission on Pornography of, 13–14, 44–45, 65, 66, 73–74, 86, 298, 311
authoritarianism, 212, 294, 306–308, 309–310, 324
  of cults, 54, 57, 306
autonomic nervous system, 157

Bakker, Jim, 26–27, 84, 239, 302, 311, 314
Barash, David, 95–96, 106, 107, 117, 118, 124–125, 144, 145–146, 226–227
behaviorism, 79–80, 81–82, 83–84, 85, 86, 112, 150, 160, 165
Benbow, Camilla, 14–15, 169–171, 180–181
Bennett, Neil, 136
biogeography, 214–216
biopolitics, 155–156, 186–205
  aggression in, 188, 198–203
  gatekeepers vs. seekers in, 189–193, 196–197, 204–205

  male dominance in, 196, 197, 201, 202–205
  power in, 186–187, 195–198, 205
  sexual desire in, 188–189, 193–195
  testosterone in, 187–198, 193–195, 197, 198–204
birth control, 31, 133, 135, 235, 243, 247, 300, 330, 331, 332
births, 98–100, 101
Blake, William, 29, 30, 46, 233, 268, 271, 313, 345
Bloom, David, 136
Bloom, Floyd, 152
Bly, Robert, 317–318
books, censorship of, 11–12, 14, 67, 68–69, 71, 73, 293, 328, 341
  see also literature
bookstores, burning of, 11–12, 235–236, 342
Booth, Alan, 133
brain, 14–15, 86, 126, 149–185, 263
  body as part of, 157–159, 160, 281–283
  as dissipative structure, 267–269, 270
  emotions in, 158, 171, 174–176, 185, 188
  evolution of, 95–96, 98–100, 106, 160, 164, 173–174, 185, 257, 291, 303–304, 329, 336, 337
  handedness and, 14, 179–181
  hemispheres of, 156–157, 160, 167–169, 170, 174, 177, 179–180, 184, 241
  homosexuality and, 183–184, 185
  hormones in, 153, 154, 158, 171, 177–184
  hypothalamus gland of, 154–155, 161, 171–173, 184, 188, 282
  mathematical ability and, 14, 168, 169–171, 179–181, 185
  neurochemistry of, 152–156, 158, 159–160, 161–162, 171, 177–179, 183–184, 185, 303, 327, 337
  orgasms and, 241–242
  pleasure in, 241, 303, 304–305, 327, 337, 338
  schools and, 176–177
  sexual desire and, 154–155, 158

brain (*cont.*)
  visual-spatial ability and, 168, 169, 170, 179, 181–183, 185
  see also imprinting; neuroscience
brain waves, 276–280
breasts, 27, 123
  as releasers, 124–125
Brownmiller, Susan, 59–60, 61, 122, 244
Budzynski, Thomas, 277, 279–280
Buss, David, 122–123

Califia, Pat, 244, 248–249
Castaneda, Carlos, 318
celibacy, 302, 306, 307, 310
censorship, 11–14, 65–74, 91, 167, 238, 260, 293–294, 297, 341–343
  anticensorship feminists and, 72, 77–78, 249, 297, 314
  of books, 11–12, 14, 67, 68–69, 71, 73, 293, 328, 341
  libraries and, 59, 66, 67, 68–69
  of magazines, 13, 62, 65–66, 69, 71, 295–296
  of movies, 71
  of rock music, 69
  schools and, 59, 66–68, 84, 91, 293, 308
  targets of, 65–67, 69
  by universities, 342–343, 344
  violence in tactics of, 11–12, 62, 69–70, 235–236, 341–342
cervical cancer, 76–77
Chance and Necessity (Monod), 253–254
character armor, 272–273, 279, 282–283, 284–285, 288, 334
Chesler, Phyllis, 139, 308
Chia, Mantak, 320–321, 323–324
Christian fundamentalists, 17, 57–59, 63–78, 86, 289, 290
  behaviorism and, 83–84, 85
  born-again experiences of, 57, 242, 283, 305, 338
  censorship by, 13, 59, 65–74, 84, 238, 293–294, 308, 341–342
  erotophobia of, 236–239, 240, 242–244, 248, 332–333
  evangelist, 26–27, 63–64, 69, 84, 239, 302, 311, 314
  feminists allied with, 13, 64–65, 69–70, 71–73, 74, 77–78, 237–239, 248
  homosexuality as viewed by, 243–244
  political agenda of, 293–296, 297–298, 307–308
  splitting among, 314
  venereal diseases as viewed by, 76, 243–244
Christon, Lawrence, 141–142, 143
civilizing process, 214, 336–337, 339
clitoris, 41, 45, 144, 147
Clutton-Brock, Tim, 110
cognitive disruptions, 192, 291–293
Cohn, Norman, 37
competition, 119–122, 188, 194, 202, 226
Concerned Women of America, 68, 293–294, 295
Constitution, U.S., 71, 73, 85, 222, 236, 237, 244, 294, 316
Coolidge Effect, 129–132

Cooper, James Fenimore, 82, 142, 218
cosmetics, 122, 123–124
Cosmides, Leda, 105
Cosmopolitan, 75, 134, 285
Craig, Patricia, 136
criminals, 44, 195, 201, 204, 208–209, 297, 309
Crowley, William, 181–182
cults, 37–39, 54, 57, 306
cultural determinism, 86, 106, 112, 140, 166–167, 176, 199, 200
  neuroscience vs., 150–152, 160–161, 163, 165, 180

Daly, Martin, 133
Darwin, Charles, 12, 90, 91, 93, 125, 335
Davidson, Julian, 188, 241–242
Davis, Murray, 240–241, 242–243
Dawkins, Richard, 90, 252, 253, 263, 303, 335
DeLamater, John, 189, 196
Dershowitz, Alan, 73
deSimone, Diane, 189, 202
DeVore, Irven, 118, 121–122, 198
Diamond, Marian, 159, 172–173
digestive track, emotions and, 158
Dimen, Muriel, 240
diseases, disorders, 177, 182
  character armor in, 272–273, 282–283
  genetics, 112–113, 161–162, 201–202
  germ theory of, 255, 258
  of immune system, 179, 180–181, 185
  of language, 167, 179, 180, 181
  venereal, *see* venereal diseases
dissipative structures, 264–269, 270, 334–335
  ecosystem as, 325, 344
Dodson, Betty, 49
dominance, male, 132, 145, 146, 196, 197, 202–205, 228, 238, 248
  serotonin in, 155–156, 160
  testosterone in, 201, 202–204
Donnerstein, Edward, 74
dopamine, 154, 159, 184
Dorner, Gunter, 183–184
double standard, 134–140
Douglas, Ann, 221
drugs, 35, 38, 42, 54, 255–256
Duggan, Lisa, 288, 289, 297
Durden-Smith, Jo, 189, 202
Dworkin, Andrea, 61, 64, 238, 239, 247, 248, 249, 311
  law proposed by, 71–73, 78, 314, 333

Echols, Alice, 61
ecosystem, 138, 150–152, 162, 325, 344
Ehrenreich, Barbara, 116
Ehrhardt, Anke, 103, 182–183, 201–202
Einseidel, Edna F., 74
Elias, Norbert, 214, 336
Elshtain, Jean Bethke, 244
emotions, 171, 174–176, 185, 188, 209
  digestive tract and, 158
End of Sex, The (Leonard), 322–323
endorphins, 153, 158, 159, 303, 304, 305, 327, 337
English, Deirdre, 83
entropy, 264, 265, 314, 315, 325

erotophobia, 191–192, 235–249, 287–298, 332–334
  altered states of consciousness and, 240–243, 289
  cognitive disruptions in, 192, 291–293
  heresy and, 236–240
  memes of, 288–291, 297
  morality in, 244–246
  normal vs. abnormal sex in, 237, 243–244, 289
  oratorical techniques and, 292–293
  political agendas and, 293–298
  psychological characteristics of, 237–240
  sex contract in, 246–248
estrogen, 178, 183, 187
estrus, loss of, 100–102, 109–110, 126, 130
evolution, 16–17, 67, 80, 86, 89–110, 178, 187–188, 202, 226, 303, 328–332
  adaptation in, 91–93, 103, 251
  of bipedalism, 94–96, 97, 98, 101
  of births, 98–100, 101
  of brain, 95–96, 98–100, 106, 160, 164, 173–174, 185, 257, 291, 303–304, 329, 336, 337
  cultural, 105–107, 110, 127, 252–253, 303–304, 329, 336–337
  of female power, 109–110, 333
  of hominids, 96
  hunter-gatherers and, 96–98, 99, 102–103, 105, 116, 135, 140–141, 175, 329, 333, 338
  kin selection in, 133
  memes and, 252–253, 257–259, 268, 303–304, 335–337, 340–341, 344–345
  natural selection in, 91, 92, 93, 95, 98, 99, 101, 102, 106, 126–127, 128, 145, 251, 327
  neuroscience and, 161–163
  physical artifacts of, 147
  punctuated equilibrium in, 328, 331
  of reproductive strategies, 91, 92, 102, 105–106, 107–110, 115–116, 119, 128, 132, 135, 216–247
  of sex contract, *see* sex contract
  of sexual desire, 193–195
  of sexual division of labor, 97–98, 99, 102, 330
  sexual selection in, 93–94, 118
  survival of the fittest in, 92–93, 102
  Type T personalities and, 210–211
Eysenck, Hans J., 195

Fallows, James, 215
Falwell, Jerry, 26, 63, 64, 66, 295, 314
Farley, Frank, 207–209, 232, 268–269
fascism, 45–46, 284–285, 298
females, 209
  assertiveness of, 116
  competition by, 120–122
  desertion feared by, 134
  effects of stress on, 120–121, 138
  loss of estrus by, 100–102, 109–110, 126, 130
  mythologies of, 143–144
  nurturance by, 102, 103, 104, 200
  orgasms of, 55, 109, 144–147, 148
  power of, 109–110, 247–248, 333
  pregnancy of, 170, 182–184, 185
  releasers of, 125–126
  sex feared by, 145, 245–246
  sexual desire of, 189, 193–194
  standards of beauty for, 123
  testosterone in, 189, 193–194, 201
  Venus figurines of, 127
  see also sex differences
feminists, 59–62, 134, 193, 197–198, 247–249, 289–290, 341–342
  anticensorship, 72, 77–78, 249, 297, 314
  behaviorism and, 83, 86
  cosmetics as viewed by, 122, 123–124
  economic goals of, 138–140
  erotophobia of, 237–239, 240, 244, 247–249, 333
  masturbation approved by, 41, 44, 49
  middle-class, 55–56
  mother-child bond as viewed by, 138–139
  political agenda of, 55–56, 296–298, 308
  pornography and, 12–13, 60–61, 62, 64–65, 69–70, 71–73, 74, 77–78, 86, 237, 244, 247–248, 296–298, 308, 333
  quota laws desired by, 139
  sex differences and, 16–17, 83, 86, 103, 110, 116–117, 138–140, 166–167, 225, 227
  in sexual revolution, 41–42, 44, 47, 49, 54–56, 58, 59, 116, 247
  splitting among, 314–315
Feminization of American Culture, The (Douglas), 221
Fiedler, Leslie, 217–218
Field, Pat, 171–172
Fisher, Helen E., 93, 96, 99, 100, 101, 103, 124, 134, 146
Fliers, E., 172
Franklin, Jon, 164–165
freedom, personal, 80, 82–83, 84–86, 106, 215, 218, 316
French, Marilyn, 238
Freud, Sigmund, 12, 43, 45, 83, 155, 207, 271, 272, 284, 299, 300, 306
Friday, Nancy, 48–49
Friedan, Betty, 77–78, 134
Friedman, Jerry, 190
Frost, Vicki, 67

Galaburda, Albert M., 181, 182
gatekeepers, 115–117, 148, 189–193, 196–197, 204–205, 333
genetics, 80, 82–83, 85–86, 134, 135, 147, 155, 250–251
  diseases caused by, 112–113, 161–162, 201–202
  of personality, 112–114, 185, 206, 209–210, 214, 246, 263, 268
  sex drive in, 195
  see also evolution
Gerrard, Meg, 192
Geschwind, Norman, 179–180, 181
giftedness, 180–181, 185
Gilligan, Carol, 225–227, 231, 244–245
Gladue, Brian, 183
Glass, S. P., 131

gnosticism, 217, 313
  definition of, 321, 323
  New Age, 316–325
  in sexual revolution, 36–39, 40, 41–42, 46,
    53, 54, 55
Godey's Lady's Book, 222
Goodall, Jane, 104
Gorski, Roger, 172
Gouldner, Alvin, 270
Goy, Bob, 187–188
Green, Elmer and Alyce, 277, 282
Greenwald, Anthony, 174
Griffitt, William, 191, 192, 193, 245
guilt, 192, 237, 285–286, 291, 293, 332, 334
Gunther, Gerald, 343, 344
Gurr, Ted Robert, 214

Hahn, Jessica, 26–27
Hall, Fawn, 25–26
handedness, 14, 179–181
Hart, Gary, 25, 230
Hawthorne, Nathaniel, 217, 222
Hearst, Patty, 283–284
Heath, Robert, 241
Held, Richard, 181
Hemingway, Ernest, 12, 68, 217, 224
Henson, H. Keith, 254, 255–256, 257, 258, 260,
    262
heresy, 215–216, 236–240, 259, 307, 315, 320,
    324, 340
  see also gnosticism
herpes, 75
Hertzberg, Hendrik, 25
Hess, Elizabeth, 116
Hier, Daniel, 181–182
Hite, Shere, 134–135, 175–176
Hitler, Adolf, 12, 238, 258, 307
hominids, 96
homosexuality, 49, 55, 131, 183–184, 185, 243–
    244, 311
hormones, 153, 154, 158, 171, 177–184, 185,
    297
  see also testosterone
Hrdy, Sarah Blaffer, 103, 109–110, 117–118,
    120, 197
Huckleberry Finn (Twain), 68, 82, 142, 177, 206,
    218, 224
Hull, Clark, 81
human nature, contrasting views of, 79–86, 225
human potential movement, 46–48, 58–59, 64,
    67, 321
Humphrey, N. K., 252
hunter-gatherers, 96–98, 102–103, 105, 116,
    135, 140–141, 175, 329, 333, 338
hyperactivity, 177
hypnagogic state, 276–277
hypothalamus gland, 154–155, 161, 171–173,
    184, 188, 282

immigrants, 214
immune system, 153, 157, 158, 160, 178
  disorders of, 179, 180–181, 185
imprinting, 271–286, 290–291, 295, 332, 334
  of American culture, 284–286
  reimprinting vs., 283–284

state-bound learning in, 275–276, 280, 281–
    283
  theta waves in, 276–280, 282, 283
  trauma in, 272, 278–281, 282–283
In a Different Voice (Gilligan), 225–227, 231
information, 250–253, 260–262, 325, 328, 344
  restriction of, 296, 297–298, 335, 338
  sex as, 334–335
  technology of, 228–229
  see also memes

Jacklin, Carol Nagy, 103–104, 168, 199–200
Jacobs, Gloria, 116
James, William, 119
Japan, 309–310
jealousy, 132–134, 154
Johnson, Diane, 224
Jong, Erica, 49, 77, 140
Justice Department, U.S., 64, 66, 70, 71
  see also Attorney General, U.S.

Kaplan, Alexandra G., 223
Kaplan, Helen Singer, 123, 144, 147–148
Katz, Sidney, 178
Kendrick, Walter, 298
Kennedy, John F., 31, 239
Kerouac, Jack, 30, 218, 224
Khomeini, Ayatollah Ruhollah, 256, 307, 341
Kimura, Doreen, 103, 167, 173
kin selection, 133
Kinsley, Craig, 203
Kirkpatrick, Martha, 60
Koedt, Anne, 41
Konner, Melvin, 104, 117, 118, 145, 188, 196,
    200, 203, 231–232, 245–246
Korner, Annelise, 103, 105, 187, 200
Kreuz, L., 201

language, 95, 168–169, 173
  disorders of, 167, 179, 180, 181
Larson, John, 278
Lasch, Christopher, 321, 323
leadership, 245, 314
  hypocrisy of, 310–312
  by Type T personalities, 212, 228, 232, 238–
    240, 309–312
learning, 267, 274, 334, 336, 338
  state-bound, 275–276, 280, 281–283
  superlearning, 277
Lee, Richard, 121
LeHaye, Beverly, 68, 294, 295–296
Leonard, George, 322–323, 325
lesbians, 49, 55, 131
Levy, Jerre, 103, 163–164, 167, 168, 173–174,
    186
libraries, censorship of, 59, 66, 67, 68–69
Liebeskind, John, 149
Lief, Harold, 189
limbic system, 171, 188, 241, 278, 280, 281,
    282, 291
literature, 82, 216–218
  gender-based mythologies in, 142, 143–144,
    217–218
  relationship problems in, 140–141, 223–225
  in sexual revolution, 30, 32, 41, 42, 44, 48–49

women's, 49, 52, 60, 143–144, 222, 223–225, 249, 285
LoPiccolo, Joseph, 190
Lovejoy, Owen, 97
Lykken, David, 113
Lynch, Gary, 278

McClearn, Gerald, 114
McClelland, David C., 105, 239–240, 337
Maccoby, Eleanor, 103–104, 168, 199–200
McGaugh, James, 277–278
McGlone, Jeanette, 103, 167
McGuinness, Diane, 103, 168, 169, 171, 176–177
McGuire, Michael, 204
MacKinnon, Catherine:
  law proposed by, 61, 71–73, 78, 314, 333
magazines, 222, 285
  censorship of, 13, 62, 65–66, 69, 71, 295–296
  see also specific magazines
Malamuth, Neil, 74
males:
  aggression in sexuality of, 145, 202–203, 246
  competition by, 119, 188, 194, 202, 226
  dominance in, *see* dominance, male
  homoerotic companionship of, 142, 217–218
  mythologies of, 140–143, 213, 217–218
  orgasms of, 144, 146
  releasers of, 124–125
  sex drive of, 148, 189, 202
  sexual desire of, 188, 194
  shyness in, 153–154
  variety desired by, 130–132, 148
  violence of, 59–62, 102, 103, 104, 105, 119, 132, 194–195, 200, 201, 204
  see also sex differences
Marcus, Steven, 42
Martin, Robert, 99
Mass Psychology of Fascism, The (Reich), 45–46
masturbation, 41, 44, 49, 55, 148, 189, 237, 311, 333
mate selection, 122–124, 136–137, 190
mathematical ability, 14, 168, 169–171, 179–181, 185
matriarchy, 54, 296
Mayr, Ernst, 93, 114, 330
Mead, Margaret, 103, 111, 116, 144
media, 59, 65, 218, 228–231, 328
  memes transmitted by, 258–259, 341
  violence in, 60, 62
Mednick, Sarnoff, 113
Meese, Edwin, 13–14, 66, 73, 74, 86, 311
Melville, Herman, 82, 217, 218, 222
memes, 250–270, 273, 274, 331–345
  about sex, 288–289, 290, 322
  about sex contract, 331–334
  about sexes, 289–290
  authoritarian, 306–308, 309–310
  brain and, 257, 263, 267–269, 270, 304, 336
  definition of, 252, 261
  dissipative structures and, 264–269, 270, 334–335, 344
  of erotophobia, 288–291, 297
  evolution and, 252–253, 257–259, 268, 303–304, 335–337, 340–341, 344–345

immunity to, 260, 261–262, 341, 343–344
  infectiousness of, 254–257, 267–268, 337, 338
  intolerance vs. tolerance of, 259–260, 262–263, 335–339, 340–345
  killer, 256–257
  mass social movements caused by, 255–257, 263
  mental transformation through, 267–270, 297–298
  metameme of, 259–260, 262, 263, 336–337
  moral absolutism in, 261, 262–263, 269–270, 342, 344
  nature of reality in, 268, 334, 339
  pleasure from, 303–305, 306, 311
  power and, 253–254, 257, 262–263, 290–293, 301–308
  transmission of, 258–259, 291–293, 297, 301, 305, 306, 341
  violence caused by, 336–337
  wealth-producing, 260–261
men
  fertility of, 138
  memes about, 290
  morality of, 226–227
  sexual frequency desired by, 135, 148
  in Wild Man Workshops, 317–318
  women's views on, 140–141, 175–176, 223, 224, 248, 290, 333
  see also males
Metzger, Deena, 319–320, 325
millennial cult, 37–39
Minnesota Center for Twin and Adoption Research, 113–114, 209–210, 246
Money, John, 188, 276, 290–291, 293, 334
Monod, Jacques, 253–254, 257, 263
monogamy, polygamy vs., 117–119, 146, 196
Moore, Jim, 120
morality, 225–227, 231
  absolutism of, 261, 262–263, 269–270, 342, 344
  in erotophobia, 244–246
Morgan, Robin, 61, 116–117, 238, 244
Morrison, Jim, 38, 43, 53
Mosher Sex Guilt Scales, 192, 237, 245
movies, 15–16, 47, 71, 82–83
  gender-based mythologies in, 141, 143, 213, 218
  Hitler and, 258
  pornographic, 12, 45
  violence in, 60, 213
murder, 200, 201
Murdock, George Peter, 117
"Myth of the Vaginal Orgasm, The" (Koedt), 41
mythologies, gender-based, 140–144
  in literature, 142, 143–144, 217–218
  in movies, 141, 143, 213, 218

Nazis, 12, 244, 258, 262, 284–285, 307, 342
neuroscience, 149–152, 160–165
  cultural determinism vs., 150–152, 160–161, 163, 165, 180
  evolution potentially controlled by, 161–163
  research in, 163–165
  see also brain

New Age gnosticism, 316–325
  ancient religions in, 316, 319–321
  cataclysm predicted by, 324–325
  esoteric knowledge in, 320–321, 323–324
  political agenda of, 325
  spirituality of, 321–323, 325
  Wild Man Workshops in, 317–318
1984 (Orwell), 68–69, 235, 307
Nixon, Richard, 35, 38, 44–45, 49, 58, 298,
    315–316
norepinephrine, 154, 184
North, Oliver, 25–26, 213
nuclear war, 230

open systems, 264–267, 334
orgasms, 35, 41–42, 45, 156, 192, 284, 285
  brain and, 241–242
  female, 55, 109, 144–147, 148
Orwell, George, 68–69, 235, 307
Owen, William, 175
oxytocin, 125–126

pair-bonding, 109, 117, 118, 122, 130, 145–146,
    195
Pally, Marcia, 78
papilloma virus, 76–77
penis, 38, 43–44, 147, 242
Penthouse, 13, 26, 27, 48, 49, 66, 285
personality, 42
  genetics of, 112–114, 185, 206, 209–210, 214,
    246, 263, 268
  neurochemistry of, 153–154
  rigidity in, 269–270, 271–273, 280, 282–283,
    285, 288, 334
  see also Type T personalities
Pert, Candace, 150, 152, 158, 159, 193, 201, 303
phenylethylamine (PEA), 154, 155
Pilpel, Harriet F., 84–85
plastic surgery, 27, 123–124
Playboy, 13, 16, 25, 26, 27, 38, 48, 49, 52, 63,
    66, 285, 295
Playgirl, 48, 285
pleasure, 241, 300, 303–305, 306, 311, 327, 337,
    338
Pogrebin, Letty Cottin, 137
polygamy, monogamy vs., 117–119, 146, 196
population explosion, 330, 340
pornography, 11–14, 17, 59, 127, 148, 192, 207,
    292, 328
  definition of, 72
  effects of, 44, 60–61, 62, 73–74, 86, 298, 333,
    342–343
  feminists and, 12–13, 60–61, 62, 64–65, 69–
    70, 71–73, 74, 77–78, 86, 237, 244, 247–
    248, 296–298, 308, 333
  governmental opposition to, 13–14, 44, 64,
    65, 66, 70–71, 73–74
  laws against, 30, 61, 70–73, 78, 298, 308, 314,
    333, 342–343
  in sexual revolution, 29–30, 35, 42, 44–45,
    48–49
  for women, 42, 48–49
  see also censorship
*Pornography: Marxism, Feminism, and the Future of
    Sexuality* (Soble), 247–248

power, 299–312, 315–316
  as aphrodisiac, 204, 300–301
  authoritarianism in, 306–308, 309–310
  in biopolitics, 186–187, 195–198, 205
  female, 109–110, 247–248, 320, 333
  force in, 301, 302
  memes and, 253–254, 257, 262–263, 290–293,
    301–308
  pleasure in, 300, 303–305, 311
  of religions, 302, 306–308
  Type T personalities and, 308–312
power motive, 239–240, 337
pregnancy, 178, 182–184, 185
prenatal androgenization, 296
Prigogine, Ilya, 263–267, 269, 325
primates, 104, 120–121, 132, 155, 200, 238
prostitution, 115, 117, 148, 239, 248, 311, 333
  sacred, 36, 316, 319–320
psychology, 43, 45–48, 83, 86
  human potential movement in, 46–48, 58–59,
    64, 67, 321
punctuated equilibrium, 328, 331

Raisman, Geoffrey, 171–172
rape, 49, 59–60, 61, 116, 148, 195, 236, 238,
    333
Raschke, Carl A., 321
Reagan, Ronald, 25, 59, 62, 64, 75, 213, 221,
    295
Reich, Wilhelm, 45–46, 272–273, 279, 282, 307
  persecution of, 284–285
Reinisch, June, 198–199
releasers, 124–126
religion, 215–216, 257, 306–308, 313–314, 324,
    330
  ancient, 36–37, 54, 316, 319–321
  celibacy in, 302, 306, 307, 310
  memes of, 254, 302, 306
  see also Christian fundamentalists; gnosticism
*Report of the Commission on Obscenity and
    Pornography, The*, 44–45, 298
reproductive strategies, 91, 92, 102, 105–106,
    107–110, 115–116, 119, 128, 132, 135,
    246–247
Rheingold, Howard, 297
Richards, Janet, 139
Ricoeur, Paul, 32
Robertson, Pat, 63, 68, 294
rock music, 32, 33, 35, 38, 43, 53, 69, 242, 258–
    259, 284
Roman Catholic church, 36, 37, 215, 307, 309,
    324, 330
romance novels, 49, 52, 60, 143–144, 222, 249,
    285
Rose, R., 201
Rosenberg, Rosalind, 139
Rossi, Alice, 103
Rossi, Ernest, 281–282
Roth, Phillip, 44
Routtenberg, Aryeh, 304
Rubin, Gayle, 314–315
Rushdie, Salman, 307, 341

Saal, Frank, 190
sacred prostitution, 36, 316, 319–320

Safer, Martin, 174
Samurai, 309–310
Schlafly, Phyllis, 67
schools, 176–177, 262
  censorship and, 59, 66–68, 84, 91, 293, 308
Scott, John Paul, 199
Sears, Alan E., 66
"Secret Side of Lesbian Sexuality, A" (Califia), 248–249
serotonin, 154, 159–160, 184
  in male dominance, 155–156, 160
sex, 299–300, 301, 315–316
  characteristics of, 308–309
  experience of, 240–243
  fear of, 145, 245–246; *see also* erotophobia
  as information, 334–335
  memes about, 288–289, 290, 322
  normal vs. abnormal, 237, 243–244, 289
  reproduction separated from, 331
sex contract, 100–105, 138, 173–174, 329
  in erotophobia, 246–248
  recent breakdown of, 330–334
sex differences, 16–17, 83, 86, 105, 110, 114–148, 166–167, 342
  in competition, 119–122, 188, 194, 202, 226
  Coolidge Effect in, 129–132
  cross-cultural studies of, 103, 104–105, 115, 117, 122–123, 132, 133, 168, 189, 200
  double standard and, 134–140
  gatekeepers vs. seekers in, 115–117, 148, 189–193, 196–197, 204–205, 333
  in gender-based mythologies, 140–144
  in homosexuality, 131
  in jealousy, 132–134
  in mate selection, 122–124, 136–137, 190
  in maturity rate, 182
  in monogamy vs. polygamy, 117–119, 146, 196
  in morality, 225–227, 231
  in orgasms, 144–147, 148
  physical, 187–188
  prenatal androgenization in, 296
  in releasers, 124–126
  in sex drive, 147–148, 189, 202
  sex-role training vs., 105, 116, 117, 122, 127, 176, 200, 225
  size differential in, 117–118, 119, 187
  statistical averages of, 114–115
  visual stimuli and, 126–128
  see also biopolitics; brain; evolution
sex drive, 147–148, 189, 195, 202, 297
sex education, 17, 58, 243, 292, 293, 308, 330, 332
sexual desire, 154–155, 158, 188–189, 193–195
Sexual Opinion Survey, 191–192, 237, 245
sexual revolution, 17, 29–50, 107, 138, 189, 193, 313
  breakdown of, 51–55, 74–77
  counterculture in, 31–39, 51–55
  counterrevolution to, 51–78
  cultural intelligentsia in, 39, 42–45
  feminists in, 41–42, 44, 47, 49, 54–56, 58, 59, 116, 247
  gnosticism in, 36–39, 40, 41–42, 46, 53, 54, 55

governmental opposition to, 34–35, 38–39, 54
human potential movement in, 46–48
literature in, 30, 32, 41, 42, 44, 48–49
millennial cult in, 37–39
pornography in, 29–30, 35, 42, 44–45, 48–49
right-wing opposition to, 17, 57–59, 63–78
venereal diseases vs., *see* venereal diseases
Vietnam War and, 34, 37, 44, 45, 47, 49, 52, 57–58
sexual selection, 93–94, 118
sexual stimuli, 191–192, 245, 291, 292
  visual, 126–128
Shannon, Claude, 261
Showalter, Elaine, 225
Shucard, David, 168–169
Sigourney, Lydia, 222
skin:
  brain affected by, 158–159
  sensitivity of, 105
Skinner, B. F., 81–82, 84, 150, 151
Soble, Alan, 247–248
Sontag, Susan, 308
Sperry, Roger, 253
Stanley, Julian, 169–171, 180–181
Stark, Rodney, 215–216
state-bound learning, 275–276, 280, 281–283
stepfamilies, 132–133
Stevens, Wallace, 233, 287
Stockholm Syndrome, 283–284
stress, 207, 232, 281
  on females, 120–121, 138
  on infants, 159
  during pregnancy, 183–184, 185
Supreme Court, U.S., 29–30, 49, 70, 261, 294
Svare, Bruce, 203
Swaggart, Jimmy, 27, 64, 69, 84, 239, 302, 311
Symons, Donald, 116, 123, 131, 146, 147

Taoism, 36, 316, 320–321, 323, 324
Tavris, Carol, 176
technology, 228–229, 258–259, 341
Tedford, Thomas, 71
Tellegen, Auke, 114
Temple of My Familiar, The (Walker), 41
testosterone, 154, 178, 187–189, 193–195, 197, 198–204
  in aggression, 188, 198–203, 246
  as aphrodisiac, 188
  in females, 189, 193–194, 201
  homosexuality and, 183–184
  in male dominance, 201, 202–204
  prenatal, 179–180, 181, 183–184, 201–202, 296–297
  in Type T personalities, 207, 208, 214, 215
  visual-spatial ability and, 182
theta waves, 276–280, 282, 283
Thompson, William Irwin, 313–314, 315
Tooby, John, 105
Toran-Allerand, Dominique, 103, 172
tournament species, 118
transmutative thinking, 209, 210, 268
trauma, 272, 278–281, 282–283
Turnbull, Colin, 97–98
Twain, Mark, 68, 82, 114, 142, 206
twins, 113–114, 209–210, 246

Type T personalities, 206–232, 294, 297, 308–312, 327–328
  in American culture, 211–232
  characteristics of, 207–209
  erotophobia in, 238–240, 242, 245–246, 249
  in evolution, 210–211
  genetics of, 209–210, 214
  leadership by, 212, 228, 232, 238–240, 309–312
  literature and, 222, 223, 224
  memes and, 263, 268–269
  morality of, 227, 245–246
  in political system, 208, 221, 227–228, 229, 230, 232
  power motive in, 239–240, 337

United States, culture of, 82–83, 211, 294–295
  feminization of, 220–232
  immigrants in, 214
  imprinting of, 284–286
  literature in, 216–218, 222, 223–225
  political system in, 213, 218–219, 221, 222, 227–232
  preoccupation with sex in, 23–28, 285–286, 295
  recent changes in, 228–231, 328
  violence in, 212–214
  warfare in, 212–213, 229–230
  western frontier in, 82, 214–216, 223, 294
  world economy and, 229
universities, censorship by, 342–343, 344

Vance, Carole, 72, 78, 333
venereal diseases, 58, 75–77
  AIDS, 75–76, 131, 162, 236, 243–244, 328, 340
Venus figurines, 127
Vietnam War, 34, 37, 44, 45, 47, 49, 52, 57–58, 151, 152, 229, 259
violence, 231–232, 235–236, 287, 314, 333
  in American culture, 212–214
  in censorship tactics, 11–12, 62, 69–70, 235–236, 341–342
  civilizing process and, 214, 336–337, 339
  dominance and, 204
  fascist, 284
  male, 59–62, 102, 103–104, 105, 119, 132, 194–195, 200, 201, 204
  in media, 60, 62
  memes as cause of, 336–337
  in pornography, 60–61, 62, 73–74, 86
  in stepfamilies, 133
  against women, 59–62, 132
  worldwide, 340–342
visual-spatial ability, 168, 169, 170, 179, 181–183, 185

visual stimuli, 126–128

Wacks, Theodore, 158, 159
Walker, Alice, 41, 68, 224
Ward, Ingeborg, 183
warfare, 119, 196, 212–213, 229–230, 313–314, 315, 339, 343
Warner, Susan, 224
Washburn, Sherwood, 98
Wasser, Sam, 120–121
Watson, John B., 81, 82, 150
Weiner, Norbert, 261
Weldon, Fay, 124
White, Lynn, 133
Whiting, Beatrice Blyth, 103, 104, 200
Whiting, John, 104, 200
Whitman, Walt, 217, 222
Wide Wide World, The (Warner), 224
Wild Man Workshops, 317–318
Wilford, John Noble, 127
Wilson, Edwin O., 114, 167
Wilson, Glenn, 130, 132, 145, 146
Wilson, Margo, 133
Wilson, Robert Anton, 216, 238, 260–261, 268, 285, 291, 293, 309
Winter, David, 239
Witelson, Sandra, 103, 167–168
women, 75, 77, 134–140, 220–232, 328
  ancient religion and, 36, 54, 316, 319–321
  church and, 221–222
  employment of, 330
  erotophobia in, 191–192, 245
  fertility of, 122, 136–138
  intimacy desired by, 75, 134–135, 140
  literature of, 49, 52, 60, 143–144, 222, 223–225, 249, 285
  marriageability of, 136
  memes about, 289–290
  men as viewed by, 140–141, 175–176, 223, 224, 248, 290, 333
  morality of, 225–227, 231, 245
  in political system, 221, 222, 227, 231–232
  pornography for, 42, 48–49
  in reform movements, 222
  relationships important to, 223–224, 226
  special protection needed by, 333
  unrepresentative, 231
  violence against, 59–62, 132
  see also females; feminists
Women's Christian Temperance Union (WCTU), 222
Womongold, Marcia, 61
Wright, T. L., 131

Zilbergeld, Bernie, 203
Zuckerman, Marvin, 207